INTRODUCTION TO ARCHITECTURE

INTRODUCTION TO ARCHITECTURE

Edited by

James C. Snyder
Anthony J. Catanese

School of Architecture and Urban Planning
University of Wisconsin–Milwaukee

Architectural Drawings by Jeffrey E. Ollswang
Associate Editor for Part 3: Tim McGinty

McGraw-Hill Book Company

New York   St. Louis   San Francisco   Auckland   Bogotá   Düsseldorf
Johannesburg   London   Madrid   Mexico   Montreal   New Delhi
Panama   Paris   São Paulo   Singapore   Sydney   Tokyo   Toronto

INTRODUCTION TO ARCHITECTURE

1234567890   HDHD   7832109

This book was set in Helvetica Light by A Graphic Method Inc.
The editors were Rose Ciofalo and David Damstra;
the designer was Merrill Haber; the cover was designed by Hermann Strohbach;
the production supervisor was John F. Harte.
Other drawings were done by J & R Services, Inc.
Halliday Lithograph Corporation was printer and binder.

Library of Congress Cataloging in Publication Data
Main entry under title:

Introduction to architecture.

    Includes index.
    1. Architecture. I. Snyder, James C.
II. Catanese, Anthony James.
NA2500.I57   720   78-12808
ISBN 0-07-059547-X

To Felicity Brogden Ollswang

Contents

PART IV BUILDING SCIENCE AND TECHNOLOGY

About the Contributors

Editors

JAMES C. SNYDER, AICP, is Associate Dean and Associate Professor of Architecture and Urban Planning, University of Wisconsin-Milwaukee. A graduate of the Ohio State University (B. Arch.) and the University of Michigan (M. Arch.; M. City Planning; Ph.D., Urban and Regional Planning), Dr. Snyder has taught at the University of Michigan, Georgia Institute of Technology, and the University of Wisconsin-Milwaukee. He is the author of *Fiscal Management and Planning in Local Government* (1977). In addition to teaching and research, Dr. Snyder has served as a planning and design consultant to numerous local governments and as president of the Wisconsin Chapter of the American Institute of Planners.

ANTHONY J. CATANESE, AICP, is Dean, School of Architecture and Urban Planning, University of Wisconsin-Milwaukee. He received degrees in urban and regional planning from Rutgers University (B.A.), New York University (M.C.P.), and the University of Wisconsin-Madison (Ph.D.). He has worked as a planner for Middlesex County and the state of New Jersey and has extensive consulting experience from Florida to Hawaii. In addition, Dr. Catanese has taught at Georgia Institute of Technology, the University of Miami at Coral Gables, and at the University of Wisconsin-Milwaukee. He is the author or editor of several books in the area of urban planning, including *Systemic Planning: Theory and Application* (1970), *New Perspectives in Transportation Research* (1972), *Scientific Methods of Urban Analysis* (1972), *Planners and Local Politics* (1974), and *Personality, Politics, and Planning: How City Planners Work* (1978). Long active in the American Institute of Planners, Dr. Catanese also has been involved in political campaigns as a policy analyst and is a Commissioner, Milwaukee City Plan Commission.

Contributors

WAYNE O. ATTOE is Associate Professor of Architecture, University of Wisconsin-Milwaukee, where he teaches in the areas of architectural design, architectural criticism, and historic preservation. Dr. Attoe has degrees from Cornell University (B.A.), the University of California, Berkeley (B. Arch.), and the Union Graduate School (Ph.D.). He is the author of *Architecture and Critical Imagination* (1978).

FELICITY BROGDEN is an Assistant Professor of Architecture, University of Wisconsin-Milwaukee, where she teaches and conducts research in the areas of environmental design, neighborhood preservation, adaptive reuse, and public housing management. Dr. Brogden has degrees from the University of Hull, England (B.A.), the University of Nottingham (M.A. Urban Planning), and the University of Wisconsin-Madison (Ph.D.). She has taught at the University of Strathclyde and the University of Wisconsin-Madison and is a member of the Royal Town Planning Institute.

URIEL COHEN is Assistant Professor, University of Wisconsin-Milwaukee, where he teaches in the areas of environment-behavior studies, human factors, research methods, postoccupancy evaluation, programming, health care systems, and design. He holds degrees from the University of Illinois (B. Arch.) and the University of Michigan (M. Arch. and Ph.D. Arch. candidate). Professor Cohen is a regional editor for *Man-Environment Systems* and has written numerous articles on environment-behavior studies and architectural programming.

STEPHEN D. DENT, AIA is an architect and a Visiting Assistant Professor of Architecture, University of Wisconsin-Milwaukee, where he teaches energy-conscious design. He has degrees from the University of Southern California (B. Arch.) and Arizona State University (M. Arch.) and has practiced urban planning and design in Los Angeles and Baltimore.

DAVID EVAN GLASSER is Associate Professor of Architecture, University of Wisconsin-Milwaukee. He received his professional education at Cooper Union for the Advancement of Art and Science in New York and Columbia University School of Architecture (B. Arch.). Professor Glasser has maintained an architectural practice since 1966 and has worked on award-winning projects throughout the United States and abroad. He has taught architectural design and building construction at Columbia University, Community College of New York, the University of Wisconsin, and Harvard University. He recently received international recognition for the Treetops Condominium Project, Hilton Head, South Carolina.

FREDERICK A. JULES is an architect and Associate Professor of Architecture, University of Wisconsin-Milwaukee, where he teaches building design. He has degrees from Carnegie Mellon University (B. Arch.) and Harvard University (M. Arch.). Professor Jules has designed numerous buildings and wrote "Form-Space and the Language of Architecture" (1974).

TIM MCGINTY is a licensed architect and an Associate Professor of Architecture, University of Wisconsin-Milwaukee, where he teaches undergraduate and graduate architectural design. Professor McGinty has degrees from the University of Kansas (B. Arch.) and the University of Pennsylvania (M. Arch.). He has written several texts, including *Drawing Skills in Architecture* (1977).

GARY T. MOORE is an Assistant Professor of Architecture, University of Wisconsin-Milwaukee, where he teaches and conducts research in the area of behavioral factors in architecture. He holds degrees from the University of California, Berkeley (B. Arch.) and Clark University (M.A.) and is a Ph. D. candidate in environmental psychology. Professor Moore specializes in the areas of children and the environment, environmental cognition, special user groups, postoccupancy evaluation, and programming. He has edited two texts, *Emerging Methods in Environmental Design and Planning* (1970) and *Environmental Knowing* (1976). He is a founder of the Design Methods Group (DMG) and the Environmental Design Research Association (EDRA) and was corecipient of 1978 and 1979 *Progressive Architecture* Citations for Applied Research.

JEFFREY E. OLLSWANG is an architect and Associate Professor of Architecture, University of Wisconsin-Milwaukee, where he teaches environmental design and environmental control systems. He has degrees from Cooper Union (B. Arch.), the University of Oregon (M. Arch.), and the University of Strathclyde (M. Science) and has taught at the Universities of Oregon, Glasgow, Arizona, and Wisconsin.

DAVID J. PARSONS, AIA, is an Assistant Professor of Architecture and Director for the Energy Demonstration Project, University of Wisconsin-Milwaukee. He holds B.A. and M. Arch. degrees from Harvard College and Harvard Graduate School of Design. Professor Parsons teaches and has written papers in the areas of building process and information systems.

HARVEY Z. RABINOWITZ is an Architect and Associate Professor of Architecture, University of Wisconsin-Milwaukee, where he is a consultant and teacher in the areas of market and feasibility analysis, building development, and building evaluation. He has degrees from Cooper Union (B. Arch.) and

Rensselaer Polytechnic Institute (M. Arch.) and has worked for the MITRE Corporation and the Building Research Division of the National Bureau of Standards.

AMOS RAPOPORT is Professor of Architecture and Anthropology at the University of Wisconsin-Milwaukee, where he was a Research Professor between 1974 and 1977. He has a B. Arch. and Postgraduate Diploma of Town and Regional Planning from Melbourne University, Australia and M. Arch. from Rice University. He is a Fellow of the Royal Australian Institute of Architects, an Associate of the Royal Institute of British Architects, and a Registered Architect in Australia. He has taught at Melbourne and Sydney Universities in Australia, the University of California-Berkeley, and University College, London. Professor Rapoport has been involved in human environment studies and has written numerous papers and books, including *House Form and Culture* (1969), *The Mutual Interaction of People and Their Built Environment* (1976), and *Human Aspects of Urban Form* (1977).

JOHN SCHADE is an Associate Professor of Architecture, University of Wisconsin-Milwaukee, where he directs academic and research interests on the subject of energy. He has degrees from Lawrence University (B.A.) and the University of California, Berkeley (M. Arch.). Professor Schade has been involved in numerous energy research projects, including the HUD-AIA Research Corporation National Building Energy Performance Standards Project. He also serves as a consultant to Johnson Controls, Inc. and is president of the Energy Consortium, Inc.

ANTHONY J. SCHNARSKY is an Associate Professor of Architecture, University of Wisconsin-Milwaukee, where he teaches computer applications in architecture. Professor Schnarsky holds bachelor's and master's degrees in architecture from the University of Illinois. He has extensive experience in computing for structural design, automated specifications, information systems, and graphics.

LANI VAN RYZIN is a research assistant and a Ph.D. candidate in behavior-environment studies, University of Wisconsin-Madison. She specializes in the areas of environments for the developing child, environmental measurement, and environmental values.

JOHN W. WADE is an architect and Professor of Architecture, Virginia Polytechnic Institute and State University. He holds degrees from Harvard University (B.A.), Harvard Graduate School of Design (B. Arch.), and the University of Pennsylvania (M. Arch.). He has practiced architecture, taught at numerous universities, and written *Architecture, Problems, and Purposes*, 1977.

ABOUT THE CONTRIBUTORS

Preface

This book is an introductory survey of the built environment. The concern is primarily with the physical elements, with the realization that there are social, economic, and political elements that shape this environment as well. While this may seem limiting, it is a realistic constraint imposed in order to achieve certain pedagogical objectives. Design and planning are considered in this physical sense in order to introduce the many facets of the built environment to entering architecture and urban planning students as well as those seeking an introductory knowledge of these fields.

Architecture and urban planning are fascinating areas for professional practice. These two fields were once one, usually called architecture or master building. Within the last century, the increasing specialization of labor in our society has led to the formation of two distinct fields of study and practice. A principal distinction is that of scale. Architecture is primarily concerned with the built environment at three scales: smaller-than-buildings, buildings, and larger-than-buildings. Although there is sometimes an overlap at the last scale, urban planning is concerned with the built environment from the larger-than-buildings scale to the regional and national scale. While architecture is primarily concerned with physical manifestations of design, and urban planning is more concerned with policy formation and management, both fields are related to the natural environment within the social, economic, and political context of civilization.

There have not yet been any convenient textbooks for these two fields, especially textbooks which deal with the full range of the built environment or the relationships between each professional area. The objective of our two companion volumes, *Introduction to Architecture* and *Introduction to Urban Planning,* is to remedy this problem by incorporating the diverse components of both fields into two interrelated textbooks. By emphasizing the broad perspective and depth of architecture and urban planning, rather than accepting artificially restrictive disciplinary perspectives, we hope to fulfill this need.

The organization and substance of these two volumes was determined largely by the results of surveys undertaken by the editors during 1976 and 1977. Questionnaires were sent to members of every accredited and recognized university-based program in architecture and urban planning. These questionnaires dealt with the content, approach, and literature of introductory courses in architecture and urban planning.

Introductory level courses in architecture can appear at different levels. Entering students in architecture may be freshmen in preprofessional, paraprofessional, or nonprofessional two-year programs; freshmen or sophomores in four- or five-year professional or nonprofessional undergraduate degree programs; juniors or seniors in five- or six-year professional programs; first-year graduate students in two- or three-year professional programs; and even first-year doctoral students. The introductory level course may range from a two- or three-hour lecture course to a nine-hour studio. This variety provides a clue to why there have been so few previous textbooks for introductory courses.

Most of the reading lists for these courses are constructed from scattered text and journal readings dealing with similar subject matter and comprehensive sets of topics. There was sufficient convergence of subject matter and substance to allow us to synthesize a general outline of topics.

Introductory level courses in urban planning sometimes appear at the freshman or sophomore level for nonprofessional undergraduate programs (only a few undergraduate professional programs exist). The more typical introduction to urban planning occurs in the first year of the two-year professional master's degree program. As with architecture courses, it was possible to synthesize an outline of the content and substance of introductory courses in urban planning. While there have been a number of attempts to create textbooks for certain aspects of urban planning (for example, methods), as well as attempts to provide guides for planning practice, there is no comprehensive treatment of the field that incorporates the range of subject matter being taught entry-level students. We hope this volume meets that need.

Most architecture curricula include introductory courses in urban planning, and many urban planning curricula allow for selection of courses dealing with the design and development aspects of architecture. There has been much interest in recent years in both architecture and urban planning programs by nonmajors, especially students in fields that are intertwined in professional practice, such as economics, management, finance, political science, social work, law, history, and anthropology. We believe that the absence of introductory level textbooks for architecture and urban planning has impeded the development of such courses for nonmajors and may well have been a source of frustration for those students who did enroll in such courses. Again, we hope these two volumes will assist with the dissemination of knowledge of architecture and urban planning to these students.

Three guiding principles emerged from our interpretation of survey results (tempered by our own experience and judgment). There is a need for introductory textbooks in architecture and urban planning that:

1 Include those subject areas regularly covered in introductory courses in schools of architecture and programs in urban planning

2 Emphasize the broad perspectives and breadth of both fields rather than constrict substantive issues

3 Are aimed at the student with little or no previous experience in either field

Thus, these companion volumes (used separately or together) are designed to provide a convenient source of readings for the varied introductory level courses offered at the university level. Each volume is sufficient for the typical three-hour, one-semester lecture course. These volumes also can be used as a base of reading for more extensive introductory courses in the studio format. In addition, the breadth of coverage, synthetic nature, and coverage of contemporary subjects should appeal to professional practitioners.

Much credit must be given to the many contributors to these volumes—who have worked together in the best academic and professional tradition. Also, much credit must be given to Mary Eichstaedt and Bruce Thomson for invaluable assistance in production, and to David Damstra from the McGraw-Hill Book Company. The editors assume full responsibility for the texts. Each chapter was edited for organization, clarity, interrelationships with other chapters, sense, and style. In addition, each author worked closely with the editors to ensure an overall level of quality and cohesiveness.

James C. Snyder
Anthony J. Catanese

INTRODUCTION TO ARCHITECTURE

Part One
Origins, Theory, and Behavior

Reservation: Monastery of the early and high Middle Ages, around Mtskheta, the Hellenistic capital of Georgia, U.S.S.R.

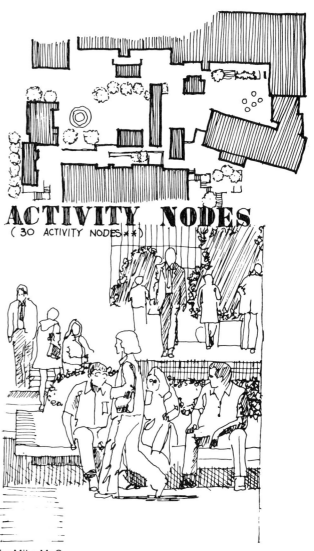

ACTIVITY NODES

(30 ACTIVITY NODES **)

by Mike McGeen

CHAPTER 1

Cultural Origins of Architecture

Amos Rapoport

Most people, if asked, would probably say that architecture began as shelter. After all, the first buildings were dwellings, and people need shelter to survive. Yet shelter is not the only, or even the principal, function of housing. In cold climates—which make stringent demands for shelter and protection—one finds great variability, ranging from minimal shelter in Tierra del Fuego through fairly low levels of protection among some American Indian dwellings in Wisconsin and Minnesota to the highly developed shelter of the Eskimo.

Built environments have various purposes: to shelter people and their activities and possessions from the elements, from human and animal enemies, and from supernatural powers; to establish place; to create a humanized, safe area in a profane and potentially dangerous world; to stress social identity and indicate status; and so on. Thus the origins of architecture are best understood if one takes a wider view and considers sociocultural factors, in the broadest sense, to be more important than climate, technology, materials, and economy.

In any situation, it is the interplay of all these factors that best explains the form of buildings. No single explanation will suffice, because buildings—even apparently humble dwellings—are more than material objects or structures. They are institutions, basic cultural phenomena.

DIFFERENTIATION OF SPACE

The more we learn about animals, the more complex their behavior appears. Animals even differentiate space and create places, which indicates to users that they are *here* rather than *there*. Among animals such places are known and marked; they include home ranges; core areas; territories; and nesting, feeding, and courting areas. Animals thus *make* places. Part of our sense of surprise at this trait is due to the fact that we rarely know wild animals, and domestic animals have lost many of these characteristics of nesting, of marking places, of observing ritual, of structuring time—even of building.[1] Animals also order the environment by abstracting and creating schemata.[2]

If this is so, we might then expect that human beings, even more than animals, should have differentiated among spaces and places from earliest times. Hominids and humans need places to meet in, to share food in, and to hold as private territories. Spatial and social relations thus are not random but ordered.[3] Distinctions are first *known;* humans then *describe* them through language and *make* them through building. In this sense language and architecture are related; both express the cognitive process of distinguishing among places.

Marking places became more important when the first hominids left their trees and began to move across the open savannahs, and later as their cognitive and symbolic needs and abilities grew. While the role of tools and language in this process has been studied, the role of buildings as ways of encoding cognitive schemata and places in physical form has received hardly any attention.

Can we fine evidence for this role of built environments? The answer is that it is difficult *not* to find it! When we consider a group like the Australian aborigines, who build few buildings, we find that they differentiate among places in an apparently featureless desert by *knowing* differences and by giving differential importance to such places. They also mark places in various ways—by attaching myths to them, by reenacting rituals at ceremonial grounds, and by using sacred paintings and engravings on rocks and in caves (as did people in Europe 25,000 years ago). They also raise temporary or permanent markers and monuments; they construct elaborate ritual or ceremonial sites; they use fires as markers; and so on. Buildings, the way we understand them, are not often built and are not very important, although various dwellings do help to further differentiate places from one another. Aborigines also use other devices; for example, around the dwellings women frequently sweep the ground in a circle 30 feet in diameter. This change in the character of the ground marks an important boundary between places of different kinds, in this case between the public camp and the private space of the family. In moving from the "outside" space of the desert (and the various parts of the desert "belonging" to particular groups), to the "semi-inside" place of the camp, and then to the "inside" space of the family unit, there are no walls or barriers. These transitions are important, however, and the invisible barriers cannot easily be passed; various rules of passage apply.[4]

We must not think that such devices are used only by aborigines. In Latin America (Colombia), in dwellings in squatter settlements, there are clear rules about who can penetrate how far. These boundaries are not always indicated by solid walls, sometimes only by bead curtains or changes in floor level.[5] In older farmhouses in Norway and Sweden, one often finds a particular beam in the ceiling that marks the point at which visitors must stop and be admitted. Up to that point, although actually in the room, visitors are regarded as being outside. This "waiting for admission" is very similiar to what happens at an aboriginal camp, or a Bedouin tent, or even among baboons.

If there are differences in inhabited spaces, one would expect *transitions* to be significant. We have just discussed admission rituals; socially there are rites of passage to mark social transitions, and these often have spatial equivalents. Architecture makes manifest spatial transitions that, of course, have

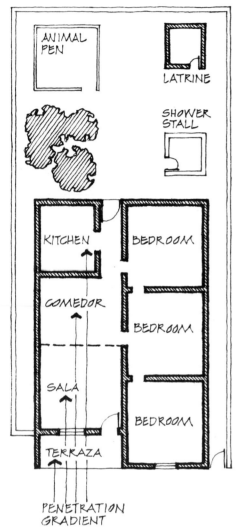

Plan of squatter house, Barranquilla, Colombia. The penetration gradient restricts visitors to the sala (based on Foster, 1972).

social and conceptual significance. Thus walls, gates, doors, thresholds, and the like often mark transitions between inside/outside, sacred/profane, male/female, public/private, and other kinds of domains; hence their importance. But even more important is the very fact of differentiation.

For example, a single-room Maya house, 23 by

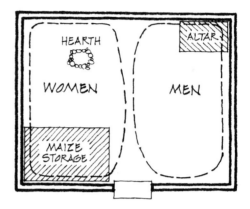

Men's and women's domains in a modern Maya house, not physically expressed (based on Vogt, 1969).

20 feet, is conceptually divided in a rather complex way into men's and women's domains, although it is not physically divided. Even tents can be very complex conceptually, so that among some Turkish tribes there is an important cognitive distinction between the round tent (the Yurt), which is women's domain, and the large rectangular black tent, which is the men's. At the same time—and we shall see this characteristic as being general—the Yurt itself is a model of the universe, the smoke coming out of the smoke hole being the *axis mundi* (axis of the world). Similiarly, the Navaho hogan, a small one-room dwelling, is extraordinarily complex in concept and is divided into several domains.[6] Two more examples should suffice. Among the Maya of Cozumel, and generally in Putun-dominated Yucatan, art was not important, yet there was a desire to impress. Houses had imposing facades of stone, smoothly plastered and brightly painted with doors leading into the dim interior under a thatched shady portico; behind this false front were pole walls.[7] The distinction here was between front and back. A similiar distinction, but one that was differently handled, is found at the Frilandsmuseet, an outdoor museum of Danish vernacular architecture near Copenhagen that includes a fisherman's cottage from Agger on the North Sea coast. If we look just at the residential

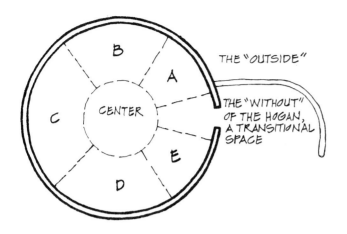

A SMALL CORNER IN THE NORTH
B NORTH CORNER
C WEST CORNER
D SMALL CORNER
E SMALL CORNER IN THE EAST

Diagram of internal layout typical of Navajo hogans.

section of the cottage (a small part of the whole) we find that *half* the space available was a formal ("best") room that could not be heated and was rarely used, and then only for formal occasions. All

the other activities—living, dining, sleeping—took place in the other half of the house. This front/back distinction communicated respectability, and it has been found in many other parts of the world.

The Antiquity of Architecture

How early in the history of the human species can evidence for buildings be found? How early can evidence for differentiation be found?

Clearly, systems like those used by the Australian aborigines will leave few traces, although archaeologists can identify camp sites used over very long periods and sometimes even individual hut sites. To use a very different culture as an example, Eskimos also differentiate among places without buildings and in ways that leave no traces. Their system of differentiation is based on a belief in various forms of evil spirits and ghosts, which differentiated the land into domains with various rules for use, avoidance, travel, residence, and the like.[8] More generally, one can show that the human mind has the need to differentiate—classify, name, and distinguish—among places; taxonomies and domains are basic to cognition and to making the world meaningful.[9]

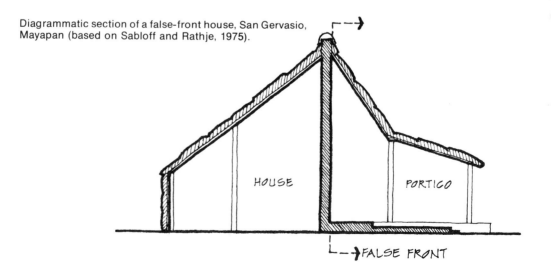

Diagrammatic section of a false-front house, San Gervasio, Mayapan (based on Sabloff and Rathje, 1975).

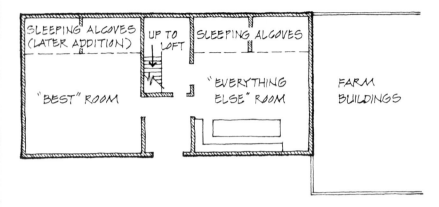

Diagrammatic plan of fisherman's cottage, Agger, North Sea coast, Denmark.

In recent years the origin of humans has been pushed back in time. Buildings also seem to go back much further than anyone would have supposed until recently. A striking example is the evidence that hominids such as the Upper Pliocene *Australopithecines* had some shelters. Semicircular stone elements that may have been either windbreaks or bases for huts 2 meters across were found in Olduvai Gorge, Tanzania, going back approximately 1.8 million years. These sites seem to have been well established by then; this is thought because home-base behavior is a fundamental feature of human behavior as opposed to that of other primates. The nonshelter function of such construction—marking *home*—is probably at least as important as its role as shelter (if not more so).[10]

The next example is much more recent—it only goes back 300,000 years! This is a camp at Terra Amata, near Nice in the south of France. There 21 superimposed huts were found in one group and 11 huts in another. The dwellings were of an elongated oval shape, between 26 and 49 feet long and 13 to 20 feet wide. It is very likely that each held more than one family, and their number suggests a group of families. The construction of dwellings to hold several families implies a complex social organization. Many tools, red ochre sticks for color, and a wide range of goods were found, and the suggestion is that there was a fairly highly developed ritual life. The dwellings were constructed by thrusting long

sticks, 3 inches in diameter, into the ground in a regular order, bending them inwards, and attaching them to a row of central posts (it is unknown whether a ridgepole was used). Stones were placed along the base of the wall. Inside, near the center, was a hearth—either a shallow pit or a pebbled surface.[11]

In the New World also the dates of dwellings, villages, and other cognitive achievements have been pushed back. Recent excavations made by Stuart Struever at the Koster site in Illinois, 50 miles north of St. Louis, have revealed a village dating from 7000 B.C.E. (Before Common Era), with houses, tools, and both human and dog cemeteries. Dogs were buried surrounded by ceremonial fires. It is significant that, since the glaciers receded from this area about 8000 B.C.E., permanent houses and villages developed very quickly. Since there are still some unexcavated layers beneath the one described, the origins here are earlier yet.

As a final example, consider Britain. Until recently its early image was one of a rather rude barbarian culture; yet already during the Neolithic era, approximately 4000 B.C.E., one finds very complex causewayed camps 1000 feet in diameter. Tombs up to 490 feet long (called "long barrows") are also found, sometimes related to "avenues" with banks 300 feet apart. At Stonehenge one such avenue is $1\frac{3}{4}$ miles long; another in Dorset is 6 miles long. It was necessary to excavate $6\frac{1}{2}$ million cubic feet of chalk from two parallel ditches to create the two banks 300

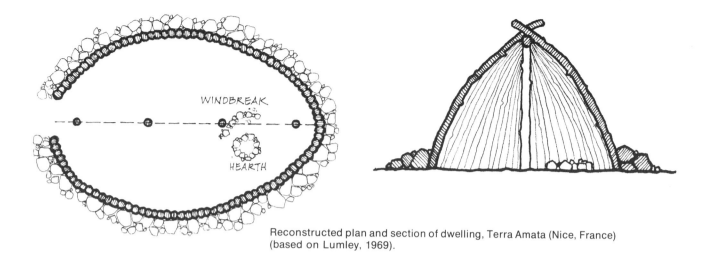

Reconstructed plan and section of dwelling, Terra Amata (Nice, France) (based on Lumley, 1969).

feet apart, which enclosed 220 acres of avenue that may have been used for processions. At about 2500 B.C.E. one finds a series of enormous wooden buildings up to 130 feet in diameter within earth enclosures, supported by concentric rows of columns and probably having conical roofs and a central courtyard. The largest ones required up to 260 tons of timber, and 9 acres of woodland had to be felled for one building.

At that time artificial hills were also built. Silbury Hill, 130 feet high, was not just heaped up but was carefully engineered and constructed of stepped layers. This hill used 9 million cubic feet of rubble, of which 6 million was excavated, forming a ditch. Finally, various megaliths, circles, "fans," and stone- and wood-henges were constructed all over Britain (and Brittany), all carefully designed using a standardized "megalithic yard" and using material brought long distances. These structures seem to have served for both solar and lunar observation in a rather complex science. They were related to landscape features and—in the case of cemeteries, burrows, and so on—to major routes. They could thus be used as markers in the landscape. At the same time one finds villages like Skara Brae in the Orkneys, with a street linking a set of circular stone houses containing stone furnishings, yet clearly

much more "primitive" than the monuments just described. Thus, the people who built these complex and vast structures generally lived in small huts or tents.[12]

Thus, dwellings and monumental buildings have been shown to be early and to be widely distributed, and so has evidence for major cognitive activity; the two seem related. We find vast resources, labor, and effort going into nonshelter constructions, and, when a conflict arises between the plan sought and difficulties of construction and economics, the former wins. Thus in the case of the Maya ceremonial center at Lubaantun in Belize, the plan was carried out at the cost of very complex and expensive site works, although small changes in the plan would have avoided those. The outcome was a development differentiated along many dimensions and in very complex ways.[13]

What Is Architecture?

People have been planning and building for a long time. But was it architecture? Until fairly recently, it was common to distinguish between architecture and "mere buildings," but this is becoming more difficult. Certainly the origins of architecture predate the first architect, who is traditionally taken to have

8

been the designer of a stepped pyramid in Egypt. Even if one includes the specialist builders of certain chiefs' houses and ritual buildings, most of what was built was not designed by professionals but was rather an expression of the same architectural impulse that prompts high-style design (that done by designers). Thus, in dealing with the origins of architecture or an understanding of what architecture is, we must be concerned with the folk or popular tradition—the buildings called "primitive" or "vernacular" that have always comprised the bulk of the built environment and that are essential for any valid generalizations, and certainly critical for a discussion of origins.

All such environments, as well as all human artifacts, are *designed*, in the sense that they embody human decisions and choices and specific ways of doing things. A person clearing a forest, putting up a roadside stand, or laying out a camp is as much a designer as an architect—such activities change the face of the earth and create built environments.

All environments result from choices made from among all possible alternatives. The specific choices tend to be lawful, reflecting the culture of the people concerned. In fact, one way of looking at culture is in terms of the most common choices made. It is the lawfulness of decisions that makes places —and buildings—recognizably different from one another; lawfulness also leads to specific ways of dressing, behaving, eating, and so on. It affects the way people interact, the way they structure space and time. These consistent choices result in *style*—whether of built environments or of life.

In making these choices, certain values, norms, criteria, and assumptions are called upon. These are often embodied in ideal schemata. Environments, in some way, reflect and encode these schemata and the order they typify.[14] The order expressed through the process of choice, the image to be encoded and given form, is some vision of an ideal environment that built environments express, however imperfectly. Such environments are conceptualized as settings for the kind of people whom a particular cul-

ture sees as being normative, and for the kind of lifestyle that is regarded as significant and typical of the group and that distinguishes it from other groups. In fact, what we call culture can be seen in three major ways (the first two of which are included above): as a way of life that typifies a group; as a system of symbols, meanings, and cognitive schemata; and as a set of adaptive strategies for survival, related to ecology and resources.

Thus, culture concerns a group of people who have a set of values and beliefs and a world view that embody an ideal. These rules also led to systematic and consistent choices. With our earlier statement that architecture is a result primarily of sociocultural factors, and with our definition of design to include most purposeful changes to the physical environment, architecture can be thought of as any construction that deliberately changes the physical environment according to some ordering schema. The difference between buildings and settlements is one of scale. As Aldo Van Eyck once said, "A building is a small city; a city is a large building."

To answer the question of why people build environments, we need to understand how the human mind works. Schemata represent one product of what seems a basic process of the human mind, to give the world meaning, to humanize it by imposing order on it—a cognitive order often achieved through classifying and naming, or *differentiating*. The world is chaotic and disorderly; the human mind classifies, differentiates, and orders. We could say that the order is thought before it is built. Settlements, buildings, and landscapes are part of this activity, which, as we have already seen, goes back a long way. When Neanderthals buried their dead with flowers they were trying to impose an order reconciling life and death. The cave paintings of Europe mark complex ordering systems and define caves as sacred spaces, different from other spaces such as dwelling caves that were *not* painted. Symbolic notational systems, in this case of lunar observations, are found remarkably early and clearly represent attempts to impose an order on time and natural phenomena.[15]

People think environments before they build them. Thought orders space, time, activity, status, roles, and behavior. But giving physical expression to ideas is valuable. Encoding ideas makes them useful mnemonics; ideas help behavior by reminding people of how to act, how to behave, and what is expected of them. It is important to stress that all built environments—buildings, settlements, and landscapes—are one way of ordering the world by making ordering systems visible. The essential step, therefore, is the ordering or organizing of the environment.

THE ORGANIZATION OF THE ENVIRONMENT

We saw above that animals structure space; they also organize time. Cats, for example, which are nonterritorial, avoid each other by scheduling their movements.[16] The purpose of structuring space and time is to organize and structure communication (interaction, avoidance, dominance, and so on). Through ritualized behaviors and various ways of marking territories, meaning is given to places and behaviors. Meaning is thus organized.

Even more strongly in the case of humans, when environments are being organized, it is these four elements—space, meaning, communication, and time—that are being organized. That is, the environment can be seen as a series of relationships between things and other things, things and people, and between people and other people. These relationships are orderly; they have pattern and structure; the environment is *not* a random assemblage of things. These relationships are also primarily, but not exclusively, spatial; objects and people are related through various degrees of separation in and by space.

Such organizations can also be seen as physical expressions of domains.[17] In fact, planning and design on all scales, from vast regions to furniture arrangements, can be seen as the organization of space for different purposes, according to different rules that reflect the needs, values, and desires of the groups or individuals doing the organizing. Rules also embody ideal images representing the congruence (or lack of it) between physical space and social, conceptual, and other kinds of space.

This is also an example of the organization of meaning, and the two can be separated conceptually and in fact. While the organization of space itself expresses meaning and has communicative properties, meaning is often embodied in signs, materials, colors, forms, size, furnishings, landscaping, and the like. Thus, meaning may coincide with space organization, and it usually did in most traditional settings. It may, however, also represent a separate, noncoinciding symbolic system through which different settings become indicators of social position—ways of establishing social identity to oneself and others, of indicating expected behavior, and so on. Meanings are naturally clearest and strongest when there is high redundancy, when spatial, meaning, and activity systems are congruent and therefore reinforce one another.

An important reason for such congruence is that the meaning of the environment and of settings within it helps social communication among people (meaning is also communication from the environment to people). Thus environments, spatially and through meanings, influence and reflect the organization of communication. Who communicates with whom, under what conditions, how, when, where, and in what context, are important factors in the way in which the built environment and social organization are linked and related. Environments reflect and control interaction, its nature, intensity, rate, direction, and so on. If people notice and understand cues in the environment identifying particular kinds of settings, they know how to behave appropriately; the social context is established. Of course, people also need to be prepared to act appropriately; but if the cues are not noticed or understood, appropriate behavior becomes impossible.

Finally, people live in time as well as in space;

the environment is temporal and can be seen as the organization of time or as reflecting and influencing behavior in time. This may be understood in two ways. The first refers to large-scale, cognitive structuring of time, such as linear flow versus cyclic time, future orientation versus past orientation, the future as an improvement over the present versus the future as a time likely to be worse, how time is valued, and hence how finely it is subdivided into units. This last consideration influences the second way in which the organization of time can be considered: the tempos, or number of events per unit time, and the rhythms, or the distribution of activities in time, for example, day and night. The tempos and rhythms may be congruent or incongruent with each other, so that people may be separated in time as well as, or instead of, in space. Thus groups with different rhythms occupying the same space may never meet, and groups with different tempos may never communicate. Clearly, spatial and temporal aspects interact and influence one another—people live in space-time.

In traditional situations these four organizations—of space, meaning, communication, and time—were more uniform and coincided more. For example, temporal organization was more uniform, being based on natural diurnal or seasonal cycles. At the same time, most people accepted the ritual/religious calendar. Temporal and spatial organization also worked together. For example, among Australian aborigines, darkness and the location of fires in front of each family's dwelling area led to an inability to see each other at night. This created a particular system of conflict resolution through verbal means, which breaks down when lighting is introduced, with consequent increases in stress and aggression.[18]

In terms of meanings, there was a much greater sharing of symbols and the cues that communicated them. Most people agreed about them, and the environment/meaning congruence was strong and clear. Space organization also clearly related to meaning. Communication was much more predictable, being

fixed and prescribed, and it related to membership in various groups.

In the case of traditional environments it therefore becomes possible to concentrate on spatial organization as reflecting and influencing all the others to a greater extent than is possible now. This is fortunate, since much of our evidence on early buildings is archaeological and exists largely in terms of space organization as revealing ordering systems.

Ordering Systems

Built environments represent physical expressions of ordering systems and schemata, a basic property of the human mind. This process is always the same, although the specific *form* of ordering and the *means* used to express it physically are culturally specific.

In all traditional situations, and particularly those at the origins of architecture, the ordering schemata are frequently based on the sacred, since religion and ritual are central (although other schemata also play a role). If built environments are humanized environments, livable places, then for most traditional peoples they must be, by definition, sacred or sanctified. Since the world view of traditional societies is religious, built environments—which encode ideals—must encode the sacred, since that represents the most significant meaning.

Thus the house of the Temne people of Africa cannot be described completely in physical and geometric terms. The decision to build a Temne house is not followed by the production of a plan, but by a communion with one's ancestors to secure their blessing. The space created is circular and *kanta* (closed), which is quite different from modern western ordering systems. Temne space is articulated not through geometry and arithmetic but through meanings. Closed space is separated, humanized, and barred against witches and demons. Cardinal directions (especially east) have great meaning in this process. Most traditional dwellings and other buildings can only be understood in this way—as part of the general process of separating the sacred from the profane.[19]

Most traditional buildings, like settlements, are earthly representations of heavenly images, incorporating world axes, navels of the world, cardinal directions, circularity, or rectangularity, and all being an attempt to differentiate a sacred, and hence human, habitable domain from the profane chaos around. As part of this process, complex and appropriate rituals accompany the starting, construction, and completion of buildings, very similiar to those involved in setting up settlements. In fact, all the characteristics just described greatly resemble those of the construction of cities. In all cases, buildings and settlements become real through schemata and rituals. For example, the houses at Lepenski Vir, a Yugoslavian settlement of the seventh millenium B.C.E., are based on the same trapezoidal shape as the settlement. The settlement is conceived as a gigantic house, and the house plan can actually be superimposed on a human skeleton in a particular position used in burials. In this way, the house expresses meaning based on the human body.[20]

It has been suggested that all symbols are based on the human body, and it may well be that architecture is, in some way, a metaphor for the human body, thus relating architecture once again to our animal origins.[21]

In any case, buildings are certainly metaphors for social situations, contexts, and schemata. Thus the North African Berber house is rectangular in plan and looks quite simple. Its description and analysis are, however, most complex. The house is a microcosm organized in the same way as the universe and is an extraordinarily complicated creation. To understand it, we need to know much about the organization of religion, symbols, schemata— about culture. Its orientation, the separation of men and women, and the importance of the threshold all make it into a place fraught with significance.[22]

Similiarly, the Thai house is a vital element in the organization of rules concerning the edibility of animals, concepts relating to marriage and sex, and

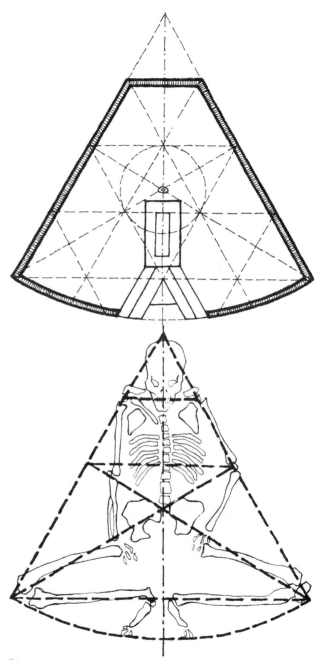

Diagram of dwelling plan based on position of skeleton buried under dwelling, Lepenski Vir, Yugoslavia (based on Srejovic, 1974).

CULTURAL ORIGINS OF ARCHITECTURE

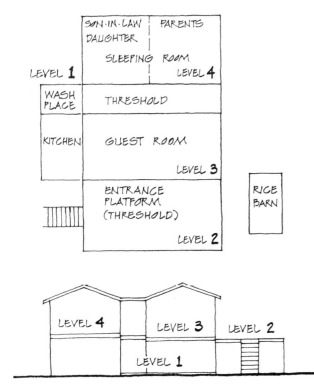

Diagrammatic plan and section of house, Mekong River, Thailand (Tambiah, 1973).

the like. The spatial ordering of the house is a domain of conceptualization that is closely related to the conceptualization of other domains; it is central in cognitive ordering generally. This spatial ordering is made evident in the physical arrangement of areas and rooms, directions, orientations, floor level differences, rules of the use of the house, and so on.[23] Yet at first glance the house seems simple.

The longhouse, in which various rituals and rites were performed, was a symbol of the universe of the Iroquois. Sacred dances occurred in the longhouse, and eating food in it was a sacrament. The longhouse symbolized the league, and its layout paralleled the league's geographical divisions. The way people were located in the longhouse represented the way the various tribes and nations of the confed-

eracy were related geographically. These parallels relate three symbolic elements—the topography of the homeland of the longhouse league (with a floor terrain 200 miles long), the longhouses in which people lived, and the spirit of cohesion that bound the members of the league like the related families in their longhouse. The Five Nations of the league seat themselves in the longhouse council in this manner today. Today, many families have moved into single-family houses but retain the longhouse for ceremonies. Very similiar ceremonial functions persist in the Navaho hogan, and sometimes new buildings are actually designed and constructed to help cultures survive. In the case of the Fang in Africa, a new building and its associated rituals miniaturize, as it were, the cognitive schemata of the group, whose traditional environment expressing these schemata was gradually disappearing.[24]

With time such symbolism is increasingly confined to nonresidential buildings and tends to disappear or weaken in dwellings. However, even then, it is possible to see new schemata and ordering systems expressed. Thus we can suggest that sun, view, space, and health are substituted for sacred directions in United States dwellings.[25] But let us turn to some examples of nonresidential buildings.

In ancient Egypt life was considered a microcosm reflecting macrocosmic processes. The physical world reflected the eternal realm. Units of space and time were miniatures of more significant spaces and times. The temple was "the mansion of the god," a replica on earth of the god's eternal dwelling. The mortuary temples of kings were called "mansions of millions of years" and were thus built of stone, while other buildings—including palaces—were built of brick. The sanctuary of each major temple was conceptually at the hub of the universe, on the primeval island on which creation had taken place. The temple *was* the residence of the creator.[26]

In traditional Hindu architecture, space, time, and matter are manifestations of the creator; material space and material things make visible ideational space. For the architectural environment, this has three consequences. First, it stresses limits of control: one changes oneself rather than the environment. Thus, building—which is a major modification of the environment—requires rigorous adherence to the appropriate cosmological model and also requires stress on ritual purity within the setting. Second, the cosmological models emphasize the center, and centrality is most important socially and architecturally. Third, ideational space can only be made manifest through symbols. Space is transformed by symbols and rituals so that the divine is made visible, and architecture is called *Vastu-Vidya,* "the science of the dwellings of the gods." To understand architecture, we must understand the divine cosmological model that underlies landscapes, towns, villages, temples, and houses.[27]

In what ways, then, do nonresidential buildings differ from dwellings? In two ways: they are more permanent and lasting, and their congruence with the ideal model is more precise. The details of temple design are not as important as the fact that architecture is a "symbolic technology," less concerned with beauty or fitting behavior than with harmonizing form with divine models.

We might suppose that in moving from India to the Renaissance, we would find a very different model, and that had once been the popular view. It now seems clear, however, that Renaissance architecture was not based on aesthetics alone but did, in fact, try to express an ideal model, which was sacred. Only thus can centrality and mathematical proportion be explained. The architectural harmony was a visible expression of a more basic, celestial harmony; "the centrally planned church was the man-made echo or image of God's universe and it is *this* shape which discloses 'the unity, the infinite essence, the uniformity and the justice of God'"—and this perfection is based on Platonic cosmology.[28] We are not so far now from the Hindu view of architecture, or the Temne view! Similarly, Gothic cathedrals, Byzantine churches, and mosques in Iran are all specific expressions of cosmic models or visions of paradise—places differentiated by being spe-

cially sacred. As a final example, Hadrian's Pantheon in Rome was cosmology expressed in architecture, sculpture, and light. There was an intimate connection between the forces of the cosmos, the ruler, and the subject. The Pantheon was not a temple in traditional terms; it expressed certain ideas, notably universality, in various ways. It expressed a universal empire reflected on earth; it was a claim to an empire, an icon of Rome's claim and mission, an order of empire sanctioned and watched over by the gods.[29]

Sacred and Profane Buildings

If all buildings and built environments in traditional societies are sacred, why do many or most cultures have buildings of special sanctity? The answer has already been suggested: the distinction is one of degree. These structures are different and try to approximate the ideal schemata more closely.

Aborigines, for example, have sites of particular sanctity, which are more protected and to which access is more restricted than to mundane sites (those containing resources). The process of ordering and differentiation implies that there is a hierarchy of sanctity; this is a clear way of differentiating among places. A Navaho Hogan is sacred, but a special Hogan is built for curing ceremonies and is sanctified through special rituals, sand painting, and so on. A Maya settlement is sanctified as a whole through ritual, but the rituals depend on relating the settlement to specially sacred sites, buildings, and monuments. As we saw, such distinctions are also found in high-style design.

How are such buildings and places distinguished? As we pointed out, the purpose is to approximate the ideal more closely and also to stress the difference. Thus special symbols are often used, even when the space organization is the same, by using the distinction among fixed feature, semifixed feature, and nonfixed feature elements.[30] The fixed feature elements are the same, but the semifixed feature ones are used to indicate the special nature of the place. For example, in Çatal Hüyük, an eighth-millenium B.C.E. settlement in Anatolia, the shrines do not differ in plan from houses, but they are much more lavishly decorated. Although even houses have decorations, in the shrines these are more elaborate; there are more paintings and sculptures, colors differ, and there seems to exist a symbolism of east and west walls.[31] These are clearly semifixed elements. Similarly, size and location may be used to stress special character. At Nea Nokomedia, a seventh-millenium B.C.E. settlement in northern Greece, the sacred building is larger (40 feet square versus 25 feet square) and located near the center of the area.[32] In the case of Dalni Vestonice, a 25,000-year-old settlement in Czechoslovakia, the sacred building is located outside the settlement enclosure. The means in these two cases are opposite, but both stress the differences among places.

In many vernacular situations, in villages in Greece, Peru, and so on, the special buildings may be distinguished by size (larger or smaller), color, form, materials, the presence of a cross or tower, and so on. The distinctive feature may be a combination of elements, such location, size, color, and decoration, as in the 60-foot high, elaborately decorated Haus Tambaran, the men's ritual place, towering above the houses built of thatch in a Sepik river village in New Guinea. It may be the form, as in the pueblos of the southwest where the kiva is generally subterranean and round, thus being distinguished from the rectangular, above-ground dwellings. It may be merely location in space, barely indicated through physical cues, as in the Maori Marae in New Zealand. It may be size, elaborateness, and materials, as in the Rumanian village church. In this case materials are most important; the church uses new ones, the dwellings, traditional ones.[33] Modernity is thus used to stress the sacred building. Such buildings change more rapidly, using new materials and techniques. The kiva changes less rapidly; it is the archaic form of the dwelling. The means differ, but the objective is the same—these places are different. Thus in each case what is important is the

distinction made, the differentiation itself.

Clearly, not all distinctions are made in terms of the sacred, although, to reiterate, at its origins that is basic. Considering materials again, we find that in the early meso-American village, adobe is first used for public buildings, then for dwellings of high-status individuals, then for all dwellings.[34] We have already seen materials used to differentiate between front and back. In Latin America generally (and elsewhere), materials and ordering systems are related to status and even to ethnicity.

Thus, in San Pedro, Colombia, the organization of houses along a grid and the use of manufactured materials such as tile, brick, and concrete indicate high status and non-Indianness, while irregular arrangements and natural materials such as thatch, earth, wattle, and so on indicate low status and Indianness. A similiar distinction is communicated by the difference between two-story and one-story buildings.[35]

THE PURPOSES OF ARCHITECTURE

To return to the original question: why do people create built environments of such elaborateness? What are the possible purposes of architecture? Even the brief analysis we have made so far suggests that its purposes go beyond the shelter function of modifying the microclimate. Architecture can provide settings for certain activities; remind people of what these activities are; signify power, status, or privacy; express and support cosmological beliefs; communicate information; help establish individual or group identity; and encode value systems. It can also separate domains and differentiate between here and there, sacred and profane, men and women, front and back, private and public, habitable and unhabitable, and so on. Although the differentiation among places is central, the purposes for which it is done and the means employed to do it may be very different.

We have already seen that domains may be separated conceptually, through changes in the nature of ground cover or its treatment (such as sweeping or covering with sand) or through symbolic devices such as ceiling beams or bead curtains. Low fences or even cornerstones may have the same effect. An example of the latter is provided by a squatter settlement in Africa, where whitewashed stones marking the corners of the lot kept people from trespassing the whole property. Changes in level or solid barriers may also be used. One particular device, such as a solid barrier, may have different purposes that are not necessarily mutually exclusive. Such barriers may screen from view, prevent movement, give shade, protect from the wind, separate domains, provide a series of distinguishable settings for distinct activities, and so on. Thus, buildings can be understood in terms of how they relate to people and natural settings and how these relationships change with culture and over time.

Also, if shelter were the only, or even the principal, function of architecture, we would find less variation in forms. We would expect a regular increase with severity of climate—which we do not find even if we take the extreme cold end of the scale. Furthermore, we find the same houses in different climatic zones, as well as form and material differences in identical climatic zones. Such differences often relate to status and degree of publicness.[36]

Again, if shelter were the principal function of architecture, we would not expect the development of specialized buildings other than dwellings to occur very early. Yet we have already seen the opposite to be the case, and one change over time is that differentiation of building types tends to increase. Thus at Olduvai the huts are similiar; at Terra Amata their sizes differ but there is no indication of different uses; at Dalni Vestonice and Nea Nokomedia we find apparently sacred buildings that at Çatal Hüyük are clearly differentiated. Later still, we find more and bigger differentiations—from one room to many rooms for different purposes, from dwelling and work combined to separation of dwelling and work, from house and shop combined to a separation of those and then to specialized work and shop settings, and so on. There is thus a general tendency towards the separation of activities in different settings. Similiarly, we would expect a tendency for materials to be used in terms of their availability, but this is not the case. We have also seen that materials come to have meaning; they have communicative functions.

Architecture makes tangible meanings; it produces concrete metaphors of the ideals and beliefs of a group. It has even been suggested that certain forms in architecture are mimetic, that pyramids, temples, domes, and towers humanize and make permanent shapes that have acquired ideological and symbolic value in perishable materials. These can be important landscapes, so that sacred places become clearly identified with their deities through temples being built, both reinforcing the relation of landscape and god and reminding people of it.[37] Such architecture also does that for behavior, by identifying a setting that reminds people of the context and of expected and appropriate behavior.

If we use the notion of behavior as drama, it follows that the proper settings and props make it easier to play appropriate roles. It is thus useful to express settings physically, to remind people of how to behave. Consider a performance, whether ritual or dramatic. Clearly it can occur any place where there is enough room for audience and actors. However, it is beneficial to mark that place in some way. Thus Australian aborigines lay out ritual grounds, prepare them, erect elements that act as scenery, and decorate their bodies as "mobile architecture." The next step is to set aside a permanent place with the proper relationship between audience and actors, reflecting notions of how performances should be given and how people should behave.

Thus buildings are ways of ordering behavior by placing it into discrete and distinguishable places and settings, each demanding known and expected behaviors, roles, and the like. Thus priests, merchants, actors, and rulers need religious buildings, markets or shops, theaters or palaces. Families need dwellings.

In ancient Egypt, the design of the royal palace can be understood only if we do not think of it in terms of Western buildings. It is not a large house, like the Vatican, Hampton Court, or Versailles (although even those had clear nonresidential meanings). The palace in ancient Egypt was primarily a device to emphasize the power of the ruler, to enhance power by creating a feeling of awe in the minds of subjects. This was done through materials and state management; arrival, entry, and movement occurred in organized spaces and settings. The palace is a "ruling machine."[38]

To reiterate, all these examples have one thing in common: they make visible differences among places and their associated behaviors. This is the meaning of the Australian aborigines' sweeping an area around their minimal dwelling, and of the behavior of the !Kung bushmen.

!Kung women take only 45 minutes to build a shelter. But frequently they will not feel like building a shelter at all. They then put up two sticks to symbolize the entrance to the shelter and build no shelter at all. This allows the family to orient themselves and know which is the men's or women's side of the fire. It also allows others to know the relationship of dwellings to camp.[39] This is clearly a mnemonic that is not even essential, since occasionally the women do not even bother with sticks. The greater the redundancy of information, however the easier social behavior becomes, the easier it is to achieve congruence of physical form and activity, and the easier it is to teach appropriate behavior to children. Thus, in pygmy camps, huts are changed around so that the relationships of doors (and the presence or absence of "spite fences") express the relationships among people and the absence or presence of communication.[40] The group is small enough to know who is angry at whom or friendly with whom, but the built environment reminds peo-

ple of these matters; it acts as a mnemonic.

Built environments thus communicate meanings to help serve social purposes; they provide spatiotemporal frameworks, or systems of settings, for human action and appropriate behavior. In the built environment, therefore, distinctions are crucial; they exist as cues for the understanding of other things. This helps explain why latent functions tend to be more important than manifest functions; most people perform similar activities but they mean different things. Also, the more complex and differentiated the group, the greater the help of built environments. In a small, isolated group, knowing settings is enough, whereas later, settings need to be marked and differentiated; finally, even that is not enough, as one finds verbal and eikonic signs—meaning systems distinct from architecture and superimposed on it.

Consider the activity of shopping. In a small group, a market is just a place; it becomes something only when it is used. Then it may become permanent, with the ground cleared in a specific location. Then shades or stalls may be added; this communicates trading and its various latent functions. We find markets, bazaars, and shops where bargaining occurs, then department stores and supermarkets where there is no bargaining behavior. In each, behavior is different, and the setting helps communicate the context and the behavior.

Thus architecture, by making visible distinctions among places, communicates information about spatial, social, temporal, and other means of ordering of society. It communicates preferences, hierarchies, lifestyles, and the like. It establishes the sacred, human domain (culture) as distinct from profane nature, or later, the profane human domain as distinct from sacred nature.[41] Architecture becomes so identified with groups, cultures, and lifestyles that it is essential in order to feel at home. Migrants bring architectural forms with them and try to recreate them, and their success in their new environment may depend on their ability to do so.

All this reinforces the basic argument—environments are thought before they are built. Tools have to be thought also. Aborigines find tools in nature, but the object only becomes a tool when matched against a mental template. When tools are made, they are made congruent with the schema. Thus any artifact, no matter how simple, must exist as an idea before it can be built. Once built, the artifact helps to remind us of that idea, and this makes it important.

The persistence of the idea can be seen in situations of cultural change. Thus in North Africa and among the Bedouin of Israel, storerooms are often the first buildings constructed, with the tent being retained as a dwelling. When dwellings are built, they tend to recreate the spatial organization of the tent, and their arrangement on larger scales persists even after dwellings themselves change in form and space organization. Certain core values are encoded at the level of settlement organization even when they are no longer encoded in buildings. Thus one cannot separate dwellings from other buildings, or buildings from settlements. The house-settlement system is a system of settings, and the separation of buildings from settlements in this discussion is arbitrary; both must be considered together.

The House-Settlement System
The importance of the house-settlement system also follows from our discussion of differentiation, the development of different settings for different purposes. Recall that the physical expression of differences is a useful mnemonic that reminds people of many important things, including behavior. The total system reminds them of the appropriate relationships and sequences of behaviors. This also follows from the fact that people live in space-time and have complex activity systems associated with specific other activities and people. Thus, cultural differences lead to different combinations of activities and hence different systems of settings for those. In Moslem cities the coffee house is central to men, while the well is central to women. In South Korea, the tearoom is an essential element for men;

among English working-class men it is the pub; and in certain Hungarian villages it is the stables (where all important decisions are made). It is not altogether clear what a particular setting is or does unless we consider associated places and settings. In fact, taking such a systems view may show that defining buildings is complex. To take the most familiar example—the dwelling—it is far from clear how to define it when we think of it in terms of activities, many of which may also take place in other, and unexpected, parts of the house-settlement system.

These differences in house-settlement systems, the relationship between high-style elements and the vernacular matrix, and differences in schemata also lead to the realization that it is very important to look at things cross-culturally. In fact, it takes us back to where we began, with a brief discussion of why it is important to look at things cross-culturally and historically, or why we should look at the cultural origins of architecture.

CROSS-CULTURAL AND HISTORICAL LESSONS

Thus far we have tried to illuminate the meaning of the concept of architecture and thus provide a more adequate basis for design, particularly design based on a full and valid understanding of human behavior as it interacts with built environments. We might ask, why should we study the remote past and all sorts of "primitive" peoples when many of us are concerned with problems of the future. The answer is simple and most important.

The ability to make valid analyses and decisions depends on the availability of a valid theory: so much has been written about architecture from all sorts of perspectives that without theory no one, not even a specialist researcher, can possibly read more than a small portion of it. The only way to deal with this mass of material, much of it scattered in many publications and in many languages, is to develop a theory whereby this material is fitted into larger elements. Such theories tend to be based on evidence from the Western tradition, neglecting many others—African, Asian, Middle Eastern, pre-Columbian, Latin American. They also tend to be based on recent developments and neglect the historical dimension, particularly the remote past and the past in the nonliterate and non-Western tradition. It is thus very important to consider built environments through time and cross-culturally.

One might reasonably still ask, however, what is wrong with concepts based on the Western, high-style tradition of the recent past? The answer—which is basic to this whole chapter and the point of view it represents—is that generalizations based on such a limited sample may be invalid. The broader our sample in space and time, the more likely we are to see regularities in apparent chaos, as well as to understand better those differences that are significant. Thus, the more likely we are to see patterns and relationships, and these are the most significant things for which to look.

Being able to establish the presence of such patterns may help us deal with the problem of constancy and change and establish certain baselines that will guide environmental design. If humans as a species have certain characteristics, and if they have done certain things for a very long time, then there may be very good reasons for these things, particularly if even animals show these patterns. It is very important to understand constancies as well as change, since our culture stresses change to an inordinate degree. Also, if apparent change and variability are an expression of invariant processes, this is extremely important because the reasons for doing apparently different things remain the same.

If we can understand these reasons and the processes they represent, then we may find that apparently unrelated forms and apparently different ways of doing things are equivalent, in the sense that they achieve the same objectives, are the result of similiar mental processes, or are transformations of each other. This helps define what architecture is, what its varied purposes (and the means of achieving them) are, and how architecture is designed.

The view developed here is that all environments reflect schemata and ordering, the antientropic processes of groups. This has tended to create environments that are highly congruent with culture—family structure, lifestyle, hierarchies or their absence, and ritual. Yet today, the same basic processes lead to settings that are not congruent with these variables.

We find that congruent environments tend to involve users in their creation, either directly (through building them) or conceptually (by sharing schemata). Not only is the fit then better, but stress is also generally lower when environments are adapted to people than when people have to adapt to environments. This leads to notions of open-endedness that are reinforced by the argument of the multiple purposes of architecture, by bringing out ideas such as the definition of domains and the organization of meaning through personalization.

An understanding of the processes that have created environments over the millenia during which people have built also has implications for the visual nature of buildings and settlements. Many designers like vernacular architecture, its appropriateness, richness, and complexity. Yet imitations, when tried, have not generally been successful. It is through using the processes (the choices of many individuals sharing some schema of an environment and giving physical expression to both schemata and cues for behavior) that environments of quality and effectiveness can be achieved. At the same time we have seen that the schemata and the means do not have to be the same (we do not have to imitate).

Thus, in effect, a discussion of the origins of architecture in the dim and distant past seems to illuminate some of the latest changes in the notion of what architecture is—the relationship of behavior to environment, the design process, and the relationship of culture to form. At the same time it helps us deepen and clarify new ideas and to place them firmly in the most basic ways in which the human mind works. After all, even animals order the envi-

ronment through abstracting and creating schemata.
Architecture can best be understood when it is seen as much more than shelter and a response to manifest functions. Thus the expression of all the other things buildings and built environments do and are becomes essential and needs to happen. The more we all think in this way, the more likely it is to happen.

NOTES

1. H. Hediger, *Studies in the Psychology and Behavior of Animals in Zoos and Circuses* (London: Butterworth, 1955); V. C. Wynne-Edwards, *Animal Dispersion in Relation to Social Behavior* (Edinburgh and London: Oliver & Boyd, 1962); and Karl Von Frisch, *Animal Architecture* (New York: Harcourt Brace Jovanovich, 1974).

2. J. J. Von Uexkull, "A Stroll through the World of Animals and Men," in *Instinctive Behavior*, ed. Claire H. Scholler (New York: International Universities Press, 1957); and Roger Peters, "Cognitive Maps in Wolves and Men," in *EDRA 4*, Vol. 2, ed. W. Preiser (Stroudsburg, Pa.: Dowden, Hutchinson & Ross, 1973), pp. 247–53.

3. Wynne-Edwards, Animal Dispersion; and A. H. Esser, ed., *Behavior and Environment* (New York: Plenum Press, 1971).

4. Amos Rapoport, "Australian Aborigines and the Definition of Place," in *Shelter, Sign, and Symbol*, ed. Paul Oliver (London: Barrie & Jenkins, 1975).

5. Donald W. Foster, "Housing in Low Income Barrios in Latin America: Some Cultural Considerations," paper presented at the seventy-first annual meeting of the American Anthropological Association, 1972.

6. Evon Z. Vogt, *Zinacantan: A Maya Community in the Highlands of Chiapas* (Cambridge: Belknap Press of Harvard University, 1969): Jean Cuisenier, "Une Tente Turque d' Anatolie Centale," L'Homme 10 (April-June 1970): 59–72; and Amos Rapoport, "The Pueblo and the Hogan: A Cross-cultural Comparison of Two Responses to an Environment," in *Shelter and Society*, ed. Paul Oliver (London: Barrie and Rockliff, 1969).

7. J. A. Sabloff and W. L. Rathje, "The Rise of a Maya Merchant Class," *Scientific American* 233 (October 1975):72–83.

8. Ernest S. Burch, Jr., "The Nonempirical Environment of the Arctic Alaskan Eskimos," *S. W. Journal of Anthropology* 27 (1971):148–65.

9. Amos Rapoport, "Environmental Cognition in Cross-cultural Perspective," in *Environmental Knowing*, ed. G. T. Moore and R. G. Golledge (Stroudsburg, Pa.: Dowden, Hutchinson & Ross, 1976), pp. 220–34.

10. L. B. Leakey, "Adventures in the Search of Man," *National Geographic* 123 (January 1963): 132–52; and Glynn Ll. Isaac, "Comparative Studies of Pleistocene Site Locations in East Africa," in *Man, Settlement and Urbanism*, by Peter J. Ucko et al. (London: Duckworth, 1972), pp. 165–76.

11. H. de Lumley, "A Paleolithic Camp at Nice," *Scientific American* 220 (May 1969):42–59..

12. Evan Hadingham, *Circles and Standing Stones* (London: Heinemann, 1975).

13. Norman Hammond, "The Planning of a Maya Ceremonial Center," *Scientific American* 226 (May 1972):82–91.

14. Amos Rapoport, *Human Aspects of Urban Form* (Oxford: Pergamon Press, 1977).

15. R. S. Solecki, *Shanidar, The First Flower People* (New York: Knopf, 1971); Andre Leroi-Gourhan, *The Art of Prehistoric Man in Western Europe* (London: Thames & Hudson, 1968); and Alexander Marshack, *The Roots of Civilization: The Cognitive Beginnings of Man's First Art, Symbol and Notation* (New York: McGraw-Hill, 1972).

16. P. Leyhausen, "The Communal Organization of Solitary Mammals," in *Environmental Psychology*, ed. H. M. Proshansky et al. (New York: Holt, Rinehart & Winston, 1970), pp. 183–95.

17. Rapoport, *Human Aspects of Urban Form*.

18. P. Hamilton, "Aspect of Interdependence between Aboriginal Social Behavior and Spatial and Physical Environment," paper presented at the RAIA Seminar on Low-cost Self-help Housing for Aborigines in Remote Areas, Canberra, Australia, February 1972.

19. James Littlejohn, "The Temne House" in *Myth and Cosmos*, ed. John Middleton (Garden City, N.Y.: Natural History Press, 1967); and Mircea Eliade, *The Sacred and the Profane* (New York: Harper & Row, 1961).

20. D. Srejovic, "Lepenski Vir, Yugoslavia: The First Planned Settlement in Europe," *Ekistics* 38 (November 1974):364–67.

21. Mary Douglas, *Natural Symbols* (New York: Random House, Vintage Books, 1973).

22. P. Bourdieu, "The Berber House," in *Rules and Meanings*, ed. Mary Douglas (Harmondsworth, England: Penguin Books, 1973), pp. 98–110.

23. S. J. Tambiah, "Classification of Animals in Thailand," in *Rules and Meanings*, ed. Mary Douglas, pp. 127–66.

24. Frank G. Speck, *The Iroquois*, 2d ed., Cranbrook Institute of Science Bulletin No. 23 (Bloomfield Hills, Mich.: Cranbrook Institute of Science, 1955); and J. W. Fernandez, *Fang Architectonics*, Institute for the Study of Human Issues Working Paper No. 1 (Philadelphia: Institute for the Study of Human Issues, 1976).

25. H. G. West, "The House Is a Compass," *Landscape* 1 (Autumn 1951):24–27.

26. H. S. Smith, "Society and Settlement in Ancient Egypt," in *Man, Settlement and Urbanism*, ed. Ucko et al., pp. 705–19.

27. Richard Lannoy, *The Speaking Tree: A Study of Indian*

Culture and Society (London: Oxford University Press, 1971); and David Sopher, "Landscape and Seasons," *Landscape* 13 (Spring 1964):14–19.

28. R. Wittkower, *Architectural Principles in the Age of Humanism* (London: Alec Tiranti, 1962), p. 23.

29. William L. MacDonald, *The Pantheon: Design, Meaning and Progeny* (Cambridge: Harvard University Press, 1976).

30. E. T. Hall, *The Hidden Dimension* (Garden City, N.Y.: Doubleday, 1966).

31. James Mellaart, "A Neolithic City in Turkey," *Scientific American* 210 (April 1964):94–104; and Ian A. Todd, *Çatal Hüyük in Perspective* (Menlo Park, Ca.: Cummings, 1976).

32. Robert J. Rodden, "An Early Neolithic Village in Greece," *Scientific American* 212 (April 1965):82–92.

33. Michael Austin, "A Description of the Maori Marae," and A. Stahl and P. H. Stahl, "Peasant House Building and Its Relation to Church Building: The Rumanian Case," both in Amos Rapoport (ed.) *The Mutual Interaction of People and Their Built Environments* (The Hague: Mouton, 1976), pp. 229–41 and 243–54.

34. Kent V. Flannery, ed., *The Early Mesoamerican Village* (New York: Academic Press, 1976).

35. Miles Richardson, "The Spanish-American (Colombian) Settlement Pattern as a Societal Expression and as a Behavioral Cause," in *Geoscience and Man*, vol. 5: *Man and Cultural Heritage*, gen. ed. Bob F. Perkins (Baton Rouge: School of Geoscience, Louisiana State University, 1974), pp. 35–51.

36. Flannery, *The Early Mesoamerican Village.*

37. Vincent Scully, *The Earth, The Temple and the Gods* (New Haven: Yale University Press, 1962).

38. E. Uphill, "The Concept of the Egyptian Palace as a 'Ruling Machine,'" in *Man, Settlement and Urbanism*, ed. Ucko et al., pp. 721–34.

39. L. Marshall, "!Kung Bushman Bands," *Africa* 30 (1960): 325–55.

40. Colin M. Turnbull, *The Forest People* (London: Reprint Society, 1961).

41. See, for example, Yi-fu Tuan, *Topophilia: A Study of Environmental Perceptions, Attitudes and Values* (Englewood Cliffs, N.J.: Prentice-Hall, 1974).

FOR FURTHER READING

Douglas, Mary. *Natural Symbols.* New York: Random House, Vintage Books, 1973.

Eliade, Mircea. *The Sacred and the Profane.* New York: Harper & Row, 1961.

Esser, Aristide H., ed. *Behavior and Environment: The Use of Space by Animals and Men.* New York: Plenum Press, 1971.

Oliver, Paul, ed. *Shelter, Sign, and Symbol.* London: Barrie and Jenkins, 1975.

Rapoport, Amos. *House Form and Culture.* Englewood Cliffs, N.J.: Prentice-Hall, 1969.

———, ed. *The Mutual Interaction of People and Their Built Environment: A Cross-cultural Perspective.* The Hague: Mouton, 1976.

———. *Human Aspects of Urban Form.* Oxford: Pergamon Press, 1977.

Ucko, Peter J., Tringham, Ruth, and Dimbleby, G.W., ed. *Man, Settlement and Urbanism.* London: Duckworth, 1972.

CHAPTER 2

Theory, Criticism, and History of Architecture

Wayne O. Attoe

Theory and history have always been essential to the study and understanding of architecture. Theory in architecture deals with what architecture is, what it should do, and how to design it. History, highly related, deals with theories, events, design methods, and buildings. Their combined impact on the future of architecture cannot be underestimated. Unlike theory and history, architectural criticism has not always been the subject of study by architects. However, as the process and record of response to the built environment, criticism relates directly to both theory and history; in fact, history can be considered as a form of criticism. This chapter integrates theory, criticism, and history and, in so doing, lays one of the essential bases for the study and practice of architecture.

THEORY

Theories are general statements dealing with what architecture is, what architecture should accomplish, and how best to design. Theories are useful to the architect at various points in the design process and are applicable to many building types. When an architect is confronted with choices, such as whether to expose the structural system in a building or to hide it within a finished wall, a theory of architecture may help in deciding.

Theory tends to be less rigorous and precise in architecture than in science. Scientific theories typically present either sets of laws that have been derived empirically, self-evident truths in the form of axioms, or descriptions of causal events.[1] One important feature of scientific theory that is *not* found in architecture is rigorous proof. To gain wide acceptance among scientists, a theory must be supported with clear evidence, and the derivation of that evidence must be explained in detail. Architectural design is in large part a synthesizing rather than analyzing activity. Instead of dissecting parts, it assimilates and integrates a wide variety of elements in new ways and new situations, so that results are not entirely predictable. Theory in architecture suggests directions but cannot guarantee results.

Some things about architecture are knowable in a scientific sense. We can determine physiological reactions to hot, humid rooms, for example. We can predict the extent of creep in concrete structures. We can anticipate auditory problems in an improperly shaped lecture hall. These bits of architectural knowledge can be explained in terms of theories of human physiology, structures, and sound transmission. Neither individually nor collectively do they constitute a theory of architecture, however. Theory in architecture is hypotheses, hopes, and guesses about what happens when all of the ingredients that comprise buildings are put together in a particular way, place, and time. Architecture is an integrative activity that is focused on affecting the future rather than on explaining isolated events in the past. It does not have rigorous theories, because buildings and their users are too complex to be knowable and predictable.

There are no laws of architecture that will allow us to predict satisfaction of residents in underground houses, for example. There was no way of foreseeing that an award-winning housing project in St. Louis would be called a symbol of wrong-headedness in planning and design after twenty years of use and be demolished. There was no way of predicting that the Eiffel Tower would at first be seen as a blemish in the Paris skyline and later become the lasting and essential symbol of the city.

One symptom of the unscientific, speculative character of theory in architecture is the tendency for theoretical statements to be manifestos and to employ evocative language. If the reader cannot be convinced with carefully argued and well-supported statements characteristic of science, perhaps he or she can be seduced with language:

The machinery of Society, profoundly *out of gear,* oscillates between an amelioration, of historical importance, and a catastrophe. The primordial instinct of every human being is to assure himself of a shelter. The various classes of workers in society to-day *no longer have dwellings adapted to their needs; neither the artizan nor the intellectual.* It is a question of building which is at the root of the social unrest of to-day: architecture or revolution.[2]

Or consider that:

In the nature of space is the spirit and the will to exist a certain way
Design must closely follow that will
Therefore a stripe-painted horse is not a zebra
Before a railroad station is a building
it wants to be a street
It grows out of the needs of street
out of the order of movement
A meeting of contours englazed.[3]

What Architecture Is

Theories about what architecture *is* are concerned with identifying key variables—like space, structure, or social processes—in terms of which buildings should be seen or evaluated. For example, Bruno Zevi advocates a theory of architecture in which space is the fundamental ingredient: "To grasp space, to know how to *see* it, is the key to the understanding of building."[4]

Those who enter upon more complex inquiry into the organic unity of man and architecture will first agree that their point of departure for an integrated, comprehensive vision of architecture is interpretation of space, and they will measure every element that goes into a building according to the space it encloses.[5]

In advocating particular ways of seeing architecture, theorists often rely on analogies. For example, we are told that architecture should be seen as "organic," or that it is a "language," or that it is

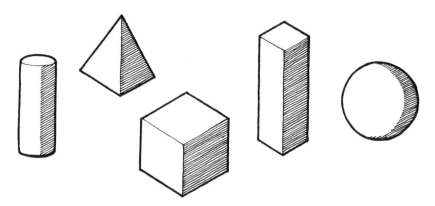

The pure forms of architecture.

"machinelike." Analogies such as these provide a way to organize design tasks in hierarchical order, so that the architect can know which things to think about first and which things can be left to a later stage of the design process.

The following are some recurrent analogies employed by theorists to explain architecture.

Mathematical Analogy. Some theorists hold that numbers and geometry provide an important basis for decision making in architecture. They have faith that buildings designed in accordance with pure forms and primary or symbolic numbers will be in tune with universal order:

> Architecture is the masterly, correct and magnificent play of masses brought together in light. Our eyes are made to see forms in light; light and shade reveal these forms; cubes, cones, spheres, cylinders or pyramids are the great primary forms which light reveals to advantage; the image of these is distinct and tangible within us and without ambiguity. It is for that reason that these are *beautiful forms, the most beautiful forms.*[6]

The "golden section" or "golden number" has most often been cited as an appropriate guide for architectural design. It is the proportion 1:1.618.

One can say that neither in the structure of this world nor in the microcosm is there anything more extensive and full of dignity than propriety of weight, number and measure from which time, space, movement, virtue, speech, art, nature, knowledge, in short everything divine and human is composed, has grown, and has been perfected.[7]

In what ways do harmoniously proportioned buildings affect our lives? They affect our aesthetic sensibilities and leave us either impoverished or enriched. Architecture whose exterior forms and interior spaces delight our eyes also elevate and enrich our minds and ennoble our spirits. It is nourishment for our inner Being and leaves a lasting imprint upon our lives.[8]

Biological Analogy. "Building is a biological process. . .building is not an aesthetic process."[9] Theories of architecture based upon biological analogies take two forms. One is quite general and focuses on the relationships between parts of the building or between the building and its setting. Following the lead of Frank Lloyd Wright, it is typically called "organic." The other form of the analogy is more specific. Called "biomorphic," it focuses on growth processes and movement capabilities associated with organisms.

Wright's organic architecture has four characteristics: First, it develops outward from within, in

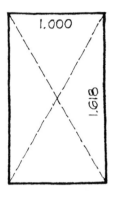

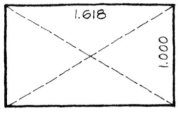

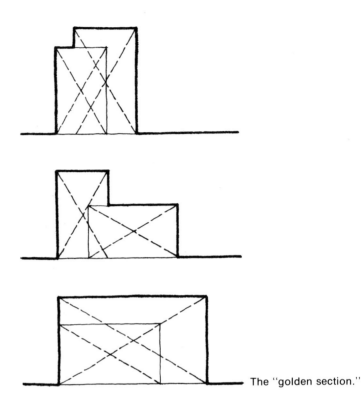

The "golden section."

harmony with the conditions of its being; it is not applied. Second, construction occurs within the nature of materials. "Wherein glass is used as glass, stone as stone, wood as wood."[10] Third, elements of a building are integral.

> The word organic refers to *entity;* perhaps integral or intrinsic would therefore be a better word to use. As originally used in architecture, organic means *part-to-whole-as whole-to-part.* So *entity is integral* is what is really meant by the word organic.[11]

And lastly, reflects time, place, and purpose: "made by the people out of the ground in ways of their own devising—true to time, place, environment and purpose. Folk building we might call them."[12]

Biomorphic architecture gained currency in the 1960s, and it focuses less on relationships between buildings and environment than on dynamic process-es associated with growth and change within organisms. Biomorphic architecture has the capacity to grow and change through expansion, multiplication, division, regeneration, and off-setting. It can be transformed in response to environmental changes and internal demands. Among schemes proposed in relation to the biomorphic analogy are an edible city (Rudolf Doernach), multicelled pneumatic structures (Fisher, Conolly, and Neumark), a self-contained living unit called a *cushicle* that can be carried on a user's back (Mike Webb), a living pod (David Greene), a travelling hall (A. Stinco), and Walking City (Ron Herron).

Romantic Analogy. The key feature of romantic architecture is that it is evocative. It elicits or unleashes an emotional response in the observer. This is accomplished in two ways—by calling up

Taliesin West, by Frank Lloyd Wright.

associations or through exaggeration. When employing associations, romantic design will make references to nature (both in the form of natural settings and in the form of natural processes, like decay), the past, exotic places, things that are primitive, or childhood associations. A motel in California exemplifies a mid-twentieth-century use of most of these associations:

> The 109 guest rooms abound with one theatrical device after another, one material after another, one refinement after another: leather bedspread and drapes in the Indian room; elaborate fireplaces in some; patent leather wallpaper here and embroidered wallpaper there; a sofa hand-hewn from tree trunks in Cabin Still; exact antique replicas in Victorian Gardens; a 4-ft crawl space tunnel which converts Daisy Mae and Cavemena into a suite; Fred and Irma Flintstone in leaded stained glass in the Flintstone Room.[13]

More subtle, yet still in accord with the romantic analogy, was Eero Saarinen's medieval solution to the problem of housing at Yale University:

> We conceived of these colleges as citadels of earthy, monolithic masonry—buildings where masonry walls would be dominant and whose interiors of stone, oak, and plaster could carry out the spirit of strength and simplicity.[14]

Critics called the colleges "justifiably artificial monasteries," and a "setting for Ivanhoe."[15]

In addition to observing specific references to other places and times, we can be affected through strictly formal devices when these are exaggerated or used to excess. We can be intimidated, frightened, or awed through the architect's use of contrast, excessive stimulation, unfamiliar scale, and unfamiliar forms. The expressionist movement in Europe in the early twentieth century employed these techniques to evoke sensuous responses in observers.

> They did not look.
> They envisioned.
> They did not photograph.
> They had visions.
> Instead of the rocket they created the perpetual state of excitement.[16]

Stiles and Morse Colleges, Yale University, by Eero Saarinen.

Linguistic Analogy. Linguistic analogies take the view that buildings are meant to convey information to observers in any of the following three ways.

Grammatical Model. Architecture is sometimes seen as being composed of elements (words) that are ordered according to rules (grammar and syntax) that allow people within a given culture to readily understand and interpret what the building is saying.

> Good architecture (is) the result of keeping to the rules; but that does not mean that good architecture (is) automatically produced by rule of thumb. It means that the architect's imagination and his artistic sense (are) exercised within the limits set by a universal architectural language.[17]

Every house worth considering as a work of art must have a grammar of its own. "Grammar," in this sense, means the same thing in any construction—whether it be of words or of stone or wood. It is the shape-relationship between the various elements that enter into the constitution of the thing. The "grammar" of the house is its manifest articulation of all its parts. This will be the "speech" it uses. To be achieved, construction must be grammatical.[18]

Expressionist Model. Here the building is seen as a vehicle through which the architect

Nella citta futurista, Virgilio Marchi (from: *Architecttura Futurista,* Franco Campitelli, 1924).

Dulles International Airport Terminal, by
Eero Saarinen.

expresses his or her attitude towards the building
project.

> Buildings can make comments about the situation,
> about their site, about the problem of holding the
> outside out and the inside in, about the problem of
> getting themselves built, about the people who use
> them or the people who made them—all sorts of
> things that can be funny, or sad, or stupid, or silent,
> or dumb.[19]

Eero Saarinen's design for the terminal at Dulles International Airport outside Washington, D.C. included several expressive concerns.

> There was also the problem of the site—a beautiful
> flat plain. In a way, architecture is really placing
> something between earth and sky. We came to the
> conclusion that a strong form that seemed both to
> rise from the plain and to hover over it would look
> best. The horizontal element, or roof, would be the
> highest element. It should be tilted forward so the
> building would be seen. The terminal should also
> have a monumental scale in this landscape and in
> the vastness of this huge airfield.[20]

Semiotic Model. Semiology is the science
of signs. A semiotic interpretation of architecture
holds that a building is a sign that conveys information about what it is and what it does. Two ways in
which this can occur have been identified by Robert
Venturi, Denise Scott Brown, and Steven Izenour.
They point out that some buildings are "ducks" and
others are "decorated sheds." Ducks are buildings
that take the form of what they sell or contain, thus
telling a visitor what to expect. A building shaped
like a duck can be expected to sell poultry; a building shaped like a piano will sell pianos. In other
cases buildings have signs that explain their meanings. Such signs are attached to an otherwise un-
distinguished shed and become façades. The signs
alone are sufficient to convey meaning; it is not necessary to mold the building into any particular form.
A steeple is a sign that a building is a church. A
painting showing pediment and columns is a sign
that a building is a bank.[21]

Mechanical Analogy. Le Corbusier's asser-
tion that a house is a machine for living exemplifies
the use of mechanical analogies in architecture. His
statement and other uses of the analogy assume that
buildings, like machines, should express only what
they are and what they do. They should not hide
these facts with irrelevant decoration in the form of

A building to sell pianos.

Security Marine Bank branch office, Madison, Wisconsin.

INTRODUCTION TO ARCHITECTURE

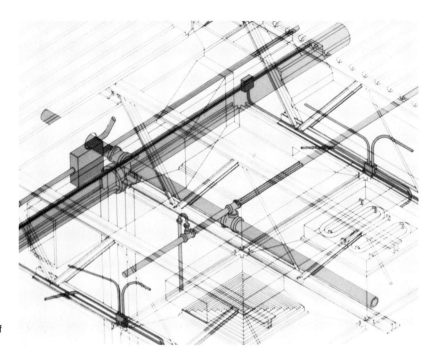

The Syncon System, by Joe White (courtesy of
Joe White and Doug Ryhn).

styles. A modern building "must be true to itself,
logically transparent and virginal of lies or triviali-
ties, as befits a direct affirmation of our contemporary world of mechanization and rapid transit."[22]

Beauty assumes the promise of function: that is
to say, objects that are straightforward, that simply
express what they are and do, will automatically be
beautiful. Locomotives, automobiles, ships, and
airplanes are cited as evidence:

> Could we carry into our civil architecture the re-
> sponsibilities that weigh upon our shipbuilding, we
> should ere long have edifices as superior to the
> Parthenon as (a modern battleship) is superior to
> the galleys of the Argonauts. . . . Instead of forcing
> the functions of every sort of building into one gen-
> eral form, and adopting an outward shape for the
> sake of the eye or of association, without reference
> to the inner distribution, let us begin from the heart
> as a nucleus and work outward.[23]

Problem-Solving Analogy. "Architecture is an
art which demands more reasoning than inspiration,
and more factual knowledge than verve."[24] Sometimes referred to as the *rationalist, logical. systematic,* or *parametric* approach to architectural design,
the problem-solving method assumes that environmental needs are problems that can be solved
through careful analysis and deliberate procedures.
Designing is viewed not as an intuitive process only,
characterized by inspirations, but as a step-by-step
process dependent upon solid information. One
requirement of such deliberate design methods is
that the problem must be well and specifically
stated. Another feature of problem-solving methods
in design is a deliberate and integrated procedure.
To be considered rational, the procedure must
include at least three stages: analysis, synthesis,
and evaluation.

> The picture of the rational, or systematic, designer
> is very much that of a human computer, a person
> who operates only on the information that is fed to
> him, and who follows through a planned sequence
> of analytical, synthetic and evaluative steps and
> cycles until he recognizes the best of all possible
> solutions.[25]

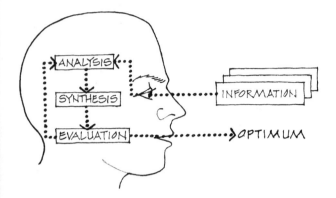

Designer as computer, based on the work of Christopher Jones in *Design Methods.*

Adhocist Analogy. While a traditionalist view of architecture would hold that the designer's task is to select appropriate elements and mold them to approximate an ideal, the *adhocist* approach is to respond to the immediate need, using materials immediately available and without making reference to an ideal. There is no external standard against which the design can be measured; one makes do.

It is a waste of time and energy for most architects to invent new forms. Rather, it is the architect's prime duty to make the best from what already exists; for creation is superfluous in the face of our industrial cornucopia. Invention is conspicuous waste; time should rather be spent cataloguing our resources, learning our area of choice. The adhocist designer is as much opposed to the radical invention which results in a space capsule as he is to the tenets of "good design" or "modern architecture." What he proposes is a lively and fumigated eclecticism.[26]

A mural in San Francisco exemplifies this approach: the artist incorporated two existing windows as part of a new mural instead of hiding them or pretending they were not there. Charles Eames's famous Case Study House in Los Angeles is a full-fledged architectural essay in adhocism, being composed of elements that were readily available from catalogs.

In some ways all architectural design is adhocist, for in most cases the architect's palette is limited to existing components. There are only so many standard windows one can choose from, and aluminum panels are available in set shapes, thicknesses, sizes, and colors. But true adhocist design limits itself even more, employing whatever is most readily or cheaply available.

Pattern Language Analogy. When we recognize that people are biologically similar, and that within a given culture there are conventions for behavior and for building, it is logical to conclude that architectural design might be simply the task of identifying standard patterns of needs and standard types of places to satisfy those needs. The typological or pattern approach assumes that environment-behavior relationships may be seen in terms of units the designer adds together to make a building or an urban setting.

Each pattern describes a problem which occurs over and over again in our environment, and then describes the core of the solution to that problem, in such a way that you can use this solution a million times over, without ever doing it the same way twice.[27]

An example of such a pattern, identified by Christopher Alexander and others, is the old-age cottage:

Old people, especially when they are alone, face a terrible dilemma. On the one hand, there are inescapable forces pushing them toward independence: their children move away; the neighborhood changes; their friends and wives and husbands die. On the other hand, by the very nature of aging, old people become dependent on simple conveniences, simple connections to the society about them.
Build small cottages specifically for old people. Build some of them on the land of larger houses, for a grandparent; build others on individual lots, much smaller than ordinary lots. In all cases, place these cottages at ground level, right on the street, where people are walking by, and close to neighborhood services and common land.[28]

Mural, San Francisco.

Ad hocism: The Charles Eames House.

Dramaturgical Analogy. Human activities are often characterized as theater ("All the world's a stage"), and consequently the built environment may be seen as a stage. People play roles, and so buildings become stage settings and props that support the life shows. One need only list a few of the dramaturgical terms architects and critics employ to see how pervasive the analogy is: behavior-setting, backstage, roles, cue, on stage, backdrop, and sight lines.

The dramaturgical analogy is employed in two ways—from the point of view of the actors, and from the point of view of the playwright. In the first instance, the architect is concerned with supplying the user with the props and settings needed to play out a particular role. The corporate executive, for example, needs to be surrounded by accoutrements that enhance his or her appearance. The executive also needs a mechanism for being off stage, "being oneself," because being on stage constantly is tiring. Furniture needs to be arranged so that a choice is available between being distant and unapproachable (behind a desk), or seeming to be equal (chairs side by side and knees exposed.) A closed door or a private washroom provides a mechanism for being off stage.

The other use of the dramaturgical analogy is from the point of view of the playwright. Here the architect's concern is not so much with the needs of the characters to appear in a particular way or to be able to drop out of character, as with directing the action. Architects can cause people to move in one direction or another by offering visual cues, for example. A lighted area in the context of darkness will attract people. Similarly, it is said that an arcade at the edge of a piazza will attract circulation. Or through proper location of entrances to an auditorium, the architect can cause audience members to fill the space in a particular way. Park benches located adjacent to and slightly higher than a playground will attract people. This use of the dramaturgical analogy has the architect acting almost like a puppeteer. The architect directs action as much as supports it.

What Architecture Should Do
Theories about what architecture should accomplish are concerned with identifying the goals that the designer and buildings should satisfy. Such theories are not concerned with a way of seeing buildings or interpreting them, but with the purposes to which they should be addressed. Goals for architecture typically take two forms—general statements about the task of architecture and statements about desired relationships between architecture and other phenomena.

General Goals. Vitruvius made the earliest widely known goal statement for architecture: "Architecture depends on Order, Arrangement, Eurythmy, Symmetry, Propriety, and Economy."[29] Subsequent theorists have developed variations on his system for identifying the objectives in architectural design. Henry Wotton, for example, took a stripped-down version of Vitruvius (durability, convenience, and beauty) and translated it into the more

familiar version, "Commodity, firmness, and delight." John Ruskin developed a variation that is more discursive:

> We require of any building, (1) That it act well, and do the things it was intended to do in the best way. (2) That it speak well, and say the things it was intended to say in the best words. (3) That it look well, and please us by its presence, whatever it has to do or say.[30]

Albert Bush-Brown formulated the Vitruvian system of goals for architecture negatively: "It may fall down. It may not accommodate its purpose. It may not be a work of art."[31]

Development of the social sciences in the nineteenth and twentieth centuries has precipitated somewhat different systems for identifying objectives for architecture. "Building is nothing but organization: social, technical, economic, psychological organization."[32] We can expect that as major changes occur in our understanding of people's relationships to the environment, goal statements for architecture will have to be modified or substantially rewritten to accommodate new insights and imperatives. Energy-efficiency and environmental impact are new considerations that have yet to be written into our statements of goals for architecture.

Relationship between the Built Environment and Other Phenomena. Goal statements about the preferred relationship of buildings to other phenomena manifest two central concerns that, incidentally, reflect a recurrent dilemma in architecture. One view is that architecture is essentially a technical field. Buildings should be logical in their structural and production systems. Among other things, this means employing materials and construction methods appropriate to the specific region and climate:

> If our designs for private houses are to be correct, we must at the outset take note of the countries and climates in which they are built. One style of house seems appropriate to build in Egypt, another in

Spain, a different kind in Pontus, one still different in Rome, and so on with lands and countries of other characteristics. This is because one part of the earth is directly under the sun's course, another is far away from it, while another lies midway between these two.[33]

The other view is that architecture's primary purpose is social. It is a background and support system to enhance ongoing life processes:

> The architect should conceive buildings not as monuments but as receptacles for the flow of life which they have to serve, and his conception must be flexible enough to create a background fit to absorb the dynamic features of our modern life.[34]

While the views that architecture is essentially technical *or* essentially social in purpose are often stated uncompromisingly, in fact both are necessary ingredients of any theory of architecture and its relationship to other phenomena. Both are necessary concerns. "The problem of the new world architecture is: *The finiteness of mechanics plus the infiniteness of life.*"[35] The most a strongly biased theory can do is to establish priorities that indicate which of the concerns should be dealt with first.

Periodically, other goal statements for architecture crop up in response to the specific needs of a period. They are too specific and time-bound to direct action on a long-term basis, but they can function to correct and redirect attention to current, pressing needs. Le Corbusier in the 1920s, for example, saw a need to revise the prevailing conception of housing and its production:

> The problem of the house is a problem of the epoch. The equilibrium of society today depends upon it. Architecture has for its first duty, in this period of renewal, that of bringing about a revision of values, a revision of the constituent elements of the house. Mass-production is based on analysis and experiment. Industry on the grand scale must occupy itself with building and establish the elements of the house on a mass-production basis.[36]

How to Design

Theories about how the architect should go about designing are concerned with identifying appropriate methods of operation. They are usually directed towards the assurance that buildings will accomplish particular ends.

Staffing. One of these concerns has to do with the relationships of individuals and groups during the design process. Is design the private, inspired act of an individual or the logical and visible effort of a team of professionals? Is it a combination of individual inspiration and cooperative verification and elaboration?

Walter Gropius attempted to integrate both views in his discussion of the tasks of architecture in the early twentieth century:

> It is true that the creative spark originates always with the individual, but by working in close collaboration with others toward a common end, he will attain greater heights of achievement through the stimulation and challenging critique of his teammates, than by living in an ivory tower.[37]

The teamwork approach has been a recurrent feature of twentieth-century theory about the design process. The assumption is that most building tasks are too complex to be understood and guided by an individual. A team of specialists—each with an area of expertise and yet with a broad understanding of the whole—will better solve complex building problems than the limited, though gifted, individual.

Procedures. Regardless who designs, what design process is best? Where should one begin? With choosing a structural system? With identifying behavior patterns? With seeking particular spatial patterns and form relationships?

Design procedures typically have two underlying biases: they are either *inductive* or *deductive*. Inductive procedures begin with details. Through accretion the details, or partial solutions, finally add up to a complete built form. For example, in a housing development one might want to make sure that the following details occur: that children's play areas are visible from kitchens; that kitchens are close to service routes (for collecting trash and for bringing in groceries); that service routes are separated from formal entrances; that formal entrances are articulated as individual places; that building costs are minimized by limiting the number and extent of symbolic articulations; that costs are reduced further by backing up plumbing walls (kitchens and bathrooms); and that threats to privacy are reduced by keeping bedroom windows away from pedestrian routes and so on. This collection of detail solutions gradually can add up to a complete built form.

Deductive design procedures begin with an overall intention or idea about the building and let details grow out of that central theme. For example, the learning resource center for a school might be seen as a "marketplace for ideas." Given that overall concept, details might be designed as follows: books, pictures, and equipment would be displayed rather than stored; circulation might be formulated to ensure that users of the resource center pass by as many of the resource items as possible; the structural system might be skeletal rather than massive in order to facilitate the exposure of items, displays, and people; and the aesthetic of a marketplace of ideas would grow from richness, variety, and complexity, not from exposing the simple beauty of a repetitive structural or geometric system.

Inductive and deductive procedures are seldom followed exclusively in designing buildings. No single process can satisfy the complex requirements characteristic of modern buildings. Even as underlying biases in designing, they can have an impact, however. Whether a building grows out of a key idea or whether it is a collection of small decisions is usually evident.

Priorities among Various Aspects of the Problem. Problems in architecture are typically complex. They are technical (requiring structure and mechanical systems, for example); social (requiring attention to the needs and wants of diverse users as well as the clients who commission and pay for the building); and aesthetic, ecological, or political as well. Some theories of architecture establish priorities among these necessary concerns, such as the following by Hans Poelzig:

> *Every real tectonic constructional form has an absolute nucleus,* to which the decorative embellishment, which within certain limits is changeable, lends a varying charm. First, however, the absolute element has to be found, even if as yet in an imperfect, rough form. *And the artist who approaches the design of structural elements solely from the viewpoint of external, decorative considerations distracts attention from the discovery of the pure nuclear form.*[38]

In this passage Poelzig asserts that in any building problem there is an underlying absolute element that needs to be expressed in structure and form before embellishment is added. For Mies van der Rohe, building form should be determined after attention has been given to internal, living needs:

> I do not oppose form, but only form as a goal. And I do this as the result of a number of experiences and the insight I have gained from them. Form as a goal always ends in formalism. For this striving is directed not towards an inside, but towards an outside. But only a living inside has a living outside. Only intensity of life has intensity of form.[39]

While many theorists advocate the primacy of one factor or another, others assert that the design process should not be prioritized but should take the form of dialectic. In this procedure each concern is considered and allowed to affect others in an iterative process. That true equality among all concerns in a design problem is possible is doubted by some, however.

CRITICISM

Criticism in architecture is the record of responses to the built environment. This includes *all* responses, not just negative ones. Criticism essentially means to sift and make distinctions. Discernment, rather than judgment, is the key feature of criticism.

Medium

The medium with which response is recorded is clearly a crucial consideration. While the written word has historically been the most familiar medium for architecture criticism, other media are equally valid. A photograph, cartoon, or set of measurements can be effective as a record reflecting the critic's point of view and concerns. In fact, our historical dependence upon the written word is unfortunate, for some kinds of criticism are not conveyed well in that medium. Residents' reactions to the design of public housing will typically not be expressed in print but in oral form or through self-directed modification of buildings—or even through vandalism. As we begin to see criticism broadly, as something more than the opinions of journalists writing once a week in the daily paper, we shall see the need to explore and exploit other methods of recording responses. A broader conception of criticism and methods for conveying responses will have a longer range and wider impact.

Method

Method is as important as medium in criticism. The critic who mixes methods or who does not understand the nature and potential of the methods he or she employs will be less effective. The following are conventional methods that critics use to record their responses to the built environment.

Normative Criticism. Normative criticism has as its basis either a doctrine, system, type, or measurement. It depends upon our believing in something outside the physical environment itself and our using that as a standard for assessing the design of buildings and cities. Because normative standards vary in complexity, abstractness, and

specificity, it is necessary to distinguish between doctrine, system, type, and measurement.

A doctrine is an abstract statement of principle. For example, "form follows function." Other recent doctrines upon which criticism may be based are: function should follow form; less is more; less is a bore; buildings should be what they want to be; they should express structure, function, aspirations, ideologies, construction methods, regional climate, materials; a building should be *of* and not *on* the hill where it sits; and ornamentation is a crime. In a specific instance of criticism based upon doctrine, Ada Louise Huxtable asserted that contemporary public buildings should avoid "those pompous pratfalls to the classical past that building committees clutch like Linus's blanket."[40] Based upon this doctrine, her critique of Boston City Hall is laudatory: "It is not Gothic. . . . It is a product of this moment and these times—something that can be said of successful art of any period."[41]

A system is an assemblage of elements or principles that are interrelated—for example, Vitruvius' principles. A systematic critique will be more comprehensive than one based upon doctrines. Buildings can seldom be evaluated in terms of one or two directives, since they are multidirectional in complexity. A twentieth-century version of the Vitruvian system views a building as "a climate modifier, a behavior modifier, a cultural modifier and a resource modifier."[42] This set of interrelated concerns provides the basis for a thorough critical assessment.

A type is a generalized model for a specific class of things, like fifteenth-century English churches, which A.W.N. Pugin felt epitomized ecclesiastical architecture and ought to be the model for contemporary (nineteenth-century) churches. Typal criticism may address itself to any of three aspects of a building: its structure, its functional organization, or its form. Pugin was concerned to have nineteenth-century church form evaluated in relation to fifteenth-century precedents. In an example of typal criticism concerned with functional organization, Philip Sawyer identifies the characteristic needs and plans of savings banks and judges a particular bank to be "a capital example," based on the type:

> The principal requirement of the Savings Bank plan is the provision for the handling of crowds; and the Commercial Bank, as it approaches to the savings institution in the character of its business . . . will find its plan coming to resemble that of a Savings Bank . . . (One) point of view requires the banking room to be as large as possible, even though the public is admitted to only a small portion of it, and comes in direct contact with only the same few persons; that a gallery or point of vantage be provided from which visitors may see every clerk in the institution, that the long lines of bookkeepers' tables may make their impression upon him and that he may overlook the various departments and hear the hum of all the parts of the great machine. Of this the United States Mortgage & Trust Co. in New York is a capital example.[43]

Measurement is the assessment of a built environment against well-defined, usually numerical standards. Is there a fire exit within 100 feet of each room? This can be determined readily with a tape measure, and the judgment made. The norms upon which measured criticism are based will be stated as either minimums, averages, or preferred conditions and reflect the variety of goals for a building, including technical, functional, and behavioral considerations. Technical criticisms will focus on the durability of the building fabric. Functional criticisms will look at the success of a building as a setting for particular activities specified. Behavioral criticism will examine the impact of the building on individuals' visual perception, general attitudes, and observable behavior.

Interpretive Criticism. In contrast to normative criticism, interpretive criticism is highly personal. The critic is an interpreter whose own vision is more important than any external standards. The critic's purpose is to make others see the built environment as he or she does.

One way a critic interprets is by suggesting a new way of seeing the object, usually by changing the metaphor or analogy through which we see the building-object. Montgomery Schuyler, for example, asserted that the design of the World's Columbian Exposition in Chicago in 1893 should be seen as a stage set, not as a city or as conventional architecture. This might be called advocatory criticism.

> The White City (the popular name for the main esplanade of the Fair) is the most integral, the most extensive, the most illusive piece of scenic architecture that has ever been seen. That is praise enough for its builders, without demanding for them the further praise of having made a useful and important contribution to the development of the architecture of the present, to the preparation of the architecture of the future. . . . It is essential to the illusion of a fairy city that it should not be an American City of the nineteenth century. It is a seaport on the coast of Bohemia, it is the capital of No Man's Land. It is what you will, so long as you will not take it for an American city of the nineteenth century, nor its architecture for the actual or the possible or even the ideal architecture of such a city.[44]

Evocative criticism is intended to arouse in an audience feelings or emotions similar to those experienced when the critic confronted the building or urban setting. The following is an evocative critique of the London Underground:

> I went down into your intestines, London, through your mouth, through your dirty lips, cracked tile, patched tarmac, down endless escalators, trundling in the half-light; strap-hanging in acheing compartments, strap-hanging across a city, across a continent, strap-hanging, balancing, reading single-handed giant newspapers, breathing again the ten times breathed air.[45]

In impressionistic criticism, the critic virtually ignores the object being assessed and instead uses it as a basis for creating another work of art. There is still an element of interpretation, but the focus of the critic's effort is in the creation of something new:

To the critic the work of art is simply a suggestion for a new work of his own, that need not necessarily bear any resemblance to the thing it criticizes. The one characteristic of a beautiful form is that one can put into it whatever one wishes; and see in it whatever one chooses to see; and the Beauty, that gives to creation its universal and aesthetic element, makes the critic a creator in his turn, and whispers of a thousand different things which were not present in the mind of him who carved the statue or painted the panel or graved the gem.[46]

Photocriticism is often impressionistic, simultaneously commenting upon the subject matter and standing on its own as a work of art.

Descriptive Criticism. The descriptive method seeks to identify facts that are pertinent to one's encounter with a particular environment. Underlying descriptive criticism is an assumption that if we know enough about what actually happened during the course of design development, and about what the building is really like, we will better understand the building. Descriptive criticism does not judge, nor does it interpret. It simply helps people to see what actually exists.

Depictive criticism points out what the building is made of and how it is organized. The following is Ada Louise Huxtable's depiction of the Ford Foundation Building in New York City:

The glass box anchored by granite piers and partially embraced by granite side walls contains a giant indoor garden—twelve-story, 160-foot high, skylit, air-conditioned, third-of-an acre park.[47]

Depictive criticism also explains how the building or urban setting works as a dynamic environment:

I discovered that one particular stretch of sidewalks, doors, and corridors in the financial-civic district was extraordinarily productive in contacts, tips, suggestions, reactions, observations, and gossip. . . . I found that by stationing myself at noon on the crowded public sidewalk outside the largest bank and office building, keeping in view

the doors of the County Court House and the second largest bank, plus the route from nearby City Hall, I was likely to meet at least two dozen news sources, men in public life or business, headed for lunch at restaurant or club, willing and sometimes eager to exchange rumor, gossip, and hard information. . . . It became clear that there was an unavoidable "Indian path" between the offices of the downtown elite and their noonday drinking/lunching/negotiating places.[48]

Finally, depictive criticism will sometimes explain the process through which the building design was generated. This can include a description of design methods employed and sequences of events in the process.

The routine redevelopment of parts of Harlem, as such redevelopment has occurred in other marginal neighborhoods, "upgrades" land potential in a way that it makes if profitable for real estate speculators to follow. What happens then is, in a sense, "takeover"; the residents are bulldozed out for an entirely different kind of institutional, commercial and residential community. Again, color it black or white; that is precisely what has happened in some of the city's other marginal neighborhoods.[49]

Biographical criticism identifies pertinent facts about the lives of architects, clients, and builders and their impact upon the final building form. For example, the influence of Gunther Froebel's games and blocks on the work of Frank Lloyd Wright is acknowledged by a number of critics, as well as by Wright himself:

(The Yahara Boat Club) was undoubtedly the simplest, most strikingly geometric design on paper by Wright. . . . Quite clearly, its blockiness owed a great deal to Froebel's games.[50]

Other biographical critiques eschew such interpretations and offer only facts, leaving the question of influences to the reader:

James Harrison Dakin was born in New York State on August 24, 1806, in the Township of Northeast, which comprises the upper corner of Dutchess County near the Connecticut border. . . . The Dakin family has a long history in America.[51]

Contextual criticism records pressures and events that accompanied design and production. How did economic, political, or interpersonal pressures manifest themselves in the final design?

Because the Premier had only a narrow caucus majority in the State Parliamentary Labor Party of 24 to 17 in favour of his visionary scheme to build an Opera House where the old tram shed stood at the end of Bennelong Point (and also had only managed to get a narrow majority at the Party's annual State Conference), he decided that it was vital to go ahead while he had the numbers, regardless of the state of the overall design. This was on the principle that once work had started it had to go ahead even if he lost the support of the four members who had made the difference between acceptance and rejection of his scheme. This explains why against the advice of Utzon (the architect) and his engineer, work began in March 1959 on the foundations of the Opera House before the building had been designed. The consequences of this quite appalling decision were not only that millions of dollars were wasted in putting things up that later had to come down, or that the work had to stop for long periods until the next lot of drawings turned up, but that relations between the principals on the project were strained from the outset under the volume of alterations to drawings.[52]

Audience
Finally, medium and method must be seen in relation to a specific audience. Just as we would not attempt to convince a group of German-speaking people with arguments framed in French or English, neither would it be effective to address social scientists with criticism in the form of cartoons or advocatory essays. Audiences for architecture criticism are highly varied. One audience is the architect of a building. In this case the critic is probably offering postconstruction feedback, a response after construction is finished and the building has been occupied. Another audience is architects in general. In this case the critic will want to generalize from specific cases in hopes of teaching a particular principle or promoting a new point of view. Clients, be they government officials, prospective home-builders, or corporate directors, are an audience, too. So are casual readers of the daily newspaper, architectural historians, and prospective occupants of new buildings. Critics do not, for the most part, write for personal pleasure, but rather to inform or mold opinion. The way criticisms are framed needs to be related to the kind of audience to be influenced.

HISTORY

In a sense history may be called a subcategory of criticism, for it employs depictive and interpretive techniques in accounting for achievements and changes in architecture over time. Since history has traditionally played a role in the education of architects, however, it deserves special attention outside the framework of criticism. There are three aspects of the history of architecture worth noting here. One is its content (what material is deemed worthy of inclusion); a second is method (how is the material formulated and presented); and the third, what impact a knowledge of history should have in the education of the architect.

Content of Historical Treatments
The raw material of history that historians mold into understandable form ranges from the abstract, in the form of theories, to the very specific, like the prescribed measurements of a room.

Theories. Theory needs to be identified and explicated by the historian because, in some instances at least, it played such an important role in generating building form.

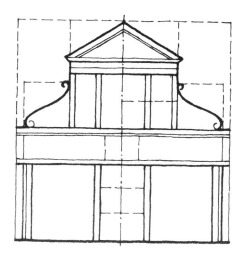

Façade of Santa Maria Novella, Florence, based on the work of Rudolf Wittkower in *Architectural Principles in an Age of Humanism.*

According to Alberti's well-known mathematical definition, based on Vitruvius, beauty consists in a rational integration of the proportions of all the parts of a building in such a way that every part has its absolutely fixed size and shape and nothing could be added or taken away without destroying the harmony of the whole. This conformity of ratios and correspondence of all the parts, this organic geometry should be observed in every building but above all in churches.[53]

The impact of this theory is seen clearly in Alberti's design for the façade of Santa Maria Novella in Florence:

Thus the whole façade is geometrically built up of a progressive duplication or, alternatively, a progressive halving of ratios. It is clear then that Alberti's theoretical precept that the same proportion be kept throughout the building has here been fulfilled.[54]

The history of theories of architecture provides a way of understanding similarities and differences in buildings that otherwise might not be evident.

Events. The impact of social, economic, political, technological, and other events is a major interest of historical treatments. The invention of nail-making machines and power-driven saws, for example, made quick construction possible, thus affecting housing form and cost in North America in the nineteenth century. Government subsidies of home-owner mortgages reinforced the growth of suburbs after World War II. The Council of Trent in the mid-sixteenth century was instrumental in the development of baroque church design:

The Church itself and the services held in it must be as dignified and impressive as possible, so that their splendour and their religious character may force themselves even on the casual spectator.[55]

One can, in fact, view the interrelation of context and building in terms of biography rather than in terms of history when the focus is on a sequence of influences and their ramifications. Alison Adburgham did this in her *Biography of a Shop,* the story of Liberty's, a department store in London:

A shop is part of the social history of its environment—in Liberty's case, of London. Its development is influenced by changes in social pressure, class patterns, governmental policies. It is affected by wars and depressions, by trade booms and enemy bombs, by changes in fashion and taste. What gives Liberty's its peculiar distinction is that it has not only reflected these changes, but has itself contributed to artistic movements and the development of fashionable taste.[56]

Design Methods. The procedures architects have employed in generating designs are an important consideration of history. Modular systems, geometries, standard typologies, or any of several other methods for designing, matter because methods have different ramifications in building form and character.

The question that the Gothic designer considered important was not "How high should the building

Liberty of London.

be in terms of the strength of the foundations and the structural possibilities of the whole?'' but rather, ''Within what figure shall it be designed?'' This was so because of the belief that with the proper geometric formula decided upon by the architect, both the aesthetic *and* structural correctness of the building could not help but be assured.[57]

The scale of the design operation and the organization of personnel also has consequences:

> Skidmore, Owings and Merrill was finally not only one of the largest offices in America, but also one of the most all-embracing in professional terms and the most integrated in terms of business operations. Horizontal integration was provided by the four units around the country, while vertical integration was accomplished by the inclusive package of design and design-related services.[58]

Buildings and Related Documents. Finally, of course, the buildings themselves are also the content of historical treatment. Plans, elevations, sections, site plans, materials, structural and mechanical systems, as well as deeds, tax records, and permits, are the raw material of history, although emphasis changes from time to time. Reyner Banham, for example, wrote an alternative history of modern architecture, stressing technological and mechanical considerations. He claimed that previous historians had erred in neglecting this important facet of the architectural tradition.

Yet architectural history as it has been written up till the present time has seen no reason to apologize or explain away a division that makes no sense in terms of the way buildings are used and paid for by the human race, a division into structure, which is held to be valuable and discussable, and mechanical servicing, which has been almost entirely excluded from historical discussion to

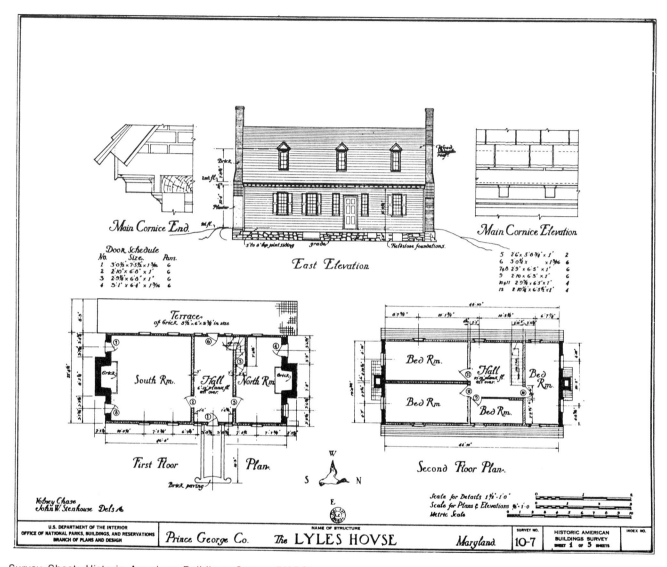

Survey Sheet: Historic American Buildings Survey (HABS).

date. Yet however obvious it may appear, on the slightest reflection, that the history of architecture should cover the whole of the technological art of creating habitable environments, the fact remains that the history of architecture found in the books currently available still deals almost exclusively with the external forms of habitable volumes as revealed by the structures that enclose them.[59]

Methods of Historical Treatment

Depictive Treatment. A familiar treatment of history is as a compendium of facts. This approach avoids interpretations. It records events as objectively as possible and lets the reader draw conclusions. For example, to continue the facts begun above about James Harrison Dakin:

THEORY, CRITICISM, AND HISTORY OF ARCHITECTURE

The Dakin family has a long history in America, tracing back to. . .the Duchess County vicinity in which the Dakin boys grew up is a very hilly area, almost mountainous.[60]

Advocatory Treatment. Like advocatory criticism, advocatory treatment of historical material requires the imposition of a particular point of view through which events are then interpreted. Charles Jencks views Le Corbusier's life in terms of tragic contradictions:

The contradictions abound, and, as is probably obvious by now, their very existence is taken here as of fundamental importance. Put simply, the interpretation is that Le Corbusier started off from a dual position which is represented by. . .his double identity (part the peasant Jeanneret, part the urbanite Le Corbusier) or his ironic building (part geometric, part biomorphic) or his tragic persona (part daemonic, part human). This last conflict, perhaps the most fundamental, is certainly the most important, because it led Le Corbusier to a basic antagonism with society which was completely beyond reconciliation.[61]

David Gebhard's characterization of Rudoph Schindler's work is in terms of reconciliation, the wedding of very different movements in twentieth-century architecture—the high and the low—into an amalgam:

First, he transformed the symbolic image of the machine (as expressed in high art) into a form or set of forms which would have the impact and vitality of low art; the language to accomplish this was to be found in the everyday building methods used around him in Southern California. Second he sought to transform low art (the building and the way it was put together) into high art; and for him the high art aim of architecture was the creation of space. . . . In concocting this mixture, he insisted that each of the symbols should contribute to the whole, but at the same time that each should not lose its basic identity.[62]

Expressionist Treatment. Expressionist historical treatment is similar to impressionistic criticism. It provides the writer with a vehicle for imagination and artistry. Historical facts are molded into a form that is more reflective of the writer's sensibility than of the subject's life. This is seen in Giorgio Vasari's expressionist treatment of Filippo Brunelleschi:

Many who Nature creates small and insignificant in appearance have their souls filled with such greatness and their hearts with such boundless courage that they cannot rest unless they undertake things of almost impossible difficulty, and bring them to completion to the wonder of all beholders, and no matter how vile and base things may be, they become in their hands valuable and lofty. Thus we should never turn up our noses when we meet persons who do not possess that grace and bearing which Nature might be expected to give to distinguished men when they come into the world, for clods of earth hide veins of gold. It frequently happens that men of insignificant appearance possess great generosity of spirit and sincerity of heart, and when nobility of soul is joined to these characteristics the greatest marvels may be expected, for they endeavor to overcome the defects of their body by the virtues of their mind. This appears in Filippo di ser Brunellescho.[63]

Clearly there is more Vasari than Brunelleschi here.

Impact in Education

An acquaintance with history has been a part of architects' training since formal programs were developed in the eighteenth century. Even before, this was seen in the form of the "Grand Tour of the Continent" made by proper architects. Walter Gropius, who was concerned about the negative effects of history on beginning students, agreed that history was useful as part of a total educational program:

Studies in the history of art and architecture, intellectual and analytical in character, make the student familiar with the conditions and reasons which have brought about the visual expression of the different periods: i.e., the changes in philosophy, in politics and in means of production caused by new inventions. Such studies can verify principles found by the student through his own previous exercises.[64]

In referring to intellectual and analytic studies, Gropius made a point that is not always acknowledged in the teaching of history in architecture schools—that the important concern should not be learning history, but learning *from* history.

CONCLUSION

Theory, criticism, and history of architecture are probably not so important in very traditional, stable societies. They become crucial in societies experiencing change. Where new technologies are purposefully developed, and where dissatisfaction with the past either occurs naturally or is promulgated in the social system, theory, criticism, and history become relevant. They are crucial because societies in change force individuals to make decisions. Appropriate decisions cannot be made without the identification of goals, and an understanding of processes operating in the society. Clearly, much construction, even in changing societies, occurs without much consideration of goals and historical contexts. As long as people are housed in tenements and in suburban tracts, in the modern-day vernacular, there is no need for reflection. But the moment that the standards change—for example, of acceptable numbers of crimes per capita, or of water pollution—then the vernacular must change. Change can occur productively, rather than at random, when there is an awareness of theory, history, and criticism.

NOTES

1. Paul Davidson Reynolds, *A Primer in Theory Construction* (Indianapolis: Bobbs-Merrill, 1971), pp. 10–11.
2. Le Corbusier, *Towards a New Architecture*, trans. Frederick Etchells (New York: Praeger, 1960), p. 14.
3. Louis I. Kahn, quoted in Ulrich Conrads, ed., *Programs and Manifestoes on 20th-Century Architecture*, trans. Michael Bullock (Cambridge: M.I.T. Press, 1970), p. 169.
4. Bruno Zevi, *Architecture as Space*, trans. Milton Gendel (New York: Horizon, 1957), p. 23.
5. Ibid., p. 224.
6. Le Corbusier, *Towards a New Architecture*, p. 31.
7. Daniele Barbaro, *Commentary to Vitruvius* (1556), quoted in Rudolf Wittkower, *Architectural Principles in the Age of Humanism* (London: Alec Tiranti, 1952), p. 121.
8. Diana Faidy, "An Introduction to the Society," *Society of the Golden Section Newsletter* 1 (No. 1, 1975):3.
9. Hannes Meyer, quoted in Conrads, *Programs and Manifestoes*, p. 117.
10. Frank Lloyd Wright, *Writings and Buildings* (Cleveland: World, 1960), p. 294.
11. Frank Lloyd Wright, *The Future of Architecture* (New York: New American Library, 1963), p. 347
12. Frank Lloyd Wright, *An Organic Architecture* (Cambridge: M.I.T. Press, 1970), p. vii.

13. Telethon, "Roadside Mecca," *Progressive Architecture* 54 (November 1973):128.
14. Eero Saarinen, *Eero Saarinen on His Work* (New Haven: Yale University Press, 1962), pp. 83–84.
15. Allan Temko, *Eero Saarinen* (New York: George Braziller, 1962), pp. 177–18.
16. Kasimir Edschmid, quoted in Walter Sokel, *The Writer in Extremis* (Stanford, Calif.: Stanford University Press, 1959), p. 51.
17. J. M. Richards, *An Introduction to Modern Architecture* (Harmondsworth, England: Penguin Books, 1948), pp. 18–19.
18. Wright, *Writings and Buildings*, p. 296.
19. Charles W. Moore, quoted in John W. Cook and Heinrich Klotz, eds., *Conversations with Architects* (New York: Praeger, 1973), p. 219.
20. Saarinen, *On His Work*, pp. 192–96.
21. Robert Venturi, Denise Scott Brown, and Steven Izenour, *Learning from Las Vegas* (Cambridge: M.I.T. Press, 1972).
22. Walter Gropius, *The New Architecture and the Bauhaus*, trans. P. Morton Shand (New York: Museum of Modern Art, 1936), p. 82.
23. Horatio Greenough, "American Architecture," in *The Literature of Architecture*, ed. Don Gifford (New York: Dutton, 1966), p. 147.
24. J.A. Borgnis, *Elementary Treatise on Construction* (1823),

quoted in Peter Collins, *Changing Ideals in Modern Architecture, 1950–1950* (Montreal: McGill University Press, 1967), p. 202.

25. John Christopher Jones, *Design Methods* (London: Wiley-Interscience, 1970), p. 50.

26. Charles Jencks, "Adhocism in the South Bank," *Architectural Review* 144 (July 1969): 28–30.

27. Christopher Alexander et al., *A Pattern Language* (New York: Oxford University Press, 1977), p. x.

28. Ibid., pp. 730–31.

29. Vitruvius Pollio, *Vitruvius: The Ten Books on Architecture*, trans. Morris Hicky Morgan (New York: Dover, 1960), p. 13.

30. John Ruskin, *The Stones of Venice*, Vol. 1 (London: Routledge, 1851?), pp. 39–40.

31. Albert Bush-Brown, "Notes Toward a Basis for Criticism," *Architectural Record* 126 (October 1959): 184.

32. Hannes Meyer, quoted in Conrads, *Programs and Manifestoes*, p. 120.

33. Vitruvius, *Ten Books on Architecture*, p. 170

34. Walter Gropius, *Scope of Total Architecture* (New York: Collier, 1962), p. 84.

35. Erich Mendelsohn, quoted in Conrads, *Programs and Manifestoes*, p. 106.

36. Le Corbusier, *Towards a New Architecture*, p. 12.

37. Gropius, *Scope of Total Architecture*, p. 78.

38. Hans Poelzig, quoted in Conrads, *Programs and Manifestoes*, p. 16.

39. Ludwig Mies van der Rohe, quoted in Conrads, *Programs and Manifestoes*, p. 102.

40. Ada Louise Huxtable, *Will They Ever Finish Bruckner Boulevard?* (New York: Macmillan, 1970), p. 170.

41. Ibid., p. 168.

42. Bill Hillier, John Musgrove, and Pat O'Sullivan, "Knowledge and Design," in *Environmental Design: Research and Practice*, Proceedings of the EDRA 3/AR 8 Conference, ed. William J. Mitchell (Los Angeles, 1972), p. 29-3-12.

43. Philip Sawyer, "The Planning of Bank Buildings," *Architectural Review* 12 (March 1905).

44. Montgomery Schuyler, "Last Words About the World's Fair," in *American Architecture, and Other Writings*, ed. William H.

Jordy and Ralph Coe (New York: Atheneum, 1964), pp. 275–93.

45. Peter Green, *Impressions* (London: Architectural Association, 1974), p. 3.

46. Oscar Wilde, *Works* (London: W.J. Black, 1927), p. 567.

47. Huxtable, *Bruckner Boulevard*, p. 86.

48. Grady Clay, *Close-up: How to Read the American City* (New York: Praeger, 1973), p. 53.

49. Huxtable, *Bruckner Boulevard*, p. 38.

50. Peter Blake, *Frank Lloyd Wright: Architecture as Space* (Baltimore: Penguin Books, 1960), p. 46.

51. Arthur Scully, *James Dakin, Architect* (Baton Rouge: Louisiana State University Press, 1973), pp. 3–4.

52. Michael Baume, *The Sydney Opera House Affair* (Melbourne: Nelson, 1967), p. 9.

53. Rudolf Wittkower, *Architectural Principles in the Age of Humanism* (New York: Random House, 1965), p. 7.

54. Ibid., p. 47.

55. Anthony Blunt, *Artistic Theory in Italy, 1450–1600* (Oxford: Clarendon, 1962), p. 128.

56. Alison Adburgham, *Liberty's: A Biography of a Shop* (London: Allen & Unwin, 1975), p. 5.

57. Spiro Kostof, "The Architect in the Middle Ages, East and West," in *The Architect*, ed. Spiro Kostof (New York: Oxford University Press, 1977), p. 87.

58. Bernard Michael Boyle, "Architectural Practice in America, 1865–1965: Ideal and Reality," in *The Architect*, ed. Kostof, p. 327.

59. Reyner Banham, *The Architecture of the Well-Tempered Environment* (London: Architectural Press, 1969), pp. 11–12.

60. Scully, *James Dakin*, pp. 3–4.

61. Charles Jencks, *Modern Movements in Architecture* (Garden City, N.Y.: Doubleday & Co., Anchor Books, 1973), p. 142.

62. David Gebhard, *Schindler* (New York: Viking, 1971), p. 189.

63. Giorgio Vasari, *The Lives of the Painters, Sculptors, and Architects*, Vol. 1, trans. A. B. Hinds (London: J.M. Dent, 1927), pp. 269–70.

64. Gropius, *Scope of Total Architecture*, p. 55.

FOR FURTHER READING

Attoe, Wayne. *Architecture and Critical Imagination.* Chichester, England: John Wiley & Sons, 1978.

Broadbent, Geoffrey. *Design in Architecture.* London: John Wiley & Sons, 1973.

Collins, Peter. *Changing Ideals in Modern Architecture, 1750–1950.* London: Faber & Faber, 1965.

Conrads, Ulrich, ed. *Programs and Manifestoes on 20th-century Architecture.* Translated by Michael Bullock. Cambridge: M.I.T. Press, 1970.

Giedion, Sigfried. *Space, Time and Architecture.* 5th ed., rev. Cambridge, Mass.: Harvard University Press, 1967.

Huxtable, Ada Louise. *Kicked a Building Lately?* New

York: Quadrangle, New York Times Book Co., 1976.

———. *Will They Ever Finish Bruckner Boulevard?* New York: Macmillan Co., 1970.

Kostof, Spiro, ed. *The Architect: Chapters in the History of the Profession.* New York: Oxford University Press, 1977.

Maharaj, Jayant T. *The Nature of Architectural Criticism.* Report No. 36. Halifax: School of Architecture, Nova Scotia Technical College, 1977.

Pevsner, Nikolaus. *A History of Building Types.* Princeton, N.J.: Princeton University Press, 1976.

———. *An Outline of European Architecture.* 7th ed. Harmondsworth, England: Penguin Books, 1963.

Scott, Geoffrey. *The Architecture of Humanism.* 2d ed. London: Constable, 1924; reprint ed., Gloucester, Mass.: Peter Smith, 1965.

Vitruvius Pollio. *Vitruvius: The Ten Books on Architecture.* Translated by Morris Hicky Morgan. New York: Dover Publications, 1960.

Whiffen, Marcus, ed. *The History, Theory, and Criticism of Architecture.* Cambridge: M.I.T. Press, 1965.

CHAPTER 3

Environment-Behavior Studies

Gary T. Moore

Since the time of Vitruvius, the goals of architecture have been expressed in terms of firmness, commodity, and delight. In more current language these values would be technology, function, and aesthetics. Architecture is a synthetic discipline, and so these inputs have traditionally come from engineering, the social sciences, and the arts, respectively. They have been integrated by architects within the design process, and good architecture has always responded to them. As the world has become more complex, and as knowledge in these three areas has become more voluminous and more specialized, architects have emphasized one or more of these values, with the best architects responding to all three. The subject of this chapter is commodity or function, or, as it is now termed, environment-behavior studies in architecture.

The term "environment-behavior studies" has a number of partial equivalents: "human-environment studies," "social ecology," "human factors," "behavioral architecture," and sometimes just "programming." The research aspect is often called "environmental psychology," while the applied aspects are called "user needs" or "social and behavioral factors." The most encompassing designation is "environment-behavior studies." It is a multidisciplinary and multiprofessional field, aspects of which are taught by most schools of architecture as well as many departments of psychology and geography, and a few anthropology, sociology, and urban planning departments. Only those aspects of the broad field that bear directly on architecture will be presented in this chapter.[1]

Environment-behavior studies in architecture include the systematic examination of relationships between the environment and human behavior and their application in the design process. The basic questions to be asked are: How do people interact with the built environment? What are their needs? How do we apply such understandings in the design process? Each time an architect moves a pencil, he or she makes assumptions about human needs and a decision about how the built environment can best serve these needs. In many cases these assumptions are unconscious, the decision-making process is not analytic, and the resulting building is not evaluated to find out how well it actually worked.

Environment-behavior studies in architecture encompass more than just function. Function in architecture often refers to dimensional concerns like the height of blackboards or the placement of wall sockets so that the building can function as it was intended to, and to quantifiable concerns like circulation flows and proximities between activities so that people can move easily from one function they have to perform to another. But behavioral factors go deeper, to the psychology of the user, how he or she perceives building form, social interaction needs, subcultural differences in lifestyles, and the meaning and symbolism of buildings.

Environment-behavior studies also include aesthetics (delight). As function is related to people's behavior and needs, aesthetics is related to their preferences, experiences, and, of course, their perception of the world. Thus, formal aesthetics is supplemented with a user-based experiential aesthetics.

Environment-behavior studies also extend to technology (firmness), for we can ask what architectural cues give a strong expression of firmness or protection as opposed to one of airiness or lightness. Because the cues may be very different from the factors that lead structural engineers to conclude that a building is structurally sound, the question of the perceptual basis for the expression of structure is grist also for the architect's mill.

Good architects, from the master builders of the Gothic period to the humanists of our time, have been sensitive to the behavioral determinants of architecture. The best buildings from historical times responded to human needs and sentiments, not only in their own time but also as social life styles evolved. There are, however, many buildings that do not work functionally or behaviorally. Others work but could have been designed more successfully if the architect had paid more attention to user needs and to ways in which the built environment and behavior interact with each other.

A great deal of useful information has emerged from the multidisciplinary field of environment-behavior studies. This has begun to document the relationships between individual behavior, social rules, cultural values, and the physical environment. A number of methods have also been proposed by architects and other professionals for using sociobehavioral information in the design process and for checking proposed designs against behavioral criteria.

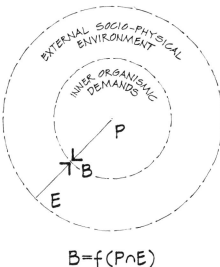

$$B=f(P \cap E)$$

Behavior as a function of inner organismic demands and the external socio-physical environment.

ENVIRONMENT-BEHAVIOR STUDIES IN THE DESIGN PROCESS

There are a number of reasons why an explicit focus on environment-behavior relations has become an important part of architecture. Considerable research has shown that the attitudes and values of professionals are very different from those of the citizens and users they purport to serve. The difference between professional designer and user is more pronounced with unfamiliar user groups and unfamiliar building types.[2] Our society has become more professionally specialized, more socially differentiated into ethnic, age-based, and special-interest groups. The professional training leads architects to see and think of the built environment in ways that are totally different from the ways most other people do. It has become necessary to close the gaps somewhat by including as integral parts of our training knowledge about a wide range of user groups, and about ways in which other less highly-trained people think about the environment. Most people are verbal thinkers, while architects are predominantly visual thinkers. Do the users of buildings therefore value the same visual aesthetics we do, or is it possible to turn this all around and base design decisions on the needs, perceptions, preferences, and values of the user? As the Dutch architect, Neils Prak said: "The 'common sense' of the architect is not the common sense of the user, simply because the one has been subjected to a professional training and the other has not. Let us, therefore, mistrust the intuition of architects and try to find out where people's needs have been thwarted, by experimenting and theorizing. There is no intuitive shortcut to knowledge."[3]

Architects who like a building or a residential area because it is "beautiful" will be inclined to excuse its functional or social shortcomings. Research has shown, however, that this aesthetic "halo effect" does not hold for most user groups and that, in fact, the architects' priorities for aesthetics over functional factors may be exactly the opposite of the users' priorities.[4]

A number of studies have evaluated buildings in use to see to what degree they meet the needs, preferences, and values of their inhabitants, and to feed this information back into new research, programming, and design. Design awards are often made before construction or just after occupancy. The AIA's awards for excellence are given ten years after project completion. Few of the awards are based on user evaluations. Rather, they are based on the prevailing architectural aesthetics of the time. Rigorous postoccupancy evaluation studies, however, have turned up shortcomings and oversights in many of these award-winning projects. Evaluations have now been conducted of a wide range of buildings, including housing, residential areas, neighborhood design, hospitals, schools, offices, children's outdoor recreation environments, student unions, and malls. This is an area of valuable information for design and one that can be expanded by architectural researchers.[5]

The best-known building to have major architecture-behavior problems was the Pruitt-Igoe housing complex in St. Louis. Pruitt-Igoe was a low-income public housing project of 33 buildings averaging 11 stories tall. It was to house 11,000 inhabitants. In the 1950s the project was touted in the architectural press as a bright new example for public housing in the United States. It was to have a number of bold design features, including a refreshing site plan, a river of open space winding through the buildings, and open galleries every third floor for children to play and for adults to meet and talk. But the area between the buildings became a desert, and the galleries became high-crime areas. A second architectural firm was contracted in an attempt to improve the project. Even so, many of the buildings were abandoned, and crime and vandalism took over completely. Finally, in 1972, large portions of the Pruitt-Igoe Housing Project were demolished by the owners, the U.S. Department of Housing and Urban Development. The predominant conclusion among those who have studied the situation was that not enough serious attention was given to the needs, preferences, and lifestyles of the urban poor who were to inhabit the project.[6]

Situations like these in many parts of the world have led to a feeling of a crisis in architecture, and to a number of issues central to the architectural profession:[7]

1 Western Judeo-Christian tradition has led to attitudes that place people over nature and the land, rather than emphasizing humans in harmony with the physical environment.

2 The structure and reward system of the architectural profession has promoted alienation from the poor, the young, the old, the disabled, and the majority who cannot afford architectural services and go forgotten, while the wealthy and politically powerful reap the fruits of society. No less critical is the client-user issue: To whom is the architect morally responsible?

3 Professional and national desire for cleanliness and order has led to sterile—though efficient—environments, rather than humane environments that first and foremost support the needs and desires of their inhabitants.

4 The architectural concern for style and a machine aesthetic has blinded many architects to human needs and behavior.

5 The architectural tradition and belief that technology could solve all environmental problems has proven to be at best only a partial solution, and at worst a crutch.

6 Although the members of the architectural avant-garde of the 1920s and 1930s paid tribute to the arts, they wished to base architecture on political and economic principles. Their manifestos suggested that modern architecture could satisfy human needs only if political and economic preconditions were met, and they called for the complete and systematic examination of human needs and for the constant reassessment of each architectural problem. But this was not to be the case. Social and economic ideals took a back seat to visual aesthetics and formalism, and this was the course of modern architecture until Pruitt-Igoe and the newer behavioral architecture.[8]

In *Design for the Real World*, Victor Papanek argues that we have isolated ourselves from the real world, that we have isolated and barricaded ourselves from real human problems, and that we have isolated very small parts of sociobehavioral-environmental problems to work on, being content to manipulate a few windows or courtyards when this does not begin to plumb the depth of human experience and human needs.[9] Until recent changes in architectural education, the system of teaching was apprenticelike indoctrination in the modern style —as if it were "truth." Fortunately, architectural education is now much broader and has again some chance of speaking to the depth of human needs in the built environment.

In order to look at environment-behavior studies in architecture, we must understand two conceptual frameworks, one illustrating the range of environment-behavior information available, and the other showing where in the design process environment-behavior information most affects architectural decision making.

The Scope of Environment-Behavior Information
A useful model for seeing the scope of available environment-behavior information, first proposed by the architectural psychologist Irwin Altman, includes three main components: environment-behavior phenomena, user groups, and settings.

Environment-Behavior Phenomena. Each of these phenomena is a different aspect of human behavior in relation to everyday physical environments. Common examples include proxemics and privacy. Proxemics are the different distances between people that are considered comfortable for social interaction. Privacy is an interpersonal control mechanism that paces and regulates interaction with others. Physical design factors affect the degree to which we can control interpersonal interaction and maintain a balance between privacy and community. Other examples of environment-behavior phenomena include environmental meaning and symbolism and the ways in which people use the envi-

Settings/
Places

World
•
•
•
Nations

Regions

Cities and towns

Urban areas

Residential areas

Complexes of buildings

Buildings of various types

Parts of buildings

Rooms

Furniture

Equipment and objects

Children

Elderly

Handicapped

Infirm

Different
socioeconomic groups

Groups with
different
ways of life
•
• •

User
Groups

Anthropometrics

Proxemics

Personal space

Territoriality

Privacy

Perception

Cognition

Meaning
• •
• •

Behavioral
Phenomena/
Concepts

The scope of environment-behavior information.

ronment in the presentation of self. Some of these phenomena, like proxemics and privacy, refer to individual behavior patterns, while others, like community and neighborhood deal with social patterns and rules. Still others, especially meaning and symbolism, refer to important culturally based determinants of design. All of these environment-behavior phenomena are important for designers in that they cross-cut each other and thus reappear as considerations in designing a variety of building types for various user groups.

User Groups. Different user groups have different needs and use patterns and are affected in different ways by the quality of the environment. Considerable information now exists about children and the environment, different ethnic groups, and special user groups like the learning disabled and physically handicapped. The importance of studying behavioral factors from a user standpoint is that it provides the architect with a wealth of understanding that can be applied in any design project involving those users.

Settings. This last component of the model includes all scales of settings, from the room scale to the region, the nation, and the world. The scale of rooms to buildings and to groups of buildings is of great interest to the architect. The scale of buildings to cities is a concern of the urban designer. Groups of buildings in relation to regions occupy the urban and regional planner, and so on. Recent developments within environment-behavior studies have seen a focus on behavioral studies and criteria for different building types; for example, residential environments for children, housing for the elderly, and residential areas and neighborhoods for different sociocultural groups. The unique feature about this orientation to behavioral concerns in architecture is the holistic focus on all of the behavioral, social, and cultural factors that need to be considered in the design of different building types.

The Place of Environment-Behavior Information in the Design Process
The place of environment-behavior information in the design process can be seen as a cyclical diagram first proposed by the architectural sociologist John Zeisel. Briefly, the design process involves applied user research, policy decisions, programming, preliminary design alternatives, selection, design development, environmental management, postoccupancy evaluation, and feedback into additional research, decision making, and programming, and into improved general design knowledge.

Environment-behavior information and concepts have no single place of entry into the design process. Rather, they inform policy decisions, programming, and overall design synthesis, and such decisions and designs are evaluated against sociobehavioral criteria in postoccupancy evaluation.

ENVIRONMENT-BEHAVIOR: PHENOMENA AND DESIGN

Environment-behavior information spans a wide range from anthropometrics to semiotics. Some phenomena, like anthropometrics, refer to human conditions that for the most part are manifest, concrete, and observable, while others, like semiotics, refer to effects of the environment that are latent, highly ephemeral, and covert. Only a few of these can be presented, but they should provide an indication of the type of environment-behavior factors architects need to know about in order to design sensitively.

Behavior Settings: Fits and Misfits
A key concept for the analysis of human behavior in architecture is the behavior setting. Based on the work of the ecological psychologist Roger Barker, a behavior-setting can be defined for architectural purposes as a basic unit of analysis of environment-behavior interactions that includes the following four characteristics:[10]

1 A standing pattern of behavior or a common recurring type of behavior, such as stopping to talk when passing a friend.

2 Social rules and purposes governing the behavior, which may be interpreted as including norms and expectations. Lengthy conversations are the norm for elderly people, and social convention allows touching and close proximities while talking.

3 Critical physical features of the setting, that is, the elements and relationships of the physical environment that are inseparably linked with the behavior, such as the

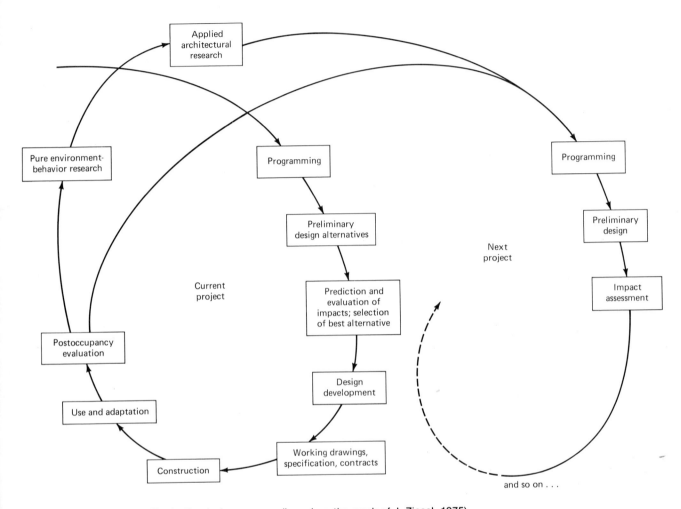

Environment-behavior studies in the design process (based on the work of J. Ziesel, 1975).

sizes and shapes of social spaces in housing for the elderly in which conversations occur, or nooks off a busy circulation path where people gather.

4 Time locus, the time frame in which the behavior occurs, for many behaviors have daily, weekly, monthly, and seasonal rhythms.

Behavior settings, therefore, include only those aspects of the physical environment that are critical to behavior. It is often better to sketch behavior settings than to photograph them, for not all photo-graphed aspects of the building may be critical aspects of the setting for the behavior being observed. It is a common observation that many standing patterns of behavior and their settings have an integrity and that, though the actors and minor props may be different or may change, the pattern of behavior and the critical relationships of the setting remain essentially the same. Classroom behavior and its setting does not differ much for the same course from term to term, despite the change in students. But people and objects are transformed as they pass from one setting to another, as when moving from a lecture room to a coffee shop.

The ultimate object of design is to create form that satisfies behavior. The rightness of a form depends on the degree to which it fits its behavioral, social, and cultural context. If the setting components are in harmony with the behavior and its rules or purposes, there is a fit between environment and behavior, between form and purpose, and the behavior setting is *synomorphic*. If the setting is a hindrance to behavior, we can say that the two are not synomorphic, or that a *misfit* exists between the setting and the standing pattern of behavior occurring within it. It is possible for a setting and its behavior to be mostly in fit, with a few misfits. For example, in housing for the elderly, socializing space may support interaction between people but may make it difficult for elderly residents to sit and watch people come and go. A central purpose of architecture, then, is to redesign settings so as to remove the sources of misfits while leaving fits intact. As the architectural theoretician Christopher Alexander has said, the process of achieving good fit between form and its context is the negative process of removing misfits or neutralizing the irritants that cause the misfits.[11]

The behavior setting concept and the twin concepts of fit-misfit are basic building blocks in architecture. They form the basis for the analysis of form-behavior relations, for the evaluation of buildings in use, and for the development of behaviorally based architectural programs. Every design may thus be seen as an array of implicit hypotheses about ways of achieving good fit between form and behavior, and consequestly every design is open to postoccupancy evaluation, reprogramming, and redesign.

Anthropometrics

Anthropometrics are the proportions and dimensions of the human body and its other physiological characteristics and abilities relative to different human activities and microenvironments. Also called "human factors" or, in applications, "ergonomics," they are concerned with such problems as the heights of work surfaces for a variety of activities, the range of heights that will be comfortable for all but the shortest and tallest, and the critical dimensions that influence the design of the micro- or space-filling elements of architecture for children, men, women, and the elderly.[12]

Proxemics, Personal Space, Territoriality, and Defensible Space

People have biological, personality, social, and cultural needs that are expressed in the environment. In addition to satisfying human needs, space speaks; it is the hidden dimension in behavior, and through it we communicate with each other.

We defined proxemics as the interrelated observations and theories about the spatial factor in face-to-face interaction. In the early 1950s, Robert Sommer, an environmental psychologist, studied the spatial factor in different types of face-to-face interactions in Saskatchewan hospitals, cafeterias, and mental institutions. Through a combination of questionnaires and experimental methods, he found that the most comfortable talking distance was 5 feet, 6 inches nose-to-nose. Studying tables of different shapes and sizes, he also found that congenial conversations most often occur when people sit at right-angle positions, cooperative tasks occur when they sit side-by-side, independent behaviors like eating alone happen at corner locations, and competitive tasks or arguments normally occur when people sit directly opposite across the short dimension of tables or other spaces.

Many other studies of proxemics have been done. The most elaborate summary has been given by anthropologist Edward Hall.[13] This work shows four distinct distances (intimate, personal, social-consultive, and public), the characteristic behaviors that occur at each distance, and the different interpersonal sense receptors involved at these dis-

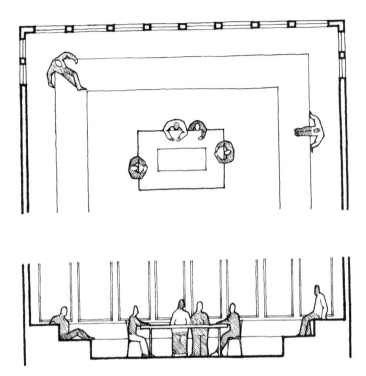

Sketches of behavior settings. (Based on the work of C. Kronser and J. Oertel)

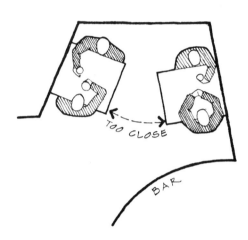

TOO CLOSE

BAR

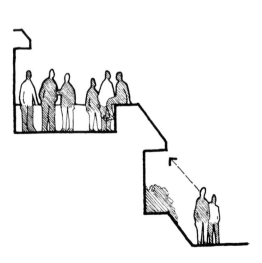

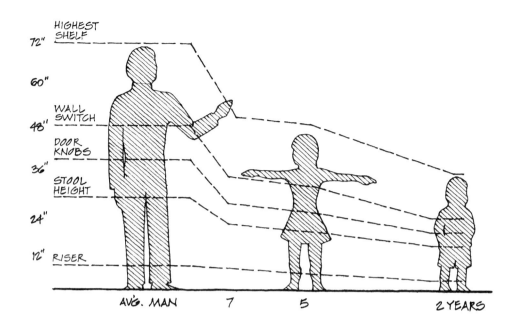

Anthropometrics: The human body.

tances. There has been some confirmation of Hall's observations under controlled conditions. There has also been some research about the effect of different physical environments on these distances. Much architectural research remains to be done on proxemics and spatial interaction in relation to characteristics of the physical environment. Even before such additional research is complete, however, the Hall generalizations are useful as a basis for making design decisions about minimum and maximum sizes of rooms, lounges, meeting halls, seminar rooms, and so on for various intimate, interpersonal, social, and public interactions.

Personal space is a specific environment-behavior concept. It has been defined by Robert Sommer as a small, invisible, protective sphere or bubble that an organism carries about and maintains between the self and others, that is, a body buffer zone of personal, not shared, space. The individual's personal space is dynamic; it changes in dimension, and stress and anxiety can result from intrusion.

Individual characteristics (personality, mood, sex, age) affect personal space, along with social norms and cultural rules associated with different physical environmental contexts. For example, men's personal space is larger when they are interacting with other men than when they are interacting with women, but women's personal space is less permeable than men's. Personal space increases with age until later life when it decreases again. United States elementary school children feel greater personal-space needs when with children of the other sex than they do with children of other ethnic or racial groups, though this trend reverses by adolescence. And people feel greater personal-space needs in formal public settings like parks and plazas than they do in informal semipublic settings like parties or picnics.

Territory and territoriality refer to a group of behavior settings that a person will personalize, mark, own, and defend. Unlike personal space, territories are anchored—they do not move. Territories have five defining characteristics: they contain spatial area; they are possessed, owned, or controlled by an individual or group; they satisfy some needs or motives, like mating or status; they are marked in either a concrete or symbolic way; and people will defend them or at least feel discomfort if they are violated in any way by intruders. Territoriality, as a concept, cross-cuts animal and human species, and indeed the concept came initially from extensive research on primates, higher vertebrates, and birds. Examples of human territories include the home, the office, one's work area and the space around it, the yard or area in front of the living unit, the "turf" of the gang, the cubbies and forts of children, and even whole neighborhoods and residential areas. These territories are protected, sometimes by fighting, sometimes by nonverbal cues, and often in architectural, symbolic ways.

Territorial behavior has been examined in a number of building settings. One interesting study looked at territoriality in mental hospitals. It found that less assertive people treated a small area as their own territory and defended it intensely, while the most dominant patients freely roamed over the entire ward but exhibited very little spatial territoriality.[14]

The concept of territoriality has been extended to suggest how housing and residential areas can be designed to be defensible against crime and vandalism. Defensible space is a term created by the architectural designer and researcher Oscar Newman, though the concept had already been set down by Jane Jacobs in her book, *The Death and Life of Great American Cities*.[15] Newman identified four characteristics of space that make it more defensible against intrusion, vandalism, and crime and that thus make it safer:

1 Surveillance, or what Jane Jacobs called "eyes on the street," which is created by mixed land uses, diversity of residents, an open plan design, and twenty-four-hour street life.

2 Perceived and defensible territory, including clear perception of public versus private zones and clear perception of the "gates" between zones.

3 Image and milieu, or the idea that certain areas have an overall image of safety or neighborhood pride.

4 Safe zones, or the separation of desired safe space from high-activity or dangerous areas, and the juxtaposition of safe and defensible areas.

Small-Group Ecology

Small-group ecology is the name given to considerations of the critical environment-behavior relations in small-group situations. Proxemic distances for various types of activities, discussed above, are a part of small-group ecology. But in addition, how do the dimensions, shape, and character of space influence interpersonal contacts? What types of spaces are best for seminars, conferences, meetings between social welfare workers and welfare recipients, informal discussions, and so on? And what types of small-group interaction happen in nooks off corridors, courts, or plazas?

Studies have shown that in a group situation, like a seminar, people tend to respond to others more if they can fully see them. Satisfaction with a work experience has been shown to be directly related to being in a central location in a group setting. Other research has demonstrated that classroom participation, and even grades, are related to seating positions. Less interaction occurs in seminar rooms that are long and narrow, but if a room has a central square area and an "escape" area, it allows both intensive discussion and the chance to escape the intensity without leaving the room.

Thus, in this context, a design for a seminar room might be a square space, windowless to eliminate distractions, with limited access to indicate the private nature of meetings, and with high visibility and interaction for all participants. Next to such rooms should be "break-out areas"—vestibulelike spaces that allow participants to linger for a while and talk with others before entering fast-moving circulation streams. These break-out areas should have easy access from other parts of the building and be convenient to major circulation spaces. They

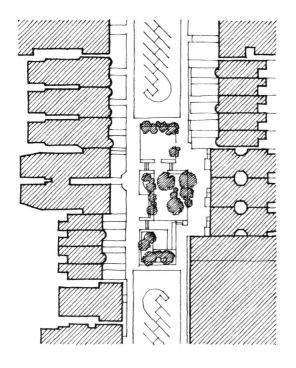

Defensible space: natural surveillance at St. Mark's Place, Brooklyn, by M. Paul Friedberg and partners.

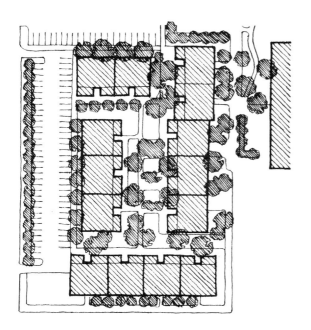

Defensible space: natural surveillance, territorial gates, barriers, and clear image and milieu at St. Francis Square, San Francisco, by Marquis and Stoller, architects.

ENVIRONMENT-BEHAVIOR STUDIES

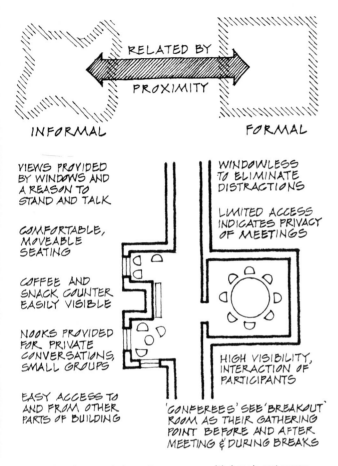

RELATED BY PROXIMITY

INFORMAL   FORMAL

VIEWS PROVIDED BY WINDOWS AND A REASON TO STAND AND TALK

COMFORTABLE, MOVEABLE SEATING

COFFEE AND SNACK COUNTER EASILY VISIBLE

NOOKS PROVIDED FOR PRIVATE CONVERSATIONS, SMALL GROUPS

EASY ACCESS TO AND FROM OTHER PARTS OF BUILDING

WINDOWLESS TO ELIMINATE DISTRACTIONS

LIMITED ACCESS INDICATES PRIVACY OF MEETINGS

HIGH VISIBILITY, INTERACTION OF PARTICIPANTS

'CONFEREES' SEE 'BREAKOUT' ROOM AS THEIR GATHERING POINT BEFORE AND AFTER MEETING & DURING BREAKS

Example of group interaction spaces with break-out areas.

should be visible immediately upon leaving the seminar room, and they should function as gathering points during and after meetings.[16]

These studies indicate how critical the spatial factor is in group interaction, and how the entire ecology of behavior and setting must be considered in the design of architectural spaces where social interaction is to occur, and how this information can be translated into behaviorally based design.

Privacy, Density, Crowding, and Stress

What are the desires of different individuals and groups for privacy versus social interaction? Is there a difference between density, crowding, and perceived density? What is the relationship between these variables and stress; that is, under what conditions do people feel stress from crowding? These are some of the questions architects must ask, especially in the context of high-density mass housing, but also in the design of many types of institutions.

Privacy may be defined as the claim of individuals, groups, or institutions to control access to themselves and to determine for themselves when, how, and to what extent information about themselves will be communicated. Thus, privacy applies to a variety of social units.

Social interaction and communication are the opposite of privacy. Chermayeff and Alexander developed a scheme of six realms of community and privacy, from individual private space to urban public space. This scheme can be applied to the analysis of existing housing and the design of new housing, and to other types of settings. The realms are the following:

1 Individual private areas, relating to the person—for example, a person's private space.

2 Family or small-group private areas, relating to the primary group—for example, home or dormitory suite.

3 Large-group private areas, relating to a secondary group—for example, management control of privacy on behalf of all residents in an apartment building.

4 Large-group public areas, involving the interaction of the large group with the public—such as semi-controlled public sidewalks or an area of group mailboxes.

5 Urban semi-public areas, that may be government- or institution-controlled with public access if purpose warrants—such as banks, postoffices, airports, city halls.

6 Urban public areas, characterized by public ownership and complete public access—including parks, malls, and streets.

The most successful urban public spaces incorporate all of these realms in a nested hierarchy of community and private spaces. A good urban, semi-public space will incorporate large-group public spaces and each of the smaller scale realms. The good home or office design will still have nested within it places for individual privacy. Designing for privacy is no easy matter, though it is vitally important for happiness and well-being.

On the opposite end of the privacy-community spectrum are density and crowding. Density is a mathematical measure of the number of people per unit of space. Crowding, on the other hand, is a psychological or an environment-behavior concept, which refers to the experience of being hemmed in, blocked, or frustrated by the presence of too many people. Crowding may result from high density. But more importantly, crowding is a function of perceived density, and this perception is also subject to the effects of mood, personality, and physical context.

Altman has advanced a model linking privacy, personal space, territoriality, and crowding. Treating crowding as a result of the failure to achieve desired levels of privacy, he argues that defending personal

space and showing territorial behavior are two mechanisms people use to achieve desired levels of privacy in crowded situations in order to avoid undue stress. As suggested above, other physical factors result in crowding, and they could be looked at in similar ways. People also use other coping mechanisms, like devising staggered schedules, avoiding crowded areas, and creating sound or sight barriers.[17]

Environmental Perception

Though architects have always made assumptions about what people see and remember about the visual qualities of buildings, and though they have always made visual design decisions, little systematic study has been given to the topic of the visual perception of the built environment until recently.

Given that architects become visually articulate through their training, it would seem unnecessary to study building perception. But quite the opposite is true. Several studies tell us that the architect's way of perceiving buildings is radically different from that of users. For example, research has shown that users

Relationships among privacy, personal space, territoriality, and crowding (from I. Altman, *The Environment and Social Behavior, 1975*).

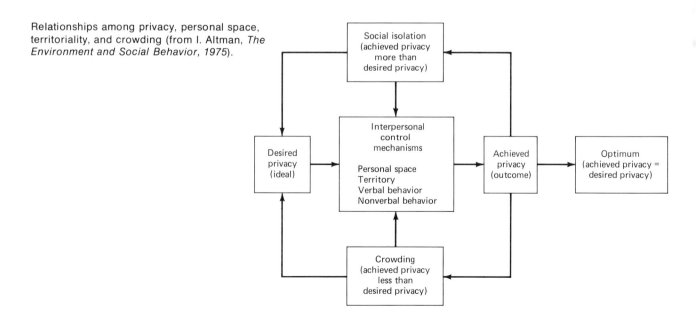

perceive wood, concrete, brick, and glass quite differently from the way architects do, and that users and architects associate these materials with different emotions. The architect may associate exposed concrete with structural expression or honesty, while the user may react negatively to the dull gray color and the unfinished or cheap look.

To date, principles of visual perception called gestalt theory have been the most used by architectural theoreticians and researchers as a basis for predicting building perception. The principles that have been most applied include figure and ground, *Pragnanz* or completeness, relative simplicity, proximity, equality, continuity, and closure. Other principles include the cues for depth perception: interposition, visual angle and distance, linear perspective, aerial perspective, light and shade, movement parallax, and texture gradients.[18]

An important question about environmental perception is how the everyday user perceives simplicity versus complexity in modern architecture and urban design. Architectural theory of the 1920s to the 1940s, and especially the concepts of the International Style, favored simplicity of form and highly regular geometric configurations. But how do users perceive such forms? First, the vast majority of users do not perceive subtlety of geometric configuration, especially when it is only noticeable in plan and cannot be appreciated without the most difficult of intellectual exercises. Nor do people prefer the stark or brutal simplicity of many modern buildings. Second, curiosity, play, exploratory behavior, and human development are stimulated by variety and complexity in the environment. Passive exposure to environments can actually be detrimental, and redundancy can lead to arrested development, while variety and complexity lead to an active commerce, exploration, and development.

The eclectic architects of the last century (Viollet-le-Duc, Renwick, and Street) had a higher preferred level of complexity than the next generations (Sullivan, the Functionalists, Gropius, Corbusier, and especially Mies and the proponents of the International Style). As a reaction to the monotony of modern architecture, architects like Aldo van Eyck, Eero Saarinen, and Robert Venturi have intentionally increased the level of building complexity and meaning since the 1950's.[19]

Environmental Cognition

People not only see the physical environment of buildings and react to what they see, but they also have memory images of the environment, and their behavior is strongly affected by these images. People will shop downtown rather than in a suburban shopping center if their image is that downtown has more variety, is more convenient, and is closer than the suburban shopping center. However, most people's images are the opposite of this. Even if the geographic distance is shorter to downtown, they often conceive of it being easier to drive out to the shopping center. Why? One reason is that the time may be shorter, and another may be that the experiential time may be shorter if there are fewer stresses associated with an outward rather than an inward journey. Thus, shopping behavior is in part a function of people's imagery, or what is called "environmental cognition."[20]

People's images of their buildings and cities serve three functions: they simplify the world into manageable chunks of memory; they give meaning to the world by personalizing buildings and making them, in effect, one's own; and they give a framework for group communication based on shared experience and sentiments about the environment. There are four types of images that are part of people's environmental cognition: urban cognitive mapping, subjective knowledge of the spatial layout of a town or the features of a building; impressions of character, or overall images of various cities or various buildings within one city; linguistic category systems or cognitive domains, basic ways of thinking about the environment and about people on the land (the native American and aboriginal Australian think of land as a communal storehouse, whereas the European immigrant views land as an economic commodity to be used or abused as one wishes for other gains); and the meanings, sentiments, and symbolism that people invest in the environment.

The basis for the study and application of environmental cognition—from building imagery to meaning and symbolism—can be summarized by the following quotation from the early linguistic anthropologist, Benjamin Lee Whorf.

> The categories and types that we isolate from the world of phenomena we do not find there because they stare every observer in the face; on the contrary, the world is presented in a kaleidoscopic flux of impressions which has to be organized by our minds—and this means largely by the linguistic systems of our minds. We cut nature up, organize it into concepts, and ascribe significance as we do, largely because we are parties to an agreement to organize it in this way—an agreement that holds throughout our speech community and is codified in the patterns of our language. The agreement is, of course, an implicit and unstated one, *but its terms are absolutely obligatory;* we cannot talk at all except by subscribing to the organization and classification of the data which the agreement decrees.[21]

Whereas perception refers to situations in which the response depends largely on the physical properties of the stimulus and to situations in which the perceptual experience follows closely after the stimulus, cognition refers to the various means of awareness or knowing that intervene between external stimuli and the entire gamut of behavioral responses. Environmental cognition, then, refers to the various forms of environmental awareness and knowing. Two aspects of environmental cognition concern architects: building imagery and urban cognitive mapping.

Building Imagery. A number of interesting architectural research studies have indicated that buildings are not remembered in the ways we often think they are. People remember buildings first and foremost in terms of their significance for use, not

their architectural characteristics, and they remember them more easily if they can pin a linguistic label on them. People also remember buildings more on the basis of visibility (siting considerations) than on the basis of physical form (contour, size, shape).[22]

Environmental cognition differs among various social and ethnic groups. One recent student research project is illustrative. Color photographs of some Chicago buildings were shown to a blue-collar group and an upper-income professional group. Each person reacted to each building and recorded a response along 52 specially constructed questions about building imagery, and then each ranked the buildings from most to least preferred. The study indicated that the most common building images were "cheap and unimpressive," "impressive and significant," and "sociable and inviting." "Sociable and inviting" was the most preferred image across all groups, followed closely by "unique and interesting." But there were strong differences between the two groups. The upper-income group's preferences were much more for the formal and high architecture and for impressive and significant imagery, while the blue-collar group's preferences were for the less formal, popular architecture and for sociable and inviting imagery. This is an example of a type of architecture research that sheds light on a little understood aspect of architecture—how different social groups respond to the same style of building. It also indicates that there is no such thing as a "right" style, but that different social groups prefer different styles of architecture.[23]

Urban Cognitive Mapping. One of the earliest and best-known studies of urban cognitive mapping is Kevin Lynch's *Image of the City*.[24] Lynch was interested in what makes a city legible for the people moving through it. He suggested that urban images have three components: a clear identity to elements that makes them stand out; spatial relationships between elements; and the meaning of those elements in relation to the observer. His research suggested that there are five types of elements and relationships that are critical to a legible environment: paths, edges or barriers, nodes, landmarks, and districts. Research on school-age children has shown that their images of the city are primarily based on paths and landmarks, such as home, school, local haunts, or what are called "fixed reference points." Preschool children's images are very egocentric; that is, they are not stable but depend on where the child is and what he or she is doing at any particular time. Teenager's images, on the other hand, are very stable and are similar to adult cognitive maps, being based upon an abstract, coordinated reference system.[25]

We also know about people's images of convenience relative to the location of buildings in the environment. For example, the social geographer Roger Downs has demonstrated that British women's images of shopping centers are comprised of eight cognitive categories. In descending order of importance, they are: quality of service, price, physical design, shopping hours, internal pedestrian movement, shop range and quality, visual appearance, and traffic conditions. These women think of service before price before design and so on in deciding which shopping center to visit.[26]

Meaning and Symbolism

A further aspect of environmental cognition is meaning and symbolism. People react to the environment through its meaning for them. Early modern architects attempted to give architecture meaning in terms of the architect's meaning, not the user's. Recent work in environment-behavior studies has begun to provide a user-oriented empirical base for meaning in architecture and is leading to the construction of a language of the built environment.

All building types have latent meanings that differ for different user groups. The environment is both a setting for communication among people and a transducer of meanings. Communication among people may be influenced by the organiza-

tion of space. But, in addition, buildings have certain meanings or nonverbal messages for people that are influenced by the layout, organization, and character of the buildings. A number of studies have shown that people are aware of the meaning that architecture conveys and sometimes (consciously or subconsciously) use it to communicate about self, shaping the environment, home, office, and corporate headquarters for the "presentation of self in everyday life."[27] For example, upper-middle class Americans often tend to their lawns before completing interior decorating in order to present a good initial impression to neighbors. Even in barrios, people put a fancy door on a house as a way of marking territory and declaring home. In Westchester County outside New York City, and even in upwardly mobile sections of India, people use styles of housing, picture windows, and a contemporary suburban style to mark their entry into the ranks of the nouveau riche.[28] These housing messages are clearly picked up by neighbors and passersby. This is evident from studies of child-environment relations, where it has been noted that children infer something about the personalities of people who live in particular houses by the nature of their gardens. People will not move into a residential area that conveys an image different from the one they wish to convey, and in choosing a home, they are even influenced by the name of a street—the sale of a home on Valley Road will bring more than that of an identical home on Prospect Avenue.

Neighborhoods and Communities

Neighborhood and its related concepts of social interaction and social networks are often poorly understood by urban planners and architects. When physical planners and architects design residential areas, transportation networks, community centers, and open spaces, they make many assumptions about the ways in which people relate to one another and the role of the built environment in influencing this interaction. Consider the design of mixed-income multifamily housing, with a client's goal of encouraging social interaction among the residents. To what degree is this an attainable goal? To what degree does the physical environment influence patterns of neighboring and friendship formation? On a smaller scale, we can ask a similar question: To what degree does physical proximity of offices or college housing rooms influence patterns of friendship? Catherine Bauer and C. A. Doxiadis expressed the two poles of this issue vividly. Bauer argued that any return to a neighborhood concept is reactionary in character and sentimental in concept, ignoring the trends of modern society away from localized groups and small parochial communities. Doxiadis, on the other hand, pleaded for the "human dimension in world cities," in which the neighborhood, a natural community as he saw it, would provide one measure of humanness.[29] But at the risk of grossly oversimplifying a very complex topic, what is the evidence for each side?

A number of studies done since the late 1950s have shown that interpersonal contacts in white-collar groups are more influenced by whom one works with and what clubs one belongs to, than they are by residential location or proximity. On the other hand, it has been found that upper-class Beacon Hill residents in Boston are aware of physical boundaries of their neighborhood, regard it as an identifiable segment of urban space, and ascribe status and social position to otherwise anonymous people by virtue of their residence in the area. All of this occurred despite the fact that most of the subjects' activities and social contacts were outside this neighborhood. It has been noted that immigrant groups in Boston's old West End identified closely with their area, and that the defined neighborhood was a setting for primary social contacts, a basis for maintaining close ties in the extended family and kinship system, and an emotionally important part of the resident's everyday life.[30]

The importance of neighborhood seems to range all the way from Bauer's position to that of Doxiadis, depending on what social group we are considering. Three dimensions underlie the differences between architectural and nonarchitectural influences on social interaction: homogeneity and heterogeneity of the population; kinship, professional contacts, and status as a basis for friendship and length of residence.

USER GROUPS AND DESIGN

As we saw earlier, the needs of different user groups and the behavioral criteria for the design of different building types may be thought of in terms of the range of behavioral phenomena and concepts expected to be important for that group in that setting. It is not possible here to summarize even a reasonable portion of what is known about familiar and less familiar user groups and about various building types. Consider, however, four examples: two user groups and two building types.

Aging and the Environment
Who are the elderly in our society, and why is it important to consider them in design? How does the environmental competency of the elderly change with age? What issues must we consider in designing for the elderly?

With an increasing life expectancy, better medicine, and more families having fewer children, the age pyramid is shifting upward markedly. That is, a larger proportion of our society than ever before is over 60 years of age, and this proportion is increasing constantly. The possibility of earlier retirement means that more middle-aged people are pursuing some of the recreational activities formerly reserved for the elderly. But mandatory retirement at a later age is keeping some older people active in the labor force. For many older citizens, the speed of social and technological change tends to be alienating.

The environment today is clearly organized in terms of young adults and the middle-aged, while older age groups have been neglected. But for the elderly, and especially the very old, most physiologically related functions begin to reverse their patterns of development; we say the person is undergoing gradual developmental dissolution. Fewer resources are available. Social roles are more narrowly defined, and health is slightly poorer for the majority. Morale and attitudes are less affected by age and physiological changes than by some of the possible consequences of aging—isolation, inactivity, denial of a meaningful role in society, ill-health, institutionalization, or some combination of these.

As these changes are happening, other changes occur in the elderly person's relation to the built environment. For example, there is a greater dependency on environmental aids (hand rails, ramps, and so on), a greater need for service and for access to services, and a greater need for protection from crime. Also, the elderly are less independent socially and have a more restricted lifestyle, while desiring more community and intense interaction spaces. These and a large number of other specific needs of the elderly can be met by good architectural policy, planning, programming, and design.[31]

Children and the Environment

At the other end of the age range, what are the special needs of children with regard to the environment? How are children affected by the design of particular buildings and of the overall urban (or rural) fabric?

The theory of the Swiss developmental psychologist Jean Piaget is recognized as the leading theory of child development and behavior. Piaget is an interactionalist; that is, he argues (and considerable research supports him) that children develop from an interaction between inner drives and external environmental conditions. Piaget also suggests that development is a product of the child's active commerce with the environment, that is, being able actively to manipulate the environment and to see the results of these manipulations. Cognitive development, for example, progresses from concrete understandings of things to abstract understandings, and this developmental process is facilitated if the young child can actively explore and experiment with the environment. At a very general level, both of these insights of Piaget have had profound impacts on the design of the physical environment and for the preservation of wild, rough, and natural environments.[32]

But what of the more concrete effects of the physical environment on children? Other than following the general concepts of providing manipulable environments and a wide range of environmental stimuli, what can the designer do to increase the richness of the experience of childhood? Conversely, what current design ideas and common lore of the profession are perhaps detrimental to children? A range of examples could be given of both, but consider just the following small sample of findings about child-environment relations:

1 In comparison with other children, and with other variables being held constant, seven-year-olds from crowded homes have been found to be nine months behind in reading age, and auditory discrimination and reading ability have been found to be lower for children living on low floors near expressway noise.

2 When families moved from crowded housing to less crowded public housing, children and parents experienced a decrease in interpersonal tension, the number of illnesses dropped, and the children were more regular in school attendance, but there were no changes in long-term interpersonal relations or scores on intellectual and achievement tests.

3 In studies of design and housing, many complaints are registered about inadequate outdoor features for children.

4 With regard to high-rise versus low-rise housing of the same density, many studies in several countries have found that considerably fewer children from high-rises play outside or even play in hallways and balconies. In high-rise buildings, the most frequent users of outdoor space are those children living on the lowest three or four floors; children living on higher floors are often not permitted to go outdoors except with strict supervision.

Traditional children's playground: a typical
school playground, Milwaukee.

5 Though it has been calculated that children are the
greatest users of public outdoor space, playgrounds and
parks do not provide for most of their needs; one study
found that children spend less than an average of fifteen
minutes in a playground during a period of several hours
spent outdoors. On the other hand, children do use
courts, sidewalks, balconies, porches, lanes, streets, left-

over spaces between buildings, and ambiguous spaces
in and around natural features much more than they do
created, sculptural playgrounds (with the exception of
adventure playgrounds). Designers and planners should
provide safe, connected play spaces linking several
house clusters, streets, paths, natural areas and leftover
places.

Contemporary-sculptural playgrounds: Buchanan School Playground, Washington, D.C., by M. Paul Friedberg and Partners, and
Heckscher Playground, New York City, by Richard Dattner and Associates.

Adventure playgrounds: Harbourfront Adventure Playground in Toronto, originated by William Rock and Huntington Beach Adventure Playground, Los Angeles, originated by Bill Vance.

Natural Playground: Washington Elementary School Environmental Yard, Berkeley, by Robin Moore.

Building Types and Design

Schools. An open-plan school, also called a school-without-walls, is strictly a planning concept whereby activity centers are open in terms of visual sight lines and circulation. Open education, however, is an educational concept that involves one or more of the following: team-teaching, performance groups rather than age groups, performance-based advancement, individualized instruction, student-initiated learning, and spatial and temporal freedoms. Thus, it is entirely possible to have an open-plan school without following an open-education philosophy, or conversely to have open education in

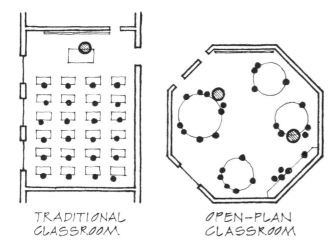

TRADITIONAL
CLASSROOM.

OPEN-PLAN
CLASSROOM

Open plan preschool renovated from a supermarket: Satalite Americana, Washington, D.C., by Paul Curtis and Roger Smith.

in several open-plan and several closed-plan schools where the educational philosophies were almost identical. Generally, the findings suggest that in open-plan schools children enter more learning settings, encounter more teachers, and work in a wider variety of group sizes. There is more observational learning among staff, greater feelings of openness, and greater feelings of unity among staff. Students were found to have more sense of the whole of the school. All of these might be considered positive. But on the other side of the ledger, students consume more nonlearning time, experience more noise, and are bothered by more visual distractions. Students and faculty also have less control over their own environment. Paradoxically, one study showed that students are guided externally by teachers and aides more in open-plan schools. Due partly to the negative effects and partly to a change in educational climate, many open-plan schools are now giving up such formats. Teachers erect walls or makeshift partitions and use furniture to define territoriality.

The design challenge is clear: to design or renovate schools to combine the best of open plans (peer-learning among staff, student's identity with the whole, a greater variety of learning settings) while solving the misfits created by open plans (increase of nonlearning time, noise, visual distractions).

Offices. The situation in offices is not unlike that in schools. The design concept of open-office planning, or office landscaping, was introduced in the 1950s, was very influential, and now is coming under heavy criticism. A number of postoccupancy evaluations of open-plan versus closed-plan offices have been conducted. For example, in Sweden a study was conducted one year after occupancy in 38 different offices—large, small, traditional, landscaped, and open-by-conversion. The researchers interviewed 2,575 people. Among other things, they found that the two qualities creating the most problems in open-plan offices were acoustics and

a closed-plan school. The open-plan school, however, was supposed to reinforce the open educational philosophy.

What are the findings? Surprisingly few studies have experimentally evaluated the many features of the open-plan layout. Systematic studies have been conducted using behavior setting observations, interviews with teachers, and interviews with students ventilation, but that light quality and layout were also critical factors. After one year of residency, worker preference for different types of open offices were in the following order: small landscaped offices, large landscaped offices, and then offices opened-by-conversion. But the clear preference was for traditional planning over all of these types of landscaped or open layouts. Other studies have shown that in open-plan versus closed-plan offices, the following apply: (1) there is no significant difference in the amount of management time spent on most activities; (2) conferences are the only activity which are held for longer periods of time; (3) there is no overall improvement in worker efficiency; but (4) there is more collaboration and communication among workers; (5) some workers feel greater amounts of tension and irritability; (6) some have a greater feeling of supervision and being checked upon; (7) many management personnel feel a decrease in stature by virtue of loss of clear territorial and status images; and therefore (8) there is more desire for visual and auditory screening; and (9) there is more use of objects and the organization of space as territorial markers; but (10) there are great individual differences, some employees definitely preferring the open structure, open visual appearance, and open information access. However, it has been found that employees moving from an open office back to a traditional office layout also have complaints and readjustment problems.

Traditional versus landscaped office plans.

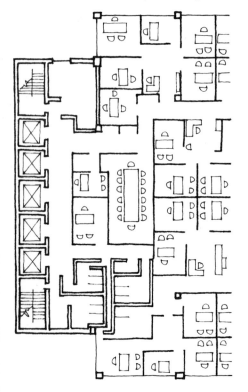 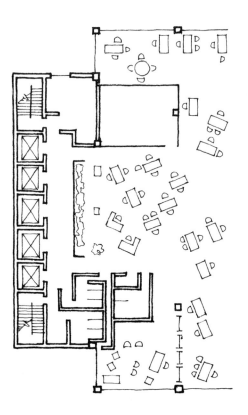

In summary, open-plan offices seem most suitable for groups not having high individual privacy or high territorial needs and for groups who are internally fairly cohesive or who are relatively homogeneous with respect to personality and tasks. Private offices and traditional layouts, on the other hand, seem best for most executives, most self-conscious people, highly individualistic people, people needing more privacy or clearly marked territory, and people pursuing very different tasks.[33]

SUMMARY

This chapter has briefly surveyed some of the environment-behavior considerations that architects take into account in building design and urban design. We refer to this as accountability in design—the architect is accountable first and foremost to people, user needs, and environment-behavior relations. We also refer to this as the behavioral basis of design, where behavioral, social, and cultural considerations are at the helm of the design process. As architecture conducted this way has as its goal the welfare and satisfaction of users of buildings, information on the role of architecture in human behavior must be incorporated early in the design process and early in architectural education.

We have looked at the crisis in architecture and at some of the roots of the failure of many form-conscious buildings. A range of concepts of multidisciplinary origin have been introduced. Four brief case study examples of the use of some of these concepts have been presented to explain the requirements of user groups (elderly and children) and behavioral considerations in different building types (schools and offices). We have also seen places in the design process where behavioral considerations have their greatest impact on form and on architectural practice: architectural programming, behaviorally based design concepts, and postoccupancy evaluation. A range of other methods exists for incorporating behavioral factors in design, but these are left to other chapters.

The application of environment-behavior considerations in the design process requires awareness, knowledge, and skill. Conducting research in environment-behavior relations requires additional awareness, knowledge, and skills. Architecture is a pluralistic profession. It needs to develop its capacity for research in environment-behavior factors and it needs to apply that knowledge more closely to the architectural design process.

NOTES

1. The field of environment-behavior studies has exploded from modest beginnings in the mid-1960s. K. H. Craik's wide-ranging review, "Environmental Psychology," in *New Directions in Psychology,* vol. 4 (New York: Holt, Rinehart & Winston), 1970, cited some 350 sources of information. The most recent review of the field counted some 500 new contributions between 1973 and 1978; see D. Stokols, "Environmental Psychology," *Annual Review of Psychology* 29 (1978).

2. For differences between professional and user attitudes toward buildings, see D. Appleyard, "Why Buildings Are Known: A Predictive Tool for Architects and Planners," *Environment and Behavior* 1 (1969): 131–156; and J. B. Lansing and R. W. Marans, "Evaluation of Neighborhood Quality," *Journal of the American Institute of Planners* 35 (1969): 195–199.

3. N. L. Prak, *The Visual Perception of the Built Environment* (Delft: Delft University Press, 1977), p. 90.

4. R. Kaplan, S. Kaplan, and H. L. Deardorff, "The Perception and Evaluation of a Simulated Environment," *Man-Environment Systems* 4 (1974): 191–192; and C.C. Cooper, *Easter Hill Village: Some Social Implications of Design* (New York: Free Press, 1975). Both discuss the differences between architects' priorities and users' needs.

5. Some of the best-known and most useful postoccupancy evaluations include C. C. Cooper, "St. Francis Square: Attitudes of Its Residents," *American Institute of Architects Journal* 66 (December 1971): 22–27; Cooper, *Easter Hill Village;* R. B. Bechtel, *Enclosing Behavior* (Stroudsburg, Pa.: Dowden, Hutchinson & Ross, 1977); Building Performance Re-

search Unit, *Building Performance* (London: Applied Science Publishers, 1972); H. Z. Rabinowitz, *Buildings in Use Study,* 2 vols. (Milwaukee: University of Wisconsin-Milwaukee, Publications in Architecture and Urban Planning, 1975–76); and J. Zeisel and M. Griffin, *Charlesview Housing: A Diagnostic Evaluation* (Cambridge: Harvard University, Graduate School of Design, Architecture Research Office, 1975).

6. For discussions of Pruitt-Igoe, see J. Bailey, "The Case History of a Failure: Pruitt-Igoe," *Architectural Forum* 123 (December 1965): 22–25; "St. Louis Blues," *Architectural Forum* 136 (May 1972): 18; and G. McCue, "$57,000,000 Later: An Interdisciplinary Effort Is Being Made to Put Pruitt-Igoe Together Again," *Architectural Forum* 138 (May 1973): 42–45. For sociological assessments, see L. Rainwater, "Fear and the House-as-Haven in the Lower Class," *Journal of the American Institute of Planners* 32 (1966): 23–31; and W. L. Yancey, "Architecture, Interaction, and Social Control: The Case of a Large-Scale Housing Project," in *Environment and the Social Sciences,* ed. J. F. Wohlwill and D. H. Carson (Washington, D.C.: American Psychological Association, 1972), pp. 126–136.

7. M. MacEwen, *Crisis in Architecture* (London: Royal Institute of British Architects Publications, 1974); B. Brolin, *The Failure of Modern Architecture* (New York: Van Nostrand Reinhold, 1976).

8. C. Heimsath, *Behavioral Architecture: Toward an Accountable Design Process* (New York: McGraw-Hill, 1977).

9. V. Papanek, *Design for the Real World: Human Ecology and Social Change* (New York: Pantheon Books, 1971).

10. R. G. Barker and H. F. Wright, *Midwest and Its Children* (New York: Row, Peterson, 1955); Bechtel, *Enclosing Behavior.*

11. See C. Alexander, *Notes on the Synthesis of Form* (Cambridge: Harvard University Press, 1964); C. Alexander, S. Ishikawa, and M. Silverstein, *A Pattern Language: Towns, Buildings, Construction* (New York: Oxford University Press, 1977); case studies in *Emerging Methods in Environmental Design and Planning,* ed. G. T. Moore (Cambridge: M.I.T. Press, 1970).

12. Complete anthropometric charts are given in H. Dreyfuss, *The Measure of Man: Human Factors in Design* (New York: Whitney Library of Design, 1959).

13. E. T. Hall, *The Hidden Dimension;* see also R. Sommer, *Personal Space: The Behavioral Basis of Design* (Englewood Cliffs, N.J.: Prentice-Hall, 1969); and T. F. Saarinen, *Environmental Planning: Perception and Behavior* (Boston: Houghton Mifflin, 1976).

14. A. H. Esser, A. S. Chamberlain, E. D. Chapple, and N. S. Chein, "Territoriality of Patients on a Research Ward," in *Environmental Psychology,* ed. H. M. Proshansky, W. H. Ittelson, and L. G. Rivlin (New York: Holt, Rinehart, and Winston, 1970), pp. 208–214.

15. J. Jacobs, *The Death and Life of Great American Cities* (New York: Random House, 1961); and O. Newman, *Defensible Space: Crime Prevention through Urban Design* (New York: Macmillan, 1973).

16. M. Mead, "Conference Behavior," *Columbia University Forum* 10 (Summer 1967): 15–19; T. McGinty, G. T. Moore, and U. Cohen, "Developing Behavioral Accountability in Architects," in *The Behavioral Basis of Design,* book 2, ed. P. Suedfeld and J.

A. Russell (Stroudsburg, Pa.: Dowden, Hutchinson & Ross, 1977), pp. 334–339.

17. For more information about privacy versus crowding, see I. Altman, *The Environment and Social Behavior: Privacy, Personal Space, Territoriality, and Crowding* (Monterey, Ca.: Brooks/Cole, 1976); W. Michelson, *Man and His Urban Environment: A Sociological Approach* (Reading, Mass.: Addison-Wesley, 1970); S. Milgram, "The Experience of Living in Cities," *Science* 167 (1970): 1461–1468; and S. Chermeyeff and C. Alexander, *Community and Privacy: Toward a New Humanism in Architecture* (Garden City, N.Y.: Doubleday, 1963.)

18. An excellent book on architectural perception is N. Prak, *The Visual Perception of the Built Environment.*

19. R. Venturi, *Complexity and Contradiction in Architecture* (New York: Museum of Modern Art, 1966); and A. Rapoport and E. Kantor, "Complexity and Ambiguity in Environmental Design," *Journal of the American Institute of Planners* 33 (July 1967): 210–221.

20. R. M. Downs and D. Stea, eds., *Image and Environment: Cognitive Mapping and Spatial Behavior* (Chicago: Aldine, 1973); G. T. Moore and R. G. Golledge, eds., *Environmental Knowing: Theories Research, and Methods* (Stroudsburg, Pa.: Dowden, Hutchinson & Ross, 1976).

21. B. L. Whorf, *Language, Thought and Reality,* ed. J. B. Carroll (Cambridge, Mass.: M.I.T. Press, 1956), pp. 213–214.

22. S. Carr and D. Schissler, "The City as a Trip: Perceptual Selection and Memory in the View from the Road," *Environment and Behavior* 1 (1969): 7–35; Appleyard, "Why Buildings Are Known."

23. This study is summarized in S. Verderber and G. T. Moore, "Building Imagery: A Comparative Study of Environmental Cognition," *Man-Environment Systems* 7 (November 1977): 332–341.

24. K. Lynch, *The Image of the City* (Cambridge: M.I.T. Press, 1961).

25. For information about children's images of cities, see chapter 12 of Moore and Golledge, *Environmental Knowing.*

26. R. M. Downs, "The Cognitive Structure of an Urban Shopping Center," *Environment and Behavior* 2 (1970): 13–39.

27. E. Goffman, *The Presentation of Self in Everyday Life* (Garden City, N.Y.: Doubleday, 1959); C. Cooper, "The House as Symbol of the Self," in *Designing for Human Behavior: Architecture and the Behavioral Sciences,* ed. J. Lang, C. Burnette, W. Moleski, and D. Vachon (Stroudsburg, Pa.: Dowden, Hutchinson & Ross, 1974), pp. 130–149.

28. J. S. Duncan and N. G. Duncan, "Social Worlds, Status Passage, and Environmental Perspectives," and "Housing as Presentation of Self and the Structure of Social Networks," in *Environmental Knowing,* Moore and Golledge, eds., pp. 206–213, 247–253.

29. C. Bauer, *Social Questions in Housing and Town Planning* (London: University of London Press, 1952); C. A. Doxiadis, "The Ancient Greek City and the City of the Present," *Ekistics* 18 (no. 108, 1964).

30. For Beacon Hill, see W. Firey, "Sentiment and Symbolism as Ecological Variables," *American Sociological Review* 10

(1945): 140–148; H. L. Ross, "The Local Community: A Survey Approach," *American Sociological Review* 27 (1962): 75–84. For the West End, see M. Fried and P. Gleicher, "Some Sources of Residential Satisfaction in an Urban Slum" *Journal of the American Institute of Planners* 27 (1967): 305–315; and H. Gans, *The Urban Villagers* (New York: Free Press, 1962).

31. For information on environments for the elderly, see M. Hoekstra, *The Aged and Housing in Perspective* (Sydney, Australia: University of Sydney, Ian Buchan Fell Research Project, 1976); and G. P. Rowles, *Prisoners of Space* (Boulder, Colo: Westview Press, 1978).

32. For information on the design of children's environments, see: R. A. Hart and G. T. Moore, "The Development of Spatial Cognition: A Review," in *Image and Environment,* Downs and Stea, eds., pp. 246–288; F. L. Osmon, *Patterns for Designing Children's Centers* (New York: Educational Facilities Laboratories, 1971); *Alternative Learning Environments,* ed. G. J. Coates (Stroudsburg, Pa.: Dowden, Hutchinson & Ross, 1974); and G. T. Moore, U. Cohen, J. Oertel, and L. van Ryzin, *Environments for Exceptional Children* (New York: Educational Facilities Laboratories, forthcoming, 1979).

33. This study by B. Wolgers and K. Wielding is cited in *Building Research and Practice* (March-April 1973): 97–99. See also F. Duffy and C. Cave, "Burolandschaft Revisited," *Architect's Journal* 161:3 (26 March 1975): 665–675, and *Office Design: A Study of Environment,* ed. P. Manning (Liverpool: Pilkington Research Unit, University of Liverpool, 1965).

FOR FURTHER READING

Alexander, C., Ishikawa, S., and Silverstein, M. *A Pattern Language: Towns, Buildings, Construction.* New York: Oxford University Press, 1977.

Gutman, R., ed. *People and Buildings.* New York: Basic Books, 1972.

Jacobs, J. *The Death and Life of Great American Cities.* New York: Random House, 1961.

Lang, J., Burnette, C. H., Moleski, W. and Vachon, D., eds. *Designing for Human Behavior: Architecture and the Behavioral Sciences.* Stroudsburg, Pa.: Dowden, Hutchinson & Ross, 1974.

Lynch, K. *The Image of the City.* Cambridge, Mass.: M.I.T. Press, 1960.

Moore, G. T., ed. *Emerging Methods in Environmental Design and Planning,* Cambridge: M.I.T. Press, 1970.

———, and Golledge, R. G., eds. *Environmental Knowing: Theories, Research, and Methods.* Stroudsburg, Pa.: Dowden, Hutchinson & Ross, 1976.

Proshansky, H. M., Ittelson, W. H., and Rivlin, L. G., eds. *Environmental Psychology,* 2d ed. New York: Holt, Rinehart & Winston, 1976.

Rapoport, A. *House Form and Culture.* Englewood Cliffs, N.J.: Prentice-Hall, 1968.

Saarinen, T. F. *Environmental Planning: Perception and Behavior.* Boston: Houghton Mifflin, 1976.

Sanoff, H. *Architectural Programming.* Stroudsburg, Pa.: Dowden, Hutchinson & Ross, 1977.

Sommer, R. *Personal Space: The Behavioral Basis of Design.* Englewood Cliffs, N.J.: Prentice-Hall, 1969.

Wapner, S., Cohen, S. B., and Kaplan, B., eds. *Experiencing the Environment.* New York: Plenum Press, 1976.

Part Two
The Context for Architecture

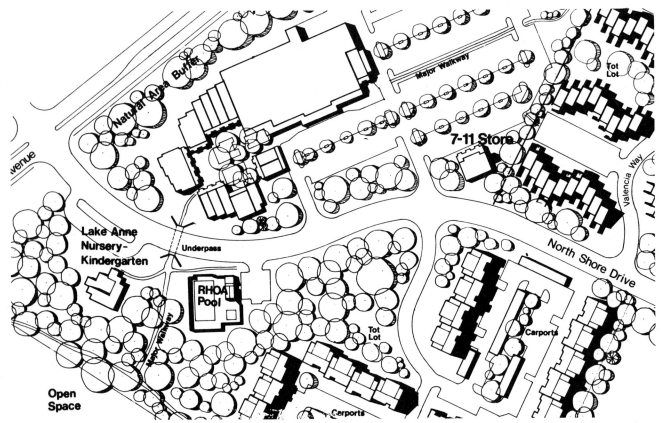

Site Plan: Tall Oaks Village Center, Reston, Virginia; by Gulf Reston, Inc.

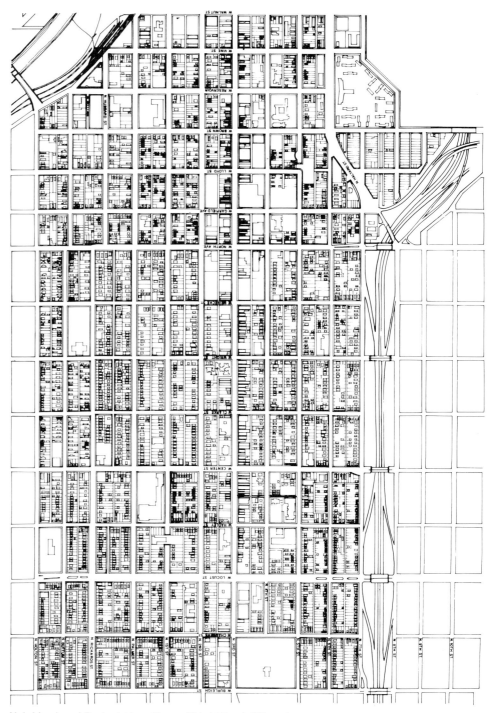

Neighborhood Project Map, Upper Third Street, Milwaukee.

CHAPTER 4

The Building Industry

David J. Parsons

The practice of architecture exists within the larger context of the building industry. This industry is unique in many ways. It is massive, accounting for 61 billion dollars in corporate income and employing over 3 million persons in the construction sector alone (1972). Unlike other major industries, which are dominated by a small number of major capital-intensive corporations, the building industry approaches each project as a new undertaking, bringing together a diverse group of local participants. Large corporations do not dominate the scene; capital investment is low while labor investment is high.

There are good reasons for this unique form. The demands of a fluctuating and unpredictable market require that the industry be able to expand and contract without disastrous financial results. In addition, construction involves a great deal of knowledge about the local situation: the land market, building and zoning regulations, and the supply of labor and materials. Because building is largely a local operation, it must respond to local economic conditions as well as to national fluctuations, such as the interest rates for long-term loans.

This chapter presents the characteristics of the building industry, with its participants and organization, and the role of the architect in that context.

PROFILE OF THE BUILDING INDUSTRY

A Local Industry

Although many basic building materials are distributed regionally or nationally, the bulk of the effort in producing a building is expended locally.[1] Many building products cannot be shipped over long distances, because the cost of shipping large or heavy products does not justify the savings that would result from centralized production. This is an increasingly important factor as assembled products require greater volumes. For instance, sheet metal is shipped in rolls from city to city, but sheet metal ductwork is fabricated in the locality where it will be installed. In addition, construction often requires detailed knowledge of local conditions. The architect must know whether there are local contractors available to bid on a project at the desired time and must be familiar with local building codes and zoning regulations. Likewise, contractors must be familiar with local subcontractors and the local labor supply. A key figure in many building projects is the land developer, often a local entrepreneur who is an expert on local markets, regulations, and building conditions.

Temporary Relationships

In the building industry, each project is a separate event that often brings the major participants together for the first time: owner, architect, engineers, contractors, and subcontractors. This is in contrast to other major industries, which depend on continuing relationships among the suppliers of raw materials, manufacturers, distributors, and dealers. This system of temporary relationships works only because, through the years, methods of working together have become relatively standardized. Standardized methods include the types of contracts used, style and content of drawings, division of responsibilities and expectations of all parties about how the other parties will act. Major industry associations such as the American Institute of Architects, the Associated General Contractors of America, and the Construction Specifications Institute have made substantial efforts to standardize these relationships.

Fragmentation

According to the 1972 census, there were over 130,000 general contractors in the United States, with no dominant firms. The 18 largest contractors account for only 2.5 percent of the total work. There are large manufacturers, such as U.S. Steel, that supply the industry with basic materials, but their part of any single building project usually represents a small percentage of the total.

Variations in Workload for Firms

Because firms in the building industry are small, individual projects often represent a major portion of a firm's workload at a given time. The firm's work is obtained sequentially, one or a few projects at a time, on a competitive basis with other firms. Thus financial failure on a single project can mean failure for the small firm. Also, clients often want the project to start as soon as possible after the participants are selected . Together, these factors produce a widely fluctuating workload for industry participants, leading, in turn, to repeated layoffs and rehiring of personnel. Because many skilled workers and laborers are hired on a project-by-project basis, mobility of the work force is a way of life. Of course, contractors usually retain a core of supervisory personnel.

The architectural profession is not well organized to respond to these fluctuations. Often, architectural firms keep capable persons on the payroll in slack periods and find themselves understaffed in peak periods. However, layoffs and staff increases are common for major projects.

Market Fluctuations

The work load of individual firms is further influenced by fluctuations in overall building activity.

Seasonal fluctuations, although predictable, create continuing problems for all building trades in regions where weather hinders construction. Local economic fluctuations are less predictable. Other industries with regional or national markets compensate for local fluctuations by shipping their goods to other regions of the country. The building industry must vary its rate of production to fit fluctuations in the local economy. National economic fluctuations are superimposed over local conditions. The building industry is particularly affected by changes in interest rates, since loans for buildings cover substantially longer periods of time than loans for other purchases. For example, the decision to borrow money for twenty-five years to finance a sizable building project is clearly much more dependent on the relative position of interest rates than would be the decision to borrow money for two or three years to buy a car.

Low Level of Capital Investment

The building industry is labor-intensive; capital investment per worker is low compared to other major industries in the United States. Of course, a low capital investment means that a declining workload does not leave the contractor with a major investment in unproductive plant and equipment. Contractors are flexible; that is, they can, on short notice, reduce the level of production substantially without becoming inefficent. If a major automobile manufacturer lost one-half of its production for a substantial period of time, the cost of having idle plant facilities would threaten survival of the company as a viable organization.

These characteristics—small local organizations, fluctuating market, projects taken one at a time, a mobile work force—are mutually reinforcing; no single factor can or should be changed without consideration of the others. The result is a flexible industry. The cost of this flexibility, however, is often high in terms of dollars, time for construction, and predictability.

PARTICIPANTS IN THE BUILDING INDUSTRY

The Owner

The building owner is a key figure in the building process but is often neglected in discussion of the subject. The owner initiates building projects and at each stage makes decisions that control the final outcome.

Owners vary widely in their experience with building. Many projects involve owners who are building for the first time. The project may be small, such as a private residence, or large, such as an industrial facility, school, or corporate headquarters. Owners building for the first time are usually surprised by the extent to which they become involved in the process. For example, if the low bid for construction of a new corporate headquarters is twenty percent over the budget , the president of the corporation becomes deeply involved in deciding whether to rebid, redesign, or increase the budget. Unfamiliar with the industry, the first-time owner undergoes an intensive "learn-as-you-go" experience. Seldom can owner's leave key decisions to consultants and contractors, since their own objectives with respect to time, cost, and quality of the building are critical. Owners without experience in building rarely are able to manage the process but can only react to crises as they arise.

Owners with experience in building are in a better position to manage and to avoid difficulties. Owners with a continuous building program, such as universities, government agencies, and large corporations, employ full-time professionals on their staffs to manage building projects. These project managers are familiar with the building process and with the importance of their role as owner. Their function is to select an approach best suited to the owner's objectives for the project. For instance, if early project completion is of high priority, setting up a direct design/build arrangement with a building contractor may be more appropriate than hiring an architect for design and a separate contractor for construction.

Owners with major building programs, such as the General Services Administration, are continually experimenting with alternatives to the traditional building process. These experiments are motivated by dissatisfaction with the industry's current difficulties in meeting time, cost, and quality objectives.

The User

Many of the people who use buildings do not own them. They often differ from the owners in their conception of appropriate building design. While owner and user are not always in conflict, they often do have a legitimate difference of perspective. For example, a university's desire for durability in its dormitories may lead to concrete block walls and built-in furniture, while students who want to personalize the space they live in may prefer warm materials and movable furniture. However, users seldom participate directly in project decisions; they must rely, therefore, on the professionalism of the architect to consider their interests. Yet time and funds are often insufficient for the architect to fully explore with future users of a building their goals and aspirations.

As researchers uncover the effects of environment on human behavior, practicing architects have incorporated these findings into their designs. Design for specific user groups, such as the elderly and the handicapped, has particularly benefited from this research. Participation by programming consultants in the initial stages of building projects is also increasing. Specialized consultants in education, health care, transportation, and housing can provide specific information about user groups and behavior patterns through interviews and direct observation.

The Architect

The traditional role of the architect has been to design buildings that reflect the interests of the client and of the public. According to the American Institute of Architects (AIA) Code of Ethics and Professional Conduct,

Members of the American Institute of Architects should serve and promote the public interest in improving the human environment (and) should serve their clients competently and exercise unprejudiced professional judgment.[2]

The architect has generally worked for the building owner on a fee basis, usually calculated as a percentage of the building cost. Table 4-1 gives a breakdown of services offered under the *basic fee arrangement.* Beyond the basic services, the architect may offer additional services including preliminary studies and programming, site surveys, special engineering studies, and construction management.

It has been considered unethical for the architect to be financially involved in the construction phase, since his or her own financial interests might prevent giving the owner "unprejudiced professional judgment." On this issue, the AIA Code of Ethics has taken a hard line:

Members shall not engage in building contracting where compensation, direct or indirect, is derived from profit on labor and materials furnished in the building process.[3]

Over the last decade, however, architects have assumed new roles in the building process, which often include taking a financial interest in construction. This has led to a continuing review of the ethical code of the profession during the last several years. At its 1978 annual meeting, the AIA voted to revise the long-standing ethical code which prohibits architects from having a financial interest in construction. The new rules, which are in effect for a provisional three-year period, allow construction activity by the architect, with careful disclosure to the owner.[3a]

Consultants

Consultants provide specialized knowledge and skills to supplement those of the architect. They are usually hired directly by and are responsible to the architect. The architect must then coordinate and control all aspects of the design process. Most con-

TABLE 4-1

Services Offered under the Basic Fee Arrangement

Phase	Percent of Fee
Schematic Design	15
Design Development	20
Construction Documents	40
Bidding or Negotiating	5
Construction	20

Source: American Institute of Architects, *Owner-Architect Agreement*, AIA Document, B131 (Washington, D.C.: American Institute of Architects, 1970).

sultants retained by architects perform engineering services—structural, mechanical, electrical, sanitary, and civil. On certain projects, such as theaters, acoustical and lighting consultants may be required. Many architectural firms incorporate one or more of these consulting specialties "in-house" reducing the need to coordinate the work of many separate firms.

Building Officials

As part of their responsibility to safeguard public health, welfare, and safety, local governments administer building codes that establish minimum standards for construction. In order to begin construction, the architect must submit final drawings and specifications to local officials who review the documents and issue a building permit. Upon completion of the building, a final inspection is made by these local officials, and they issue an occupancy permit. The primary concern of building officials is that the building meet health and safety requirements, particularly those related to structural and fire safety, as well as local zoning or land use requirements. Although building codes are administered locally, model codes have been developed at the regional and national levels to guide local governments. The first of these was the Recommended National Building Code, published in 1905 by the National Board of Fire Underwriters, an association of fire insurance companies. Subsequently, the Uni-

form Building Code was developed and widely adopted in the West in 1927; the Southern Building Code was developed in 1945 for application in the Southern states; and the Basic Building Code was adopted widely in the Midwest and the East beginning in 1950. These three codes were prepared by associations of building officials. In an attempt to reduce arbitrary building code variations and inconsistencies from one municipality to the next, many states have taken an active role in writing and administering codes for statewide application. These vary from the mandatory statewide building code in California to a model state code in New York that may be adopted at the discretion of local governments.[4]

Lending Institutions

A significant portion of the cost of a building is the cost of borrowing money. Table 4-2 indicates the loan amounts and sources for both long-term mortgages and loans to finance construction. In 1972 the total paid for general construction contracts was about 62 billion dollars. Using an approximate interest rate for construction loans of 10 percent, building owners paid about 3.5 billion dollars in interest during the same period. Thus, between 5 and 6 cents of every construction dollar goes for interest on construction loans. This does not include interest paid by general contractors and subcontractors on money they have borrowed to finance their operations. Contractors must have operating capital, since they pay their employees, and often their subcontractors and suppliers, before they receive payment from the owner.

The institution providing construction financing, usually a commercial bank, requires that commitments be made for long-term financing prior to the start of construction. This ensures that the construction loan will be paid off by the long-term mortgage, upon completion of the project. The institution providing the long-term mortgage is, therefore, very concerned with the financial soundness of the project. The mortgage lender reviews the project care-

THE BUILDING INDUSTRY

TABLE 4-2

Holdings of Construction and Long-Term Mortgage Loans by Lender: 1972 and 1974 (in Billions of Dollars)

	Total 1972	Total* 1974	1974 Breakdown by Lender				
			Savings & Loans	Commercial Banks	Mutual Savings Banks	Life Insurance Companies	Federal Credit Agencies
Construction Loans	35.7	42.8	9.0	17.1	1.0	0.4	
Long-Term Mortgages	498.6	616.9	237.7	109.8	73.7	83.2	63.6
1- to 4-unit Homes	326.4	394.0	196.5	66.6	48.8	18.4	34.7
Multifamily	61.2	76.8	21.7	3.3	12.4	18.9	11.4
Nonresidential	87.5	115.8	19.1	34.0	12.4	39.6	3.6
Farm Properties	23.5	30.3	0.4	6.0	0.1	6.3	13.9

Source: U.S. Department of Commerce, Bureau of the Census, *Statistical Abstract of the United States: 1976* (Washington, D.C.: Government Printing Office, 1976), p. 489.
*Includes lenders not shown separately.

fully prior to construction to ensure that it will have a value that justifies its cost. Obtaining project approval from the lender can be a crucial step in the building process.

Insurance Institutions

All participants in the building process are concerned that events may not go as anticipated. In many cases they buy insurance to guard against unforeseen circumstances. The owner is generally responsible for fire and liability insurance during the construction phase. Contractors and subcontractors buy insurance to provide protection in case they are held liable for injury or property damage. Also, owners often require that contractors have bid bonds to guarantee that they will sign a contract for which they have bid, and performance bonds to guarantee that they will carry out the work for which they have contracted.

The architect and other consultants carry errors and omissions insurance to protect themselves against law suits alleging that responsibility for design or construction errors lies with them. In 1976 an estimated 40 million dollars was paid in insur-

ance premiums by architects and their consultants for errors and omissions insurance. Although it is impossible to determine what part of the total building dollar is required to pay for insurance, the concern for risk by all participants clearly translates into a significant cost, ultimately paid by the owner.

General Contractors

On most major building projects, construction is managed by a single contractor selected through a process of competitive bidding. General contractors usually have several key trades working directly for them such as carpentry and concrete work, but subcontract much of the construction work to specialty contractors such as plumbers, electricians, masons, and drywall contractors. An average project may involve 25 different subcontractors, all hired, managed, and paid by the general contractor. The primary function of the general contractor, particularly on large jobs, is the management of construction work performed by others. This includes coordinating the initial bid, planning and scheduling the project, supervising work at the site, coordinating work involving more than one subcontractor, and overseeing quality control.

Many contractors prefer to get work through direct negotiation. This is particularly true in highly competitive markets, where the contractor would be bidding against ten or more competitors. Owners seldom negotiate with more than two or three contractors at the same time, making it a more attractive process for the contractor. Even in a negotiated design/build job, where the contractor invests substantial time in developing a preliminary design proposal, the probability of getting the project can be relatively high. This arrangement is attractive to the contractor since it means having control over detailed design and construction. Contractors also offer construction manager services, working for the owner on a fee basis, much as the architect does. In this arrangement, the contractor coordinates the construction process without financial risk.

Specialty Contractors

Many contractors specialize in particular areas of building construction. Table 4-3 indicates the range of specialties and the amount of work they perform. In 1972 approximately one-half of the 55.7 billion dollars in specialty construction work was performed directly for building owners; the other half was subcontracted by general contractors.

When projects are bid competitively, subcontractors prepare their bids and submit them to general contractors. The subcontractor is hired by the general contractor after award of the contract. The general contractor schedules and supervises the work and pays for it upon completion. The subcontractor is primarily concerned with clear definition of the work that is to be performed, sufficient notice as to when the work is to be done, and timely payment for work that has been completed.

Fabricators

Fabricators of building products are generally local companies that process and assemble materials produced by others. Their work is usually produced for individual jobs, and they work closely with specialty contractors. In some cases fabricators are also materials suppliers, such as lumber yards that produce prefabricated trusses. Other fabricators produce precast concrete, steel structural members, roof decks and other shapes, and mechanical and lighting system components (such as ducts, ceiling grids, and diffusers).

Indirect Participants

The participants discussed above play direct roles in building projects. There are others who contribute substantially to the industry in an indirect way. For example, research and testing agencies, such as the National Bureau of Standards, provide vital information about the safety and performance of building products. Environment-behavior researchers are responsible for the growing body of knowledge about the relationship between the physical environment and human behavior. The information industry itself publishes books, journals, and specific information services regarding building project activity, building products, and construction costs. Educators in all building industry disciplines also play an important role. These are but a few examples of indirect participants.

ORGANIZATION OF THE BUILDING PROCESS

In most industries, goods and services are distributed through established channels. In the building industry, a new combination of participants is brought together on each project. They are often working together for the first time. For this reason, relationships among participants are governed by customs and habits that allow each to have a set of expectations about how the others will behave. Architects expect manufacturers' sales representatives to promote products. Contractors expect to receive drawings with specific content and organi-

TABLE 4-3

Specialty Contractors

Special Trade Contractors	Number of Firms	Construction Workers	Construction Receipts ($1,000)
Plumbing, Heating, and Air Conditioning	53,301	371,113	15,321,135
Painting, Paper Hanging, and Decorating	29,011	125,807	2,382,301
Electrical Work	32,455	271,441	9,448,881
Masonry, Stone Setting, and Other Stonework	23,896	156,395	3,085,759
Plastering, Drywall, and Insulation Work	13,415	151,825	4,084,687
Terrazzo, Tile, Marble, and Mosaic Work	4,270	26,600	703,114
Carpentering	23,524	115,464	2,329,145
Floor Laying and Other Floorwork	9,052	36,402	1,175,846
Roofing and Sheet Metal Work	18,535	134,189	3,940,243
Concrete Work	17,772	135,041	3,650,338
Water Well Drilling	4,159	14,598	534,171
Structural Steel Erection	2,760	49,983	1,457,836
Glass and Glazing Work	2,459	14,175	593,658
Excavating and Foundation Work	15,981	92,592	2,956,531
Wrecking and Demolition Work	1,027	7,544	219,412
Installing Building Equipment, N.E.C.	1,945	31,058	1,408,192
Special Trade Contractors, N.E.C.	15,420	82,899	2,440,265
Totals	268,982	1,817,216	55,731,514

Source: U.S. Department of Commerce, Bureau of the Census, *1972 Census of Construction Industries, vol. 1: Industry and Special Statistics* (Washington, D.C.: Government Printing Office, 1976), pp. 1—8.

zation as the basis for bid preparation. Consulting engineers expect to make a specific set of engineering decisions. Subcontractors expect to divide the work according to established boundaries.

The traditional process has strengths and weaknesses. Its appropriateness for a given project hinges on the objectives of the owner. If the owner places high priority on control over quality, the traditional process may be suitable. If the owner wants to put full responsibility for construction in the hands of *one* general contractor, the traditional process may also be appropriate. If, on the other hand, the owner is most concerned about early project completion or wants to know the construction cost for the project prior to investing in the design services of an architect, alternatives to the traditional processes must be considered.

In addition, to select an appropriate building

process, the owner must ask questions about industry context. Are there enough contractors prepared to bid on the project to make bidding truly competitive? Are there one or more sufficiently reliable contractors with whom to negotiate a construction contract? Are parts of the project so specialized that only one subcontractor or supplier is capable of bidding on them, thus eliminating competitive pricing? The answers to these questions could undermine the strength of the traditional process in providing the owner both control over quality and the best price through competitive bidding.

As a building project begins, the owner should review objectives and the building industry context and select the most suitable approach. But there are two obstacles to this ideal. First, there is no systematic body of knowledge about the building process.[5] Second, the system of mutual expectations that allows project participants to function together on each new project is a strong conservative force. No individual can change a role in the process without making complementary changes in the roles of others. A contractor can redefine an area of work only by simultaneously redefining the work of at least one other contractor. If a team of participants worked together from one project to the next, it could develop new relationships by mutual agreement. The team could redefine areas of responsibility and test them over a period of years. This opportunity is rarely present in the building industry.

The Traditional Building Process

Relationships among the major participants in the traditional building process are indicated in the adjacent figure. The owner hires an architect who, in turn, hires engineers. The owner selects a general contractor through competitive bidding, and the general contractor selects subcontractors who work directly for the contractor. The architect supervises the work of the general contractor and the subcontractor, but payments are made to the general con-

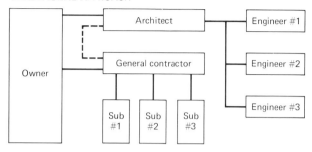

TRADITIONAL APPROACH

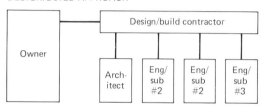

DESIGN/BUILD APPROACH

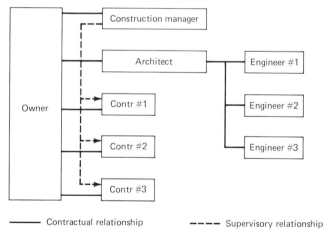

CONSTRUCTION MANAGEMENT APPROACH

——— Contractual relationship   - - - - Supervisory relationship

Three approaches to the building process.

tractor through the owner. The traditional process consists of four phases: project initiation, design, bidding, and construction (see figure, page 84).

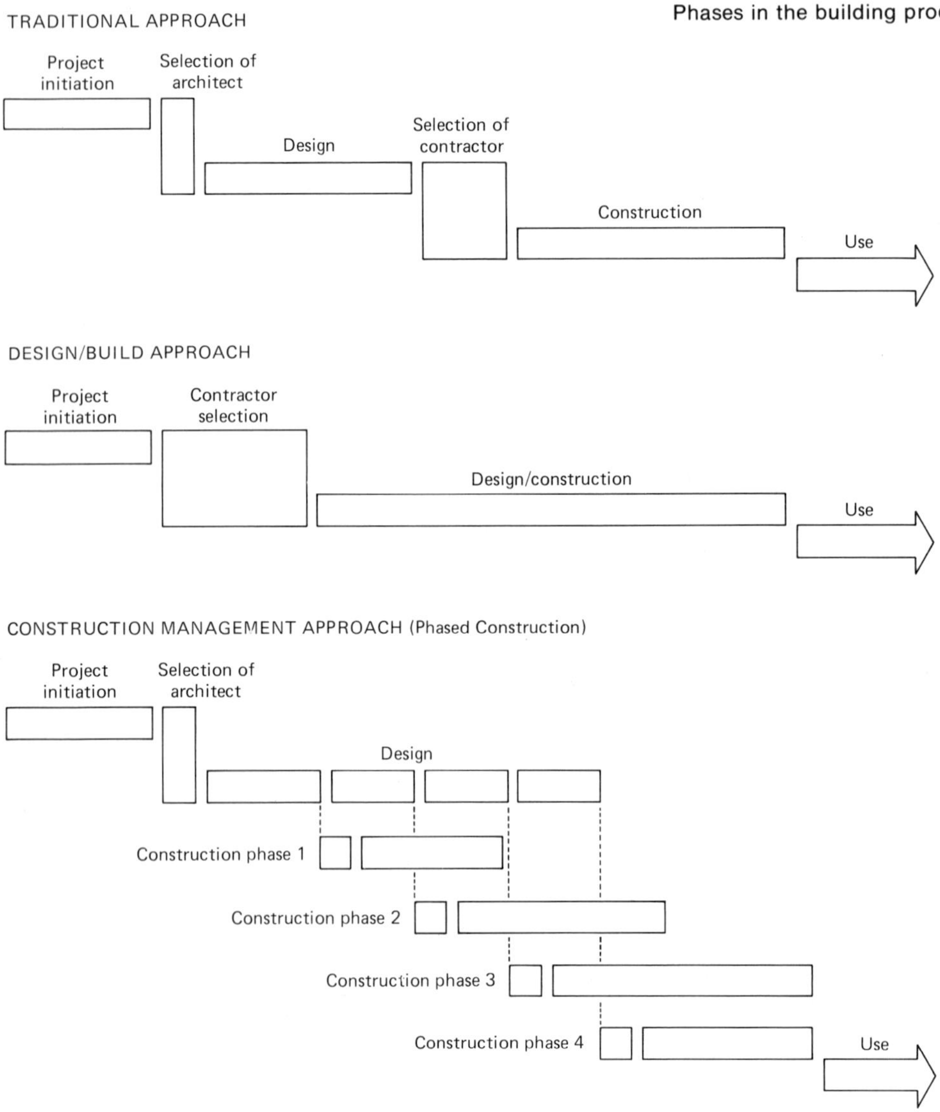

TRADITIONAL APPROACH

Phases in the building process.

Project
initiation

Selection of
architect

Design

Selection of
contractor

Construction

Use

DESIGN/BUILD APPROACH

Project
initiation

Contractor
selection

Design/construction

Use

CONSTRUCTION MANAGEMENT APPROACH (Phased Construction)

Project
initiation

Selection of
architect

Design

Construction phase 1

Construction phase 2

Construction phase 3

Construction phase 4

Use

Project Initiation. The project initiation phase is critically important to the eventual success of the project. During this phase, the owner's initial ideas for a new building are transformed into specific objectives for space, building quality, budget, and delivery date. This transformation requires an economic analysis to determine budget levels needed, and behavioral analysis to determine what activities are to be accommodated by the new building. The level of effort expended in project initiation may be very great, as in the case of hospital projects where extensive programming studies and thorough economic feasibility analyses are prepared. On a simpler project, such as a private dwelling, these questions may have been considered only informally prior to the hiring of an architect, with detailed answers emerging through the dialogue between client and architect during the design phase.

During the project initiation phase, the owner makes a commitment to an approach to the building process. He or she has the opportunity to analyze the characteristics of the project and select an appropriate approach. For this reason, the project initiation phase is not unique to the traditional building process but is the common starting point for all approaches.

The next step in initiation of the traditional building process is the selection of an architect. This step may be informal, involving personal contact between individuals or formal, with several prospective architects making presentations to a panel representing the owner (such as a school board or a hospital building committee). When the architect is selected, a fee is agreed upon, and a contract for architectural services is signed. The contract delineates the responsibilities of the architect and the manner and frequency of payment. The fee is usually based upon a percentage of the total construction cost of the project, ranging from about 5 percent to 10 percent as a function of project size and complexity. Small projects often require a greater design effort in proportion to their size and therefore call for a higher percentage fee.

The American Institute of Architects is developing a data bank on the time required to design projects of all types and sizes. These data provide a systematic basis for architects and their clients to estimate the appropriate fee for a specified set of design services.[6]

Design. During the design phase of the project, the architect and consulting engineers develop schematic designs, detailed designs, and construction documents. The engineers are hired by the architect and paid from the architect's fee. At the end of each phase of design, a presentation is made to the client, and approval is given for further design development. These approvals give both architect and client confidence that design is proceeding on a mutually agreeable basis.

As the design progresses, sales representatives of product manufacturers make regular appearances at architectural firms to promote use of their products and to prepare more detailed information about products of particular relevance to projects that are underway. This communication is almost always made directly with representatives of the manufacturer of the product and not through the contractors or subcontractors who will eventually install the product. The architect seldom communicates directly with potential bidders on the project.

When the construction drawings and specifications are complete, they are submitted to local building officials for their review and issuance of a building permit. These documents are also reviewed by the lending institutions that are providing financing for the construction period and for the long-term ownership of the building.

Bidding. During the bidding period, construction documents consisting of detailed drawings of the project, construction specifications, instructions to bidders, and construction contracts are made available to interested general contractors. A period of four to eight weeks is allowed for preparation of bids. During this period each general contractor gives portions of the drawings and specifications to one or more subcontractors in each area of work to get their bids. As indicated in the figure on page 86, subcontractors may be approached by more than one contractor and, therefore, may participate in more than one final bid to the owner.

During the bid period, subcontractors also request prices from fabricators and manufacturers for products that are not simple catalogue items.

General contractors often ask the architect and the related engineers for clarification of the drawings and specifications when they appear unclear. These questions often lead to addenda or changes

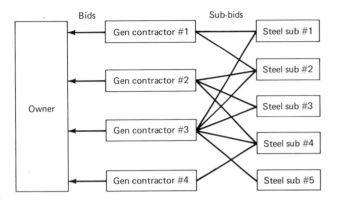

Bids		Sub-bids

Owner — Gen contractor #1 — Steel sub #1
Gen contractor #2 — Steel sub #2
Gen contractor #3 — Steel sub #3
Steel sub #4
Gen contractor #4 — Steel sub #5

Relationships during bidding for one subcontract area.

in the bid documents issued to all bidders during the bid period. Since addenda can invalidate bid preparation efforts based upon previous versions of the drawings and specifications, contractors will often delay bid preparation until they feel that the last addenda have been issued.

As the deadline for submitting bids approaches, the general contractor pressures the subcontractors to submit their bids. Subcontractors are reluctant, often suspecting that the amount of their bid might leak to a competing subcontractor, who can then simply underbid without absorbing the considerable cost of preparing a bid. A subcontractor may give different prices to different general contractors based on experience in working with them and confidence in their fairness.

The bid period culminates in a flurry of phone calls between the general contractor and subcontractors, with the final bid prepared moments before the deadline for submission. The bid opening is a ritual at which each sealed bid is opened by the contract officer, usually an employee of the owner, in the presence of all interested parties. The contract is usually awarded to the lowest qualified bidder.

The general contractor identified as low bidder will review the bid in detail to check for errors. If a major bidding error is found, usually the bid can be withdrawn. If major errors are not found, a contract is

signed for the bid amount. However, the bidding may not stop there. Subcontractors do not yet know if their bid to the winning general contractor was lowest. A new round of bidding may be opened up between general contractor and subcontractors, which the contractor hopes will yield lower prices in each area of work. This practice, known as bid-shopping, may in the long run have the effect of giving the general contractor a bad name with subcontractors. A bidding backlash may result, in which the original bids are padded to allow for the second round; or worse, some subcontractors will not submit bids to the general contractor at all.

Often these negotiations between contractors are unknown to the architect or owner of the project. They are important to the owner, however, because they result in hidden costs, such as the increased overhead or contingencies added to the basic bid by subcontractors, or the costs resulting from an uncooperative mood among contractors during the construction phase.

Construction. During construction, the architect periodically reviews the work to ensure its conformance with the construction documents. The contractor makes monthly requests for payment from the owner, based upon the work performed during that period. The architect is usually responsible for verifying that the work claimed by the contractor and subcontractors has actually been accomplished. Five to ten percent of each monthly request is withheld as *retainage* to be paid upon completion of the entire project. As the project proceeds the general contractor and subcontractors often ask the architect for interpretations of the drawings and specifications and for minor design decisions in situations that were not anticipated.

At the conclusion of the project, the architect systematically reviews the entire project for conformance with drawings and specifications and prepares a *punchlist* that indicates any items that do not conform. In most states there is a one-year period following completion of a project during which any defects in construction must be rectified by the appropriate contractor. In addition, particular parts of the work, such as the roof, are insured or warranteed for as long as twenty years.

The traditional process has the advantages of tight control over quality by the architect and commitment on a price for the building prior to the start of construction. When all participants are familiar with the process, relative agreement about their responsibilities and a willingness to enter into the project in the first place are usually assured. The weakness of the traditional process is the lack of overall management. This leads to a number of specific problems that are reflected in unnecessarily high project costs and long completion times. Separate contracts for design and construction can lead to uncertainty over responsibility for problems that arise on the project. This separation also leads to duplication in design effort. Many detailed drawings prepared during the design phase by the architect and engineers are redone as shop drawings by contractors during the construction phase. This duplication is costly and time-consuming. Communication between engineers and the contractors who will install their work is indirect. The bidding process, designed to provide the owner with the lowest possible price for the building, can often have the opposite effect. Costly duplication of effort by the many contractors preparing bids, confusion and mistrust among contractors, and problems with the timing of a bid in relation to other projects being bid by the same contractors can all lead to an artificially high price. All of these difficulties reflect the lack of management control over the traditional process.

Modifications of the Traditional Process

Within the framework of the traditional process, owners have modified the methods of selecting and contracting with architects and contractors. These modifications give owners some flexibility in dealing with specific characteristics of the project for which the traditional process is not well suited.

The design competition is an alternative approach to selecting an architect that gives the owner an indication of the architect's design direction before the architect is selected. Such competitions are particularly attractive to young architects because they provide opportunities to obtain major projects that normally go to well-established firms. The approach is time-consuming and must involve a project of architectural significance to attract serious interest among architects. Occasionally, a limited competition will be held, in which a small number of architects will be paid to develop schematic designs, and a winner will be selected to complete the project. This involves additional expense to the owner and would be appropriate only for the most prestigious buildings.[7]

Owners also employ alternatives to the traditional architectural fee arrangement. Instead of being based on a percentage of total building cost, the fee can be fixed at an agreed-upon dollar amount. The fixed fee removes uncertainty about what the final fee will be; it also removes an apparent incentive on the part of the architect to increase total building costs in order to increase the fee. When the amount of design effort is difficult to predict, the architect can be paid on an hourly basis at an agreed-upon rate. This approach is used only on small projects or when the extent of construction work is undetermined, such as on a renovation project.

There are many variations in the process of selecting and contracting with the general contractor. One or more specialty contractors may be asked to bid directly to the owner thereby removing them from the supervision of the general contractor. This gives the owner greater control of these subcontractors, but also it puts the owner, rather than the general contractor, in a position of overall responsibility for coordination of the project. Contracts may be negotiated with one or more general contractors rather than being bid competitively. This speeds up the selection process but may result in a less favorable price to the owner. The construction contract may be based upon a price per unit of construction rather than on a price for the total project. This is appropriate under circumstances in which the total quantity of work is not known, as in excavation or pipeline construction. The unit priced approach allows the owner to get a fair price for work where the quantity is difficult to estimate, but it is an approach that requires careful supervision by the owner to determine the actual quantity of work performed.

When a price per unit of work is difficult to estimate, the owner can turn to the time and materials approach, in which the contractor is paid for materials and labor hours, with a mark-up for overhead and profit. The owner must supervise work on a time and materials contract very carefully to determine the quantities of labor and materials actually expended, and to see that the labor is productive.

These approaches put the owner in a stronger position to manage the traditional process, but they dilute one of its major advantages: single responsibility for construction in the hands of one general contractor.

The Design/Build Approach

A previous figure indicates relationships among the major participants in the design/build approach. The owner hires a design/build contractor based on a preliminary design and specification. The contractor employs an architect either as staff or as a consultant. Engineering work is usually done by the appropriate subcontractors—structural, mechanical, and electrical—who work directly for the design/build contractor. The design/build approach consists of three phases: project initiation, contractor selection, and design/construction.

Project Initiation. In the design/build approach, the owner must prepare a statement of objectives for the building as a basis for the development of proposals by contractors during phase two. As in the traditional approach, the owner may con-

duct extensive financial and behavioral studies or make a brief and informal statement of needs. In either case, the end product of this phase is the issuance of a request for proposals to potential design/build contractors.

Contractor Selection. The design/build contractor can be selected either through direct negotiation with the owner or through competitive bidding against several other contractors. In either case, contractors prepare schematic designs, brief specifications, and a bid for the construction price. Subcontractors develop preliminary designs and estimates for their areas of work. The general contractor usually works with only one or two subcontractors in each area. Engineering and construction estimating are usually done by the subcontractors, largely eliminating the communication problems that exist between engineers and subcontractors in the traditional process. Based upon these proposals, the owner selects the contractor who, in his or her judgment, has offered the best combination of price and quality. The contractor with the lowest price is not always selected. Then a contract for design and construction based upon the selected proposal is signed.

Design and Construction. During the design/construction phase, the contractor's architect develops a detailed design and construction specifications. Engineers working with subcontractors develop detailed designs for structural, mechanical, and electrical work. There is no need for the rigorous construction contract documents of the traditional building process, since no further bidding is required.

During construction, the owner should retain an independent architect or engineer to review the work for compliance with the design/build contract and to authorize monthly progress payments to the contractor. The project architect cannot fulfill this role since he or she only works for the contractor and should not be expected to give an independent judgment.

Advantages of the design/build approach stem primarily from the single responsibility for design and construction it places in the hands of the contractor. The owner gets a firm price for construction without the risk in time and money of developing a detailed architectural design. Duplication of effort between engineers and contractors is largely eliminated, since they are working together from the beginning. The division of responsibility for design and construction is also eliminated, since the design/build contractor is responsible to the owner for both phases of the work.

The major problem of this approach is lack of control by the owner over the quality of design and construction. The schematic design and preliminary specification on which the design/build contract is based do not provide a detailed description of the work to be done. This is not a disadvantage if the project is simple, or if it is similar to other projects done by the contractor that can be used as a standard of quality. This explains the widespread use of this approach for industrial buildings. It is increasingly employed for building types such as medical clinics, branch banks, and small office buildings, in which some design/build contractors have specialized. The approach is also being applied to larger and more complex projects, although this requires more careful analysis of the owner's financial and behavioral needs.

The Construction Management Approach

While the design/build approach puts greater control of the process in the hands of the contractor, the construction management approach puts control in the hands of the owner and the owner's consultants. The construction manager (CM) is a professional working for the owner under a fee arrangement, much the same as the architect does. The CM takes responsibility for managing the construction process and for supplying the architect with information about construction costs and scheduling during the design phase. As indicated in previous figures, there is usually no general contractor, and specialty contractors work directly for the owner. As indicated, there is the potential for phased construction, in which some parts of the project begin before others have been designed.

Project Initiation. The CM may be hired early in the project initiation phase, before an approach to the building process has been selected. The label "construction manager" is actually a misnomer, since the CM may advise the owner on all phases of the project, including selection of an overall approach. The CM may assist in the preparation of initial project budgets and in the selection of an architect.

Design. During the design phase, the CM assists the architect and engineers in reviewing project cost estimates and making decisions with important cost and scheduling ramifications. The CM must be aware of the availability and interest of contractors in each category of construction and must take into account the effects of seasonal construction activity. If there is pressure for early completion of the project, the CM will establish a schedule for phased construction, also known as *fast-track scheduling,* in which work on early stages of construction such as excavation and foundations will proceed while design of the later stages of construction is still underway. This puts pressure on the architect and engineers to make decisions on structural layout and design early in the project without knowing the details or even the materials to be used in later construction work.

Contractor Selection. Contractors may be selected by any of the methods outlined for the traditional or modified traditional building process. In the phased construction approach, contractors are selected as soon as the design work is completed for that portion of the work. The CM is responsible for the coordination of these independent selection processes.

Construction. During the construction phase, the CM plays a role very similar to that of the general contractor in the traditional building process. The CM plans the overall project and schedules arrival of each contractor at the site. The CM coordinates work involving more than one contractor and reviews all work for conformance with drawings and specifications. He or she differs from the general contractor by working for the owner on a fee basis and by having no financial interest in the final construction cost. Therefore, the CM can represent the interests of the owner, review the progress of construction work, and authorize payments to contractors by the owner.

The chief advantage to the owner of this approach is that, by gaining greater control over the construction process through the CM, he or she may save both time and money over the traditional approach. The owner pays for these potential savings by taking the risk of committing funds to the early stages of construction without knowing what the total construction cost will be. Even if all contracts are bid at one time, the owner is taking the risk of managing the building process.

There is a clear trend toward application of the CM approach to large, complex building projects such as major office buildings and hospitals. One indicator is that previously conservative government agencies, such as the General Services Administration, have moved to the CM approach on all of their major projects.

ROLES FOR THE ARCHITECT IN THE BUILDING INDUSTRY

Architects perform a wide variety of functions within the building industry. Table 4-4 indicates the number of registered architects in each sector of the economy according to the 1970 census. This section presents a more detailed picture of the role of the architect in the architectural firm, government, man-

TABLE 4-4

Architects in Each Sector of the Economy

Engineering and Architectural Practice	38,242
Agriculture	4,901
Public Administration	3,280
Construction	2,343
Manufacturing	2,289
Education	1,099
Finance, Insurance, Real Estate	793
Transportation, Communications, Utilities	744
Business, Retail, Wholesale, Business Services	1,051
Health Services and Hospitals	188
Personal Services	208
Others	1,036
Total	56,214

Source: U.S. Department of Commerce, Bureau of the Census, *1970 Census of Population: Subject Reports* (Washington, D.C.: Government Printing Office, 1972), table 8, Occupation by Industry.

ufacturing, construction, and construction management.

The Architectural Firm

Architectural firms can take several legal forms affecting their tax status and ownership. The simplest form of ownership is the *sole proprietorship*, common for small firms. Under this arrangement responsibility for the work of the firm rests with a single person who has complete control over the firm's operations. There is no corporate tax on the income of the organization, and the sole proprietor is personally liable for the debts of the firm and any legal action taken against it. In a *partnership*, several people share ownership of the firm, and again there is no corporate tax on income. The partners are also personally liable for debts of the firm and for legal action taken against it. The third major form of organization is *incorporation*. The corporation is treated legally as a person, insulating the owners of the corporation from possible indebtedness of the corporation. Profit earned by corporations is taxed by federal and state governments. If the remaining income after taxes is passed on to shareholders as dividends, it also is taxed as personal income. An advantage of corporate organization is that the architects who own the corporations are also empolyees and are eligible for employee benefit programs not available to them under the other forms of organization.[8]

Table 4-5 shows the number of firms in six size ranges, their income, and number of employees. It also shows the number of architects who share in the ownership of their firms and the number who are simply employed by them.

In any architectural firm there is a wide range of functions to be performed. The services being offered by the firm—architectural programming, schematic design, detailed design, and construction supervision—are the primary function of the architect. But equally important for the firm's survival are the management activities of securing work, hiring and firing employees and consultants, managing finances, and planning for the future. In small firms many or all of these activities are performed by one person. In larger firms, people often specialize in phases of the design process, in types of projects, or in management functions such as development of new business, personnel management, fiscal management, or project management.

The architect is often visualized as a loner or individualist who pits idealism against the realities of the financial and social world. In fact, as can be seen from Table 4-5, there are still a substantial number of architects who practice either alone or with very small firms. The unique advantage of the very small organization is its flexibility. The architect is not burdened with a large staff for which a continual flow of projects must be supplied. In larger firms this pressure to generate new business often puts the partners in the position of salespeople with little time for involvement in design.

The small organization is often able to take on jobs that would not make financial sense for larger firms. For example, in the design of a $100,000 house, a 10 percent fee will result in a gross income to the architect of $10,000. For an architect working alone, only a small portion of the gross fee is required to pay the modest expenses incurred. In a large firm, overhead expenses such as salaries for receptionists and secretaries, rent, and the costs of management personnel who do not work directly on projects account for 50 percent or more of the gross

TABLE 4-5
Architectural Firms by Size

Size (Number of Employees)	Number of Firms	Total Income ($1000)	Payroll ($1000)	Total Employees	Architects as Employees	Architects as Partners
0–3	5,503	387,245	101,388	8,464	1,804	4,532
4–7	2,394	366,683	123,971	12,875	3,443	2,182
8–19	1,595	535,077	212,000	18,996	5,027	1,308
20–49	531	427,408	191,353	15,292	3,828	444
50–99	102	185,164	84,364	6,878	1,706	85
100+	54	302,416	156,350	11,178	1,605	88
Totals	10,179	2,203,993	869,426	73,683	17,413	8,639

Source: U.S. Department of Commerce, Bureau of the Census, *1972 Census of Selected Service Industries,* vol. 1: *Summary and Subject Statistics* (Washington, D.C.: Government Printing Office, 1976), pp. 5–14.

fee. On small projects, particularly single-family houses, the time required to design and supervise the project is barely justified by the gross fee and can seldom be profitable in a firm with a large overhead.

For the architect operating a small office, life is varied and often exciting. The architect is in constant motion, performing all of the functions handled by more specialized personnel in a larger office, from promotion and client relations to detailed design, specifications writing, and job supervision. The workload of the firm will change from feast to famine, particularly if the architect has a few large projects rather than many small ones.

In offices of more than a few people, it is necessary to organize the flow of projects through the firm. There are two basic approaches to office organization. As illustrated in the adjacent figure, in the vertical approach each project is assigned to a project team that has responsibility for all phases of the work. The team is managed by a project architect, and its members should be generalists in order to provide the full range of services required by a project. In the horizontal approach, projects pass from one department to the next where they are worked on by people specializing in one phase of project development. Each department has a manager who takes overall responsibility for projects in a given area.

Many architectural offices mix these two basic organizational approaches, attempting to combine the advantages of specialization and those of project continuity. The mixed approach shown is typical. Projects pass through a programming department and are then taken over by project teams. The project team is responsible for schematic design, design development, construction documents, and cost estimating. The project then goes to the contract administration department, which manages it through bidding and construction.[9]

Architects in Government
As indicated by Table 4-4, over 3,000 architects are employed in federal, state, and local governments. Government agencies at all levels are responsible for a major proportion of building construction in the United States each year. Many of these agencies maintain a staff of professionals, often architects, who are responsible for managing their building programs.

In the role of owner, the architect is presented with both a challenge and an opportunity not available in the conventional role of the professional architect. Establishing the priorities of the owner and selecting a building process to fit them are decisions of utmost importance occuring during the project initiation phase, usually before the professional architect is hired. The challenge for the architect as the owner's representative is to think in terms of designing the building process rather than designing the building. The architect should show an understanding of the relationship between alternative approaches to building and the owner's priorities. As an owner's representative, the architect can have a major influence over the ultimate quality of the built environment through understanding of the building process. Major building programs of state and federal agencies have been the source of many innovations in the building process. Architects have often been in a leadership role on these projects.

Architects also do research within individual public agencies and at the National Bureau of Standards, where studies are conducted on the properties of materials and systems of construction, energy conservation, and methods of writing building specifications and codes. Government agencies also have building design groups that perform functions similar to those handled by design teams in architectural firms.

Architects in Manufacturing
There are many roles for the architect in industry. These are associated with the industrial firm's construction of buildings for its own use and with the production of building products. In the first case, the architect plays a role similar to that of the architect

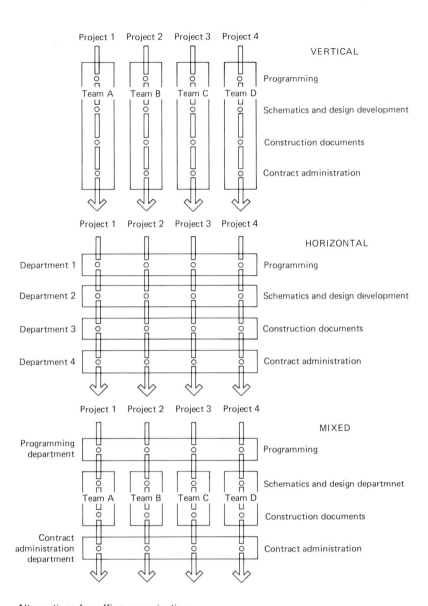

Alternatives for office organization.

in government, as the client's or owner's representative. Many large industrial concerns have ongoing building programs that require a full-time management group for their direction. In some cases outside architects are hired; in others, a complete architectural and engineering design capability is staffed within the company.

Roles for the architect with manufacturers of building products include sales, design, and production management. Every building product must at some point be designed, and the skills required are often similar to those required to design a building. Marketing of building products usually means making contact with the architects who will specify them and also requires an understanding of the relationship between the product and the building as a whole. This role is often filled appropriately by an architect.

Architects in Construction

Many architects work for or are themselves developers and general contractors. They may have retained their functions as building designers or moved into other roles having to do with the management of construction. Many developers do their own design work, and building contractors are participating increasingly in design/build projects, where it is necessary either to hire an architect or to have one on their staff. In the context of the construction or development organization, the architect can become an advocate for environmental quality in the face of the considerable pressures for financial survival.

Architect as Construction Manager

Construction management is a new function in the building industry, and there is disagreement over both the scope of services to be offered by the construction manager and the appropriate professional background for people who fill the role. Building contractors tend to emphasize the role of the CM in the construction phase of design and argue that contractors have the proper grounding in construction supervision. Architects tend to emphasize the importance of the CM's participation in the early phases of a project and point to the architect's understanding of design issues as well as of construction. There is clearly an opportunity for architects to offer building owners comprehensive professional services that would guide the building process from beginning to end, reflecting the owner's objectives for cost, time, and quality. To compete successfully with contractors in this area, the architect should demonstrate expertise in the construction field or form an affiliation with an expert.

EXPECTATIONS FOR THE FUTURE

During the postwar era of the 1950s and 1960s, building construction benefited from a period of high and undiscriminating demand. Growth in population, increasing government services, and general economic expansion stimulated construction of housing, schools, and commercial and industrial facilities. A decade of economic depression during the 1930s and five years of a war-based economy created a vacuum that the building boom of the following twenty years filled.

The building industry did not respond with innovations in either its products or its procedures. Early postwar efforts to stimulate industrialized housing failed.[10] The industry expanded within the framework of fragmentation, low capital investment, local operations, and ad hoc organization. Industry organization remained the same because the market, although it was expanding, remained fluctuating, seasonal, and subject to local economic conditions. The primary effect of the increasing demand for building was a rate of increase in cost higher than that for other consumer products.

In 1969, the time was ripe for a major change in housing, or so thought George Romney, then Secretary of the Department of Housing and Urban Development (HUD). He felt that the slowdown in the United States space program left many aerospace firms looking for major markets in which their management skills and capital could be applied. Operation Breakthrough was designed to encourage these firms to take a fresh look at the challenge of housing the American people. With an emphasis on factory production, twenty-two firms were selected to build prototypes of the new products at nine sites around the country. Little attention was given by either HUD or the housing producers to the problem of matching large-scale factory production with the fluctuating and unpredictable marketplace for housing. As of 1976, only five of the Operation Breakthrough Housing Systems were still being marketed by their manufacturers.[11]

The situation in the 1970s has changed substantially from that of the previous twenty years. Population growth in the United States has come to a standstill. Children born during the post-World War II baby boom have grown up, leaving many school districts with a classroom surplus. The combined recession/inflation of the mid-1970s had a sobering effect on business, resulting in a lasting reluctance to commit capital to plant facilities.

In addition, more exacting demands are being placed upon the design and construction of new buildings. Deterioration of air and water quality during the 1950s and 1960s has led to higher standards of performance for buildings. Environmental impact statements must be prepared for buildings to spell out their effects on water and air quality, sewage systems, ecological systems, and even the amount of sunlight that reaches other buildings.

Increased sensitivity to human needs in other areas has put further pressure on building design.

Design standards recognizing the special needs of the handicapped have become law. Research has shown that design for the elderly, for the very young—in fact, for all people—requires more careful consideration for the relationship between environment and behavior than has been given to it in the past.

The latest and perhaps the most profound constraint on building design is the recognition of our dwindling supplies of energy. During the 1950s and 1960s, minimal concern was shown for energy conservation. Fuel was cheap and expanses of glass were in vogue. We are now paying the price. The long-term energy picture has forced not only a reevaluation of building design in terms of energy conservation but also a new look at the construction of buildings and the production of building products in terms of energy efficiency.

Another resource that has been squandered in the past is the supply of existing buildings. Buildings that in the past would have been plowed under are now carefully considered for adaptation to new uses. Rehabilitation of existing buildings will grow dramatically in proportion to other construction during the remainder of this century.

In sum, the market for building construction today and in the foreseeable future will be characterized by a moderating demand that is far more discriminating than in the past. As we saw earlier, this has already led to experimentation with alternatives to the traditional building process. Efforts to introduce management tools developed in other industries, in particular the use of the computer, have been limited by the lack of overall management control in the building process.

Currently, attention has been focused on construction management as the solution to organizing the building process, but no one approach will fit the variety of situations faced by building owners. The future will bring a new category of professional who can look beyond any single method of organizing the process and see that it must be organized to reflect the objectives and situation of the building owner. The process must be designed. In the opinion of Ralph Nash, the only appropriate source for these new professionals will be the schools of architecture.[12]

NOTES

1. U.S. Department of Commerce, Bureau of the Census, *1972 Census of Construction Industries*, vol. 1, *Industry and Special Statistics* (Washington, D.C.: Government Printing Office, 1976).

2. American Institute of Architects, *Code of Ethics and Professional Conduct*, AIA Document J330 (Washington, D.C.: American Institute of Architects, 1977), pp. 1–2.

3. Ibid., p. 2.

3a. American Institute of Architects, MEMO (Washington, D.C.: American Institute of Architects, July, 1978), p. 4.

4. Richard L. Sanderson, *Codes and Code Administration: An Introduction to Building Regulation in the United States* (Chicago: Building Officials Conference of America, 1969), pp. 7–11.

5. Aldo Norsa, *Answers for the Building Community: Optimizing the Choices*, IF Occasional Paper no. 3 (Montreal: Université de Montreal, 1976; Urbana: University of Illinois, 1976).

6. American Institute of Architects, *Compensation Management Guidelines for Architectural Services* (Washington, D.C.: American Institute of Architects, n.d.).

7. American Institute of Architects, *Architects' Handbook of Professional Practice*, vol. 1, *The Selection of an Architect* (Washington, D.C.: American Institute of Architects, 1963).

8. Robert Allen Class and Robert E. Koehler, eds., *Current Techniques in Architectural Practice* (Washington, D.C.: American Institute of Architects, 1976; New York: Architectural Record Books, 1976), pp. 5–8.

9. Ibid., pp. 10–16.

10. Charles Lewis Owen, *Design and the Industrialized House* (Chicago: Institute of Design Press, 1965), pp. 95–113.

11. U.S. Comptroller General, *Operation Breakthrough: Lessons Learned about Demonstrating New Technology* (Washington, D.C.: U.S. General Accounting Office, 1976), p. 17.

12. Norsa, *Answers for the Building Community*, p. 56.

FOR FURTHER READING

American Institute of Architects. *Architects' Handbook of Professional Practice*. Vol. 1. Washington, D.C.: American Institute of Architects, 1963.

———. *Code of Ethics and Professional Conduct*. AIA Document J330. Washington, D.C.: American Institute of Architects, 1977.

———. *Compensation Management Guidelines for Architectural Services*. Washington, D.C: American Institute of Architects.

———. *Owner-Architect Agreement*. AIA Document B131. Washington, D.C.: American Institute of Architects, 1970.

Bender, Richard. *A Crack in the Rear-view Mirror*. New York: Van Nostrand Reinhold Co., 1973.

Class, Robert Allen, and Koehler, Robert E., eds. *Current Techniques in Architectural Practice*. Washington, D.C.: American Institute of Architects, 1976; New York: Architectural Record Books, 1976.

Glover, Michael, ed. *Alternative Processes: Building Procurement, Design and Construction*. IF Occasional Paper no. 2. Montreal: Université de Montreal, 1976.

———, ed. *Building Procurement: Proceedings of a Workshop*. IF Occasional Paper no. 1. Montreal: Université de Montreal, 1974; Champaign: University of Illinois, Construction Engineering Research Laboratory, 1974.

Gutman, Robert. "Architecture: The Entrepreneurial Profession." *Progressive Architecture* 48 (May 1977).

Heery, George T. *Time, Cost, and Architecture.* New York: McGraw-Hill Book Co., 1975.

McCue, Gerald M., Ewald, William R., and The Midwest Research Institute. *Creating the Human Environment.* Urbana: University of Illinois Press, 1970.

Norsa, Aldo. *Answers for the Building Community: Optimizing the Choices.* IF Occasional Paper no. 3. Montreal: Université de Montreal, 1976; Urbana: University of Illinois, 1976.

Owen, Charles Lewis. *Design and the Industrialized House.* Chicago: Institute of Design Press, 1965.

Sanderson, Richard L. *Codes and Code Administration: An Introduction to Building Regulation in the United States.* Chicago: Building Officials Conference of America, 1969.

U.S. Comptroller General. *Operation Breakthrough: Lessons Learned about Demonstrating New Technology.* Washington, D.C.: U.S. General Accounting Office, 1976.

U.S. Department of Commerce. Bureau of the Census. *1972 Census of Construction Industries.* Vol. 1: *Industry and Special Statistics.* Washington, D.C.: Government Printing Office, 1976.

————. *1972 Census of Selected Service Industries.* Vol. 1: *Summary and Subject Statistics.* Washington, D.C.: Government Printing Office, 1976.

————. *Statistical Abstract of the United States: 1976.* Washington, D.C.: Government Printing Office, 1976.

CHAPTER 5

Development and Building Economics

Harvey Z. Rabinowitz

The practice of architecture takes place within the context of the building industry, as presented in Chapter 4. It also largely takes place within the context of the process of *development* and its associated economic constraints. That is, a large portion of building projects are initiated by developers—for their own use, ownership, or management, and/or for resale. Obviously, the economic and financial parameters of such projects are extremely important; the architect must be familiar with, and work within, this process. Most importantly, he or she must understand the relationship between the development process and architectural design. This chapter describes the building development process and the relationship between economics and design.

Building projects are initiated, implemented, and built by developers for their own use or ownership. A developer is an entrepreneurial individual, or legal entity such as a partnership or corporation, who is engaged in the highly speculative business of creating buildings for investment purposes. Developers can be engaged in renovating a small house or creating a new town; building an industrial complex or a tennis club; selling a building immediately upon completion or holding it throughout its life. Except for public or quasipublic buildings, such as police stations, libraries, schools, and hospitals, most of our environment is built by these individuals and organizations.

The context in which the developer works is primarily one of money and economics. The architect, hired by the developer to design a project, should be responsive to the economic context that is so critical to the project's success. The economic context is the most difficult among the many factors the architect must consider, because economic factors are often the most restrictive, pervasive, and difficult with which to work. They are the *bottom line.*[1]

In this difficult role, the architect must be aware that design solutions and decisions bear directly on the success of the building project. The architect, responsible for the physical design solution, is the resolver of these many, and often contradictory, forces. The developer counts on the architect to provide a responsive design solution in a limited time and within a strictly limited budget. The architect's decisions at all levels, from a judgment on the overall form to the location of an electric outlet, should be based on a knowledge of the variety of solutions available and their consequences.

The nature of the development context is changing. Developers and architects are at present experiencing and recognizing an even broader spectrum of relationships between economic factors and design that can critically effect the success of a development project. Whereas strict budgetary concerns were once considered primary, a more flexible approach is now necessary. The new approach also includes:

- Alternative use of land resources.
- Marketing factors and amenities.
- Alternative building systems and construction methods.
- Energy, life cycle costs, and tax consequences.

A knowledge of the solutions in these areas and their implications is now required to achieve feasible building projects. This, in effect, makes the architect's relationship with the developer symbiotic, and even more difficult. The architect should be adept in these additional areas and be able to reconcile them with the technical, functional, behavioral, and aesthetic factors already being considered. Such additional factors add more constraints and complexity. The architect's main task of synthesis, never easy, is made more difficult and yet all the more important.

Unfortunately, some architects who have had difficulty with the previous process, complex and convoluted as it was, cannot cope with the influx of these additional, unfamiliar factors in the economic realm. A growing number of architects, however, are becoming knowledgeable in these areas. Some are not only becoming stronger participants in the process with developers but are also becoming developers themselves.[2]

THE CONTEXT OF DEVELOPMENT

How are specific decisions concerning the form and design of buildings made? To answer this question, we will need some perspective on what is built and the process of creating a building.

What Is Built?

In the United States, the great bulk of building, some 85 percent of the dollar volume, is done by the private sector—that is, primarily by developers. This includes housing, industrial buildings, offices, stores, hotels, and warehouses. Public-sector buildings are governmental, such as libraries, firehouses, airports, and military facilities. We will be concerned with private-sector building, since it is the source of most architects' work.

Economic Forces on Development

In the private sector, there are a number of large-scale economic and social forces that influence the potential for development and even the type and shape of buildings. The availability and control of land, size and location of population growth, costs of construction, availability of financing, tax laws, and the state of the economy are some of the most important of these forces.

These economic forces have affected the development of the United States. An abundance of resources, a booming population, and economic expansion had created a history of continuous growth, optimism, and exuberance. In the 1950s and early 1960s, this incredible affluence attained its highest levels. For the first time, however, in the late 1960s, conditions prevailed that produced a psychological tremor in the previously consistent optimism.

Many of the factors fueling the previous history of expansion seemed suddenly and inexorably reversed. The always-available land, which by the 1970s had resulted in half the United States population living in low-density suburbs, was now largely developed. Suburban land scarcity; the absence of water, sewer, and utility service; and the need for governmental and community approvals and land use controls have all ended the era of cheap and available land for development. Land can account for as much as a third of the cost of developing a building project because of these factors. To compound this situation, a questioning of the validity of continued suburban expansion and rising land values was reinforced by the energy crisis, which made our car-centered culture suddenly obsolete and our detached houses potential white elephants.

The oil scarcity triggered increased inflation. Numerous products became considerably more expensive; in some cases they were even allocated. Following inflation, interest rates reached new heights—as high as 10 percent, from which the unspoken assumption was there would be no return to cheap money. Borrowing money for speculative building projects became unfeasible in this situation.

Competition in the development area has changed. In an expansive economy there is space for all. However, the negative forces we have mentioned make the climate for development extremely competitive, with many organizations vying for fewer possibilities. Such competition means that buildings must be able to attract users and tenants and results in design requirements for image, amenities, form, and size. The formulas and conventional wisdom suitable in the past do not suffice when it is necessary to probe market interstices and when innovation is necessary.

The Architect's Role

The architect's role in this new development context is critical and very different from what used to be. In the past, when a development project was more assured of success, there existed a greater tolerance for variances in architectural design. Conceptual, stylistic, and form decisions, among others, could be based upon a broad array of ideological foundations. These could be—and were—quite unrelated to the context, whether developmental or physical, and still not affect the presumed success of the project in an expanding and free economy. In the current new context, more rigor, knowledge, and accurate decisions are necessary to make development projects workable, successful, and attractive.

This changing role of the architect has important implications for the future of the profession. Economic-design parameters will be severely tightened on the one hand, but a larger number of variables will be available for manipulation. Innovative solutions will be necessary to respond to site, community, market, environmental, constructional, and life cycle constraints, and these solutions have the potential of producing buildings of strength and richness in design.

THE DEVELOPMENT PROCESS

The developer is the key to the development process—the catalyst, fuel, and engine. The developer initiates the process, hires the experts (including the architect), supplies the money, signs all contracts, takes final responsibility for all the decisions, and eventually owns the completed building. Development can be a highly rewarding business, but it has great risks.[3]

Unlike manufacturing, service, or retail businesses, where national sales can be measured, trends extrapolated, and expansion (or contraction) more rationally weighed, virtually all new building developments are high-risk undertakings. This is because of the long duration of such projects; many legal and political pitfalls; technical difficulties; and, after completion, the imponderables of the marketplace and the developer's typical lack of liquidity. Local conditions and the fragmented nature of the building industry impose rules that typically necessitate a development entity very different from the prototypical corporation. In fact, developers, even when they are large organizations, focus on the single top individual who possesses intuition, knowledge, contacts, and energy. Of the large corporations contemplating and/or entering the housing and development field in the late 1960s (such as Boise-Cascade, General Electric, American Standard, and Behring), all abandoned many of their large-scale efforts after very few years.

Developers often specialize in a certain building type, for example, office buildings, hotels, housing, or stores. Most are even more specialized within these categories, emphasing certain size buildings, locations, and construction types. The initiation of a new project often is circumscribed by the developer's expertise.

Site Selection

The developer's first task is to look for a suitable building site, screening numerous sites. Many criteria enter the site selection decision, including the following.

1 *Zoning.* Will the applicable local jurisdiction (city, town, or country) allow this type of use and size of building

The development process.

- Site selection
- Feasibility and financing
- Marketing
- Design and construction
- Operation/life cycle

on the site? Required parking, maximum building height, setback restrictions, and numerous other constraints must be considered.

2 *Utilities.* Water, storm and sanitary sewers, gas, electricity, and telephone hookups are needed. Are they available? Are improvements needed?

3 *Technical Factors.* How will the soils, topography, and drainage affect building design and cost? Acoustical factors, microclimate, and orientation will affect site usage.

4 *Location.* This is a very strong consideration. Is a market for the proposed use available? Is the site visible and easily accessible? Other variables to be considered are the neighborhood and the amount of traffic (auto and pedestrian) passing the site.

5 *Aesthetics.* Are there views? Landscape conditions, existing and proposed, are important aspects.

6 *Community.* What will be the community reaction to the proposed development? Can it be made compatible with the neighborhood? Will it produce more traffic and noise? What will be the effect on property values in the area?

7 *City Services.* Can the police, fire department, refuse collection, and local schools be utilized?

8 *Cost.* Is the land cost within a range that allows the development to meet all of the criteria and yet remain affordable by potential tenants and users?

Given these many and varied criteria, along with the competition among developers and the paucity of available sites, it is readily apparent that the site-search aspect of the development process is by no means quickly or easily done. When a developer does find a developable site, the next step is a more careful examination of its feasibility.

Determining Feasibility and Obtaining Financing

When a suitable site has been selected, more in-depth investigation is required to probe its feasibility, that is, whether the proposed development project makes sense from economic, market, and technical standpoints. This detailed probe includes approaching the community and testing its potential acceptance of the project; considering in more detail the technical solutions to special site problems, including soil tests; careful market analysis; and finally, the creation of schematic designs by the architect. During this feasibility phase, economic projections, which are estimates of the building's operation after completion, are produced, based on the many alternative designs and modifications. Finally, after many alterations of these estimates, the income generated by the project must meet the project's total expenses, including an allowance for profit, projected during a typical year of operation. If these criteria cannot be met, the project will be dropped and the site search recommenced.

A further and more objective test of feasibility is provided by the financial institution from which the developer hopes to borrow the money for the project. Virtually all buildings—even public-sector buildings—are financed in some way. (For instance, a school board may attempt to obtain financing through a bond issue, necessitating community approval.) The private developer or owner typically contributes 25 percent of a project's total value. This is called *equity*. The financial institution lends the remaining 75 percent of the total development cost, to be paid back over the life of the project, about twenty-five years. This is called a *mortgage loan.*

The financial institution may be a bank, insurance company, pension fund, or even an individual. The lender's experience in reviewing and financing proposed building projects, both successful and unsuccessful, makes their evaluation of the development proposal especially acute. Many proposed projects are rejected. Review criteria are principally economic. Lenders must be convinced of the future success of the project; they sometimes require that a project be partially or substantially rented, or preleased, before committing funds. This loan is usually critical to the implementation of a development, and the lender's suggestions have great weight. They may even suggest changes in the building design. Once a commitment to finance a project is obtained, however, the implementation of the project is virtually assured.

Design and Construction

The detailed design of the building can now proceed, followed by construction. In the early stages a number of alternative designs for the site are produced, and the most viable are chosen for schematic or preliminary drawings. These schematics are then modified after review by the lenders, consultants, and the community, and are then further refined by the architect. Eventually design development drawings are made, incorporating the final modifications. At this point the architect begins the working drawings and specifications. These are *contract documents* that detail every aspect of the building so that it can be constructed.

The developer, with contract documents in hand, will hire a general contractor on the basis of bids received from a number of these contractors, usually by choosing the lowest bid. The general contractor is a construction coordinator and manager who hires, schedules, supervises, and pays a host of specialized subcontractor firms. As many as 30 subcontractors can be working on one project (for instance, electricians, plumbers, or masons). Sometimes general contractors only manage the project and do no actual construction. However, most have crews that participate in some aspect of construction.

The developer is quite active during this stage of the process. Approvals for substitution of materials will be necessary; delays will inevitably occur and construction must be expedited; quality must be constantly reviewed and contractors paid. For the construction phase the developer usually obtains an interim or construction loan, because the permanent mortgage will not be given until the project has been completed. The construction loan may be from the same source as the permanent mortgage or from another source specializing in this type of loan. It is somewhat more risky and carries a higher interest rate.

Marketing

From the time a site has been selected, the developer has been marketing the project by attempting to find tenants or buyers. Aspects of many decisions (site location, landscaping, and building design) can be significant in attracting tenants or users. Advertisements in newspapers, personal contacts, and real estate brokers are all used to attract tenants. If a certain break-even level of rentals has not been reached within perhaps a year of completion, the project is likely to fail. The developer will lose the project to the financial institution holding the mortgage.

Building Operation

Building operation is the longest period in the life cycle of the building—it may be from twenty to more than a hundred years. The building is now almost fully occupied; the tenants are paying rents; and the developer, now owner, is paying the project's expenses such as, water, sewer, gas, maintenance, and administrative costs.

Income tax considerations become important during this phase in the development process. The United States tax system allows interest on the mortgage and an important factor called depreciation to be subtracted from the income from the building. This can result in a *tax shelter,* in which some actual profits are not taxed. This shelter was originally enacted by Congress as an incentive to encourage investment in buildings, but it also provides an advantage to a small group of building owners and investors that is not shared by the general public. Although such tax shelters are becoming more restrictive, they remain the target of much political criticism.

HOW BUILDING ECONOMICS AFFECTS DESIGN

As we have seen, changes in large-scale economic forces have resulted in considerable changes in the parameters and difficulty of development. The developer and architect should approach many of these factors in a cautious and deliberate manner for they seriously affect design decisions.

Land Factors and Site Planning

The first categories we shall examine in which economic factors are strongly related to design decisions are land factors and site planning. We mentioned earlier the increasing scarcity of developable sites and the extensive site search made by the developer. When a suitable site has been located, the architect plays a key role in planning the site so it can be a feasible development.

The cost of land is high and growing faster than any other cost factor in development. It can reach as much as a third of total development costs.[4] The developer, then, is required to use the land efficiently. Inefficient use can almost always make the development unfeasible. For example, if there are two acres selling for $100,000 in a modest neighborhood of $50,000 homes, a proposal for two homes would be unfeasible. The land alone would be $50,000 for each house, and the total cost for each completed house would be about $90,000. This would not be salable in that location. Ten homes on the two acres would sell. The land would be $10,000 per house, bringing the total cost to about $50,000, matching neighborhood values. If 20 houses were developed, the land cost for each would be $5,000 and the total cost of the house $40,000, producing an even higher probability of success for the project. If such zoning were permitted, and if the designs at such density found consumer acceptability, these latter proposals might work. In this way economics directs a proposal toward more intensive development or the *highest and best use* of the land.

The inducement for intensive land use presents difficult site planning problems for the architect. Many factors should be balanced by the architect and developer in producing site plans, including the following.

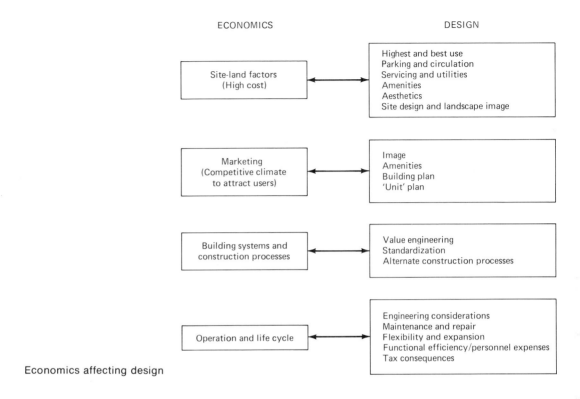

ECONOMICS   DESIGN

Site-land factors
(High cost)

Highest and best use
Parking and circulation
Servicing and utilities
Amenities
Aesthetics
Site design and landscape image

Marketing
(Competitive climate
to attract users)

Image
Amenities
Building plan
'Unit' plan

Building systems and
construction processes

Value engineering
Standardization
Alternate construction processes

Operation and life cycle

Engineering considerations
Maintenance and repair
Flexibility and expansion
Functional efficiency/personnel expenses
Tax consequences

Economics affecting design

1 *Highest and Best Use.* Can the intensity of the proposed development and its ancillary requirements (roads, parking, servicing, and amenities) be accommodated physically and aesthetically on this site? Here many basic assumptions about the project may be questioned and modified; among these might be the size of the project, the type of buildings proposed, and the amount of parking facilities required. A number of site-planning alternatives are usually proposed, and each is evaluated in terms of cost, function, and design considerations. The architect should be able to develop these alternatives and know the development implications of each. While it may be possible to accommodate intensive development legally and physically, the negative design implications may be economically harmful if potential tenants or buyers are not receptive to the project.

2 *Parking.* The type of parking (indoor, surface, or ramp) is a key decision, as is the number of spaces to be provided. Other considerations are the location of the

parking and automobile and pedestrian circulation. Site planning is too often oriented to parking, but it is also an important factor in project cost and user acceptance.

3 *Servicing.* How much is needed? Where should it be located? In some buildings, such as hospitals, servicing is a high-priority factor, and savings due to good planning can be significant.

4 *Amenities.* The quality and image of the amenities may be as important an economic factor to the user as cost. What types, if any, should be included? Where should these be located?

5 *Design.* Community and neighborhood concerns, such as materials, privacy, noise, and even style, should be addressed at the earliest stages of the development project. Community acceptance of the development, as well as user acceptance, is directly tied to design. Views should be a consideration, with the best views demanding a premium rate.

These problems associated with the use of land and their resolution, are the first, most inclusive, and least changeable decisions to be made. They determine the continuance of the development project, and, if it is continued, the pattern of many subsequent phases and decisions. Knowledge of all the economic and design variables and the scope of applicable solution types and of the consequences of the alternatives are critical in developing a workable design solution. The first detailed economic projections are made at this point and are based upon these land planning factors.

Market Factors

Notwithstanding the aptness of decisions related to land factors, judgments in the sphere of market factors can significantly affect the success of a development project. The architect's design solutions at all levels—site, building, and unit, and even correct choice of project signage—can generate interest and enthusiasm in potential tenants and users. Knowledge of the types of users, their characteristics, their needs and desires, and the design implications of these attributes are the basis for solutions.

The location of the project is often outside the architect's control. Experience with many projects, and many failures, has shown this to be the major influence in marketing the building. An old real estate adage is that the success and value of a project are determined by three things—location, location, and location.

The type of user to be attracted by the development is another key decision. Whatever the building type—housing, offices, stores, recreation—it does attract specific user groups. Examples in housing include the elderly, adults, families, and singles. Each implies a different set of design solutions in the areas of site, building, and unit.

The architect's role, once a site and user group has been defined, consists of responding to the relationships between the physical form of the building and the needs of the user groups with respect to the following categories.

Image of the Development. The provision of a distinct image for different user groups is a part of our culture. The image of a development project, especially in its façade and public places, provides strong cues to passersby, users, and potential users of the building. This image has the power to produce strong reactions and suggest connotations. These are the portions of the building that have proven to be the major focus for architectural experimentation, intellectualization, and creativity, sometimes in conflict with the layperson's image of the building or what the building should look like. The location, dominance, monumentality, modesty, materials, sounds, entrance, scale, and style are some of the stimuli to which the user or visitor responds.

This aspect of design is so sensitive that often the choice of architect is made on the basis of image alone, all else being equal. For instance, the architectural firm of Skidmore, Owings and Merrill is often chosen as architect for large corporate headquarters. Its designs are typically machinelike, precise, conservative, and predictable. Roche, Dinkeloo is another architectural firm doing work for corporate clients, but its product is strongly conceptual, more aggressive, or overwhelmingly modest, in any case unordinary. Confidence and precision will be present, but a less familiar, more exciting building may result. A corporation requiring a more innovative image might choose the latter firm, while a stable, established firm might choose the former.

Landscaping and site design provide strong signals for prospective users. Formality, scale, sequence, and image may go so far as to make the building secondary to the site and landscape, especially if the site has existing vegetation. The Ford Foundation Building in New York, by Roche, Dinkeloo, offers public spaces inside that are filled with junglelike trees and plants, thereby minimizing the interior building form. Similarly, the Oakland Museum in California (by the same firm) provides many terraces and plantings covering the building and downplaying its hard physical form and image.

Amenities. Amenities of various types offer a direct appeal to specific user groups. Extreme privacy and security can be one kind of amenity, opportunities for socializing and excitement can be another. An amenity can be a facility (a club or a pool) or a service (a doorperson). It can be private or in a public area. In some cases, the lack of amenities can be a plus because of the cost savings.

Building Plan. The means of circulation into and through the building is a design facet related to the market factors. The architect should manipulate it to respond to the user groups. In some buildings, notably stores, long circulation paths are preferred in order to expose the user to the most impulse-type merchandise. Some specialized stores may prefer circuitous and somewhat disorienting circulation. Gambling casinos are a prototypical example of this, using disorientation to the extent of not even providing clocks or a view to the outside. In housing, the type of circulation may vary widely. For instance, design for the same user groups may be different depending on whether the project is a rental or condominium. The length of the building, location, number of entries, and stair design are some other factors affecting marketing decisions related to building design.

Unit Plans. The unit is the area actually rented or purchased by the user or the tenant. This can be an apartment or condominium, hotel room, office space, or store. In each case specific design features will aid considerably in attracting or putting off potential tenants. The size and shape of the units, exposure and views, and finishes and equipment provided all affect rentability.

Given the parameters and tolerances within which to manipulate the form of the physical environment, the architect has a plethora of choices. This is the architect's primary role and dilemma—providing the judgment needed to be the most responsive to users. In the areas of land and market, we have seen how strongly these judgments and design solutions affect the development. In technical areas, the architect's judgment is also a key factor in the success of the building development.

Building Systems and Construction Processes
The final product of the architect's work is a set of detailed plans for putting the building together. Brick and mortar are the architect's final concern and the development's single highest cost. Though the developer will take an active role in decisions related to design and marketing, the architect is often deferred to in construction and technical factors. Because achieving project savings is so important to the developer, the architect's role is critical.

The architect's choices for construction systems and processes are based upon cost, time, and effect on the technical performance of the building. Analyzing alternatives and making choices in this area is sometimes called *value engineering*. A typical example is the choice between a steel or reinforced concrete structure. Steel can be erected rapidly, compared to concrete, but it could be a more costly material. It must be fireproofed to meet criteria set in building codes, whereas concrete is inherently fire resistant. The installation of utilities, floor thicknesses, size of floors, required spans, and building height are other criteria that must enter into this decision on the structural system. The decision may change from project to project, and from developer to developer, and as the costs of the various materials change, even from year to year.

The architect's judgments in the area of construction methods and processes, as distinct from subsystems choices, are strongly related to the economics of development. Prefabricated building components are often used. These large building elements, such as exterior wall panels, are factory-produced and delivered to the site for installation.

Savings in costly site labor and time can result, as well as better building quality. The effects of this method on design, the proximity of plants that manufacture these components, shipping costs, familiarity of on-site contractors with these products, and local regulations must be considered, however.

Some developers employ design/build firms for their projects. These firms combine both architectural and contractor activities and are adept at producing buildings especially responsive to the technical aspects of the development process. Their experience in construction is used to produce design solutions that can provide time and cost savings.

Some other construction processes that provide efficiency in the building process include fast tracking, in which portions of the building are constructed before final plans are completed. This can expedite the process to a significant degree. By eliminating the general contractor, the developer's organization is left to supervise, coordinate, and manage the building process, thereby providing some savings. Standardization within and even among development projects can effect cost and time savings by allowing the purchase of large quantities of materials and by making labor more efficient. For instance, the School Construction System Development project (SCSD) combined a number of California school districts and developed thirteen schools using many standardized components from six manufacturers.

The ultimate test of decisions in this technical area occurs when the bids come in. If the bids greatly exceed the estimated budget, the project, even at this stage, may be dropped. If they are somewhat over budget, careful modification of the design and specifications may occur so as not to impair the marketability of the project. These implications point out the vital role of the architect.

Life Cycle Cost Factors and Energy Considerations

Architectural decisions affect the building, its users, and its owners throughout its useful life—for 30, 40 or even over 100 years. All the decisions made in the areas previously mentioned—land, site, marketing, and construction—will contribute to the success of the project, both initially and throughout its life. The developer, often the owner of the project for years after its completion, is concerned with many expenses during this period of continued ownership, such as maintenance and repair, heating, modification and expansion, and personnel and administrative costs. Once again, decisions made by the architect and affecting building and site design will have crucial consequences during the life of the building.

The consideration of these factors, yet another layer of knowledge and expertise the architect should provide, is called *life cycle analysis*. It too has a significant impact on the project.

1 *Energy.* Initial design and technical decisions concerning orientation, perimeter, massing, exterior cladding, roof, insulation, mechanical equipment, controls, and lighting are some of the areas that affect energy use. Energy cost is now a significant percentage of total operating costs and will continue to rise. Savings or losses can be critical to the financial soundness of a project.

2 *Maintenance and Repair.* Certain design solutions that may have low construction costs may also have short useful lives. These can result in extensive repairs, eventual replacement, and tenant and owner discontent. On the other hand, higher initial costs can sometimes reduce or eliminate later replacement and repair. Carpeting, for instance, costs more than typically specified resilient tile flooring but hides dirt better. Thus it does not necessitate daily cleaning, thereby saving personnel costs, one of the highest expenses in building operations.

3 *Flexibility and Accommodation of Change.* Built-in flexibility, at considerably higher initial cost, may pay for itself many times over during the life of the building. Studies of hospitals, for instance, pinpoint the radiology area as the most rapidly changing and expanding area and one where flexibility is warranted. Other parts of the hospital need lesser degrees of flexibility.[5] The architect's knowledge of the actual experience of change in different functions for various building types can provide insights into the need for flexibility. On the other hand, flexible solutions may be developed and never utilized, costing more than they ever will save. For example, in some schools originally designed for flexibility, neither the present administration nor the teaching staff is aware that many components can be moved or changed.

4 *Functional Costs.* Initial design should take into account lifetime costs related to the functioning of the building. Again, using the example of a hospital, the largest single cost of running a hospital is personnel, and a major part of the personnel cost is involved in the circulation of food, linen, medicine, and equipment. Some recent designs have included complex and expensive automatic delivery systems that require fewer employees for their operation. The high initial cost of these systems is recovered quickly during the payback period, because of the savings in personnel expenses.

5 *Tax Considerations.* Tax considerations seriously affect design decisions, often in an adverse way. Owners of investment property are allowed to depreciate their buildings over their useful lives, to account for wear and tear on the structure. Typically, the useful life allowed is 40 years, although in reality the building would probably appreciate in value and perhaps be used for over a hundred years. Owners, anxious to make the most of their depreciation and tax shelter (including sheltering their nonbuilding income) attempt to show that their buildings have shorter useful lives. The primary means of proving a shorter life is to indicate that the construction used was less than the usual quality, or even poor quality. Thus, the built-in incentive for the developer and/or the owner is to cheapen the building. This is further reinforced because the tax law reduces the allowable shelter within 8 to 13 years, at which time the owner may find it advantageous to sell the building. The original owner, knowing of this relatively short-term benefit of ownership, will not encourage quality in the building construction even though the building may house occupants for many times this period of ownership. The architect, responsible for design in these circumstances, is certainly in a quandary.

Today these tax considerations often result in buildings of artifically low quality. This especially affects rental housing. Residents of this type of housing, often unable to buy their own homes, are relegated to lower-quality buildings, eventually resulting in major problems of maintenance, cost, and habitation.

ECONOMICS AFFECTING DESIGN: EXAMPLES

The increasingly adverse climate for development has nevertheless generated some positive responses. One response, as we saw, has been the necessity for more discriminating decisions by architects and developers in order to produce successful projects. This leads toward innovative developments—very different building types, processes, and designs—that seek out unexplored markets. These innovative responses are not only vital and exciting, but they are also beginning to have a major influence. Examples of these innovations are trends toward higher density housing, recycling of buildings, and the growing utilization of large interior spaces.

Higher-Density Housing
Some 69 percent of United States families presently live in single-family detached housing. But many families in following generations will not be able to afford this kind of housing. It will not be feasible, because of higher cost factors for land, construction, financing, and operation. A large part of future housing needs, therefore, will be met by higher-density housing, probably at two to three times current densities.[6]

Before the 1960s, multifamily housing starts (buildings with four units or more) were an inconsequential part of new housing, averaging about 10 percent of all new housing starts. As conditions for feasible developments grew more restrictive, multifamily units became for many families and developers the only recourse. Today this type of unit averages 40 percent of all housing starts. In some recent years, more multifamily housing has been built than single-family units.

A concomitant trend paralleling the growth of multifamily units has been the growth of condominiums. These allow persons to own a home—even in a multifamily building—say a unit on the thirtieth floor, for example. This ownership mitigates

Ponce de Leon Mews, Atlanta, by Surber-Newton-Barber. Thirteen condominium units on one acre, with one renovated unit, built around a well-landscaped courtyard (photo by Clyde May; owner/developer, Mews Development Corp.).

with some success the higher-density conditions in multifamily, semidetached, and townhouse developments. This form of ownership has other advantages, notwithstanding the density or form of the building. Exterior maintenance, painting, repairs, lawnmowing, and snow removal are taken care of as a service. Certain tax advantages, equivalent to those of home ownership, are retained. The unit can appreciate in value and it can be resold at any time.

It is no coincidence that the higher-density forms of housing and condominium ownership are growing in direct response to new economic circumstances. Expectations and lifestyles, and the ways buildings are developed and designed are changing. A growing portion of the population will be living in closer proximity yet will still require all the characteristics of "home"—image, identity, privacy, outdoor living areas—all within a neighborhood and community context.

Condominium or homeowners associations bring people together to share experiences and decisions about the community, its maintenance, amenities, and activities. An exciting potential here

is that this trend of higher density combined with condominium ownership will help the residents relate to each other in positive ways. The responsibility of common ownership, the ability to decide the future of a community, and the forming of commitments to influence the larger decisions are in a sense rejuvenating an American tradition of the town meeting.

That houses will be denser implies the increasing use of *maisonette housing,* as commonly found in England. In essence, a maisonette is a two-story unit, including the traditional separation of living and sleeping spaces but being entered from an upper floor—a townhouse in the air. This has already been used at several recent projects in the United States, such as Riverbend Housing on Roosevelt Island in New York City, the Coldstream Project in Baltimore, Maryland, and Cedar-Riverside in Minneapolis, Minnesota.

While higher densities and condominium ownership are a *fait accompli* in terms of their institutionalization and market penetration, there are still many unresolved issues, especially considering the

Islandia Townhouses, Alameda, California by Fisher-Friedman Associates (photo by Joshua Freiwald).

probability of their increasing pervasiveness. In a real sense these types of housing are still experimental. They have been widely used for only a few years, and they are still to be uniquely posited to respond to the United States culture in physical, social, and political terms.

Building Reuse

Another trend with dramatic impact on the environment is building reuse, also referred to as *adaptive reuse, recycling* or, more practically, *renovation*. The economic forces that have made development so difficult in the cities, primarily on the outskirts, have ironically provided an incentive for the redevelopment of older buildings, many with historical and architectural importance. Older sections of many cities, passed over in the eras of leapfrogging concentric development, are being rediscovered as bargains. Their lack of an attractive image, disrepair, age, high vacancy rate, and functional obsolescence (in terms of their originally intended use) make them attractive investments because of low

purchase prices. These older buildings are often in the original city cores, near present downtown areas, and are excellently built and crafted. They have a strength of character, scale, and architectural interest that are impossible to reproduce today. Innovative developers and highly imaginative architects have transformed many of these buildings, some on the brink of demolition, into successful enterprises. In the process they have preserved parts of the cities' building heritage and made them highly visible and accessible to the community.

Some of the first such developments were in San Francisco. Ghiradelli Square, an old chocolate factory, and the Cannery, an old canning factory, were redeveloped in the mid-1960s. Well located (near Fisherman's Wharf and San Francisco Bay), obsolete in terms of their original uses, and in disrepair, they were relatively inexpensive for the developer. Sophisticated shopping centers were created in both. The masonry of the original buildings was preserved to create a strong image. This was reinforced by the interior improvement of

The Cannery, San Francisco, by Esherick, Homsey, Dodge and Davis. In this retail center that was once a cannery, the existing brick walls are penetrated by circulation to reinforce the project's image (photo by Kathleen Kershaw; owner, Leonard V. Martin).

circulation and new construction in the same material and scale. Landscaping and site design, lighting, graphics, and amenities were included to provide excitement and vitality in these developments. They have become among the most popular and successful environments in San Francisco, generating other such projects there and elsewhere.

Other cities have experienced reuse of older structures. Pioneer Square in Seattle, Butler Square in Minneapolis, Canal Square in Washington, the Century (formerly a theatre) in Chicago, Fanneil Market in Boston, Trolley Square in Salt Lake City, Quaker Square in Akron, Ohio, and Larimer Square in Denver are all major examples of significant older buildings recycled into shopping environments.

Housing too has been developed in older buildings with previously different uses. In Boston, Long, Mercantile, and Lewis Wharfs have been converted into housing, just near downtown, with incredible harbor views. A large piano factory outside Boston was developed into housing. In New York City a former manufacturing plant was renovated into the Westbeth Artists Housing Cooperative. The Soho District, also in New York, is a historic area of early cast-iron manufacturing plants and now a prestigious location for loft living. As in San Francisco, all of these examples are well located in inner-city areas where buildings could be acquired inexpensively because of their economic and functional obsolescence. Of course, as these areas become fashionable again, the purchase price will increase.

The development potential of these older buildings has had an auspicious beginning. Many wonderful old buildings all over the United States are threatened because of their obsolescence—an obsolescence due in many cases to shortsightedness. The economic advantages of developing these older buildings are outstanding. Redevelopment costs can be less than those of new construction, because the land needs no improvements and foundations and exterior cladding are already in place.

Butler Square, Minneapolis, by Miller, Hanson, Westerbeck, Bell: Mixed use in a 1906 warehouse (photo by Phillip Mac-Millan James).

DEVELOPMENT AND BUILDING ECONOMICS

Long Wharf, Boston, by Anderson Notter Feingold Associates, one of a number of wharfs on Boston's waterfront converted to housing and retail use (photo by Randolph Langenbach).

Furthermore, construction and renovation time are much shorter, thereby reducing interim financing costs and producing income much earlier than in conventional new developments.[7]

The architect's role in the reuse of buildings is especially critical. Setting up apartments, shops, or offices in a building originally intended to be a factory, garage, or wharf is extremely difficult. It often involves devising imaginative design solutions, solving building code problems, evaluating the existing building in great detail, providing modern services, and completely revising circulation, while at the same time preserving as much of the original fabric as possible.

Special Interior Spaces

Before mechanical ventilation and satisfactory artificial lighting became common, courtyards and arcades were often used to bring natural light and air to the interior of buildings. This produced an era of magnificent interior building spaces, such as the Arcade Building in Cleveland, the Plankington Building in Milwaukee, the Pension Building in Washington, and Berlage's Bourse in Amsterdam. Turn-of-the-century railroad stations and many hotels are also examples of the use of these spaces. Technological advances and an inexorable economic squeeze on building development largely eliminated this spatial phenomenon. "Less is more" was taken more seriously by developers than architects. What began as a spatial and technological necessity, however, has been rediscovered as a feasible amenity in many new building projects.

This was made explicit first in architect and developer John Portman's Hyatt Regency Hotel in Atlanta, Georgia. A grand, 22-story, glass-covered atrium is the central focus of the project. It contains exposed, glass-enclosed elevators, hanging foliage everywhere, bars and restaurants, and appropriately large-scaled works of art.[8] The unparalleled success of this risky venture spawned more than a dozen other such atrium hotels. Many were designed and developed by Portman himself, including the Hyatt Regency Hotel in San Francisco and the Renaissance Center mixed-use complex in Detroit. These hotels are all in the luxury class, charging the highest rates and achieving very high occupancies. Much of this success is due to the atrium design and its amenities.

Larger interior spaces have also been used in regional shopping malls. The first was Southdale in Minneapolis, designed by Victor Gruen in 1956. The success of this innovation was immediate and over-whelming. Virtually all markets in the United States are now saturated with these centers. These shopping malls are typically linear, two-story spaces, with one or more focal areas along the spine. Large skylights in the public spaces are common, but few amenities are necessary, with the stores providing the entertainment. This formula is now changing in a variety of interesting ways, primarily because of economic pressures and competition.

Having saturated markets, such large centers are now forced to compete for public attention. Almost every weekend such events as antique shows, auto shows, children's shows, choirs, and bands are scheduled to attract patrons. Recently designed malls have even included ice-skating rinks in their large spaces, drawing crowds of both spectators and skaters. As the malls become more vital and attractive places, sales per square foot also increase substantially.

A third generation of shopping mall—the vertical mall—is now being developed in the center city, to compete with the suburban malls that had drained shoppers from these central areas. Water Tower Place in Chicago and Eaton Place in Toronto are recent and successful examples. Water Tower Place includes seven stories of shops around a glittering open space in which a set of four gemlike ele-

Hyatt Regency Hotel, San Francisco, by John Portman (photo by Alexandre Georges).

DEVELOPMENT AND BUILDING ECONOMICS

Water Tower Place by Warren Platner. The elegant mall of this vertical shopping center.

vators silently glide. Two vertical department stores are anchors in this mixed-use development that also includes a hotel, apartments, and offices.

Finally, the concept of malls is beginning to be used in a number of other building types. The Ford Foundation Headquarters pioneered its use in office buildings, and it has now filtered down to even modestly scaled office projects. The first instances of interior arcades in smaller community and neighborhood shopping developments, previously thought unfeasible, are beginning to be seen.

The growing use of this innovation is not entirely unexpected, given the many recent economic pressures on development. Competitive pressures in more saturated markets required innovations. Consumers appreciated the convenience and comfort of these spaces; land and site development costs required vertical centers; operational cost factors, especially the cost of energy, required fewer windows, emphasizing an interior orientation; building cost factors led to a central concentration of articulation and amenities; and developers saw that it worked. Such successful innovations have been quickly disseminated, developed, and institutionalized in a wonderful way.

THE ARCHITECT AS DEVELOPER: A TREND

We have seen the intimate ties between architectural and development decisions. Innovative, sensitive, and stimulating concepts lead to projects that reflect a synthesis of these two areas. Architects who are taking a strong role in this process are producing meaningful buildings, sometimes with themselves as developers. John Portman, an architect

and developer, has already been mentioned, but many other firms are participating in this trend. Kaplan and McLaughlin of San Francisco have developed and designed a number of building reuse projects; Miller, Waltz, Diedrich of Milwaukee have designed a number of handsome downtown structures developed by Jordan Miller, one of the firm's principals; ELS Design Associates of Berkeley and New York have become specialists at working with developers in complex, mixed-use, in-town projects. These are but a few, more familiar examples. The times are demanding special expertise, and these and many other firms are producing a new generation of projects in response.

Water Tower Place by Warren Platner. Greenery and water attract shoppers and enhance the approach to the atrium space.

NOTES

1. Because economic factors are ubiquitous in building development, the phrase "bottom line" is often used to refer to the economic consequences of development and design decisions. The bottom line literally means the last line on a building's estimated operating statement, indicating the profit (or loss) remaining for the owner as in, "What will adding a fountain do to the bottom line?"

2. The most often cited example is John Portman, whose projects are well described in *The Architect as Developer* (New York: McGraw-Hill, 1976) by John Portman and Jonathan Barnett.

3. C. W. Griffin's *Development Building: The Team Approach* (Washington, D.C.: American Institute of Architects, 1972) is an excellent introduction to the development process. One of the few texts portraying the reality of development situations is *Case Studies in Building Development* (Menlo Park, Calif.: Property Press, 1973) by Stephen E. Roulac.

4. Land costs exceeded 25 percent of the cost of new single-family detached housing in 1976, compared with 12 percent in 1950, according to Federal Housing Administration figures.

5. A strong case for built-in flexibility in certain functional areas of hospitals is made by H. McLaughlin, J. Kibre, and M. Raphael, "Patterns of Physical Change in Six Existing Hospitals," in *Environmental Design: Research and Practice,* Proceedings of the 3d EDRA Conference, ed. William Mitchell (Los Angeles, 1972).

6. A pungent and concise summation of these trends is found in *The Nation's Housing, 1975–1985* (Cambridge, Mass.: Joint Center for Urban Studies of M. I. T. and Harvard University, 1977) by Bernard Frieden and Arthur Solomon. See especially chapter 5, "The Costs of Homeownership."

7. Herbert McLaughlin, "Preservation Costs in Commercial Buildings," in *Economic Benefits of Preserving Old Buildings* (Washington, D. C.: Preservation Press National Trust for Historic Preservation, 1976).

8. Portman and Barnett, *The Architect as Developer.*

FOR FURTHER READING

Frieden, Bernard, and Solomon, Arthur. *The Nation's Housing 1975–1985.* Cambridge, Mass.: Joint Center for Urban Studies of M.I.T. and Harvard University, 1977.

Golemon , Harry A., ed. *Financing Real Estate Development.* Washington, D. C.: American Institute of Architects, 1974.

Griffin, C.W. *Development Building: The Team Approach.* Washington, D.C. American Institute of Architects, 1972.

McMahan, John. *Property Development.* New York: McGraw-Hill Book Co., 1976.

National Trust for Historic Preservation in the United States. *Economic Benefits of Preserving Old Buildings.* Washington, D.C.: Preservation Press, National Trust for Historic Preservation, 1976.

Portman, John, and Barnett, Jonathan. *The Architect as Developer.* New York: McGraw-Hill Book Co., 1976.

Roulac, Stephen E. *Case Studies in Property Development.* Menlo Park, Calif.: Property Press, 1973.

Seldin, Maury, and Swesnik, Richard H. *Real Estate Investment Strategy.* New York: John Wiley & Sons, Wiley-Interscience, 1970.

Zeckendorf, William, and McCrary, ed. *Zeckendorf.* New York: Holt, Rinehart & Winston, 1970.

CHAPTER 6

Site Planning and Design

Felicity Brogden

The architect's primary responsibility lies with the design of buildings, enclosures for human activities. However, buildings do not exist in isolation; they exist in a spatial, behavioral, and perceptual context. Thus, the architect has a direct responsibility for the relationship between building design and the building site and locale. This area of concern is termed site planning or site design. In fact, professional roles are sometimes defined in terms of scale, with parallel dimensions of building-site-locale-community and architect, landscape architect, urban designer, urban planner. Site design, then, involves the architect, landscape architect and urban designer, focusing on the relationships between the building and its site, and between the site and its locale. Specifically, the architect's role may involve site selection (finding the best site for a given activity), site evaluation (evaluating the suitability of a particular site for different activities), and site design (making the appropriate fit between building and site, and between the exterior spaces between buildings). This chapter addresses the process and substance of site planning and site design.

Site planning is the art of ordering the man-made and natural environments to support human activities. The study of site planning is often organized into two related components, the natural environment and man-made environment. The natural environment is conceived of as an ecological system of water, air, energy, land, vegetation, and life forms that interact to form a community that adapts and evolves as the environment changes. Human activities form an important part of this ecological system. In development, therefore, the concern is to maintain an essential harmony and to avoid exceeding the natural capacity of the system to support human activity. For example, a good site design enhances human activity settings while respecting the indigenous qualities of the site.

The man-made environment comprises the built forms of the city, the physical fabric and its spatial arrangement together with the social, political, and economic behavior patterns that shape the physical environment. These two perspectives are interdependent. Often, the built environment involves a deliberate overriding of the natural environment. For example, cities involve extensive infrastructure systems for water, power, transportation, storm and sanitary sewers, and such. The concern here in site design is to ensure that a site relates appropriately to these man-made systems. Thus, site design involves relationships with both natural and made systems.

Site context may be categorized also as exurban, suburban, and urban. Obviously, the natural environment is most important in exurban sites. Human activity must be accommodated without damage to the ecosystem. At the other extreme, urban site design deals primarily with relationships with built environment systems, where the natural system has been purposely overridden. In this case, the local override depends on an environmentally balanced larger area. Planning suburban sites, where environmental damage has too often been the rule, involves sensitivity to both concerns, including the design of infrastructure systems.

THE SITE-PLANNING PROCESS

In site planning, as in other forms of architectural problem solving, a rational and critical process is required. Although the process shown here appears to be linear, in reality it is iterative. For example, while the client sets the basic objectives, these cannot be defined fully until the site analysis has been completed, with site potentials, constraints, and design concepts identified. At the same time, the site analysis cannot be conducted until the basic objectives have been established. Similarly, site analysis and program development are integrally related.

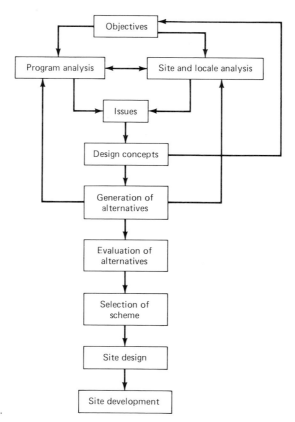

The site-planning process.

Objectives

An understanding of the client and the client's role in the planning process is the first step. The client sets the general goals for the program; the architect has a direct responsibility to the client. However, the client may not be the final user. For example, many large residential developments are packaged by developers for sale to final residents. In such a case the architect must recognize a responsibility to both the developer and the ultimate user, identifying and balancing their needs. The architect must also work within the institutional framework of the community, including a range of public policies and fiscal and legislative controls that affect the use of the site. For example, zoning and subdivision regulations and building codes control the use to which a site may be put. The objective of this public intervention is the regulation of individual free-market actions to protect the general health, safety, and welfare of the larger community. The final group involved in site design objectives includes the local and adjacent residents and/or land owners; they are concerned with the impact of new development or redevelopment on the immediate area. The architect-site designer must consider the objectives of all these (sometimes competing) interests.

Program Analysis

Program development is based on an understanding of the needs of all the client groups in relation to the activities to be accommodated (internal and external spatial requirements), and the spatial and temporal relationships among activities and the physical connectors (paths, roads, walkways) needed to make these linkages.

The process of site programming is essentially that of all architectural programming—involving the systematic determination of required activity patterns and the physical or functional responses to those patterns. Program patterns are often studied and presented in diagrammatic form and are developed and refined concurrently with the site analysis.

Site Analysis

All spaces, interior and exterior, are designed to support one or more specific activities. The behavioral qualities of an activity will influence the form that the space takes. Conversely, the form of the space affects people's perception of the space and hence the way they use it. Thus, there is an integral relationship between behavior, perception, and form. Site analysis and design focuses on these relationships in terms of the building on the site, and of the site in the community.

Site analysis requires the systematic consideration of three major contexts:

1 The spatial context of the site (natural and made).

2 The behavioral context (the social and economic activity patterns of site and locale, with the public policies that affect site development).

3 The *perceptual context* (perceptions and use of space).

The task is to develop an ordered arrangement of spaces with a coherent visual image, compatible with the carrying capacity of the site and behavioral needs of the users and the locale.

THE BEHAVIORAL ENVIRONMENT AND PUBLIC INFRASTRUCTURE

The site designer must look beyond the boundaries of the site to study the spatial distribution of social and economic activities and linkages in the locale. Every land use reacts to, and functions within, a multidimensional environment, both spatially and institutionally. The spatial environment for a site includes both the larger community within which the subject activity functions, and the more immediate, adjacent area. In each case, the concern is with the nature of the relationship, the type of flow (vehicles, pedestrians, goods), the direction of flow, and the type of access route needed to accommodate the flow.

Urban Activity Patterns

Urban areas are characterized by population concentration around one or more central points and along major transportation routes, with a gradient of concentration from the highest densities in the center to the lowest at the fringe. Concentration occurs because of the need for people to interact economically and socially; hence the need for accessibility due to the friction of distance. Friction of distance refers to the time/distance costs imposed on access by the prevailing transportation technology. For example, the friction of distance was much greater in the nineteenth century walking city than in the automobile metropolis of today. The tendency to concentrate produces competition for the centrally located sites with high accessibility, traditionally the downtown or central business district in a radial city. This competition is reflected in the land values and in the density of development.

Traditionally, three related models have been put forward as generalized explanations of the spatial organization of activities in urban areas, based on the concept of competition for accessibility.[1] While the patterns they suggest differ, most of the differences can be accounted for by the different times in which they were developed and thus the differing transportation and economic conditions. It is important for the site designer to understand the forces that create an urban activity pattern of zones, sectors, and nuclei. In selecting a sector or locale for a specific program, the site designer should understand that each use attempts to locate itself within the city to maximize its environmental conditions at a price it can afford.

Local Activity Patterns

Every sector and the locales or neighborhoods within it constitute a unique location and environment. Each is composed of a set of stra-

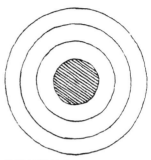

CONCENTRIC RING

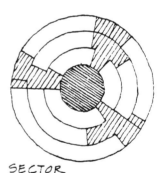

SECTOR

MULTIPLE NUCLEI

Urban spatial patterns.

tegic characteristics in terms of the activity mix and physical setting. Individual activities and groups of activities react to the specialized sector and neighborhood environments and their spatial distribution within the urban network, since all activities have different needs in terms of the activity mix that can provide the best support. For example, residential areas tend to be homogeneous; homes are predominantly single-family, duplex, or multifamily. The compatible uses in a single-family neighborhood are those that help support the nuclear family lifestyle (schools, convenience stores, churches, community centers, neighborhood bars). Incompatible uses include those that generate heavy traffic, reducing the safety of the streets and invading the privacy and quiet of the neighborhood (heavy industry or major public institutions such as a hospital or university). Alternatively, some activities rely heavily on a heterogeneous use mix for survival. For example, a retail shopping center depends on a broad mix of complementary activities for success (professional offices, banks, restaurants, entertainments), and heavy traffic circulation and parking is essential.

One technique for analyzing both the local and urban activity environment of a site involves mapping the spatial distribution of the related activities and the nature of the access linkages. Such a diagram notes the following factors:

1 The location of the related activities in the locale and urban area.
2 The location of incompatible activities in the locale.
3 The direction of the flows (inward, outward, two-way) among activities.
4 The frequency of interaction (daily, weekly, monthly).
5 The access route (pedestrian, bus, automobile, train).

This type of diagram may be used as a basis for evaluating the suitability of different locales in terms of the compatibility of the use mix, proximity of related activities, and quality of access. In site design, these diagrams form the basis for evaluating opportunities, constraints, and deficiencies in the local activity and access pattern, all of which must be addressed in the site design.

Finally, in analyzing the spatial distribution of activities, the site designer should be aware that the pattern of zones, sectors, nuclei, and locales is not a static one. It is subject to constant change for a variety of reasons:

1 Changes in the location of related activities.
2 Changes in transportation technology.
3 Obsolescence of the site plan or structures.

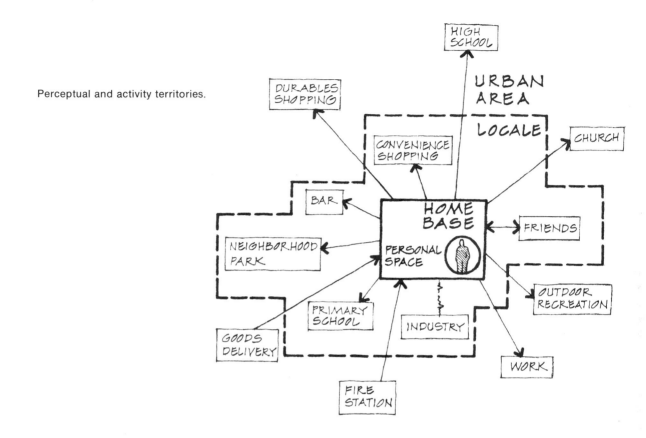

Perceptual and activity territories.

4 Changes in market demand for the activity.

5 Changes in the activity mix through infiltration of incompatible uses.

6 Changes in public policy.

Thus, in site selection and evaluation, the search is for an environment that can provide a compatible activity mix and complementary physical setting in the long term.

Transportation and Circulation

The utility of any site is largely a function of its accessibility; circulation systems facilitate linkages that relate activities in space. Flows of different types use different systems. Traffic flow, parking facilities, and pedestrian flow are essentially part of a pattern of flows of people, while utilities are flows of energy, waste, and water.

The vehicular circulation system is a primary element in structuring a site plan. Circulation systems are not haphazard; they form distinct hierarchical patterns. The spatial pattern that this hierarchy takes varies. The major patterns are the grid, radial, linear, organic, and combinations of these.

The street system is one of the most expensive and visually intrusive elements of site design. It must form a logical hierarchy of flow within the site, while connecting with the existing local and community transportation system. In general, street systems should be efficient in terms of cost, minimal in visual impact, sensitive to the site's natural features, and easy to comprehend. The storage of vehicles is as important as their movement. Most municipal codes demand self-sufficiency for parking in any large-scale development. Given the size of automobiles, storage can become a major use on a site. Car storage can be visually obtrusive unless it is located sensitively in relation to the topography. Yet, it must also be related to the activity pattern. The layout of a parking lot is dictated by the movements and dimensions of automobiles and must accommodate the largest vehicles using the site, generally fire and service trucks.

Walking is still the most frequent means of movement for many people, particularly the young and the elderly. Thus, the pedestrian system forms an important link, relating activities on site to the local network. It may be a major structuring element in site design. Like a flow of water, pedestrian movement has a fluid momentum. Pedestrians will follow the line of least resistance, shortening distances by cutoffs, sweeping wide on curves, eddying about obstacles, and forming pools above and below restrictive channels such as stairs or corridors. In analyzing pedestrian movement it is important to differentiate between different types. Pedestrians may be purposeful (walking to work) or they may be casual (taking a Sunday afternoon stroll). The purposeful pedestrian takes the line of least resistance, while the cas-

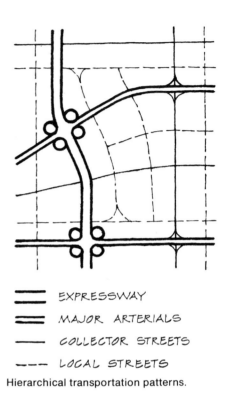

EXPRESSWAY

MAJOR ARTERIALS

COLLECTOR STREETS

LOCAL STREETS

Hierarchical transportation patterns.

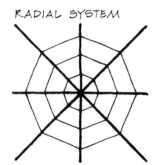

RADIAL SYSTEM

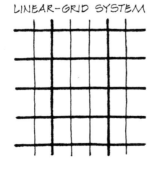

LINEAR-GRID SYSTEM

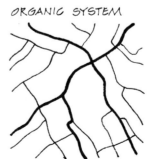

ORGANIC SYSTEM

Diagram of transportation patterns.

ual pedestrian may take a meandering course. Slow, casual movement engenders interest in detail; the stroller explores with the senses and may be deflected or encouraged by visual attractions, changes in level, or the texture of the paving. Deliberate movement, however, demands safe, direct, functional access between activities.

In this context, the site design can fix the path, control the flow, and shape the environment. The objective in designing the pathway system should be to develop a safe, legible, functional sequence that is visually stimulating and expressive of the character of the site. An excellent example of a well-designed pedestrian path system is the site plan for Radburn, New Jersey, a residential development designed by Clarence Perry in the 1920s. The plan provides a safe pedestrian environment by separating the pedestrian and vehicular systems. The pedestrian system is also legible, visually stimulating, and socially functional, linking the groups of houses together.

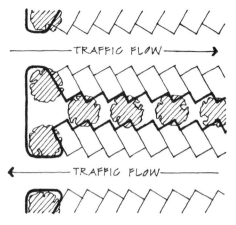

Sixty-degree parking and traffic flow

Radburn, New Jersey.

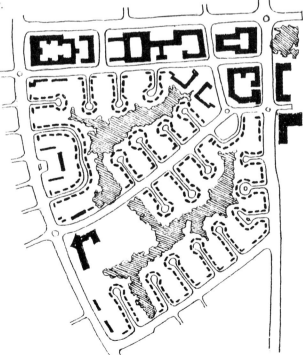

Utilities

Utility systems are important to site design because they often represent a major cost of site development; they must accommodate the urban environment where the natural system has been overridden. Storm and sanitary sewers, water, and energy (gas or electricity) must all be available on the site and be accommodated in the site design. The availability of such utilities on a site cannot be assumed; lines may or may not exist, with or without capacity. For example, as concerns over energy and the environment grow, many communities are refusing to extend their already overloaded sewer systems out to the suburbs. New hook-ups for natural gas are limited. Therefore, it is important to check the availability and capacity of all utilities in the site analysis.

In site design, the utility lines should be integrated with the other circulation systems in order to develop an efficient site plan. Increasingly, the trend is to place utility and communication lines underground, directly related to the street and sidewalk system and utilizing the same right of way.

Institutional Controls

The site designer exercises only partial control over the design environment in relation to the spatial distribution of related activities and linkages. The design environment is limited by a range of land use and environmental public policies and controls that specify the type of development allowed in an area and the way a specific site may be developed for any one use. These controls range from federal programs controlling the quality of the environment (for example, the National Environmental Policy Act of 1970 requires that any development receiving federal funding submit an environmental impact statement)[2] to state and regional land use and environmental programs (many of which are based on federal programs), to local municipal zoning and building codes (which control the use of the land and the design and layout of the site plan and structures).

Most of the legislative power to control the use and development of land has traditionally been vested in the local community as the appropriate level of government to deal with the detailed issues of land use planning and control. These policies and controls have a major impact on site design, although it is important to note the trend to increased state and federal control of land use in ecologically sensitive areas and areas subject to intense development pressure.

At the local level, a range of policy plans and legislative controls place significant restrictions on the site design environment. First, many municipal governments and planning commissions prepare master land use and transportation plans as official policy guides for future development decisions. These are generally comprehensive but flexible blueprints for the future development of the community that both protect and enhance the public welfare and serve as a basis for the development of related municipal policies and controls. In general, all private and public development should coincide with the master or comprehensive plan. A series of regulating policies and legislative controls, including the official street map, capital improvements program, zoning ordinance, subdivision regulations, and the building code, serve as tools to implement the master plan.

The official street map contains the layout of all existing and planned streets and street right-of-ways. New developments must be designed with reference to this map, providing streets where appropriate and connections between the site and the street system.

The capital improvements program is a plan for public infrastructure investment, in five-year increments, and includes sewer systems, water systems, streets, sidewalks, tree planting, municipal buildings, parks, and other public facilities. Often, schools are considered separately, although they are a vital part of a comprehensive capital expenditure program in a growth area. The capital program is a plan for the provision of facilities and services that are necessary for site development. In suburban fringe site situations, the capital program affects the development potential of different locations based on the staged construction of new public services. In urban sites, it contributes to the analysis of the local environment, detailing the level of maintenance and continued commitment to the area by the municipality.

The zoning ordinance is a legal document dividing land in a community into broad use areas or districts (commercial, residential, industrial) in conformance with the master plan. The ordinance, by separating activities and classifying properties, enhances the security of property owners by helping to shape the land values and prevent certain conflicts of safety and nuisance. In addition, the ordinance regulates the way that a site is developed; it may control the location of buildings on the site, their size and height, the parking requirements, and acceptable signage.

Broadly speaking, the zoning ordinance is as important to the site as the building code is to the building. In recent years zoning has played a growing role in structuring the site designer's decisions. Rapid urban growth has led to increased use of this legal tool to control the direction, rate, and type of growth. Yet, the isolation of land into homogeneous zones can be contradictory to the nature of human activity patterns. Activities typically mix and interact as one contributes to another or succeeds it in space. For this reason, recent years have seen the introduction of performance zoning. Performance zoning outlines a set of acceptable environmental standards for an area relating to noise level, traffic flows, density of development, and the like, but it is flexible about the permitted use mix, providing that the mix meets the environmental standards. This trend is of advantage to site designers in that it increases flexibility in an otherwise increasingly rigid institutional environment.

Subdivision is the legal process of dividing undeveloped land into lots for development and providing the lots with public improvements such as streets, utilities, and open space. Subdivision regulations ensure the orderly relationship between private development and the required public infrastructure. They set the minimum design standards for required improvements which include the following:

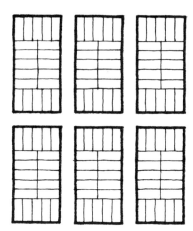

Rigid subdivision pattern.

1 Streets—street layout, street grades, curbs, gutters, sidewalks, street signs, and tree planting.

2 Lots—lot sizes, building lines, and setbacks.

3 Utilities—sewer, water, electricity, gas, and telephone.

The regulations specify which physical improvements the developer must provide and which will be provided by the municipality. Within this framework, the site designer controls the location and design of both public and private improvements. As with zoning, subdivision regulations have tended towards uniformity and rigidity, resulting in large-lot, low-density development and/or monotonous site plans.

Recent trends in response to this have seen the introduction of planned unit development ordinances that suspend the zoning and subdivision regulations, setting up instead a set of environmental performance standards relating to overall density of development, provision of public space, noise, traffic flow, and so on. This allows greater flexibility in the design of the site plan.

Planned unit development pattern.

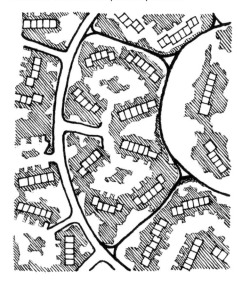

The building code, like the zoning ordinance, is based on police power. Although the zoning ordinance is often specific to an individual community, the study and preparation of a tailormade building code has proved too difficult and costly for most municipalities to undertake. Therefore, many communities have adopted regional or national uniform building codes. These codes regulate minimum standards for structures with regard to fire protection, safety, plumbing, structure, heating, ventilation, and location of the structure on the site.

Finally, restrictions may be placed on the use of the site through the property rights of the freehold deed. The controls may be restrictive covenants that limit the uses to which the site or structure can be put. Alternatively, the control may be an easement, or the sale of a single property right for a specific purpose, for example, the right of access across a site or the right of an unrestricted view.

THE SPATIAL ENVIRONMENT

Natural Elements
An understanding of the natural elements of the site and its locale (climate, water, soil, topography, vegetation, and animal life) is important to site design. The locale must be seen first as a functioning ecosystem with a natural carrying capacity to be respected in site development, and secondly as a set of indigenous spatial qualities to be related to the activity program and expressed in the site design.

Climate. Climate may be viewed at two levels—regional and site. Each site has a characteristic regional climate that is beyond the control of the designer but that affects the relationship between the building and the site. This regional climate is expressed as a series of average data that includes winter and summer sun angle (azimuth), days of sunlight, amount of sunlight, days of precipitation, amount of precipitation, wind direction, wind force, and wind frequency. To ignore the effects of climate and the natural or passive siting mechanisms available for the design of energy-conscious usable space is to overlook a vital set of elements that shape the way a space is understood and used. In this context, the regional climate will influence the orientation of structures and spaces and their exposure or protection from the summer and winter sun and the prevailing winter and summer winds.

Microclimates are site specific, varying within the site itself. On an undeveloped site the microclimate will be affected by two factors—the ground surface and the landform. Site design for comfortable activity spaces requires that the designer directly observe and measure the microclimates generated on the site. Ground-surface materials absorb heat, store it, and radiate it back into the atmosphere over a period of time. However, not all heat is absorbed; some is reflected back into the atmosphere immediately. Different materials have different reflection, absorption, and radiation characteristics. For example, surface water absorbs heat, stores it, and radiates it back into the atmosphere very slowly; this acts to even out the daily and seasonal temperature variations on adjacent sites. Vegetation ab-

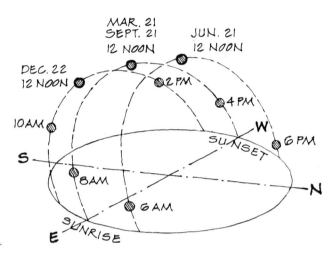

Sun path: equinox and solstice.

sorbs heat, air, and moisture for its nutrition cycle; it then slowly transpires through its leaves, emitting oxygen and pure water back into the atmosphere. This has a cooling effect on the air temperature and may alter a microclimate in the summer by several degrees. Trees and plant cover can also modify a microclimate by providing shade from the summer sun. Deciduous trees are ideal for this purpose, since they provide shade in the summer but shed their leaves in the winter, allowing the warmth of the winter sun to filter through.

The landform of the site (its depressions, plains, hills, and valleys) is critical to the microclimate for two reasons—as it affects air movement, and orientation to the sun. The impact of topography on air movement is twofold. First, winds are greater on the leeward side of a slope than on the windward, which makes the lee slope a sheltered site location. Second, as air cools at night it becomes saturated with moisture and sinks towards the bottom of the valley or depression, thereby leaving the higher slopes warmer at night. This can be advantageous when siting in either hot or cold climates. In relation to the sun, depending on the latitude, season, and hour of the day, maximum solar radiation is received by the ground surface that is perpendicular to the sun's rays. Therefore, a southern slope will receive more sun than a flat plain.

The study of urban microclimates is a new and complex field. In general, urban microclimates are affected by several factors. First, the high reflectivity and low conductivity of manufactured materials such as concrete, brick, and asphalt and the high density of buildings generate large amounts of heat, creating a "heat island" effect that results in upward air currents. Second, these convection currents generate

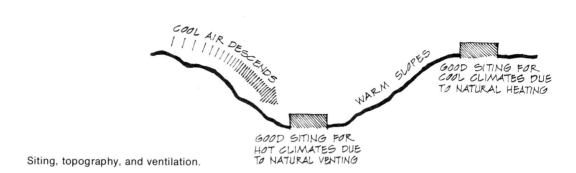

Siting, topography, and ventilation.

clouds; the air pollution created by industry and automobile exhaust emissions adds impurities to the clouds, creating a haze that reduces the amount of solar radiation reaching the earth's surface. Finally, the massing, siting, and form of buildings affect air flow. In general, tall, thin buildings create intensive eddying and turbulence on their downwind sides if placed in the path of the prevailing wind, while thicker buildings reduce the eddying effect. Airflow between buildings is very complex and requires wind tunnel studies.[3]

Vegetation and Wildlife. In analyzing the plant and animal life existing on a site, the designer must address two issues—first, the nature of the ecosystems and their sensitivity to development, and second, the design potential that these natural forms offer.

As an ecosystem, the vegetation on the site must be viewed as an interdependent association that will vary with the climate, region, and soil type. All plant associations are a delicate balance of competing and cooperating species, occupying three levels or niches in the habitat: trees, shrubs, and ground cover. All such associations are also sensitive to change, and their survival will depend on the way that the site is developed; some are more sensitive than others. For example, wetlands constitute one of the most sensitive associations. They play

Plant community.

a major role in the hydrological cycle, acting as a sponge to provide a long-term source of replenishment for groundwater. Because development inevitably brings about change in even the hardiest communities, the site analysis should identify the most sensitive communities that must be respected in the site design.

Vegetation is also a major indigenous site potential. Plants are a primary landscaping material; the variety of scale, texture, color, and shape, together with the seasonal changes, make them an ideal material for defining exterior space. There are three levels that can be manipulated. Trees can be used to create a vertical plane for enclosure, to screen objectionable views, to create privacy, and to protect the climate of the space. Shrubs may be used for texture, color, and variety in a vertical plane and to create partial enclosure. Groundcover (grasses) forms the base plane and in this context is an important surface element, defining the quality of the space by its texture and color. In site design the choice of new planting must be guided by the fit with the existing plants.

In addition to plant associations, each site supports an animal community in interdependent association with the plant community. The equilibrium of the animal habitat will be upset by development. The existing animal communities must be located and identified, and their basic needs for survival must be understood and respected (for example, migration trails that may cross the site should be accommodated).

Topography. The landform or topography of a site shapes its development in three ways. First, it represents an ongoing geomorphological system subject to change through weathering. Second, it includes a slope or plane that sets engineering constraints on development. Last, it represents an indigenous site potential.

Spatial landscaping material.

ORNAMENTAL TREES TO VIEW   TREES AND SHRUBS TO PROVIDE BOUNDARY   TREES TO PROVIDE PRIVACY   SHADE TREES TO WALK UNDER

The topography of a site is the result of two processes. First, geological processes have affected the site, its formation, landform, and the type of rock beneath the soil surface (volcanic action, metamorphic action, etc.); and second, various weathering processes of erosion and deposition (chemical, fluvial, glacial, and wind) mold the landforms into characteristic new forms. It is important to understand the geomorphological processes at work on a site, and to understand the origins of the landforms that should be respected in the site design. The relationship between the surface and subsurface strata is also important in identifying the engineering capabilities of the site (that is, its bearing strength).

When the engineering capabilities of a site are analyzed, the slope characteristics play an important part in identifying areas suitable for development. The ability to use a slope varies in relation to the activity. The site analysis should categorize the site in terms of areas of different percentages of slope and their ability to support different activities. (The percentage of slope is calculated by estimating the vertical fall in a horizontal distance of 100 feet.) In general, slopes under 4 percent are classified as flat and suitable for intense activity and development. Slopes between 4 and 10 percent are moderate and suitable for light activity, while slopes over 10 percent are steep and unsuitable for activity development. Finally, when analyzing the engineering characteristics of slopes, we must remember that topography and soil are integrally related; different soil types have different structures and hence different abilities to maintain slope. For example, clay is a fine particle soil that slumps at a low percentage of slope.

The indigenous landform can be strong design element. Each site has a unique topographical form and an identifiable character or pivotal feature to which the design should respond. The site analysis should map these pivotal features (views, overlooks, enclosures, or sequences).

The topography may dictate the basic spatial relationships between activities on the site, if the design is to take full advantage of natural features. If the given topography is unacceptable in some way, then it may be altered. The ground can be molded to enhance the design, providing that the ecological transition between existing and new forms is harmonious. Landscape grading may be used for a variety of purposes—to provide visual stimulation, to ensure privacy, or to serve as insulation from winter winds.

The site designer must work in three-dimensional space, represented in models or on two-dimensional plan drawings. The third dimension is represented on a plan drawing by the use of isolines

Topography and contours.

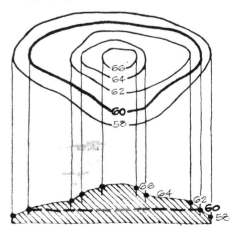

(lines of equal distance) called "contour lines." The contour lines represent elevations above mean sea level and are drawn at equal intervals to form a topographic map.

Soil. Soils are derived from the parent material or landform and thus vary widely. The basic composition of soil is a combination of weathered rock and plant remains. The type of soil strongly influences the location, form, and structure of human settlement but does not dictate it. Soil structure qualities limit development potential only until the economic demand for dense use development is sufficient to permit extensive investment in foundations and structures capable of overcoming the limitations of the soil. Particles of soil are classified in two major ways—by grain size, and as being organic and inorganic. The soil has importance for the site designer for three reasons—first, ecologically, as a medium for the support of plant life; second, architecturally, as a medium for the support of structures; and third, as an indigenous site potential.

The U.S. Department of Agriculture Soil Conservation Service classifies and surveys soils with respect to support of both plant life and development. Soils are categorized in broad types based on geology, climate, and their organic origins; these types are subdivided into regional and subregional series and still further, according to the texture of the surface soil. The surveys are most important to site planning. In addition, many sites are surveyed by a series of test borings, which reveal the important attributes of the soil (bearing strength and presence of subsurface water) at exact locations.

The important soil attributes for plant life are drainage, organic content, acidity (pH value), and the availability of nutrients such as nitrogen. Suitability for development is based on stability, drainage, and load-bearing capacity. In this context, the size of the particles of soil—from gravel to silts to sands to clays—is important. For example, gravel soils are generally well drained, stable, and capable of bearing heavy loads, while silt becomes unstable when wet, heaves when frozen, and has limited bearing capacity.

Finally, as a fundamental site amenity, earth and rock symbolize the relationship of people to the natural environment. Rock outcrops and other topographic features that are indigenous to the site may be used to impart this relationship of continuity and harmony.

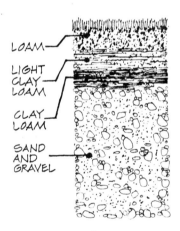

Typical soil profile.

Water. The site designer must have a knowledge of the properties and presence of water on a site for several reasons. First, water is important as a base element in the support of all life forms; second, surface and subsurface water affect the development potential of the site; and third, water can be an indigenous site amenity.

One important aspect of site water involves the runoff and percolation of surface water to the groundwater table. Runoff occurs when the precipitation exceeds the infiltration of water into the soil. The amount of runoff will be affected by the amount and timing of the precipitation, the nature of the ground surfaces, the amount of vegetation, and the topography. When surface water runs off, it flows downslope, perpendicular to the line of the contour, first as a film across the land and then gradually under natural conditions, collecting in gullies, streams, and rivers. Therefore, an understanding of the natural drainage pattern is important in site analysis. A runoff diagram constructed from the contour map can quickly demonstrate the drainage pattern.

In addition, it is important to note where drainage from other upstream sites crosses the subject site, and the impact of the subject site drainage on downstream sites. In general, the rate of surface runoff from a development should not exceed the rate of runoff from natural cover. The designer should try to maintain a positive drainage pattern with minimal modification to the natural pattern. Water should flow away from buildings and roads and should not be concentrated in gullies or valleys unless additional provision has been made for the flow. The intent is to keep water flowing freely but not so fast as to cause erosion. This often requires recontouring of the surface and the provision of storm sewers where the volume would otherwise cause erosion.

The source of most subsurface water is rain and snow. After runoff, evaporation, and transpiration, the remaining water infiltrates the soil. Some of this water collects in the root hairs of plants and around soil particles as soil moisture. The rest percolates through openings in the soil and rock until it reaches a zone where all voids are completely filled with water; this is called the "water table," and the water in this zone is called "groundwater." Normally, the water table is a sloping surface that approximates the ground level above, sloping down gradually to surface water bodies where it reaches the ground surface. Its depth below ground varies significantly, depending on the season and the amount of rainfall.

Groundwater is important for sustaining water supply and vegetation. It provides the base supply for surface rivers and streams in periods of drought. It also provides the water supply for human settlement, through artesian wells and pumps. While the amount of groundwater is large, it is not inexhaustible. Yet, human development has been depleting this resource, both by tapping it with wells and by building impervious structures that create higher rates of runoff and do not allow water to percolate into the soil. Site development must respect the ecological sensitivity of this valuable resource.

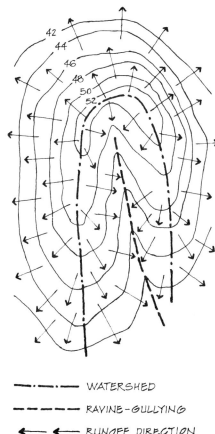

—·—·— WATERSHED

—————— RAVINE-GULLYING

◄—— ◄—— RUNOFF DIRECTION

Drainage diagram.

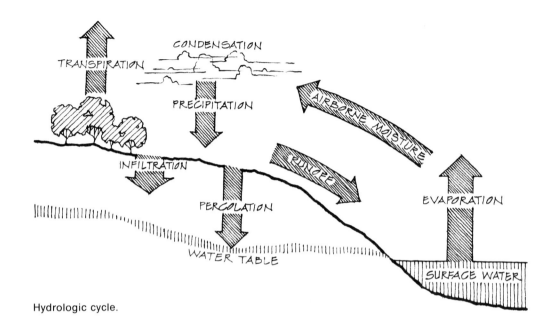

Hydrologic cycle.

Groundwater also has important impact on the development potential of the site. Areas where the water table is high (wetlands) are not only ecologically sensitive, but they also present structural problems. Excavation can be a problem, foundations are liable to be unstable, and the buildings may be subject to flooding. The height of the water table on a site can be obtained from a soil survey and mapped to show areas unsuitable for development.

Often, surface water is used as a major site amenity. It is a natural and flexible element and can take a variety of forms to create a variety of effects: repose, reflection, activity, and so on. Running water from fountains, streams, and waterfalls can create sound and movement as part of a site design. Existing bodies of water can be preserved and

Surface and groundwater.

enhanced or new bodies can be created—sometimes from the increased runoff caused by development. Containment of surface runoff on the site can facilitate increased percolation to the water table, as a way of minimizing environmental drainage.

Architectural Elements

In addition to the natural elements we have discussed, space is defined by made, or architectural, elements. That is, the placement of buildings creates exterior space, and that space must be designed with the level of care usually associated only with interior spaces.

Architectural Elements That Define Spaces. An understanding of space rests with the basic two-dimensional planes: the base, vertical, and overhead. These planes can be manipulated to enclose three-dimensional volume or exterior space. The base plane is the earth and its landform. On an urban site, the original landform may have been modified to accommodate intensive activity. In this case, the base plane may still be made a strong definitional element through the use of material, textures, and colors.

Vertical planes are the most important in articulating an exterior space. In site design, the mass and placement of buildings in relation

Michelangelo's Campidoglio, Rome.

Piazza del Campo, Siena, Italy.

to each other or in conjunction with natural elements is used to create vertical planes that articulate the enclosure of a space. The vertical planes need not be buildings; opaque barriers and walls may also be used to define a space.

In an exterior space, the sky is perceived as the overhead plane. However, buildings can also be used to give definition to the height of a space with vertical line elements that pierce the sky. Linear vertical elements can also act as points of reference or landmarks.

Elements That Influence The Qualities of Space. Exterior spaces are designed with respect to enclosure, scale, shape, and proportion. Three-dimensional enclosures are formed by two-dimensional planes, and, of course, different activities have different space requirements. The volume of space enclosed should be related to the intended use and the human scale. Scale refers to relative size. That is, the size of an exterior space should relate to the larger context (an urban plaza in midtown Manhattan or a pocket playground in a residential neighborhood) and to the planned human activity (a small space for relaxing with a newspaper or a large space for a parade).

The shape of a space can affect the type of activities that can

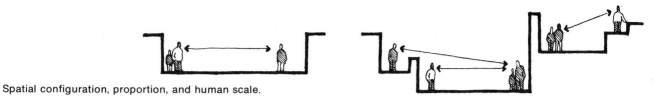

Spatial configuration, proportion, and human scale.

occur separately or simultaneously within the space. Different shapes provide qualities that reinforce the formation of behavioral territories. For example, a space of simple configuration allows different activities to occur simultaneously, if they do not require visual or acoustical separation.

Proportion is an internal volumetric relation, the comparative ratio of the space-defining elements (height to width to length). The proportion of a space has an affect on the way that the space is perceived by individuals and thus on the way it is used. Lynch has developed a rule of thumb for perceptual qualities that can be assigned to the size and proportion of comfortable spaces and that is based on the size of the user and the ratio of vertical to base plane dimensions. For example, "an exterior enclosure is most comfortable when its walls are one-half or one-third as high as the width of the space enclosed, while if the ratio falls below one-fourth, the space ceases to seem enclosed."[4]

The quality of space can be reinforced by light and shade and by the color and texture of the materials used. Light can sharpen or blur a definition, emphasize or silhouette an element, conceal or reveal a feature, and contract or expand dimensions. The designer can manip-

The pond, Hampstead Heath, London.

Hard and soft textures, colonial Williamsburg, Virginia.

ulate outdoor light by using building placement to cast shadows or by using reflective surfaces such as glass and water to mirror images.

All materials used for surfaces or planes have texture, whether architectural or natural; they may be rough-surfaced building materials such as brick or soft, natural materials such as grass. Texture provides a human scale in the environment by supplying a recognizable dimension that may be perceived by touch or by sight. A simple example of textural difference is a path across a grassy open space; the soft texture of the grass is juxtaposed with the hard texture of the path, thus inviting movement.

All materials have color as well. Color may aid in creating an atmosphere in a space. Bright colors symbolize gaiety and excitement,

Sequential views.

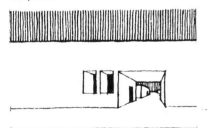
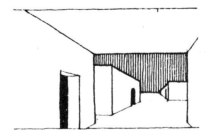

INTRODUCTION TO ARCHITECTURE

while more subtle tones may be used to suggest warmth and quiet. Thus, color may be used to create a diverse environment, aiding in the definition of space by accentuating scale and proportion. The color contrast of a building with its surrounding environment can aid in delineating the vertical planes of the building from the overhead plane of the sky and the base plane of the ground. Alternatively, the repetition of color can create harmony. This can be used to integrate a new building or space with its locale.

Elements That Order Space. All spaces, interior and exterior, are experienced by people passing through them in a definite sequence. Spaces do not occur in isolation; they are linked together. Thus the effect of a space depends on the spaces that come before and after it. All spatial sequences should be functional and legible. Significant sequences existing in the site locale may be important organizing elements in the site design. Cullen's technique of serial-vision sequential sketches is an excellent analytical tool here.[5] Sequence is continuity in the perception and understanding of spaces, and it is achieved by the use of spatial elements to provide a succession of visual experiences. As an individual is experiencing space by moving through it, that space is revealed as a chain of

A series of spaces, Washington, D.C.

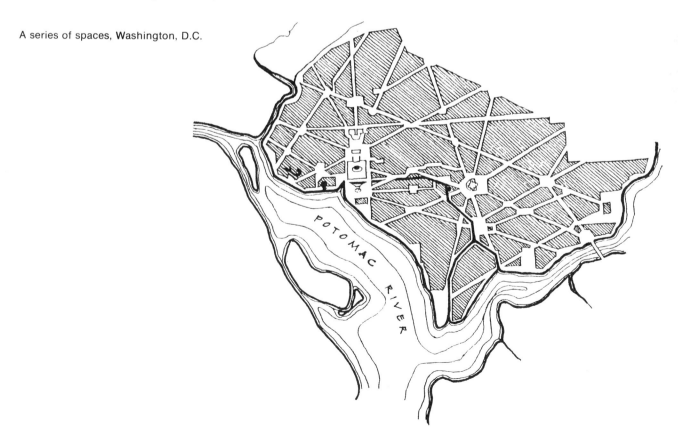

events. These events may be divided into the existing view and the merging view (Cullen's terminology).[6] Each element in the chain should lead to the next—without necessarily revealing it. The objective is to excite curiosity as to what lies beyond, and to create drama through the juxtaposition of different types of space.

A simple type of organizational structure for a sequence is a hierarchy (such as in the size of spaces). The spaces may increase progressively in size (and hence in importance) until one reaches the primary space. Alternatively, the use of repetition may order a sequence. The repetition may be based on the regular occurrence of open space or of a color, texture, or shape. To develop a rhythm, the repetitous sequence must be interspersed at recurring intervals with a contrasting element to create variety.

Finally, continuity may be used to structure a spatial sequence. Continuity will depend on the quality of the transitions between spaces (for example, between an interior and exterior space or between two exterior spaces). At the site design scale, entry and exit transitions are major features that must be articulated if the adjoining spaces are to read as a cohesive, legible entity.

Hierarchy of entry, Oxford, England.

Calder sculpture in Chicago.

Contained Elements. The quality and appearance of a space can be modified by a range of objects placed in the space, in addition to the people and their activities that possess the space. Street furniture, graphics, artificial lighting, and sculpture are all contained elements that can alter the quality of a space. For example, an honorific space can be given a human scale by the use of sculpture. A site and its locale contain many made details: benches, sculptures, trash cans, signs, lights. Their human scale and habitual use make them an integral part of the total behavioral and visual experience of a space.

Artificial light can reinforce the familiar daytime setting or transform it. Most outdoor lighting is provided to enhance personal safety. However, it can also be used for dramatic effect if varied in color, intensity, direction, and motion. It can produce new visual experiences, changing the basic character of a space. Artificial lighting includes signage. The idea of signage and advertising unfortunately evokes the picture of the "American Strip" and the symbols that are a dominant, chaotic, and often ugly part of the everyday townscape. Yet signs are necessary to explain and direct activity, and they can also add interest to a space.

The designer's task is to simplify and regulate the delivery of vital information and to use this signage creatively to express the image of the place as a positive element in the townscape.

THE PERCEPTUAL ENVIRONMENT

The visual form that an activity space is given will affect our understanding and use of the space. Our understanding of a space is based
upon our perception of that space—through the visual environmental
stimuli sent from the eye to the brain and cognition, the process of giving meaning to stimuli based on our storehouse of experience.

Individuals move through and occupy space in response to their
generalized image of the environment. The environment suggests
distinctions. The perceived environmental cues and the manner in
which they are sorted, organized, and stored varies with the individual,
depending on a variety of factors including the activity or trip purpose,
home location, job location, social class, income, education, occupation, stage in the life cycle, and cultural and ethnic background.
Research studies have shown that people organize the spatial and
behavioral elements of the environment into a mental map. Lynch has
found that the following basic elements are used to structure the mental map: paths, edges, districts, landmarks, and nodes. These elements are organized in relation to their perceptual structure, legibility,
and meaning.[7] The capacity of a space to foster and sustain an activity depends on the congruence between these elements and the activity function. The size, shape, scale, proportions, and enclosure of the
space must be appropriate for the intended behavior.

Perceptual Structure
In site analysis and design, the designer should consider the perceptual structure of the site and locale, first, in terms of the way people
perceptually divide space into a hierarchy of territories, which affects
the way the space is used and second, in terms of the ways in which
the arrangement of space and space-defining elements affect the
manner in which people interact in the space. Territorial behavior
occurs at three distinct spatial, hierarchically nested levels: personal
space, home space, and urban space.[8]

At the lowest level, personal space is individual space—the bubble of privacy around an individual's body which may not be penetrated without the person's feeling threatened or invaded. It is the
minimum space needed to maintain individual integrity. Home space
is a fixed space that may be controlled by a regular user. The degree
of control allows the user a feeling of intimacy and a degree of
freedom of behavior. It may be individual or relate to a small primary
group (the family or a collective group). Thus, a home space may be a
private space, the family residence, or a public space taken over

through regular use (such as the neighborhood bar). In either case, the area operates as the home base for the individual or group.

Finally, there is urban space, which an individual occupies selectively, in relation to workplace, shopping, recreation, and socializing. The total area traversed by an individual is called the "urban range." Unlike personal space and home space, urban space is not a discrete unit of space completely occupied and defended by an individual or a group. Rather, it is public space, free to everyone. Within this space individuals traverse selective paths, districts, and nodes, coalescing into groups and separating again according to their respective activities.

In conclusion, it is important that the site designer understand the site and the locale in terms of the psychological territories perceived by people. Lynch's cognitive mapping technique is an excellent analytical tool.[9] Territories must be respected in site design and they must be appropriate to the activity—public, semipublic, or private. Each territory must be visible and distinct. To be distinct, places should have a clear perceptual identity—a sense of place—unique and differentiated from other places, memorable, and recognizable. This does not mean that all territories have to be physically separated; for example, it should be possible to enjoy and sense the presence of other people while maintaining personal territory.

Meaning and Legibility

For a space to have a clear meaning, the perceptual structure must affirm the activity function of the space. For example, a visual climax should be consistent with the most intense activity location, the key visual sequences should be along the major circulation routes, and the perceptual territories should fit the social territories. The environment should be capable of being perceived as meaningful, and its visible spatial elements as being related to other aspects of life—the functional activities; the social structure; the institutional structure; and the individual psychological needs, values, and aspirations.

The legibility of the spaces of a site design is an important issue. Spaces should be arranged so that an individual can understand their pattern and organization. Sequencing is one way of achieving this spatial legibility. A legible spatial structure aids in the perception and cognition of a space and provides psychological support. It can be a source of emotional security and a basis for self-identity. A legible environment is one in which the main circulation system is clearly articulated and congruent with the major activity patterns. The major activity centers should be easily read, not only by the resident but by the stranger as well.

THE GENERATION OF DESIGN CONCEPTS

Returning to the general site planning process, recall the initial steps of setting objectives, program analysis, and site analysis. Site analysis is conducted concurrently with program analysis and is used to evaluate alternative sites for a given program, to evaluate a given site for alternative programs, or for site design. In each case, the focus is on the relationships between the building and the site, and between the site and its larger environment. The major contexts for site analysis include the behavioral environment and public infrastructure, the spatial environment (natural and architectural), and the perceptual environment.

Site analysis involves the inventory and analysis of all these factors in an attempt to identify constraints and opportunities for design. Once completed, the objectives and the program and site analyses are integrated. This allows the clarification and revision of basic objectives and sets the stage for the generation of site design concepts.

A typical technique used in site analysis involves mapping the various dimensions of behavior, space, and perception in an attempt to identify key issues that will structure the environment and thus, the design process. Important elements represented on successive overlays or a composite map will form patterns that provide a basis for site evaluation and any subsequent design intervention. For example, a soils-water-vegetation composite map may indicate an ecologically sensitive area of the site that should not be disturbed, while a map of roads, traffic capacity, and volume may indicate the best location for vehicular access to the site. Likewise, a topographic-vegetation map may indicate locations for significant views of and from the site.

Once the site analysis has been completed and the objectives and program have been made final the process of site design can proceed. This usually involves the generation of alternate design concepts that can be evaluated in terms of meeting objectives and programs. The general process of design is covered in some detail later in this text. However, in site design, the elements of design are the same as the elements of site analysis. Once a site has been selected, the task is to organize both the interior and exterior spaces of the site to satisfy the program requirements. The basic elements of

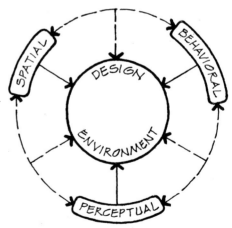

Interactions in **design environment.**

site organization—the behavioral structure of activity patterns, the space-defining elements (both natural and architectural), and the psychological perception of space—must be melded together in the site design to achieve a spatial, behavioral, and perceptual unity.

NOTES

1. E. W. Burgess, "The Growth of the City: An Introduction to a Research Project," *Publications American Sociological Society* 18:85–87; Homer Hoyt, *The Structure and Growth of Residential Neighborhoods in American Cities* (Washington, D.C.: Federal Housing Administration, 1939, Chauncy Harris, and Edward Ullman, "The Nature of Cities," *Annals of the American Academy of Political Science* 242:7–17
2. An assessment of the long- and short-range environmental impact of the development, including an evaluation of alternative approaches, a statement of adverse effects that cannot be avoided, and a statement of any irreversible effect such as depletion of natural resources.
3. For further discussion of urban microclimates, see Thomas Detweyler, Melvin Marcus, et al., *Urbanization and Environment* (Belmont, Calif.: Duxbury Press, 1972).
4. Kevin Lynch, *Site Planning*. 2d ed. (Cambridge, Mass.: M.I.T. Press, 1971), p. 194.
5. Gordon Cullen, *The Concise Townscape* (New York: Van Nostrand Reinhold, 1961), pp. 7–21.
6. Ibid., p. 9.
7. Kevin Lynch, *The Image of the City* (Cambridge, Mass.: M.I.T. Press, 1960).
8. Robert Sommer, *Personal Space: The Behavioral Basis of Design* (Englewood Cliffs, N.J.: Prentice-Hall, 1969.
9. Lynch, *The Image of the City*.

FOR FURTHER READING

Cullen, Gordon. *The Concise Townscape*. New York: Van Nostrand Reinhold, 1961.

Halprin, Lawrence. *The RSVP Cycles: Creative Processes in the Human Environment*. New York: George Braziller, Inc., 1969.

Hurst, Michael E. *I Came to the City*. Boston: Houghton Mifflin, 1975.

Lynch, Kevin. *The Image of the City*. Cambridge, Mass.: M.I.T. Press, 1960.

———. *Site Planning*. 2d ed. Cambridge, Mass.: M.I.T. Press, 1971.

McHarg, Ian. *Design with Nature*. Garden City, Doubleday & Company, Inc., 1971.

Porteous, J. Douglas. *Environment and Behavior*. Reading, Mass.: Addison-Wesley, 1977.

Simmonds, John Ormsbee. *Landscape Architecture*. New York: McGraw-Hill, 1961.

Part Three
Building Design

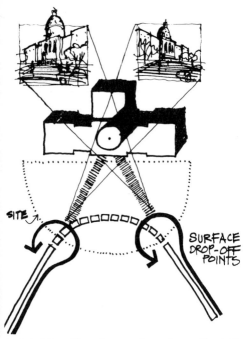

Serial vision: View from surface drop-off points.

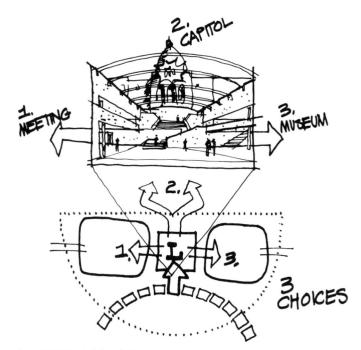

Serial vision: Lobby view.

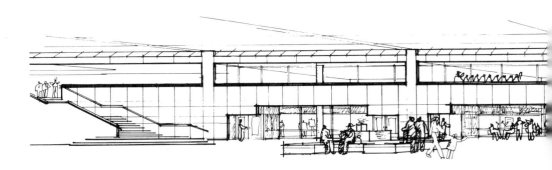

Perspective and diagrammatic design sketches, Minnesota State Capitol Annex Competition: Jules-McGinty, Architects

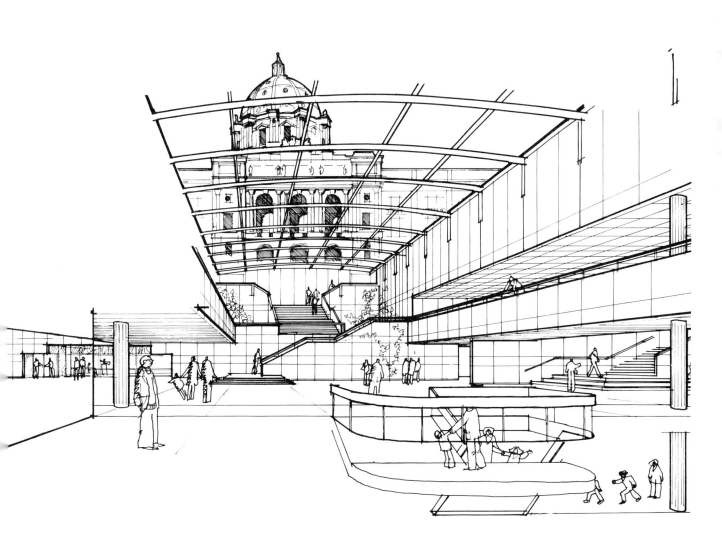

CHAPTER 7

Design and the Design Process

Tim McGinty

This chapter, the first of several that cover architectural design, presents an overview of design and the design process without advocating a particular view. A number of attitudes toward design and the design process are reviewed, including the basic format for the delivery of services suggested by the American Institute of Architects. Finally, a short section on applicable skills is included. The chapter is presented in full recognition that architecture happens within a broad social, environmental, behavioral, and economic context, and that design and the design process respond to that context.

DESIGN

Design, in the context of architecture, is simply the activity of generating proposals that change something that already exists into something that is better. Design can be viewed as a three-part process consisting of an initial state, a method or process of transformation, and an imagined future state. These components also define the functions of the architectural designer—to identify problems, identify methods for achieving solutions, and implement those solutions. In more practical terms, these functions are programming, generating alternative building designs, and implementing plans.[1]

Design in Education

Although design is a broadly based activity touching everything from the visual arts to engineering to business management and the study of logic, the potential for a unified introduction to design is usually unmet. Most art schools have so-called basic design classes that everyone—including painters, ceramists, and sculptors—takes. These basic classes introduce a series of fundamental visual and problem-solving experiences. At some schools, architects, landscape architects, product and industrial designers, and interior designers join the art majors in the same design program. More typically, however, the basic design courses for architects are taught within architectural schools.

The model for an integrated design education was a pre-World War II school in Germany called the Bauhaus. The Bauhaus teachers conducted an initial workshop and visual studies program for all the arts. Architecture, painting, dance, and theater students shared the basic design experience. The teachers and the curriculum had a tremendous influence in the United States, through the immigration of its faculty to the United States during and after World War II. Ironically, while Frank Lloyd Wright, the great American architect, had little influence on architectural education in the United States, the publication of his work in Europe greatly influenced many designers there who had started in the Bauhaus. Nevertheless, the pattern and direction of architectural education in the United States, from World War II to recent times, has clearly been influenced by the Bauhaus.

The Bauhaus was, in part, a reaction to the traditional approach to architectural education offered by the Beaux Arts system of France. The Beaux Arts system, with its initial studies of the classical styles, had its origin in the 1800s and continued in France and the United States as the predominant form of architectural education until the mid-1950s. The Beaux Arts system differed dramatically because it emphasized the study of historic architecture as a pattern for future architecture, rather than the study of abstract principles as the basis for architectural design. The Beaux Arts dealt with preserving and enhancing the authority of historically proven forms, while the Bauhaus promoted a search for unique solutions and forms that reflected both the type of building designed and the materials and methods of construction. Typical Beaux Arts student projects were designed to be built in stone, while student designs at the Bauhaus were to be built in concrete, steel, and glass. Both schools influenced architecture in the United States, but the Bauhaus more clearly influenced architectural education in the mid-1950s and early 1960s.

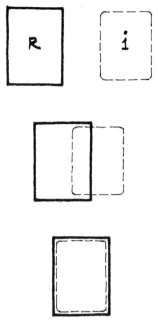

The design process

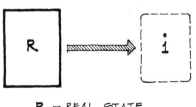

R = REAL STATE
i = IMAGINED STATE
⟹ = PROCESS

Several additional changes have influenced education in the last fifteen years. First, there has been less emphasis on the engineering aspects of architecture in response to a need for a broader education in the arts, the sciences, and the expanded practice of architecture, which now includes urban planning and design, business management, construction management, marketing, and the like. Architectural education, like the profession itself, has expanded to include a broader base of knowledge and specializations; no longer are all architectural students assumed to be architectural designers. Consequently, there is less emphasis on structures, technology, and building design as the only core of architectural education. Certainly, individual students (perhaps even the majority) can and do specialize in these areas, but not to the exclusion of a broader education.

A second major change in recent years has been the emergence of the study of human behavior as a basis for beginning architectural education. Traditionally, architects had to make numerous assumptions about the relationship between their buildings and human behavior. Some factual information supporting or challenging those assumptions is now available. Thus, basic courses in psychology, sociology, and anthropology and applied courses in environment-behavior studies are now integral parts of most architectural curricula.

A third but less widespread innovation in beginning design education uses a total immersion in a building design problem as the student's initial contact with architectural design. This is a contrast to most introductory curriculums, which separate the various issues that architects manipulate—social, visual, technical—into separate introductory experiences and courses. Traditional curricula try to ensure that each principle is understood before the student attempts to integrate them. The goal of total immersion is just the opposite; the students are first taught through experience to appreciate the problems and excitement of an integrated experience to prepare them for subsequent coursework in which the principles are taught.

Finally, there is a trend toward beginning design education that includes instruction in the design process as an abstract experience. The emphasis is on creative problem solving as taught in logic courses or in introductory problem-solving courses in engineering, often called systems design. The goal is to make the study of design and problem solving the base intellectual activity of the profession. This strategy was stimulated by changes in professional practice in the 1960s, when architects found themselves contracting to solve management, programming, and other problems not directly related to building design and construction. However, the studio case study, where the student concentrates on designing a single building type for a specific site, is still the dominant teaching mode used to develop the student's ability to design.

Design Process Theory

Although a number of disciplines, such as systems design, logistics, planning, and engineering, have influenced the architectural profession, the design process, as a distinct area of study, did not receive full attention until the 1950s. Later, J. C. Jones' *Design Methods* (1972) identified the study of the design process as a search for methods that would improve design quality.[2] Most of the subsequent activity in this area of design methods has been done in England, Scotland, Australia, Czechoslovakia, Poland, and the United States. methods and rational strategies in the United States can be attributed to Christopher Alexander.[3] His *Notes on the Synthesis of Form* (1964) had a major impact on the attitudes of faculty and students. The key words in Alexander's view of the design process are *atomistic* and *fit*. Just as all material things in the universe are formed of basic building blocks (atoms), so is architecture composed of basic components. The requirements for a building can be atomized or reduced to the simplest components. Solutions can be built or constructed from appropriate combinations of these small elements. The idea that problems could be reduced to long lists of very small bits of information paralleled an increasing interest in the role of programming in design. Programs that were once simply lists of rooms and room sizes became extensive descriptions of functional elements, relationships, and performance requirements. This development occurred both in schools and in architectural practice.

Fit was the term used to describe the appropriate assemblage of the atomized parts in a way that fulfilled the prescribed needs of the problem. A match between an activity and an environment is described as a fit. In *Community and Privacy* (1963), written with Serge Chermayeff, Alexander further describes a process of searching for matches between groups of requirements called "constellations." The goal of the process is to develop an appropriate hierarchy of matches between requirements and the physical solution.[4]

The more recent work of Alexander and his colleagues also focuses upon combinations called "patterns," which are roughly analogous to molecules. A pattern is a collection of fits in a single setting that supports a specific activity or behavior. The product of recent studies in this direction is called a "pattern language."[5] Pattern language is general, in that it relates to a variety of situations rather than

156

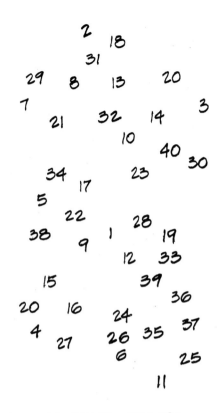

A. APPARENT CHAOS:
THE PROBLEM UNSTRUCTURED

B. CONSTELLATION:
THE PROBLEM STRUCTURED

Constellation: problem
structuring

to a particular building type. Yet it is also specific, in that it suggests
formal solutions for particular functions. Although pattern language
may appear to some to infringe on the designer's ability to innovate, it
does summarize useful information about the behavior of people in
specific functional activity settings. Certainly it goes well beyond
traditional architectural standards, because it introduces supporting
information in addition to advocating a specific recommendation.

Several additional views and values have also dominated the
focus of architectural design education over the last few decades. The
first of these is the form-giver approach to design. Great architects
such as Frank Lloyd Wright, Le Corbusier, Mies van der Rohe, and
others are admired for their creative contributions. Their work is seen
as the product of personal genius, and the role of schools is seen as
the teaching of general principles from their work and the cultivation

of the seeds of genius that may lie within each student. Students, in turn, are expected to internalize these design principles, develop their genius, and make subsequent form-giving contributions to architecture.

A second tradition is embodied in the term "functional architecture." The assumption here is that there is an efficient and functional configuration for any given program. The configuration of a design is based on the activities that must be accommodated and the relationships between those activities. A successful design packages these elements, listed or deduced from the program and context in an efficient arrangement.

A third attitude affecting design education is called the "realm of architecture." This attitude holds that the functional aspects of a design are relatively easy to resolve, and that functional aspects should be subordinated to the more difficult questions. The specific characteristics or attributes that presumably make a design proposal "architecture" vary from school to school. Two typical but different themes in this tradition are "buildings as symbols" and "user satisfaction." Buildings may be seen as important artifacts that satisfy their users because they symbolize something that the users value. users because they symbolize something that the users value. Monuments like the Lincoln Memorial in Washington are valued not because they function well but because they symbolize important public values. Other buildings can also be symbols, can have symbolic meaning, and can be designed in such a way as to present an appropriate image and convey a specific meaning to the public. Likewise, building design can focus on forms that appropriately accommodate the immediate needs of the users. Unfortunately, many buildings have failed to do this, and the failure of many publicly financed buildings—from housing to prisons—is in part traceable to the inappropriateness of their appearance and what that appearance symbolizes, as well as to their ability to satisfy the behavior and needs of the people who inhabit them.

All these traditions and design attitudes often exist within a given school of architecture, especially if the school is related to or includes urban planning, landscape architecture, environmental design, or environmental psychology. Although this variety of points of emphasis may present some confusion for the beginning student, it is clear that the field of architecture is too broad and complex to be encompassed by a single approach.

A final variation of design education involves a faculty's attitude about the role of design within the larger context of architectural practice. Some schools may view design as the central focus of architectural practice, with each student expected to be a designer "first"; other subjects in the curriculum are thus made subservient to design. Some schools view design as a more general problem-solving activity and advise students to concentrate simultaneously on a variety of areas, including structures, environmental systems, urban design, economics, and human behavior, as well as design. Still other schools view design and design methods as only one of several specialized areas of study, allowing students (especially at the graduate level) to omit building design entirely in favor of other academic areas, including architectural history, criticism, and research methods. Given the breadth of architecture, it is fortunate that variety exists, but students should be aware of the type of school they select.

THE DESIGN PROCESS

The description of the design process as going from an initial state to a future imagined state does not explain fully the activities undertaken along the way. These activities are described in the following sections first as a five-step process, then as a contractual arrangement, and finally as a list of questions for students.

The Five-Step Design Process

Design process, as conceptualized and taught in schools of architecture, includes a number of sequential problem-solving steps. Basically, the steps are initiation, preparation, proposal making, evaluation, and action. Typical variations, from a number of sources, are shown in Table 7-1.

Initiation. Initiation involves the recognition and definition of the problem to be solved. Although architects are often expected to identify problems and opportunities, the tradition is of the client bringing the problem to the architect. As Jane Holtz Kay suggests, "A gentleman waits to be asked."[6] The traditional image has the client walking unannounced into an office to tell the architects that they have been picked because the client admires their work. Both clients and architects know this isn't the usual process. Projects are almost always awarded after competitive interview. Sometimes the interviews are open to anyone who can meet the minimum qualifications, and sometimes the client limits the interviews to three or four preselected firms. Architects also have begun to take more initiative in making contacts with potential clients, and many have formed working associations with developers, especially in the housing and commercial fields. Although limited advertising has recently been approved by the AIA, a variety of restrictions still exist on the ways architects can solicit services. Nevertheless, architects are often directly involved in the early stages of problem identification. Another aspect of the initiation step involves the role of imagination and aspirations. That is, architects attempt to raise the aspirations of society in terms of the quality of the built environment. They identify general problems, educate the public, and suggest alternative solutions. They supply critical imagination in their area of expertise that stimulates the client's aspirations. More than one architect has reflected that "good clients make good buildings."

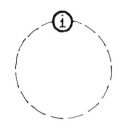

Preparation. The second step of the design process, preparation, includes the collection and analysis of information about the problem to be solved. In a broad sense, professional education is itself a preparation for delivering design services. Professional architects are constantly preparing to deliver services—informally, by learning from each successive commission, and formally, by continuing education. More specifically, preparation involves the systematic collection and analysis of information about a particular project. This activity is called "programming"; the product is a building program in the United States and a brief in England and Europe. Programs generally include a written report summarizing the needs of a project and can include extensive analysis that identifies the important issues to be resolved.

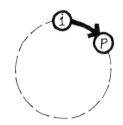

Other preparation activities include the gathering of base maps, of site and areal data (about the natural and made environment, traffic, utilities, and so on), of information about legal constraints and economics, and of finance data. Another product of the preparation stage is a list of criteria that describes the desired characteristics of an architectural solution. Solutions are measured against these criteria as the project cycles through the proposal making and evaluation stages.

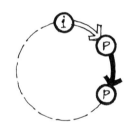

Some preparation activities are integrated into other stages of the design process. The designer may find that certain types of information are required at various stages of design. For example, the criteria for a hospital design may change due to technological innovation during the eighteen or more months of design time that such a project might require. Thus, information collection and analysis is both an initial step in design and one that continues throughout the design process.

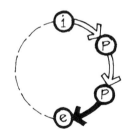

The five step design process Initiation, preparation, proposal making, evaluation, and action.

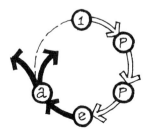

TABLE 7-1

Various Views of the Design Process

Five-step design process	R. Whitaker's eight- step design process	H. Rittle's summary of design process	J. C. Jones's design method	AIA basic and supplementary services	Guenter and Corkill, *Systematic Approach to Architectural Design*
Initiation/ imbalance	Recognition	Identify the problem	Idea		Basic definition
	Definition				Preliminary program
Preparation	Preparation	Collect information	Information	Predesign services	Investigation, analysis
	Analysis	Analyze information	Analysis		Program abstraction
Proposal making	Synthesis	Creative leap	Synthesis	Schematic design	Synthesis and development
		Work out solution		Design development	Volumetric design proposal
Evaluation	Evaluation	Test solution	Evaluation		Reevaluation and modification
Action	Execution	Communicate and implement	Optimization	Contract documents Bidding Administration of contract Postdesign services	
	Reevaluation				

Richard Whitaker, "Eight-Step Design Process" (unpublished), Department of Architecture, University of Wisconsin-Milwaukee, 1971).

H. Rittle, "Summary of Standard Descriptions of the Design Process" (unpublished student handout, Department of Architecture, The University of California-Berkeley, 1970).

J. C. Jones, *Design Methods* (London: John Wiley and Sons, 1972), p. 50.

The American Institute of Architects, *The Architects Handbook of Professional Practice* (Washington, D.C.: The American Institute of Architects, annual).

P. A. Corkill and Robert F. Guenter, "Systematic Approach to Design" (unpublished, Department of Architecture, University of Nebraska-Lincoln, 1970).

Proposal Making. An informed architect is prepared to generate ideas and make building proposals. Valid ideas can come at any time in the design process, from the first meeting with a client to the end. The complexities of contemporary buildings and their sites make initial, intuitive, or naively conceived solutions highly suspect. Preconceived solutions represent an unfortunate tendency among beginning students and experienced practitioners alike. Too often, the client, student, or architect proposes what the building should look like and then tries to force the required activities into that image.

Student design process: Thornley #1	Student design process: Thornley #2	G. T. Moore's design process	M. Asimow, engineering design process	RIBA Architecture services
	Program formulation	Problem identification		Inception
Accumulation of data	Investigation	Analysis of user needs	Feasibility	Feasibility
	Assessment of design possibilities	Programming		
Isolation of general concept or form	Creation	Design synthesis	Preliminary design	Outline proposals
			Detailed design	Schematic design
Development of form	Refinement and presentation		Planning	Detail design
		Selecting from alternatives		
Presentation of solution		Implementation		Production information
				Bills of quantity
		Postoccupancy evaluation		Tender action
				Project planning
				Operation on site
				Completion
				Feedback

D. G. Thornley, "Design Method in Architectural Education," in J. C. Jones and D. G. Thornley, eds., *Conference on Design Methods* (New York: Macmillan, 1963), p.48.

G. T. Moore, "The Design Process" (unpublished, Department of Architecture, University of Wisconsin-Milwaukee, 1974).

M. Asimow, "Engineering Design Process," in J. C. Jones, *Design Methods* (London: John Wiley and Sons, 1972), p. 24.

Royal Institute of British Architects, Architectural Services, in J. C. Jones, *Design Methods* (London: John Wiley and Sons, 1970), p. 24.

There is considerable debate among faculty and practitioners as to just how much preparation is appropriate before proposal making begins. Some designers argue that the quality of the design is proportional to the length of time that the intuitive decision is delayed while others contend that the parallel development of program and schemes ensures the appropriate interaction of requirements and design solutions. Many architectural school faculty allot little time in design studios to preparation activities because preparation is thought to be both relatively simple and time-consuming while idea generation is allowed more time because it is more difficult. Other teachers do the reverse, contending that the core of design is finding the right problem. This difference of philosophy which exists within many schools causes considerable confusion among design students.

The actual process of making design proposals is often called "synthesis." That is, design proposals must bring together a variety of considerations from the context (social, economic, physical), the program, the site, the client, current technology, aesthetics, and the values of the designer. Proposals are expected to be physical demonstrations of the integration of a very large number of issues. The designer often makes initial drawings as overlays to record the impact of information on the solution and to explore the potentials of different physical arrangements and forms. The drawings and notes together form a tool for successive explorations and iterations that converge on a solution. The inspection of these drawings leads one from the designer's initial assumptions to the proposed solution. At various stages, the design under study can be presented to the client to confirm or revise program intentions.

Typically, the beginning design student is not expected to juggle and resolve the whole range of issues that must be addressed by the experienced architect. The time frames of formal education and practice vary; the student must address a large number of design problems in a span of four to six years, while a single large project might stay in an architectural firm for several years. Design teachers resolve this dilemma by focusing attention on particular issues that are critical to design in general or to the educational needs of students at various stages.

Evaluation. Evaluation in architectural design occurs at several scales and includes a variety of participants This discussion focuses on evaluation of alternative proposals by the designer, although designs are typically reviewed by clients, certain review boards (building inspectors, zoning and subdivision boards, or financial institutions), and the building's users, and in published newspapers, magazines, and journals. In addition, buildings are sometimes evaluated after they have been built and occupied for some period of time. In this case, both the original program and the design can be evaluated in terms of actual, measured performance. However, evaluation of proposals by the architect involves comparing proposed design solutions with the goals and criteria evolved in the programming stage. We can visualize the preparation-design-evaluation cycle as a three-part process, consisting of the establishment of goals and criteria for the design, the generation of potential designs, and the measurement of the proposed solutions against the program criteria In addition, proposals or designs may be evaluated in terms of implicit criteria, unstated in the program but generally accepted in the profession. Most important, however, is the designer's ability to evaluate his or her design proposals in terms of a large number of design issues and in an iterative fashion that converges on an appropriate and successful proposal.

Action. The action stage of the design process includes the activities associated with preparing and implementating a project, such as readying the construction documents and acting as the liaison between the owner and the contractor. Construction documents include working drawings and written specifications for the building.

Cycles, Feedback, Iteration. Although each designer develops his or her own style of working within the five-step design process, some procedures appear to be typical. First, the process is cyclic. That is, a designer may run through the sequence quickly at the advent of a project to generate a range of preliminary or limited proposals. This, in turn, may help to focus programming activities such as the identification of appropriate information needs or client reactions. The word "feedback" also describes the cyclic nature of the design process. New information causes the designer to reconsider existing information as the design proposal progresses. Second, the process is iterative. The designer runs through the cycles a number of times; each cycle incorporates a larger number of issues and the synthesis becomes more sophisticated. Successive iterations converge on a satisfactory solution. Lastly, the process is highly graphic. Typically, students and architects use inexpensive tracing paper as overlays, tracing base drawings or features from previous iterations and continuing exploration. Intermediate drawings are not discarded; rather, they form an important documentation for the design.

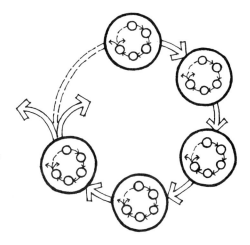

The design process: cyclic.

THE DESIGN PROCESS IN STANDARD PRACTICE

Basic Architectural Services

The American Institute of Architects (AIA) is the primary professional organization of practicing architects in the United States. The AIA provides a variety of services to its members including standard forms for various contracts. One of the forms describes the basic services that the architect is expected to deliver to a client.[7] Items may be

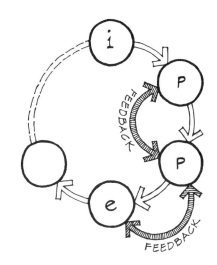

The design process: feedback.

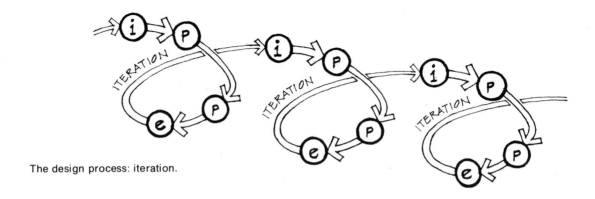

The design process: iteration.

deleted or added to the standard contract forms through negotiation, but the basic description of what the profession thinks clients should expect as typical services provides a useful reference for looking at the design process.

The profession proposes that the architect's basic services can be divided into five sequential phases: *schematic design, design development, preparation of construction documents, bidding or negotiating, and administration of the construction contract.* Architects can provide additional services and a major change in the architect's self-image is reflected in the variety of predesign, postdesign, and supplementary services that are now listed.

Progress through the five steps depends on the approval of each stage by the client. This protects both client and architect, since work does not proceed until all agree on the products to that point. For example, changes in a building program during the construction documents stage might require considerable reworking of the schematic design development stages. The architect can require additional compensation if the changes significantly deviate from items approved at earlier stages. Thus, professional services are designed to function as elements of a legal contract as well as a process of design.

Schematic Design. The goal of schematic design is to establish the general characteristics of the building design, such as the scale required to satisfy the basic program requirements, disposition on the site, and estimated costs.[8] Often, schematic designs are presented as alternatives for the client, including the general image of the building

Schematic Design: The Milwaukee Art Center, an addition to Eero Saannen's Milwaukee County War Memorial Building, by Kahler, Slater & Fitzhugh Scott; David Kahler, project designer.

Schematic Design: section and perspective sketches

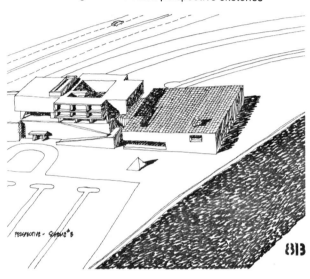

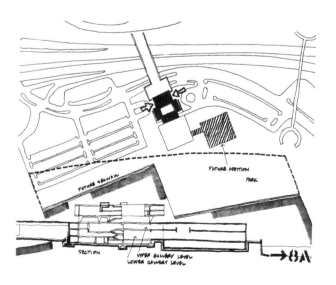

Schematic Design: studies in plan.

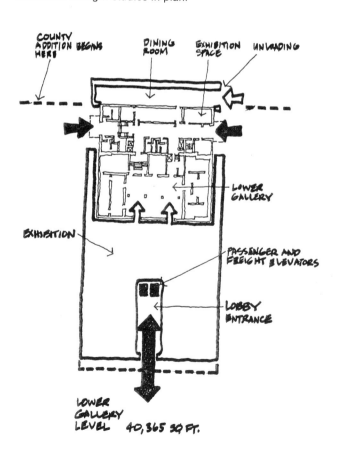

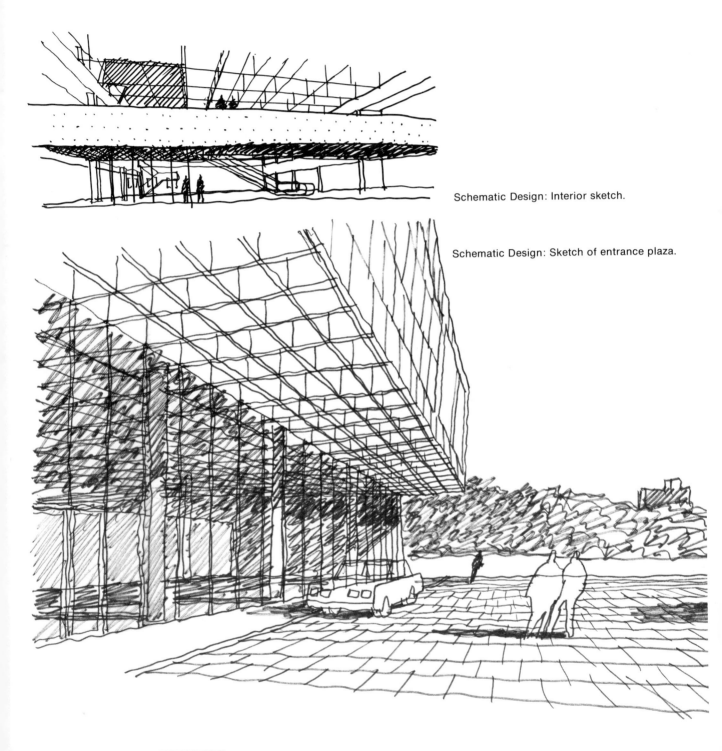

Schematic Design: Interior sketch.

Schematic Design: Sketch of entrance plaza.

Schematic Design: Model of plaza alternative.

as well as the sizes and organization of spaces, circulation, and siting. The purpose of this is to identify major issues and make initial decisions that serve as the base for subsequent stages. This is the point at which the architect has an opportunity to raise the aspirations or capture the imagination of the client. It is also the phase where the architect identifies the concept for the building. Schematic designs can be presented as a series of informal sketches, a simple report, or as an elaborate and dramatic visual presentation, depending upon the type of client and the working relationship between client and architect.

Design Development. An architect begins additional design work after approval of the schematic design. The purpose of the design development phase is to describe the specific character and intent of the entire project. The documents produced include a site plan, floor plans, elevations, and sections, with notes that describe the major materials. The drawings and notes also show or summarize the

Design Development: The Milwaukee Art Center, by Kahler, Slater & Fitzhugh Scott.

Design Development: Interior courtyard alternative.

Design Development: Study of exhibit space.

Design Development: Alternative structural system.

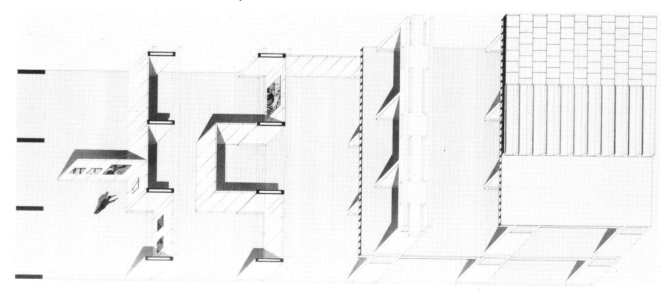

DESIGN AND THE DESIGN PROCESS

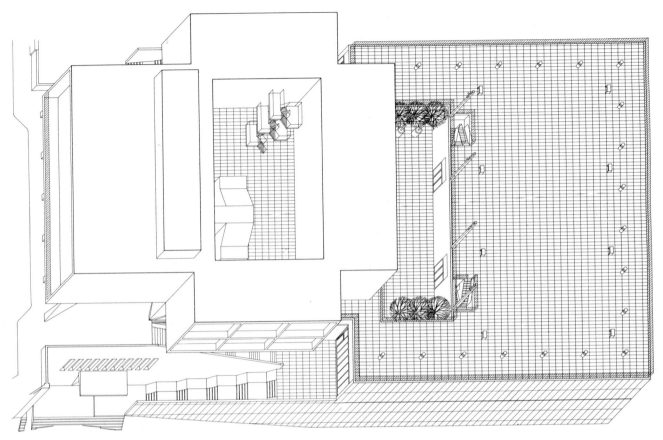

Final design presentation: roof plan.

mechanical and electrical requirements of the building and include a refined statement of probable costs.[9] In determining the specific scope and character of the project, the client is frequently involved in a series of discussions and decisions. These cover probable cost, appearance, quality, and performance. Alternatives are identified, and decisions must be made about basic structural, mechanical, and other technical elements, especially because of the impact these decisions have on the interior furnishings, flexibility, and final costs of the building. Some clients prefer to let the architect, as a specialist, make most of these decisions, while others demand that they be involved.

Architects see this phase as the heart of the design process. It requires the coordination of technical information and the work of a

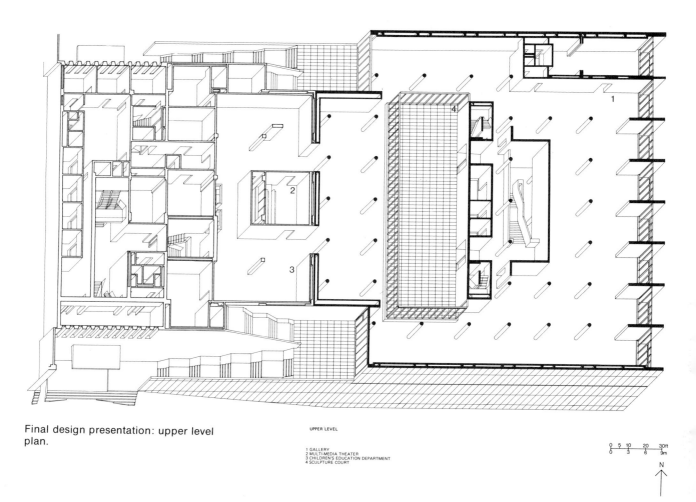

Final design presentation: upper level plan.

UPPER LEVEL

1 GALLERY
2 MULTI-MEDIA THEATER
3 CHILDREN'S EDUCATION DEPARTMENT
4 SCULPTURE COURT

0 5 10 20 30ft
0 3 6 9m

N

large number of people, especially in a complex project. The establishment of smooth interactions and the coordination of information and personalities are required if the remaining stages are to progress with any efficiency. The large-scale drawings done at this stage are necessary for studying choices and for detailing materials and methods of construction. The estimates of probable costs done in this stage can be accurate and based upon the use of certain materials and specifications. Presentations to the client of work done at this stage are usually keyed to the various detailed decisions that have to be made.

Construction Documents. The phrase "construction documents" reflects the fact that construction is based on a com-

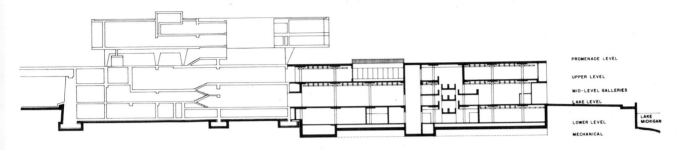

PROMENADE LEVEL

UPPER LEVEL

MID-LEVEL GALLERIES

LAKE LEVEL

LOWER LEVEL

MECHANICAL

LAKE MICHIGAN

LONGITUDINAL SECTION

Final design presentation: section and elevation.

Final design presentation: model.

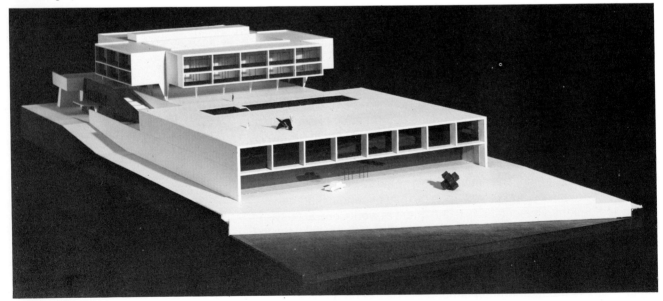

INTRODUCTION TO ARCHITECTURE

bination of drawings called "working drawings" and written requirements called "specifications." In general, the drawings show location and quantity, and the specifications identify quality and recommended procedures. Variations are possible, and in some offices standard detail drawings appear in the specifications. On small projects (such as homes) the specifications may appear on the drawings. The purpose of the construction documents is to show clearly and concisely the information that the contractor needs to know in order to bid on and construct the project. While there are addenda (instructions for changing the original drawings) and other supplementary drawings, like shop drawings that are done by each materials fabricator, the project should be buildable from a set of construction documents. More specifically, the working drawings show what is involved, where things are located, and what the physical dimensions are, while the specifications communicate what the materials are, how they are expected to function, and where they can be obtained.[10]

Bidding or Negotiating. With the owner's approval, the construction documents are released for bidding or negotiation. Several general contractors may bid on the contract or the owner may prefer to negotiate with a single contractor. The architect has the role of facilatator. The construction contract is drawn up between the general contractor and the owner, rather than between the architect and the contractor.

Administration of the Construction Contract. This final phase of the basic services has gone through a number of changes in recent years. Traditionally, architects were responsible for supervising all aspects of construction, ensuring that the building was constructed according to the drawings and specifications. Problems or failures in this regard were the responsibility of the architect. This standard has changed, and the contractor is now responsible for building according to the documents. The architect acts as the agent of the client and interprets and supervises the correspondence between owner and builder. In addition, the architect must interpret documents and make the inevitable day-to-day decisions and modifications that are required in any building project. In negotiating differences between the client and the contractor, the architect does not favor either. Instead, the architect advocates for a building that will serve the client. The contract wording regarding the activities and responsibilities in this phase is explicit: "The architect is responsible for the administration of the contract between the owner and the contractor."[11] Further, it requires that the architect interpret changes, establish standards, and judge performance.

174

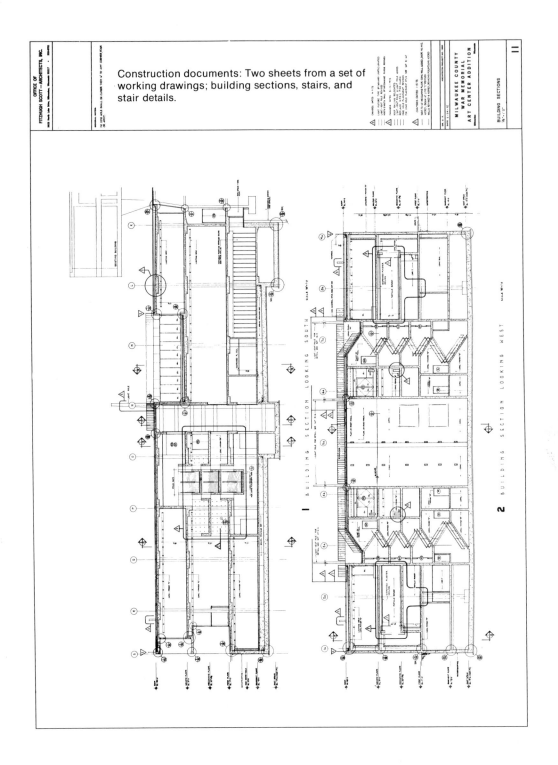

Construction documents: Two sheets from a set of working drawings; building sections, stairs, and stair details.

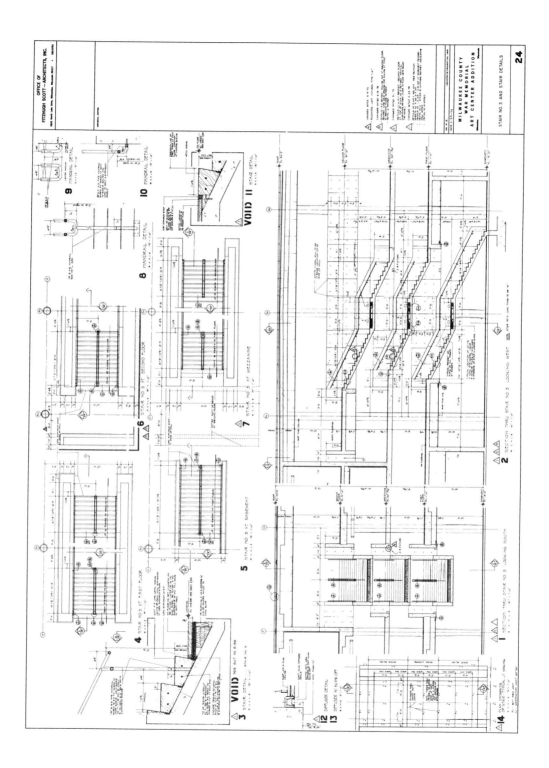

Construction drawing: stair detail

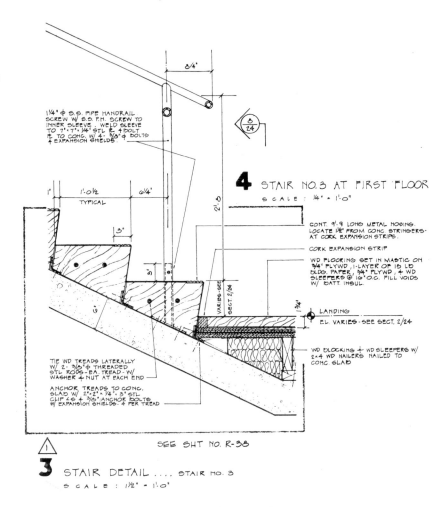

1¼" ø S.S. PIPE HANDRAIL
SCREW W/ S.S. P.H. SCREW TO
INNER SLEEVE . WELD SLEEVE
TO 7"×7"×¼" STL ℄ & BOLT
℄ TO CONC. W/ 4- ⅝"ø BOLTS
& EXPANSION SHIELDS.

4 STAIR NO.3 AT FIRST FLOOR
SCALE: ¼" = 1'.0"

CONT. 9'.9 LONG METAL NOSING.
LOCATE 1½" FROM CONC. STRINGERS·
AT CORK EXPANSION STRIPS.

CORK EXPANSION STRIP

WD FLOORING SET IN MASTIC ON
¾" PLYWD, 1-LAYER OF 15 LB
BLDG. PAPER, ¾" PLYWD, & WD
SLEEPERS @ 16"O.C. FILL VOIDS
W/ BATT. INSUL.

LANDING
EL. VARIES - SEE SECT. 2/24

WD BLOCKING & WD SLEEPERS W/
2×4 WD NAILERS NAILED TO
CONC. SLAB

TIE WD TREADS LATERALLY
W/ 2- ⅜"ø THREADED
STL RODS-EA. TREAD- W/
WASHER & NUT AT EACH END

ANCHOR TREADS TO CONC.
SLAB W/ 2"×2"×¼", 3" STL
CLIP ℄s & ⅜" ANCHOR BOLTS
W/ EXPANSION SHIELDS. 4 PER TREAD

SEE SHT NO. R-38

3 STAIR DETAIL .... STAIR NO. 3
SCALE: 1½" = 1'.0"

Administration of the Construction Contract:
the construction sequence

The completed building
(Photo by Richard Eells).

Additional Services

Architects provide a number of services in addition to the basic services described above. If, in any project, these services constitute a substantial commitment of resources, then they are covered under an additional contract. While many of these services are not considered basic, they reflect the breadth of architects' skills as well as the requirements of contemporary building design. The AIA suggests that such services may include:

    1 Predesign activities, including project administration, facilities programming, marketing studies, and project budgeting.

    2 Site analysis, including site planning and development, utilities studies, property rezoning assistance, site analysis, and site selection.

    3 Postconstruction services, including programs for maintenance, training of users, and the production of record or "as-built" drawings.

    4 Other supplementary services, including construction management, selecting and placing art, value analysis, interior design, environmental monitoring, demonstration projects, graphics design, and energy studies.[12]

    Of course, the full list of potential skills of architects and their application is quite extensive and continually expanding. In fact, some professional practices develop around one or more specific but supplementary services. For example, some firms specialize in interior design, site analysis, market analysis, or architectural research. Contrary to lay belief, tempera renderings of buildings are usually considered an additional service requiring supplementary compensation.

Artist's rendering of the project.

PROPOSAL MAKING: GRAPHIC EVIDENCE

Even with the various descriptions of the design process, the actual
activity of generating design proposals is elusive. It is as complex as
the human mind, responding to needs as broad as society itself. The
particulars of the process vary with project size, complexity, required
detail, and the familiarity of the designer with the problem, as well as
the size and character of the architectural office, its management
strategy, and the intentions of its client. It is no wonder that beginning
architectural students (and even accomplished architects) must
struggle to develop design strategies and ideas and to manage the
time devoted to design. While the traditions of the Beaux Arts and the
Bauhaus, various descriptions of the design process, handbooks, and
even the examples in architectural journals all contribute to the generation of design proposals, the student looking for a step-by-step
procedure will be disappointed. It simply does not exist. The complexities of designing are beyond simple step-by-step descriptions.

Thus, clients and teachers often rely on graphic evidence to evaluate the success of a design proposal. Drawings and notes generated
in a design studio comprise the most direct evidence of the process of
design. At the inevitable risk of oversimplifying and overgeneralizing
the issue, there are eight critical questions that must be answered.

1 How big is the building?

2 Does it fit on the site?

3 Is there a good match between the site and the proposed activity?

4 What are the required interactions and relationships among the activities in the building and on the site?

5 Does the designer have an image of the activities that take place in the
building and on the site?

6 What additional information is needed?

7 What issues are most important?

8 Can everything known be combined in a single drawing? .

These questions can be summarized as size, site, siting, interaction, images, importance, information, and integration. The first, *size,*
appears deceptively simple but has an important impact of one's
image of the project. An answer facilitates comparisons with other
more familiar projects and serves to establish scale relationships for
design work. Required spaces measured in square feet or meters (as-
signable and nonassignable, interior and exterior) are drawn to scale

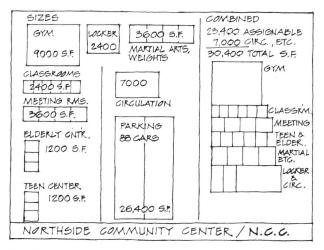

Graphic evidence: size.

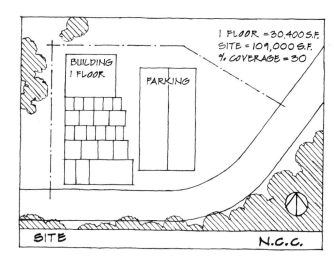

Graphic evidence: site.

for each program function or activity. Some design implications immediately become apparent, for two-dimensional area drawings have some of the attributes of plan drawings.

In addition to the building itself, the *site* of immediate importance. This question, answered in a simple site plan drawing, must include consideration of zoning and subdivision requirements (height, setback, easements, and so on). Alternate building massing and location alternatives can be explored at this point.

The third question, *siting,* requires a series of drawings that record data about the site; its location and its man-made and natural features—especially vegetation, slope, orientation to the sun and wind, access, utilities, and so forth. In contrast to the previous questions of size and fit, siting deals with identifying site factors that will affect the design solution.

Next, the designer graphically explores the relationships among components of the program, usually with a series of "bubble diagrams." This graphic technique translates functions or activities into spatial arrangements in consideration of the relative scale of spaces, the connections among spaces, their orientation to the site, and the like. Successive iterations of these diagrams cenverge on approximate floor plans and vertical arrangements that represent the building design.

Graphic explorations also address issues of the *image* of building spaces. For example, the designer explores alternative ways in

DESIGN AND THE DESIGN PROCESS

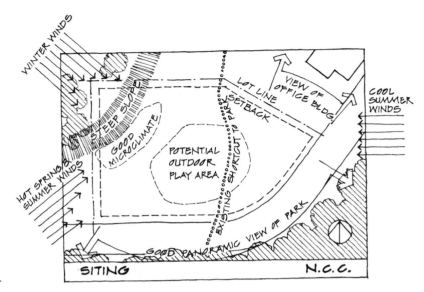

Graphic evidence: siting.

which functions might be accommodated, or alternative physical forms that respond to program activities. What should a classroom be like, or what should an entrance be like? Here it is useful to imagine oneself as a user of the building and to scan one's memory for examples of similar situations. Plan, section, and perspective sketches facilitate this study.

Unscaled interaction bubble diagram.

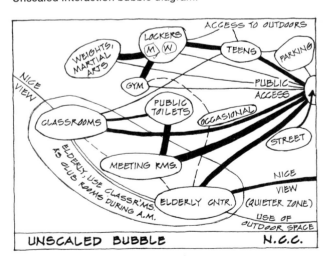

Scaled interaction bubble diagram.

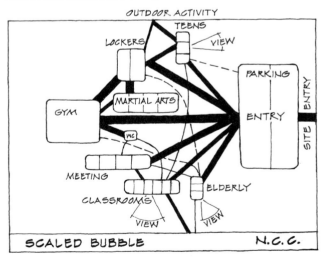

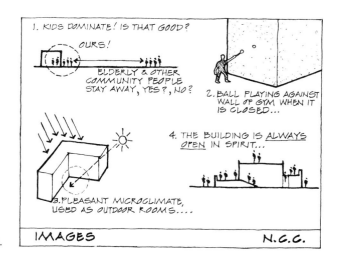

Images.

The designer seldom (if ever) starts the design process with complete *information.* One constantly finds the need for additional information. What does the zoning code require? What was the north part of the site like? Will that particular space be used for some particular activity? These questions should be recorded so that the required information can be collected efficiently.

Next, the designer must attempt to synthesize of all of the previous studies. This requires that the designer make decisions as to what is important and what is not. There are inevitably tradeoffs among objectives. The key is to identify the important issues for the design. (The concepts chapter presents a variety of ways designers go about deciding what is important in a project.)

While there are no set rules for making design proposals, combining all the information into a single drawing is an excellent way to review the factors that should affect the final solution. Some architects and students find they can literally translate their bubble diagrams and their siting information into a solution, but others use this drawing as preparation for making a "creative leap." This leads to a proposal that accommodates the needs and issues without being a literal translation of the diagrammatic studies. Finally, while the eight questions imply a general order to the design process, the influence of iteration and feedback eventually dominates the design activity.

The graphic exploration described above is simply a guide that is fairly common to architectural practice. There are, however, several additional concepts that serve as an aid to understanding the design process. They are alternatives, hierarchial order, and least effort.

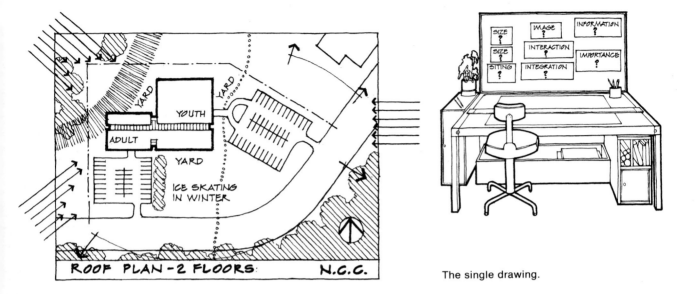

ROOF PLAN – 2 FLOORS: N.C.C.

YOUTH

ADULT

YARD

YARD

YARD

ICE SKATING
IN WINTER

SIZE ? IMAGE ? INFORMATION ?

SIZE ? INTERACTION ? IMPORTANCE ?

SITING ? INTEGRATION ?

The single drawing.

The concept of alternatives presumes a willingness on the part of the designer to explore multiple ways in which a building can be designed. One should fight off the inclination to accept and continue the development of only the first feasible solution that emerges. Part of design education involves exploring alternative ways a design could be in order to learn how a design should be. The same is true for the experienced designer.

The concept of hierarchy relates to the idea that a building is more than the sum of its parts. A building is an integration of a number of parts (materials, functions, and images), organized in a way that exceeds the mere sum of those parts. A design proposal should integrate the smallest parts into a whole, and the whole building into its site and environment. Some designers see this as a literal sequence where the pattern or configuration of the smallest part is embodied in the whole and vice versa; others emphasize an abstract composition of the various parts that requires the observer or user to speculate on just how the building makes a complete entity. The work of Earl Fay Jones typifies the "literal hierarchy" approach. The work of Hardy, Holzman, Pfeiffer typifies the "ambiguous hierarchy" approach.

The last concept—that of least effort—deals with the search for the most efficient way to achieve a desired result. For example, a building that achieves its function with a simple structure is often better than one that requires a complicated structure. Likewise, a building that minimizes energy use is better than one that uses more energy. Many of these factors relate to building costs, but least effort is also an aesthetic issue. This concept holds that simple, straightforward solutions that clearly respond to various issues are often the most sophisticated. The concept of least effort does not mean that architecture is the result of least effort on the part of the designer.

SKILLS

The designer should have knowledge of a wide variety of issues and methods, and a set of specific skills that facilitate the application of that knowledge to the client's project. While knowledge, feelings, and

House in Arkansas, by E. F. Jones: literal hierarchy (photo by Richard Payne).

Private school by Hardy, Holzman, Pfeiffer: ambiguous hierarchy (photo by Norman McGrath).

point of view are critical aspects of design, they are different from skills Knowledge is supported by skill, but skills do not substitute for knowledge. Architects are expected to have professional knowledge about buildings and the physical environment, and the skills to manipulate that knowledge in the service of the client and society at large. Thus, one large part of architectural education is devoted to transmitting knowledge and problem-solving methods, and another large part is devoted to the development of appropriate skills.

Unfortunately, there are many misconceptions (romantic and otherwise) about architects. For example, some beginning students expect to do a great deal of drafting and making of blueprints. Drafting is an applicable skill, but it is certainly not a dominant one. In fact, blueprints have not been in common use for twenty years. Another misconception holds that architects spend much time drawing finely detailed renderings of their projects. Perspective drawings are common, but fine renderings are most often done by specialists who work as consultants to architects.

The following sections attempt to provide a short description of the skills that are appropriate and typical in the design process.

Graphic Skills

Graphic skill in architecture basically means drawing, but it also includes a variety of other skills associated with model building, printing, photography, and the graphic arts. These skills can be categorized as visualization skills and generative drawing skills.

Every client—whether an executive from a large corporation or a family armed with ten years of clippings from magazines—wants to see what a building will look like before it is built. Clients want pictures. Drawings and models are therefore basic to communication between client and architect. Models, aerial perspective drawings, and slide or graphic presentations all have direct appeal to clients because they are usually easier to understand than the standard architectural graphics used by architects (plan, section, and elevation). The other type of graphic skill involves drawings used to generate design proposals and includes diagraming and abstraction. Diagrams are useful in planning circulation flow, site topography, surface water drainage, sun angles, and structural systems. This category also includes sketches—simple drawings that represent various aspects of a building design (such as the massing and arrangement of the major parts of a building).

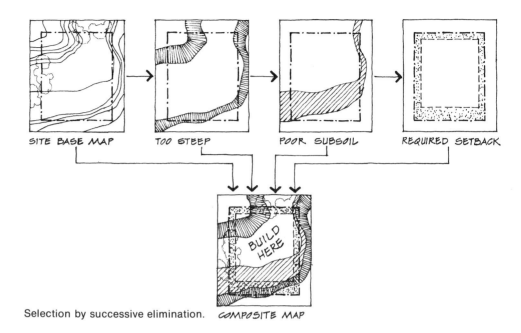

SITE BASE MAP TOO STEEP POOR SUBSOIL REQUIRED SETBACK

Selection by successive elimination. COMPOSITE MAP

Intellectual Skills

Architecture is both rational and intelligent; building design is the product of considerable knowledge and the appropriate application of that knowledge. There is no substitute for clear and concise thinking. Thus, the general skills associated with college-level education (the ability to think clearly about problems and methods for solving problems) are clearly appropriate. However, a number of specific skills are worth mentioning.

For example, designers must work in situations with some degree of ambiguity. They must often make decisions when they do not have enough information. This in turn can lead to high levels of frustration. A rational person expects to collect and analyze information and thus discover a solution. Unfortunately, in architecture, not only is there often a lack of sufficient information, but also the process by which a solution is to be derived is often uncertain.

Architects must use both deductive and inductive reasoning. Deduction derives a conclusion from an initial premise or general belief; it generates a specific conclusion from a general situation. An architect might feel that his or her design solution is the necessary and appropriate result of responding to building program requirements. For example, "Regular structural bays make efficient architecture; therefore, this particular building design should have regular structural bays." A variation of this type of reasoning is Ian McHarg's site planning method whereby a number of criteria are applied to a site.[13] It is a reduction process in which successive applications of various criteria eliminate portions of the site as being inappropriate for building or some other use. Each variable is mapped and combined in a composite map that reveals the appropriate places for the proposed activity. The specific conclusion necessarily follows from the general situation.

Conversely, inductive reasoning or inference generates a general belief from one or several individual observations. Evidence is collected from various sources to support a general rule. For example, "Every office building I have seen has regular structural bays; therefore, all office buildings must have regular structural bays." Inductive reasoning takes a leap of faith. General beliefs so derived can seldom be proven; a single exception destroys the rule. Designers often take such creative leaps, generating a building design inductively from a limited number of specific points rather than deductively from following the rules. John Portman's exciting hotels with their gigantic interior spaces certainly accommodate the applicable functions, but they are not the logical and necessary results of analyzing those functions.

Self-Criticism

Another important skill for designers is self-criticism. If criticism is a judgmental response to an idea or solution, then self-criticism is the ability of the designer to pass critical judgment (positive and negative) on his or her own work. This skill requires that the designer be able to redescribe any idea in several different ways so that original ideas can be compared to alternatives. On the one hand, this involves manipulating elements of the building—orientation, organization, massing, size, and so on. On the other hand, it means continuing to ask general questions about the project at various stages of the design: does the design still solve the basic program objectives? This type of criticism and evaluation is a traditional part of academic and professional design.

Thus, a variety of skills are required of architectural practice. Certainly, graphic, intellectual, and self-criticism skills are central to design. The expanding scope of architectural practice is placing increasing emphasis on written and verbal communication, however, as well as on management skills. Obviously, any number of specializations within the architecture require different skills. If all of this seems too much for any one individual, it is only because architecture is a broad and complex field of endeavor, with little consensus as to objectives and means. It also explains why the team approach has become common in architectural practice.

NOTES

1. John Wade, *Architecture, Problems and Purposes* (New York: John Wiley and Sons, 1977), p. 88.

2. J. C. Jones, *Design Methods* (London: John Wiley and Co., 1972), p. xii.

3. Christopher Alexander, *Notes on the Synthesis of Form* (Cambridge, Mass.: Harvard University Press, 1964), pp. 15–45.

4. Christopher Alexander and Serge Chermayeff, *Community and Privacy* (Garden City, N.Y.: Doubleday and Co., 1963), p. 145.

5. Christopher Alexander, Sara Ishikawa, and Murray Silverstein, *A Pattern Language* (New York: Oxford University Press, 1977).

6. Jane Holtz Kay, "Sizing Up Boston Architects," *Boston Magazine* (November, 1974), p. 113.

7. American Institute of Architects. *Architects Handbook of Professional Practice,* Chapter 9, "Owner Architect Agreements" (Washington, D.C.: American Institute of Architects, 1973), pp. 4, 5.

8. Ibid., Chapter 9, p. 4.

9. Ibid., Chapter 11, "Project Procedures" (Sept. 1969 ed.), p. 8.

10. Ibid., Chapter 12, "Construction Documents-Drawings" (April 1970 ed.), p. 3.

11. Ibid., Chapter 18, "Construction Contract Administration" (Jan. 1973 ed.), p. 3.

12. Ibid., Chapter 5, "The AIA Handbook: The Architect and Client" (Jan. 1975 ed.), pp. 3, 4.

13. Ian McHarg, *Design with Nature* (Garden City, N.Y.: The Natural History Press, 1969), pp. 31–41.

FOR FURTHER READING

Adams, J. L. *Conceptual Block Busting*. San Francisco: W. H. Freeman and Co., 1974.

Alexander, Christopher. *Notes on the Synthesis of Form*. Cambridge, Mass.: Harvard University Press, 1964.

Alexander, Christopher, Sara Ishikawa, and Murray Silverstein. *A Pattern Language*. New York: Oxford University Press, 1977.

The American Institute of Architects. *The Architects Handbook of Professional Practice*. Washington, D.C: The American Institute of Architects, annual.

Asimow, M. *Introduction to Design*. Englewood Cliffs, N.J.: Prentice-Hall, 1962.

Attoe, Wayne. *Architecture and Critical Imagination*. London: John Wiley and Sons, 1978.

Broadbent, Geoffrey, and Anthony Ward, ed. *Design Methods in Architecture.* London: Lund Humphries, 1969.

Chermayeff, S., and C. Alexander, *Community and Privacy: Toward a New Architecture of Humanism.* Garden City, N.Y.: Doubleday, 1963.

Ching, Frank G. *Architectural Graphics.* New York: Van Nostrand Reinhold, 1975.

Design Methods and Theories. Berkeley, Dept. of Architecture, University of California, quarterly.

Gordon, W. J. J. *Synectics: The Development of Creative Capacity.* New York: Harper and Row, 1961.

Gregory, S.A., *The Design Method.* London: Butterworths and New York: Plenum Press, 1966.

Hanks, Kurt, Larry Belliston, and David Edwards. *Design Yourself.* Los Altos, Calif. William Kaufmann, Inc., 1977.

Jones, J. Christopher. *Design Methods.* London: John Wiley and Sons, 1970.

Jones, J. Christopher, and D. G. Thornley, eds. *Conference on Design Methods.* London: Pergamon and New York: Macmillan, 1963.

Koberg, D., and J. Bagnall. *Universal Traveller.* Los Altos, Calf., William Kaufmann, Inc., 1977.

Lockhard, W. K. *Drawing As a Means to Architecture.* Tucson, Ariz.: Pepper Publishing, 1977.

McHarg, Ian L., *Design with Nature.* Garden City, N.Y.: The Natural History Press, 1969.

McKim, Robert H. *Experiences in Visual Thinking.* Monterey, Calif.: Brooks/Cole Publishing Co., 1972.

Moore, G. T., ed. *Emerging Methods in Environmental Design and Planning.* Cambridge, Mass.: M.I.T. Press, 1970.

Prince, G. M. *The Practice of Creativity.* New York: Harper and Row, 1970.

Sanoff, Henry. *Methods of Architectural Programming.* Stroudsburg, Pa.: Dowden, Hutchinson & Ross, 1977.

Wade, John. *Architecture, Problems and Purposes.* New York: John Wiley and Sons, 1977.

CHAPTER 8

Architectural Programming

John W. Wade

Architectural design includes programming, planning, and design phases. Programming is concerned primarily with the collection and organization of information that is required for building design. While some programming is simple, recording only what the client says about the building, other programming can be very complex and requires extended procedures and complex techniques. This chapter presents a step-by-step approach to the task of architectural programming.

PROGRAMMING

The work of architects can be divided into several very different areas. In the first part of their work, called *programming,* architects determine the concerns of the client for whom they are to design a building and what it is that the client needs. In the second part, they divide the client's general problem into a number of "standard" smaller problems that have known solutions or that are easily solved. This is sometimes called *planning.* In the third part of the work, architects use the information from the first two stages as a guide in developing a total idea and a proposal for the form and construction of the building. This part is called *design* (the entire process is also referred to as design). Architects then work out all of the details of the design and develop drawings and specifications that the builder will use for the construction of the building. In the last phase, architects oversee the process of construction and approve the manner in which the builder has carried it out.

When architects give a technical description of the design work that they will perform in a contract, they describe it in a somewhat different manner, in order to identify different parts of their work clearly for the client. The technical description is as follows.

Architects say, first, that the client must furnish

them with a program for the building. They call this first phase of work *schematic design*. In this phase, architects do a good deal of what will be described later as programming, and they develop a simplified proposal for the building. Since such a proposal is often exploratory and intended to elicit more information from the client concerning his or her likes and dislikes, this phase is really a form of research.

Architects call the second phase *design development*. During this phase they are guided by information from the client and by a schematic design that the client has accepted. They begin to work on a number of problems that must be solved in order for the building to function properly. When these problems have been solved, they develop an entire detailed scheme for the building. After this has been approved, architects proceed to a *construction documents* phase, during which detailed drawings and specifications are developed for the building. Then they proceed to the *construction* phase, where the contract for construction between the client and the builder is administered.

Although these two descriptions of the architect's work are different, they are not in disagreement; they simply emphasize different aspects of the work. The first description emphasizes the conceptual development of the work, while the second description emphasizes the products that result from different parts of the conceptual development. The two descriptions are useful in different contexts. Although you should keep both descriptions in mind, the following material will refer most often to the conceptual definition.

Architectural programming is concerned with information. The architect must know what the client is like, what the client's needs and purposes are, and what kind and quality of building the client must have.

It used to be true, and it sometimes is still true, that the client could determine what kind of building (whether a school, church, or city hall) was needed, the approximate size, and where it was to be located, and the architect could proceed with work.

The more important thing in architecture was the style that the architect imposed on the building; in those times usually the architect could not ensure that the building would function in exactly the way that the client intended. Engineering procedures were not so exact, and the client was not so knowledgeable about the needs of the building. Gradually, things changed. Very precise degrees of engineering control have been achieved over heating and cooling systems, electrical systems, structural systems, and all parts of building construction that affect the building functions. Clients have grown more and more exacting in their requirements. Thus, architectural programming has grown into a more important part of the design process than it once was. It can be a relatively simple or a relatively complex and extended part of design, depending on the kind of building and the kind of client for whom it is being designed. It has grown so important that some architectural firms have begun to specialize in programming services, using special techniques where the programming of a building is especially difficult or complicated.

A flow chart (based on the kind of flow chart that computer programmers use) can be used to show the range of different programming processes. By inserting different questions (or decision points) into the chart, it is possible to learn when some of the more complicated operations must come into effect, and when they can be neglected. The adjacent flow chart diagrams such a programming process.

The most important steps in the diagram are:

1 Beginning a program.
2 Developing a program.
14 Preparing the program.
15 Presenting the program.

These four are important because they must all be done regardless of the simplicity or the complexity of the program. Then, depending on how each of four questions is answered, other steps can come into use. The four questions are:

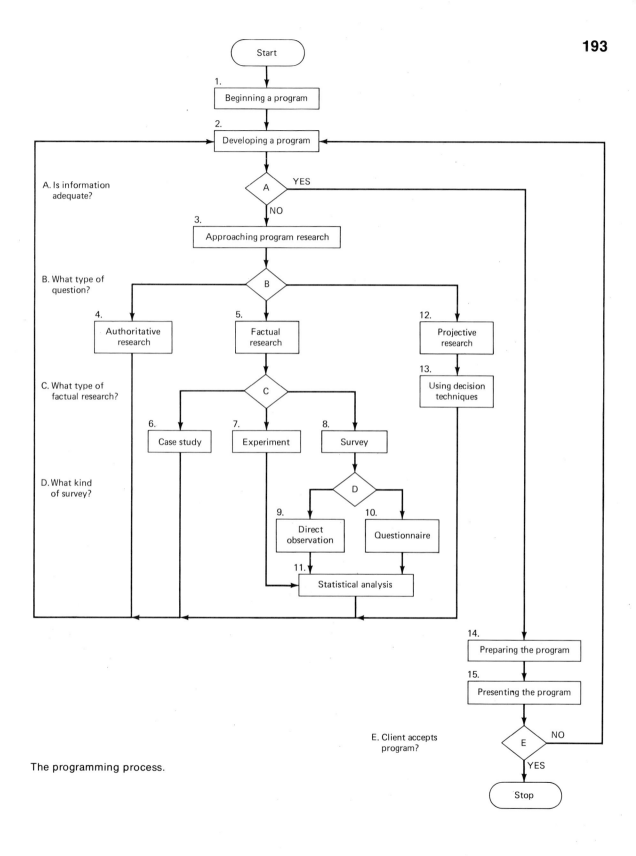

The programming process.

1 Is the information adequate?
2 What kind of information is needed?
3 What type of factual research is required?
4 What kind of survey should be used?

BEGINNING A PROGRAM

Programming usually begins in a tentative fashion when architects have their first conversations with their client or clients. If they are familiar with the building type, architects can assist the process by using prepared lists of questions about the building. If not, they might need to become familiar with the building by undertaking a type study. Building design is a well-understood process, and architects normally know what information they will need to undertake a successful design. If the building is unusual, they might need to obtain additional information. In either event, the initiation of the programming process should identify the full information that will be required. Classifying known information according to a spectrum (person, purpose, behavior, function, object) shows what information is missing and establishes the architects' information-gathering task.

When architects begin discussions with a client about the building they are to design, they must accomplish a number of tasks. First, they must learn as much as possible about the client's problem. This includes such things as identifying the building type, learning what is wrong with the existing building, estimating how severe the client's problems are, estimating the design effort required, and learning the client's needs (for a long-range plan, for a feasibility study, or for plans for immediate construction). They must also obtain an approximate budget for the building.

After the architect and his or her staff have obtained an initial knowledge of the client's problems, they might need to become familiar with the building type in question. If the firm has designed similar buildings in the past, a review of the recent periodical literature may be sufficient. However, if they have never designed such a building, a more careful and formal building type study may be required, consisting of collecting plans of the building type, sorting them into groups, and deriving from these groups the several basic schemes that have been used to design buildings of that sort. Such a study might be carried further by a logical expansion of these basic plans into the possible plans that could be used. Such familiarization is essential since it helps to identify the questions that still need to be asked of the client.

After this familiarization, architects proceed to somewhat more detailed questions about the client's problems. Has the client organization changed in size or character? Have the purposes of building changed? Does the client want to be able to do different kinds of things in the proposed structure than were planned in the past? Must the new building provide for different functions? Should the building have a different character? Has the present building become physically, functionally, or economically obsolete? Or has something about the environment of the building changed? Is there now too much noise, pollution, or traffic? While inquiring about the client's problems, the architect has in mind the kinds of information needed for the building design. This type of information is shown in Table 8-1.

A usual way of organizing questions is by classification—by grouping together questions on the same subject. There are several different forms of classification that are useful. The most common of these is a hierarchic scheme, whereby questions about the building are organized in the same way that the building will ultimately be organized. Thus there are questions about the building as a whole, about different departments or major subdivisions of the building, about each subdivision, and about individual rooms.

Programming statements by a client will take on a limited number of different forms: statements

TABLE 8-1

Types of Programming Information— A Classification System

1. Objectives of the master plan
2. Special restrictions and limitations on design
3. Characteristics of the site
4. Site development requirements
5. Functional requirements for the facility
6. Characteristics of the occupants
7. Specific facility requirements
   a Spaces and sizes
   b Number and character of occupants
   c Relative location and interrelations
   d Essential architectural equipment features and services
8. Relative location and interrelation of spaces
9. Budget
10. Flexibility for future growth and changes in functions
11. Priority of needs among the various requirements

Derived from Harold Horowitz, "The Program's the Thing," *AIA Journal* 47 (May 1967): 94–100.

about clients, their purposes, their desired behaviors, functions that are needed, or physical characteristics that the building should have. Because these statements can be converted from one form to the other, it is often useful to classify program statements into several categories.

There are several advantages in using standard forms of classification in collecting program information. First, architects can see the completeness of the information. Second, with a bit of experience, they can discover whether all the information is consistent or whether some is contradictory. Third, they can begin to determine which information is important. Fourth, at a later programming stage, they can amplify their information by inference or assumption.

After architects have had first conversations with a client, they can begin to develop a program outline. Such an outline is useful because it shows what must be done in order to complete the total programming that the building will require. The pro-

gram outline is affected by two principal considerations: how much information the client has to impart, and how the architect's design strategy will make use of that information. The flow chart in the figure below summarizes the procedure that has been described for initiating program development.

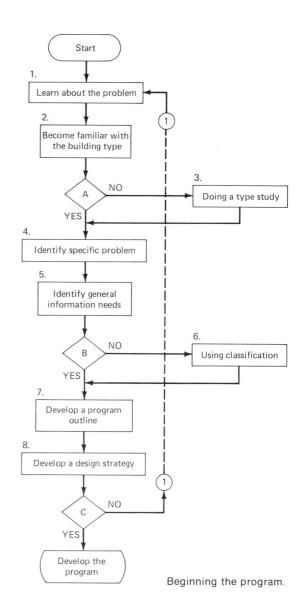

Beginning the program.

TABLE 8-2

Program Information Demands

Person (Person-structural properties)	Client, client organization
	Organization structure, line and staff, major departmental division
	Organization personnel, rank and role of personnel
	Informal organization, social structure
	Related organizations: serving or controlling organization, code agencies, lending institutions
	Users, clients, customers, patients, etc.
	Characteristics of users
	Changes in client, client organization, organization staff, users, desired changes, projected future changes
Purpose (Event-functional properties)	Public information about social impact of type organization
	Client philosophy, mission, goals, subgoals, objectives
	Departmental objectives
	User goals, objectives
	Objectives in master development plan
	Safety considerations
	Changes in purpose, objectives
	Desired changes, projected future changes
Behavior (Event-structural properties)	Operation of organization
	Operation of organization in relation to organization structure
	Operation of organization in relation to goals, objectives
	Behavior of organization personnel (structured, unstructured)
	Behavior of users (structured, unstructured)
	Changes in behavior
	Desired changes, projected future changes
Function (Object-functional properties)	Operational system, task system
	Information systems, circulation systems
	Material movement systems
	Utility systems, environment systems
	Space enclosure, division systems, structure systems structural load requirements, fire rating, alarm system, ventilation
	Changes in function, changes in function demand
	Desired changes, projected future changes
Object (Object-structural properties)	Existing and past projects of similar function, condition, size
	Existing building, facility, furnishings, equipment
	Site description and requirements, site access, utility access, land contours features, foliage, soil conditions, surroundings, climate
	Special restrictions, limitations on design exit requirements, materials, ventilation openings, toilets, sprinklers
	Requirements of lending institutions, insurors
	Requirements of planning, zoning boards
	Changes in objects, maintenance considerations
	Desired changes, projected future changes

Adapted from E. T. White, *Introduction to Architectural Programming,* Tucson, Ariz.: Architectural Media, 1972.

DEVELOPING THE PROGRAM

Before architects can proceed further with programming, they must plan the programming procedure. First conversations with the client have indicated what programming is necessary. Now, steps must be outlined that will let the architect accomplish the programming task. If the client has furnished a preliminary program, the task will be relatively simple; architects need only check the program for completeness, consistency, and accuracy. However, if the client has asked the architects to program a kind of building that has never been built before, it can be an extremely complex task. Even when the building is of a familiar type, if little is known about the people who will use the building, the task of finding out can impose a difficult programming problem.

In order to plan the programming procedure, architects must take into consideration what kind of data are needed, what form the data should be in to be most useful, whether the data are available in this form, when the different kinds of data will be needed, who will be available to collect the data, and who the data must be collected from. Architects must select an approach to data collection based upon the above considerations, outline the form in which the organized data are to appear, outline the data analysis task, and outline the data collection task. In effect, the architects work backward from the information needed through the different steps they must take to develop the information in the right form. Effort can be saved if some parts of the data are available from the client or some other source in an already organized form; examples include plans of the existing building, an organization chart of the company or institution that will occupy the building, flow charts of such a company's production process, and the like. When these sources are exhausted, the architect must next determine who has the information that is needed. While major policy questions must be directed to top management, many detailed questions must be addressed to those persons who are closest to the problem.

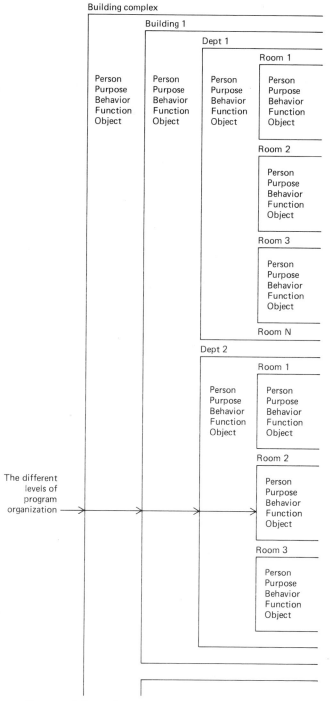

Program information organization.

198

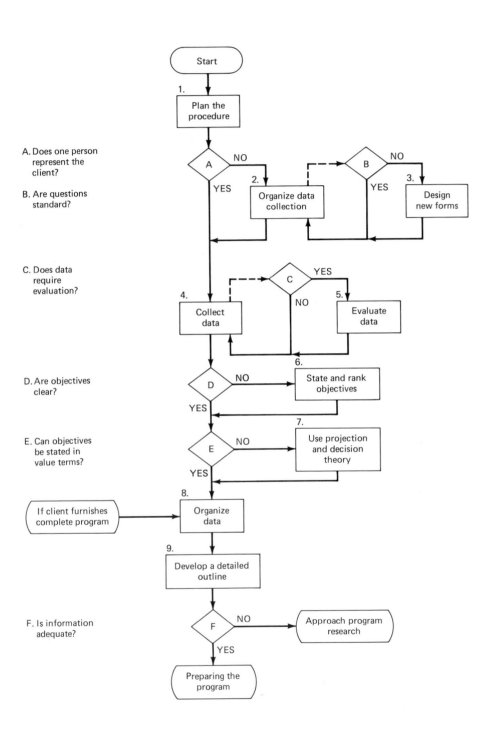

A. Does one person represent the client?

B. Are questions standard?

C. Does data require evaluation?

D. Are objectives clear?

E. Can objectives be stated in value terms?

F. Is information adequate?

Developing the program.

INTRODUCTION TO ARCHITECTURE

Data needs must be matched to data sources. As with the initial interviews, questionnaires are used at this stage. When a questionnaire is to be distributed to a number of persons, considerable care should be taken in its development. Devising such a questionnaire calls for considerable specialized skill. If the architects do not have such skill, the services of a consultant may be required to assist in preparing an effective and economical questionnaire. When appropriate questionnaires have been devised for the different data sources, interviews must be scheduled and conducted with individuals and groups. If the data fit into one of the standard classification schemes that the architects have used in the past, and if there is no conflict between different parts of the data, little effort will be required to evaluate the data. If the data are complete, they can confirm the data with the client and proceed with development of the program.

If the data cannot fit into a standard format, considerable effort must be directed to data evaluation. A new classification may have to be developed. For example, the data might show a stronger need for building staff and maintenance personnel than the usual building requires, and a reorganization of classifications to accommodate space and equipment for such persons might be needed. With an appropriate classification scheme, architects can examine information for completeness, for notable distinctions between different parts of the data (which could suggest that different parts of the building might need to be very different in character), or for conflicts between different parts of the data. If there are conflicts, they must determine whether these are the result of inaccuracy in data collection, or whether there are real conflicts of interest and purposes on the part of the client or of different segments of the client organization. If conflicts are the result of inaccuracies, a revised process may be appropriate. If real conflicts exist in the client's objectives, architects might work with the client in stating objectives more clearly and ranking those objectives to clear the conflicts that exist. If the objectives

can be stated in value terms, it may be useful to project possible future conditions that could affect the client's objectives. Decision theory techniques might be used to assist in making a choice of objectives. If the architects are not skilled in these techniques, operations research or systems theory consultants may be used.

When the data are available and complete, they can be organized in a manner that will assist the first design effort. In simpler buildings, architects can go directly to the development of a graphic "bubble diagram" that shows the relationship between the various spaces in the building. They are guided in the development of a bubble diagram by the earlier building type study.

By contrast, if the building is complex, or if there are no previous buildings of a similar type to guide the work, the architects will need to use some of the techniques developed recently (within the last fifteen years), using matrices, clustering techniques, and graph theory to define the interrelationships that must exist between the different parts of the building. Matrices are used in one form or another (interaction matrix, role-interaction matrix, service request matrix, function context matrix) to define the separate relationships between all the different spaces that have been defined for the building. Clustering techniques are used to form those individual spaces into groups of spaces with strong interactions and to separate them from other spaces in groups with which there are only weak or negative interactions or no interactions at all. For example, the serving-served relationship between a dining room and a kitchen is a strong interaction, the serving-served relationship between a janitor's closet and any single one of a suite of offices is a weak interaction, the relationship between library activities and kitchen garbage-disposal activities is a noninteraction, and the relation between a noisy play area and a quiet study or library space is a negative interaction. Finally, graph theory can be used to organize all of these interactions (and clusters of interactions) into a graph or di-graph that shows the

ARCHITECTURAL PROGRAMMING

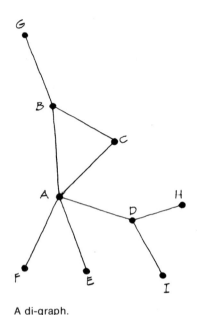

A di-graph.

A dual graph.

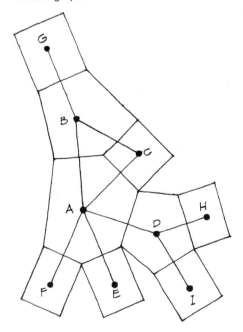

space relationships that need to exist in the building. Such a graph is a more sophisticated version of a bubble diagram; more complex graphs of this sort must be developed with the aid of a computer. When the bubbles in a bubble diagram have been placed in scale with the sizes of the spaces that they represent, the architects have developed a first approximation of a building plan. In a similar fashion, a dual-graph technique exists that converts a graph or di-graph into a first plan approximation.

Given adequate data and the process described on page 198, the architect is now ready to write a program and present it to the client and other applicable groups. However, before describing that process, let us return to the situation in which the information is incomplete. The architect cannot proceed with data organization but must undertake program research activities.

APPROACHING PROGRAM RESEARCH

When adequate information is unavailable from the client, architects must find a way to collect it.

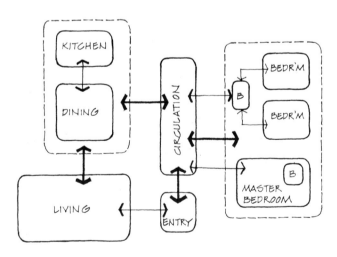

A simple bubble diagram.

Depending on the kind of information needed, data collection can be approached in several different ways. If more than one kind of information is missing, a number of approaches may be required. In terms of program research, there are three kinds of information: authoritative, factual, and projective. Authoritative information is that which the client can and does furnish about personal preferences if a question is asked about those preferences in a way that permits an answer. Factual information is what the client does not have but that can be obtained by the usual behavioral research methods (case studies, surveys, or experiments). Projective information is data the client does not have and that is not avail-

able by conventional research. Rather, it must be obtained by developing a mathematical representation of the client's circumstance. The representation can then be used to describe the impact of different conditions that the client might face and the value of different choices that the client could make under those conditions.

Before the architects can say just which kind of information they need, questions must be stated very clearly. The first step in stating a question is to find the problem area, perhaps by use of an ends-means information classification scheme. That classification scheme is based on two facts: that buildings are tools that help people do things, and that people do

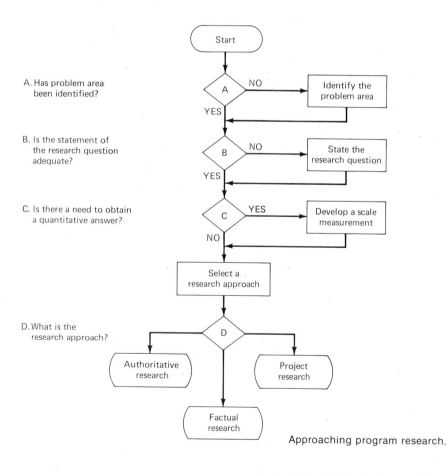

A. Has problem area been identified?

B. Is the statement of the research question adequate?

C. Is there a need to obtain a quantitative answer?

D. What is the research approach?

Approaching program research.

things because they have purposes. Stated in a formal way, designed objects (including buildings) have functions (or capabilities) that assist behaviors in order to achieve the purposes of people (or their organizations).

These words form the classification scheme, with each word being a label for a part of the classification. The scheme is useful because each of its parts is a typical way in which people describe their needs; they can say who they are, what they want, what they want to do, how their buildings should help them, and what qualities their buildings should have. As it happens, different professional disciplines focus their interests around one or the other of the different parts of this classification scheme:

Person (or organization)	Organization studies
Purposes	Operations research
Behaviors	Environment-behavior studies, environmental psychology
Functions	Systems engineering
Object	Design research

Each of these disciplines has techniques for answering a number of different kinds of questions associated with its area.

When the research question has been stated with as much accuracy as possible, the architects must then select the manner in which they believe the question can best be answered. If the question is one of preference, they will undertake authoritative research; if it is one of simple fact they will choose a factual research approach; and if it is about the value of alternative courses of action under different conditions, they will choose a projective research method. If they do not have appropriate skills in these different methods, they must obtain the assistance of consultants from an appropriate disciplinary area to assist their research. These matters are summarized in the figure on page 201.

Undertaking Authoritative Research

If the information needed is something that the client can provide, the architect must find ways to ask questions in a way that the client can answer. Of course, the most usual way is by a direct question, but if this fails (as it often does), the architects can undertake a schematic design of the building based upon assumed answers to those questions. The way the client responds to the schematic design proposal usually answers the architect's question.

Authoritative research (about client's preferences) can be undertaken by the process just outlined. The architects develop their information as far as possible by inference and by assumption. They then develop a schematic design to show the several things in a context. They review the schematic design with the client, making explicit the quality of the information on which the design was based in order to get the client's reaction to the design and to the information. Depending on the client's reaction, the architects keep or change the information that they have developed.

Undertaking Factual Research

When the information that architects need is factual information that the client does not have, then an entirely different approach must be taken. The architect must approach such research in the same manner that the behavioral sciences have approached it—by means of the case study, the survey, or the experiment. Sometimes architects have the skill to undertake a simple survey by use of a questionnaire, but if the research question is at all complicated, they will need to call on the services of behavioral scientists.

If the question is in an exploratory stage and only tentative answers are needed, then a *case study* exploring the entire area of the question might be most appropriate. By contrast, if the question is more specific and deliberate and is already based on an exploratory knowledge of the area in question, then a more precise form of study (either a survey or an experiment) will usually be required. If the question is about causal relationships between different subjects or different events, then an experiment is probably most appropriate. If the question is about the distribution of different kinds of events or different properties of a subject, then a survey is the appropriate research device.

Regardless of the kind of study, there are some basic rules guiding the manner of its execution. If the question is about some stable and visible condition, then more accurate information can usually be obtained by direct observation made by the researchers. By contrast, if the question is about something that is not stable but is fugitive in occurence, or if it is about something that is not visible (like an opinion), then the researchers will have to rely upon inquiries from persons who were present when the fugitive event occurred or who are knowledgeable about the nonvisible event.

Finally, if the set of questions is relatively simple, the research can be carried out in a nonparticipative way (even by a mailed questionnaire), but if the question set is very complex, or if the questions that are asked depend in a strong way on the answers to questions that have gone before, then the researchers must be present and must participate in the research procedure, guiding its course until all of the questions have been answered.

Undertaking Projective Research

When the research question is complex and when it depends on future events, the architect will need to call upon projective research. The help of professional consultants may be needed, because the projective research procedure is even more complex than with factual research. Some of the techniques are similar to those of factual research, but

the most important element in this form of research is quite different. The technique is called *modeling*.

In this technique, an abstract model of the situation under study is developed. Usually the model is a mathematical representation of all of the different variable conditions that affect the situation. For example, in dealing with the selection of a site for a shopping center, alternate sites would be described in terms of costs (land acquisition, taxes, construction costs at that site, and so on), market area (the number of customers within a certain driving time), the possibility of other development in the vicinity, the potential mix of stores interested in occupying a shopping center at that site, and so on. These several factors would be put together in a model to represent the profitability of the center under different kinds of economic circumstances in the future. Each different economic circumstance would be dealt with as if it were more or less likely to occur. Its mathematical probability would be applied to the model, and a probable outcome for each future circumstance could be derived from the model.

In effect, such a model abstracts in mathematical terms the important features of the real situation that affect the operations of the system under study. A model like this has several uses. It can demonstrate how the system will respond to different outside influences. It can permit the decision maker to choose the course of action that will produce the best outcome (in terms of the model). It can locate the most sensitive internal components of a system (those that have the strongest influence on an outcome) and permit a detailed study of those components. This kind of study can then lead to a reconsideration and a redesign of that component.

Such projective research (which has been called *operations research, systems research,* and *decision research*) depends upon techniques of factual research. Usually substantial amounts of factual research are required in order to construct an adequate mathematical model of the situation. Because of this, projective research is a time-consuming and costly process. It should be used only when there is clear and strong evidence that there is no other way to obtain the required information.

PREPARING THE PROGRAM

As the required research efforts are completed, each new piece of information is fitted into the overall information collection effort. As each piece of information is added, the collected information is compared with a detailed list or outline of the required information. When this list is complete, actual program preparation proceeds. In fact, the development of the completed program usually begins before the last piece of information has been secured. The advantage of an organized program format is that work can proceed on the parts while other information is still being collected.

The completed program often takes the form of a printed book or brochure. The form in which the contents of the program are arranged should follow the basic logic by which the program was developed. A useful form for this is a modification of the information spectrum described above. That spectrum should include who the client and/or user is, the client's purposes, the behaviors that will accomplish those purposes, the functions that are required in the building to assist those behaviors, and the physical characteristics of the completed building.

The program can then take the following outline form:

1 *Front matter:* Title, foreword or preface, table of contents, purpose and scope of the document, program organization, and programming methodology.

2 *Client/User:* Who the persons and institutions are for whom the building is to be designed.

3 *Problems and Purposes:* What the existing condi-

tions are and what problems they make for the client. What the client's purposes are that require a change in those conditions.

4 *Desired Behaviors:* What the client and/or user wishes to be able to do in order to carry out those purposes. What specific objectives the client has for the building.

5 *Function Criteria:* What functions the building should supply that will assist those behaviors. Function criteria for the different operating systems of the building, room-by-room lists of requirements, bubble diagrams, or other such devices that show the important relationships between different parts and rooms of the building.

6 *Object Criteria:* Physical requirements, as imposed by local codes, client's preferences, and the like.

7 *Approaches:* Type studies, patterns, organizing ideas, and other forms of recommendation that suggest how the architects can approach the design of the building.

8 *Back Matter:* Index, appendices, exhibits, definitions, bibliography, credits, and so on.

Under the head *Client/User* the program can deal with such matters as identification of the client and/or user or of the client institution, the client's background, the client's and/or user's demographic characteristics, the client's philosophy, a history of the client institution's operations and development, and the like.

Problems and Purposes can include a description of the client's current operation, an analysis of existing conditions, the facts that willl affect an architectural solution to the client's problems, the existing constraints and limiting conditions, the general client purposes and goals, the purposes that motivate the specific project, and the general trends that exist among institutions of the client's type.

The section on *Desired Behaviors* must discuss specific project goals and objectives, what the project should accomplish for the client in operational and behavioral terms, the social and behavioral constraints that exist on the project, which behaviors are task-related and highly structured, and which are more socially oriented and less strongly structured. There can also be subsections that deal with the condition of the project, time schedules and time constraints on the project, project priorities, and a project budget.

Function Criteria can include general precepts for the arrangement of functional areas and their disposition on the site; performance requirements for each of the different functional systems described in a room-by-room manner; environmental and operational requirements for the different functional areas; and various means for describing the interrelationship between spaces, including bubble diagrams, relationship graphs, interaction matrices, and the like.

Object Criteria consist of architectural design criteria; lists of physical characteristics for the building and its parts; equipment, products, or materials that the client would like to have used in the building and the manner in which they will influence the building design; lists of code requirements; and zoning ordinances and other physical standards that will affect building design.

The *Approaches* can include typological studies that display the usual manner in which similar buildings have been designed, patterns of solutions to specific problems within the building, a statement of design philosophy or design approach that indicates how the architect expects to approach the problems, and basic organizing ideas by which the problems can be solved.

A booklet or brochure of the kind that we have described requires considerable degrees of skill in several areas. While the development of the program information required the exercise of logical and mathematical skills, the development of the program itself requires writing, editing, and organizing skills. The publication of the booklet or brochure requires artistic and graphic design skills and experience with reproduction processes. It is not enough

to have written the material in an orderly manner; the material must also be displayed on the page in a manner that distinguishes different parts from each other, emphasizes the most important points, and makes the program easy to read and to understand. Illustrations must be used to reinforce the written material.

PRESENTING THE PROGRAM

Ordinarily, the architect is required to make an oral presentation of this program to client groups. While the written program can provide the enormous detail that a building program entails, an oral summary or presentation of the program can help the client to better understand the program.

Architects often present programs to user groups in addition to the primary clients (they are often different groups). While the client group is not always receptive itself to a proposal for change, it has become a commonplace event over the last two decades for user groups to be outspokenly hostile to possible change. Architects often face a dilemma. In whose interest must they speak? Must their motive be to seek the quickest acceptance of the program proposal, assuming that to be in their client's direct interest? If this is so, should architects use their skill in public presentation to highlight the most acceptable aspects of the program, and to underplay or downplay the least acceptable aspects? Do they speak in their own self-interest, demonstrating the professional qualities that will ensure their acceptance in positions of trust and to ensure quality projects? Or, by contrast, should they adopt a more neutral stance?

It seems clear that a neutral stance is best. Not only must architects present the different points of view clearly and fairly, they must also make sure that their manner of presentation does not inadvertently favor one position over others.

There is a certain skill required in presentation that depends for its development on being able to imagine what the listener needs to hear.

SUMMARY

Architectural programming (depending on the complexity of the design project) passes through a number of distinct phases and requires a number of different skills. Some of these skills are very different from those usually associated with the work of an architect.

When architects first approach a client they must develop a quick understanding of what kind of building the client needs. If they are not familiar with that kind of building, they must be able to develop a quick familiarity. They can be helped in the initial program stages by checklists and by lists of standard questions to ask the client. After initial interviews have established the general character of the building, architects usually proceed by developing an overall outline of the information that will be needed for the design of the building. They are helped in this by their former experiences in programming. It is especially helpful if they can classify program information according to persons, purposes, behaviors, functions, or objects. Such classification permits them to see what information is missing and what must be supplied.

One kind of information that can be missing involves the client's preferences. Such information is most easily obtained by developing schematic design proposals. This is called authoritative research—determining within a context of other known preferences what the client's remaining preferences are.

The other kind of information that can be missing is factual information. Such information must be supplied by factual research after the manner of the behavioral sciences, or where the information is complex by projective research that uses the technique of mathematical modeling.

When the information is complete, architects must then organize it into a written and publishable form and make both written and oral presentations of this material to their clients and sometimes to user groups. When the program has been fully accepted by the client, it becomes a basis for the later stages of the building design process.

In the early phases of programming, architects must make use of analytic, logical, and mathematical skills, and they must make use of several specific programming techniques (interaction matrices and graphs of relationship). In the later phases of program development, architect must be able to use writing and editing skills. They might need to develop clear diagrams, drawings, or maps, and they will need to organize this material for printing using skills in graphic design. Finally, they must be able to make an orderly oral presentation of their program before groups of clients and users.

FOR FURTHER READING

Pena, William M., and J. W. Focke. *Problem Seeking: New Directions in Architectural Programming.* Houston: Caudill, Rowlett & Scott, 1969.

Sanoff, Henry. *Methods of Architectural Programming.* Stroudsburg, Pa.: Dowden, Hutchinson & Ross, 1977.

Wade, John W. *Architecture, Problems, and Purposes: Architectural Design as a Basic Problem Solving Process.* New York: John Wiley & Sons, 1977.

White, Edward T. *Introduction to Architectural Programming.* Tucson, Ariz.: Architectural Media, 1972.

CHAPTER 9

Concepts in Architecture

Tim McGinty

A simple definition of a concept suggests that concepts are ideas that integrate various elements into a whole. In the context of this text, these elements can be ideas, notions, thoughts, and observations. In architecture, a concept suggests a specific way that programmatic requirements, context, and beliefs can be brought together. Thus, concepts are an important part of architectural design.

This chapter explores the place of concepts in architectural design, including the five types of concepts: analogies, metaphors, essences, direct response (and problem solving), and ideals.

CONCEPTS

Concepts do not have to be invented by the architect. Probably the best example of a response to a concept already stated in the client's program is Le Corbusier's design for the Carpenter Center of the Visual Arts at Harvard University. The Center for the Visual Arts is an undergraduate division of the university and is open to all students, not just art majors. The concept in the program was that if more students were aware of the programs, and if they could see the activity and life of the Center, then they would be more likely to enroll in the Center's classes. Le Corbusier's response was to make a ramp out of a pedestrian circulation path that already passed through the site, to have it tunnel through the middle of the building, providing views into many of the studios and workshops.

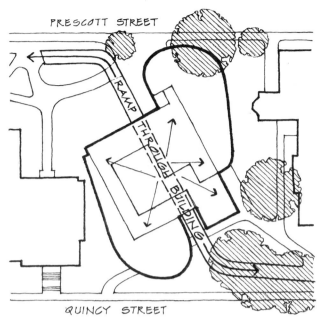

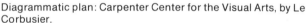

Diagrammatic plan: Carpenter Center for the Visual Arts, by Le Corbusier.

Carpenter Center, by Le Corbusier. (Balthazar Korab)

The following six synonyms have been used by various designers to describe their search for concepts: architectural ideas, themes, superorganizing ideas, *parti* and *esquisse,* and literal translations.

Architectural ideas are concepts that have been reduced to a formal architectonic concern like daylight, space, sequences of spaces, integration of structure and form, and siting in the landscape. Each can influence the general design of a building. The specific architectonic concern is then used as the basis for the design decisions that follow. A theme is a specific pattern or idea that recurs throughout the design of a project. It can be narrow in intention, like a specific geometric theme that appears throughout the project, or it can be more general. Charles Moore suggests that his work is a search for the particular way in which each of several themes or principles that interest him can be developed.[1] The title of a booklet on Louis I. Kahn's Kimbell Art Gallery in Fort Worth, Texas, is "Light is the Theme." Kahn argues that the changing mood of daylight over the seasons, as well as during a single day, is the key to complementing a great work of art. In designing the gallery he concentrated on bringing that changing quality of daylight into the building.[2]

Kimbell Art Gallery, Fort Worth, Texas, by
Louis I. Kahn. (Marshall D. Meyers)

Superorganizing ideas refer to the general geometric configurations or hierarchies that the parts of a project should respect. Urban
design and campus planning provide some clear examples in which
an overall organizing pattern is established and the pattern filled in. A
superorganizing idea allows variations among the parts, just as long
as they reinforce the overall pattern. Thomas Jefferson's plan for the
campus of the University of Virginia is a good example. The goal of
the superorganizing idea was to give enough structure to the pattern
so that the individual parts could be developed with their own idiosyn-
cracies and still support the whole. This was true in Jefferson's
design, where there is a clear overall pattern yet the individual houses
have their own identities.

The design of circulation in large projects sometimes constitutes
the superorganizing idea. In the case of the Air and Space Museum in
Washington, D.C., by Hellmuth, Obata, and Kassabaum, the decision
to develop the scheme around a circulation pattern proved to be a
wise one, because the number of visitors has exceeded peak predictions.

The *parti* (scheme) and *esquisse* (sketch) are the conceptual and
graphic products of a particular method of instruction developed in
the Beaux Arts Schools of France during the nineteenth century. This
method demanded that students develop their conceptual skills to a
high level. They were expected to develop a concept and preliminary

University of Virginia Campus, by Thomas Jefferson. (Ed Roseberry)

National Air and Space Museum, Washington, D.C. by Hellmuth, Obata, and Kassabaum. (Kiku Obata)

sketch of the building configuration in the first few hours of work on a project and to hold to that *parti* throughout the project.

Literal translation is a phrase used by Edward Larrabee Barnes to describe the goal of developing a concept and diagram that can become the simplified plan for the project. To Barnes, the concept for a project should be expressible in the kind of sketch one might do on a napkin. Presumably, that original diagram would be just as visible and identifiable in the finished building as it was on the napkin. According to Barnes:

> A building must have a strong idea that is architectural rather than sculptural or painterly—one that is related to the activity in the building. . . . When one architect asks another: 'What kind of building are you doing?', one should immediately be able to draw an abstraction, or a diagram, of the architectural idea.[3]

Concepts are the antithesis of notions, which do not make any pretense about being appropriate. A notion for the design of a bird cage at a zoo might be that of a bird in flight. The fact that the design might not have enough unobstructed space in it to actually allow the birds to fly and get the exercise they need would be of no concern. As a notion the idea would be acceptable and, perhaps, amusing; as a concept, it would not be appropriate. A concept implies appropriateness; it supports the main intentions and goals of a project and respects each project's unique characteristics and restrictions.

Diagrammatic plan of National Air and Space Museum, Washington, D.C.

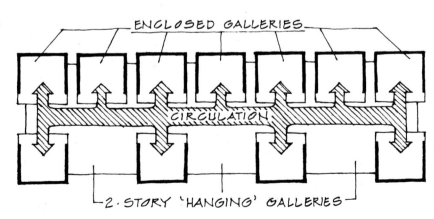

CONCEPTS AND ARCHITECTURAL DESIGN

Concept formulation is not an automatic activity. It takes a concentrated effort to develop a concept that appropriately integrates things not previously brought together. Bringing things together is a creative act—one that designers, architects, critics, artists, musicians, and writers have identified as being about 10 percent inspiration or genius and 90 percent hard work. Concept formulation is an unfamiliar activity for most people, and students of architecture have as much trouble mastering it as they do other aspects of design. Three problems block skill development in conceptualizing. The first block deals with problems of communication, the second with inexperience, and the third with the problems of generating hierarchies.

The first problem the student encounters is communication. Surprisingly, the most difficult communication problem is not in explaining our concepts to others, but in explaining our ideas to ourselves. Designers learn to develop a dialogue within their own minds as a prelude to explaining ideas to others. Another communication problem that influences concept formulation is graphic communication. Ironically, many students are hesitant to sketch as part of their process of developing concepts. In architecture, everything must get drawn if it is to be built, and drawings comprise half of the contract documents for building. The process of sketching should begin early so that the proposal and its concept can continually be criticized and improved.

Louis Kahn offers an anecdote suggesting that the communication problem between the imagined building and one's first sketches is a universal problem for students:

> A young architect came to ask a question. 'I dream of spaces full of wonder—of spaces that rise and evolve flowingly without beginning, without end—of a jointless material white and gold. . . . Why is it that when I place the first line on paper to capture the dream, the dream becomes less?'. . . . This is a good question. . . . This is a question of the measurable and the unmeasurable. . . . To express oneself in music or architecture one must employ the measurable means of composition or design. The first line on paper is already a measure of what cannot be expressed fully.[4]

The second problem area of unfamiliarity is an extension of the first. Concepts are difficult to invent if they are an unfamiliar aspect of architecture. Since many buildings are built without the benefit of a concept, and since most critics and many architects avoid writing about them, it is relatively easy for the beginning designer to have no ambitions for concepts and no understanding of the role they play in building design.

The third problem area can be simplified as the problem of identifying appropriate hierarchies. This is especially a problem for the beginning student who, because of lack of experience, has difficulty deciding if an idea is a brilliant concept or an awful one. The architect must be able to make discerning judgments. An understanding of the relationships among ideas, notions, and concepts can help resolve all three problems.

Ideas

Ideas are specific, concrete thoughts we have as the result of an understanding, insight, or observation. In architecture we have ideas about many things, including ways to orient a building, the placement of a kitchen, the best means to benefit from natural ventilation, the value of energy conservation, the importance of durable materials, transitions between forms, the best way to develop a spatial sequence, and the like. Buildings and building design are composed of many small decisions, and it is important to develop skills in generating ideas and concepts that respond to the wide variety of issues that emerge.

Frank Lloyd Wright is a good example of an architect who had many ideas about how things should be done. In his book, *Wright's Usonian Houses,* John Stewart reprints an article from *House and Home* (a magazine primarily for builders) that identified 35 ideas that Wright had about the design and construction of small homes. Likewise, Christopher Alexander and his colleagues, in *A Pattern Language,* have identified more than 1,000 ideas, mostly about human behavior and reactions to environments, which they call patterns. These are collected as an "ideas bible" for building designers. Neither the ideas listed by Wright nor the patterns devised by Alexander are unified. While Wright shows how his ideas could go together in his completed buildings, the ideas are offered as individual words and are not linked together. In each case the conceptual linkings are left to the individual designer or builder.

Notions

Notions are very similar to ideas except that there is a connotation of randomness. Notions are ideas that are presumed to be insubstantial, unsubstantiated, or often trivial when tested against other ideas. Still, there is always the possibility that there is an important germ of truth hiding in even a glib remark. Given this definition of notion, one might expect that notions have no role to play in concept formulation. This is not the case. One of the basic tenets of scientific problem solving, or *synectics,* as it is called by Gordon, is random idea generation.[5] When one is working on a problem that has evaded resolution, any idea or notion might contain the germ of the solution. Synectics and other idea-generation techniques depend on the ability of a small group of people to generate many ideas—some of them apparently absurd, irrevelant, and notional—as the initial and critical step in a process aimed at resolving the problem.

In architecture, an appropriate concept for a project may persistently resist articulation, and it may be necessary to invent notions as a step in formulating an appropriate concept, both as a key technique in conceptual blockbusting, and as a necessary result of inexperience in design and concept formulation. Students can expect to be inventing notions when they wish they were inventing concepts.

Concepts and Ideas

Concepts are similar to ideas, in that they are specific thoughts we have as a result of an understanding, except that a concept has this particular characteristic: it is a thought concerning the way several elements or characteristics can be combined into a single thing. In architecture, a concept also identifies how various aspects of the requirements for a building can be brought together in a specific thought that directly influences the design and its configuration. A concept in architecture is an ambitious thing, the result of a concentrated and imaginative effort to bring apparently dissimilar things together.

Two American architects associated with concepts are Eero Saarinen and Edward Larrabee Barnes. Saarinen advised:

> The character or expression of any building can only be achieved if it is itself a total expression. Like any work of art, it must be dominated by a strong, simple concept. All of its parts must be an active part of one dominant attitude. This is true whether the elements and decisions are big, early ones, like plan and structural systems, or later ones, like interior color and door knobs. This challenge of making a building a total expression seems to me the highest and most difficult one. But it is the one that I think must concern all of us most.[6]

Barnes suggests a similar view:

> There is an essential oneness about every job. In the best solutions there is a strong central idea involving activity. It may be static or mobile, but it has to do with the human being in space.[7]

Conceptual Scenarios

Given that the requirements for a building can number in the hundreds, supplemented by additional requirements and goals that the architects themselves incorporate, it should be apparent that a single concept statement that ties all the elements together could be both ambitious and elusive. Architects, in their writings and lectures about the concepts behind their designs, often offer short essays or scenarios that tie together all the important factors and ideas that influenced their solution.

While the goal in developing a concept appropriate to a project is to integrate the various parts into a unified whole, a designer expects the final building itself to be the integrated statement of several concepts. The name for this design strategy based on concepts for individual parts is incrementalism. An incremental attitude toward design suggests that architecture comes from resolving individual issues according to their own needs, and not by searching for overall concepts.

Another strategy or resolving this dilemma is for the architect to be less demanding about how much a concept should include. Saarinen, although known for his enthusiasm for using concepts, typically generated only very general conceptual statements for his buildings. For example, he identified the following conceptual image for the John Deere Company's world headquarters. While it offers some insights into the intentions behind the project, it does not help us answer other basic architectural questions about why the building is broken into parts or straddles a valley.

> Deere and Company is a secure, well-established, successful farm machinery company, proud of its Midwestern farm-belt location. Farm machinery is not slick, shiny metal but forged iron and steel in big, forceful, functional shapes. The proper character for its headquarters' architecture should likewise not be a slick, precise, glittering glass and spindly metal building, but a building which is bold and direct, using metal in a strong, basic way.[8]

Saarinen often developed concepts only for one or two issues in a project, leaving the development of other aspects of the design to circumstances. The strategy of developing only very general concept statements is also similar to the Beaux-Arts method of developing an initial *parti* and then finding ways of carrying out that idea throughout the rest of the project.

The conceptual scenario expands the concept statement, turning it into a short essay that includes more than one major issue and identifies more than one set of visual images for the project. The conceptual scenario can be used to identify how all the important ideas and

John Deere offices, by Eero Saarinen. (Ezra Stoller/ESTO)

issues that might be left out in a briefer conceptual statement could be brought together in a longer prose statement. The following three excerpts from lengthy scenarios by architects with different styles of building show a shared interest in concepts. Wright's discussion of Unity Temple is just as inventive and exciting now as it was when it was written during the first decade of this century. Kevin Roche's scenario was offered as part of an interview about his work on the Ford Foundation Building, and Barnes' statement is about the design of the Walker Art Center in Minneapolis. Frank Lloyd Wright:

> Why not, then, build a temple, not to GOD in that way—more senti-mental than sense—but build a temple to man, appropriate to his uses as a meeting place, in which to study man himself for his God's sake? A modern meeting-house and good-time place.

> Build a beautiful ROOM proportioned to this purpose. Make it beautiful in this *simple* sense. A *natural* building for natural Man . . .

> That ROOM; it began to be that same night. Enter the realm of archi-tectural ideas. The first idea—to keep a noble ROOM in mind, and let the room shape the whole edifice, let the room inside be the architec-ture outisde.[9]

Kevin Roche:

> We were trying to create a sense of community. . . . In an organization, the problem of common purpose is critical. A group of people spends

Unity Temple, Oak Park, Illinois, by Frank Lloyd Wright. (Hedrich-Blessing)

Unity Temple floor plan, by Frank Lloyd Wright.

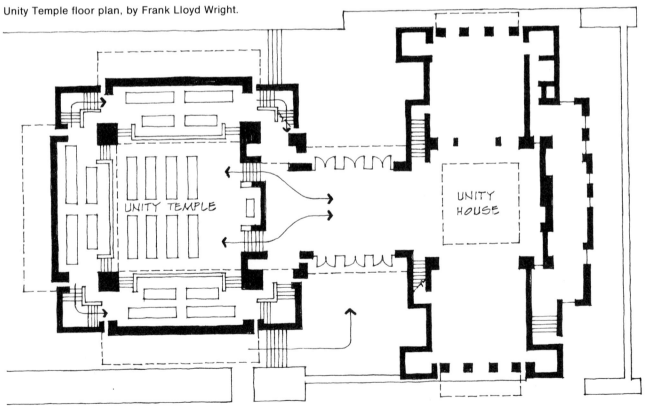

working hours dedicated to some purpose. . . . Let's say that they are in fact people concerned about making a contribution to the world in which they live. Within the Ford Foundation, they are a part of an instrument which has a lot of money which can, if properly directed, be a fairly substantial contribution to many areas. So, let's make the assumption that we're dealing with dedicated people, who have gone out of their way to join this organization. It's not just another job for them.

Now, we have 300 people with this common aim. It's really very important in that kind of community for each to be aware of the other, for their common aim to be reinforced . . .

We're building a house for them. One of the main purposes is to stimulate the sense of community, and we start with the proposition that this is not just another office building but an entirely new animal.[10]

Edward Larrabee Barnes:

We are trying to create architecture that does not compete with art—to put the priorities in the right order. We want the visitor to remember paintings in space, sculpture against sky, and a sense of continuous flow. It is flow more than form that has concerned us. The sequence of spaces must be seductive. There must be a subtle sense of going somewhere, like a river. At the same time the architecture must be relatively uneventful and anonymous.

Interior court, Ford Foundation Building, New York, by Kevin Roche and John Dinkeloo. (Ezra Stoller/ESTO)

CONCEPTS IN ARCHITECTURE

Interior Garden, Ford Foundation Building, New York, by Kevin Roche and John Dinkeloo. (Ezra Stoller/ESTO)

Walker Art Center, Minneapolis, by Edward Larrabee Barnes. (George Cserna)

> The generating idea behind the design is the helical plan which provides sequential flow from the lobby to the roof whether going up or down. At the same time, direct access to individual galleries is possible by using the elevator or core stairs. This circulation system is the armature of the building.[11]

A conceptual scenario such as those excerpted above is the product of an evolutionary process, and while concepts themselves are often the product of flashes of insight, the examples quoted represent the final versions of a process that went through a series of development and clarification stages. Even though parts of each scenario may have been clearly established from the beginning, the scenario uses insights gained during the design process to tie it together.

A practical example of a design process based on the incremental development of a scenario is the *charette* design process. A *charette* (in schools of architecture) is a last-minute push during a design project to get everything done on time. It derives from the French word for "cart," such as those in which nineteenth-century architecture students carried their designs to a central point for evaluation, often finishing them en route. It is also a technique used by practitioners to involve various individuals and organizations of a community directly in the planning, programming, or design of a project. A community design *charette* implies a marathon work session that compresses decision making into a few days. Various interest groups, often competing with each other, participate in the idea and concept formulation. The role of the professional designer is to coordinate and stimulate the participation and suggestion making of the participants.

Circulation: Walker Art Center, Minneapolis.

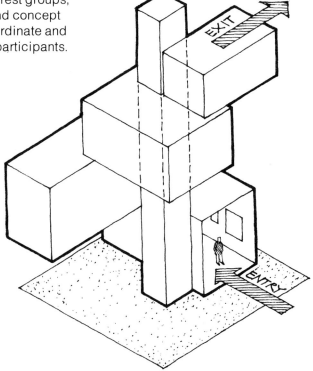

Over the course of a marathon session, the professional encourages an initial rush of ideas from all the interested groups and then directs discussion so that the important issues are identified. Finally, he or she directs the discussion towards setting priorities. An effective leader helps resolve apparent conflicts and directs the group towards making decisions or compromises.

CONCEPT HIERARCHIES

An understanding of the hierarchical relationship between notion, idea, concept, and conceptual scenario becomes the foundation for developing a process for generating appropriate concepts for buildings. The sequence is ordered as: *notion, idea, concept, and scenario.* This is based on a pattern of increasing complexity, appropriateness, and depth of thought. In the early stages of a project, ideas have a good chance of being notionable, especially if minds are open to innovative, unusual, and imaginative thoughts that might help resolve unique or difficult design and programmatic requirements. At some point architects become more informed and familiar with the project and begin to identify some notions as more important and more appropriate than others. Finally, similarities, potential interactions, and groupings of ideas become apparent. These observations create the base from which a sustained argument for doing things is developed.

Appropriateness and Self-Criticism

The problem of choosing an appropriate form for concepts—whether metaphors, analogies, or scenarios—is less important than the self-criticism applied to those concepts as they are formulated. The key question in critical dialogue is still, "Is this idea appropriate to the project?" Both the concept and the solution should ultimately be appropriate and integrated with problems and activies of the building.

Another interesting variation on the question of appropriateness is whether or not concepts are necessary and appropriate for all building types. Are they appropriate for some buildings and not others? Both architects and critics have argued that not all buildings are "sculpturally" important or "foreground" buildings, that some buildings deserve to be "background" buildings. George Baird, an architect in Toronto, answers that concepts are at least as important in background buildings as they are in foreground buildings. He has worked on modest projects in which the search for concepts was critical to bringing enough intensity and order to the building to make it good architecture. For example, his concept for an addition to a very small house was to maintain the intimacy and homeliness of the existing house while doubling its size by reinforcing the sense of hearth in his proposal.

FIVE TYPES OF CONCEPTS

There are five types of concepts: analogies (looking at other things), metaphors (looking at abstractions), essences (looking beyond the programmatic needs), programmatic concepts (looking at the stated requirements, and ideals (looking at universal values).

Analogies

Of the five categories analogies are probably the most frequently used device for formulating concepts. Analogies identify possible, literal relationships between things. One thing is identified as having all the desired characteristics, and thus it becomes a model for the project at hand. Until the rise of the modern movement in the first half of the twentieth century, it was assumed by clients and architects alike that all the great architecture of the world had already been built. The task of the architect was to figure out which previous building was the appropriate model for the new building being designed. At one point the intial assumption was that Gothic was the appropriate model for churches, colleges, and universities; Greek Doric was the appropriate model for banks; and St. Peter's Basilica was the appropriate model for capitols from Washington, D.C. to Madison, Wisconsin.

Some analogies seem to turn up more than others. One of the most frequent is the village street or a covered shopping street like the Galleria in Milan. A recent example is Diamond and Meyers' use of both a village street and the Galleria as an analogy for the design of a building for the University of Alberta in Edmonton that combines a student union with married students' housing. The apartments are located along the interior street with a curved dome and daylighting similar to the Galleria in Milan. In developing this project, the architects were concerned with the basic validity and how to develop and carry out the analogy. An example of one refinement of the original analogy is in the use of panel windows that open onto the street. The architects noticed that the perspective view down the street in an early version of the design did not match the vitality and colorfulness

St. Peter's Basilica, Rome. (George Gerster, Rapho Photo Researchers)

Student Union Housing, University of Alberta, Edmonton, by Diamond and Meyers.

United States Capitol Building. (the U.S. Department of the Interior)

INTRODUCTION TO ARCHITECTURE

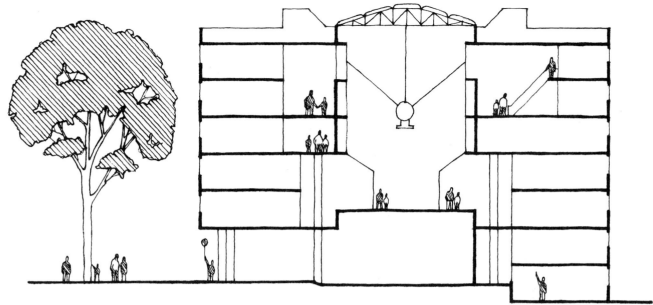

Section: Student Union Housing, University of Alberta.

of other streets they had seen. They remembered picturesque images of wash hanging from the windows, but this particular scheme did not have that friendly clutter. To introduce that visual vitality, they designed and developed special windows for the rooms overlooking the street. The windows were solid, brightly painted panels, not glass, and were opened to provide extra cross-ventilation and views of the street activity below. The colors of these panels and the posters attached to them provided the visual vitality the architects were seeking.

Another example of the use of a direct analogy in which one building provides an appropriate image for another project is Treetops by David Glasser of Marquis, Stoller, and Glasser, on Hilton Head Island, South Carolina. In this example, the gangway and bridge system of circulation in the warehouse area of Savannah, Georgia, was identified as having characteristics that would solve a variety of siting and circulation problems. The gangway system seemed applicable to the new design, even though the Tree Tops project was on a flat site and the activity was housing rather than warehousing.

Analogies do not have to relate to other specific buildings. Kahn, in discussing the concept behind the Richards Medical Research Building at the University of Pennsylvania, made several analogies. He talked about the need for researchers to communicate and share their ideas. Thus, he developed an analogy of the research building as a community where people could see each other and become aware of the activities within the building. This concept is very similar to Roche's Ford Foundation Building. Kahn observed that the medical researchers on the University of Pennsylvania campus were

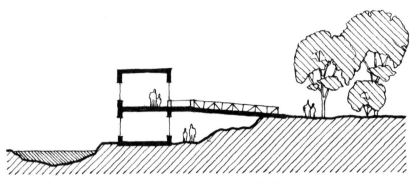

WAREHOUSE DISTRICT, SAVANNAH, GEORGIA

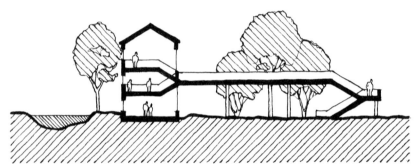

'TREETOPS', HILTON HEAD ISLAND, SOUTH CAROLINA

Treetops, Hilton Head Island, South Carolina, by Glasser, Stoller, and Marquis. (David Glasser)

INTRODUCTION TO ARCHITECTURE

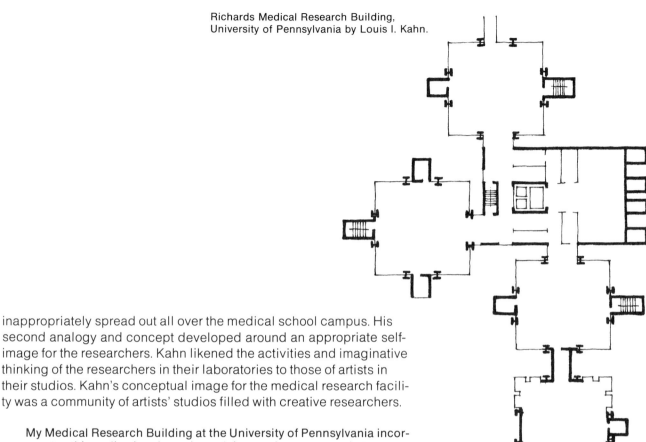

Richards Medical Research Building,
University of Pennsylvania by Louis I. Kahn.

inappropriately spread out all over the medical school campus. His
second analogy and concept developed around an appropriate self-
image for the researchers. Kahn likened the activities and imaginative
thinking of the researchers in their laboratories to those of artists in
their studios. Kahn's conceptual image for the medical research facility was a community of artists' studios filled with creative researchers.

> My Medical Research Building at the University of Pennsylvania incor-
> porates this realization that science laboratories are essentially
> studios . . . . This design, the result of consideration of the uniqueness
> to be made of its spaces and their service requirements, expresses the
> character of the research laboratory.[12]

Kahn may have developed an inspiring and appropriate analogy
as his concept for building, but according to some reports the building—while heralded by some as the most important structure of the
1960s—is difficult for researchers actually to use. Researchers do not
appear to be enamored of the concept of a community of scientists
or of their visual accessibility to each other; many choose to close
their blinds for privacy and to control heat gain from the sun. Neither
do they seem to be inspired by the analogy that their research spaces
are artists' studios with two walls of windows for light. They need walls
on which to hang experimental equipment, and they do not need the
kind of light that an artist might require. Still, the building has some
important achievements.

Jonas Salk visited research buildings around the United States as part of the process of selecting an architect for his new research building. He studied the Richards Building, observed it in use, talked with its users, and learned of its problems. Despite its drawbacks, this building was the only facility he visited that tried to include the philosophical issues of creativity, and he chose Kahn to do the Salk Institute in San Diego.

Metaphors and Similes

Like analogies, metaphors identify relationships between things. However, the relationships are abstract rather than literal. Similes are metaphors that use the words "like" or "as" to express a relationship. Metaphors and similes identify possible patterns of parallel relationships while analogies identify possible literal relationships.

Charles Moore, in a discussion of his interests, suggested that he likes buildings to be like geodes. He develops that metaphor in a brief scenario:

> At St. Simon's Island, Georgia, [the] condominiums by the beach do something in response to this [geode-like] image. It is apparently an old Georgian plantation, but huge, on the outside; inside it is an orgiastic, brightly colored and decoratively formed set of walls surrounding an interior space.[13]

Richards Medical Research Building, University of Pennsylvania, by Louis Kahn.

Salk Institute, San Diego, by Louis Kahn. (Ezra Stoller/ESTO)

The geode is a conceptual metaphor that suggests how the building could have two simultaneous images. When viewed from the outside, the building could have an image that would match the image of the neighborhood. It could have a different image on the inside, such as an entertaining, theatrical, and dramatic environment appropriate to a resort. Other examples of metaphors include Gio Ponti's provocative list of definitions and explanations of various aspects of architecture. His definition of architecture itself is a simile: "Architecture is like a crystal." Other metaphors discussed in his book, *In Praise of Architecture,* include: "The obelisk is an enigma," "The fountain is a voice," "The room is a world," "The door is an invitation," "The colonnade is a choir," and "The house is a dream."[14]

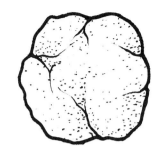

Essences

Essences distill and concentrate aspects of more complex issues into terse, explicit statements. Essence connotes insights into the most critical and intrinsic aspects of the thing being analyzed. A statement of the essence of something can also be the result of discovering and identifying the roots of an issue.

Stanford Anderson wrote about and quoted Kahn's interest in essences and his use of metaphors.

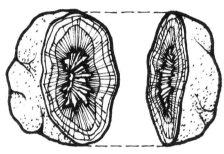

Geode-architecture analogy.

Kahn is concerned with form, what things are, with essences, with elements and their articulation. "I'd think of the nature of something, see the emergence of what kind of institution it would be . . . every building . . . answering to an inspiration it serves, and the environment of spaces which express the place of one man and another. It is almost the first duty of the architect, you might say, to take a program and to translate its areas programs to spaces, so that the lobby becomes a place of entrance, the corridor becomes a gallery, and the budget becomes an economy."[15]

Geode-architecture analogy: St. Simon's Island, Georgia, project by Charles Moore and Associates.

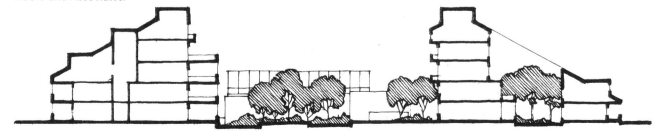

Designers have developed several methods for searching for the essence of a project and for transforming it into concept statements. The search is to identify ideas that tie together the various parts of the building and, as Kahn has suggested, that allow the designer to overcome the circumstances of each project and to accomplish what is really important to accomplish. A pragmatic method of identifying the essence of a project is to analyze the program and identify a hierarchy of issues for the project. The assumption is that the most important things are the most essential. This search can be an analysis of the program or it can be a graphic analysis in which the project is diagramed in different ways.

Placing emphasis on essences and roots runs contrary to the one other major philosophical approach to creativity and architecture popular in this century. This philosophy is based upon the idea that each individual architect has a unique, innovative contribution to make. Architects from Frank Lloyd Wright to Eero Saarinen have valued this belief, as did Walter Gropius, one of the founders of the Bauhaus.

The general willingness to use precedent—whether historical or recent—other than vernacular sources has only regained respectability since Kahn's emergence as a form-giver in the 1960s. Kahn unabashedly identified the architecture of ancient Rome and the work of Le Corbusier as his major inspirations. While not always candid about his contemporary sources, Kahn did modestly suggest, in the middle of designing the library at Phillips Exeter Academy, that Hugh Stubbins' Medical School Library at Harvard was a "very good library." A comparison between the plans and interior spaces shows a remarkable similarity.

The work of John Portman of Atlanta illustrates another version of the search for essences. Portman's most famous buildings are hotels with dramatic, innovative interior spaces. As concepts they integrate image, interest, function, and—whenever possible—an urban-design plan for the city in which they are built. The proof that they capture the essence of a hotel is their popularity. The main multistory lobbies, especially in San Francisco, are essentially public places belonging to the city as well as to the hotel. Portman's understanding of what interests and excites people is developed in his detailing, especially in his elevators, which are decorated with tiny light bulbs and pierced by windows for a view of the dramatic space. Another insight is his willingness to build architecture that includes decoration, something that has been missing from almost all twentieth-century structures. Judging from its role in the success of these buildings, decoration is an essential element in an architecture admired by the general public.

Hyatt Regency Hotel, San Francisco, by John Portman. (Alexandre Georges)

INTRODUCTION TO ARCHITECTURE

Section of Phillips Exeter Academy
Library, by Louis Kahn.

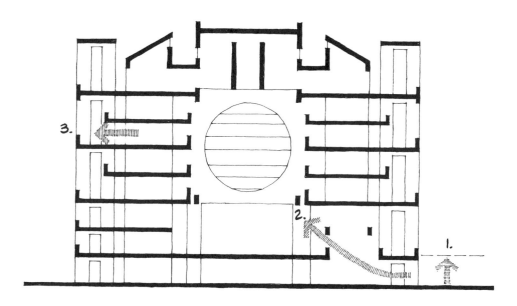

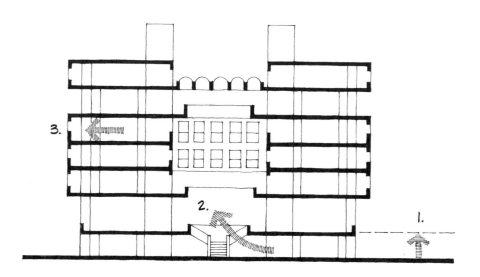

Section of Medical Library at Harvard
University, by Hugh Stubbins.

CONCEPTS IN ARCHITECTURE

Another kind of essence architects look for is the essence that they can express in the design of the building. Eero Saarinen interpreted the conceptual challenge at the TWA Terminal at Kennedy International Airport to be the expression of movement and travel as the key idea that could hold the whole project together. According to Saarinen:

The challenge of the Trans World Airways Terminal was twofold. One, to create, within the complex of terminals that makes up Idlewild [now Kennedy International], a building for T.W.A. which would be distinctive and memorable. . . . Two, to design a building in which the architecture itself would express the drama and specialness and excitement of travel. Thus, we wanted the architecture to reveal the terminal, not as a static, enclosed place, but as a place of movement and of transition. . . . The fact that to some people it looked like a bird in flight was really coincidental. That was the last thing we ever thought about. Now, that does not mean that one does not have the right to see it that way or to explain it to laymen in those terms, especially because laymen are usually more literally than visually inclined.[16]

Trans World Airlines Terminal Building, John F. Kennedy International Airport, New York, by Eero Saarinen. (Ezra Stoller/ESTO).

In contrast to the philosophical musings about essences and expression, another pragmatic and diagrammatic method of discovering essences has been suggested by Lars Lerup. His technique combines analogies and essences. Given a particular design problem to solve, he begins by identifying famous places that have characteristics matching aspects of his design problem. Pictures of several famous places are chosen, and each is expected to have at least one aspect that would be highly desirable in his own solution. Next, Lerup analyzes each picture in a series of steps. First, he redraws the image, then he edits to bring out its salient characteristics. The characteristics are further abstracted into a hypothesis about the important design lesson to be learned from the original setting. That hypothesis is combined with others distilled from the other photographs. The collection of hypotheses is then used to focus and direct the synthesis and design of the actual proposal.

Symbols are a subset of the essences category. Symbols imply that the essences can be characterized in specific forms and images that the public can understand. Why, after all, would anyone try to manipulate the design of a building to symbolize that which was not important, critical, or essential? Symbols in architecture are images that evoke automatic responses to a set of stimuli, usually visual. Thus, symbols have to do with expectations. Many building types can be designed to match expectations. The building can be both the place for an activity and the image that symbolizes that activity.

Direct Responses and Problem Solving

Not all concepts capture the essence of a project, nor do they all symbolize the function of all the activities in a building. Concepts can be developed around more pragmatic issues often explicitly identified in the building program. While many architects take pride in their ability to solve a client's problems, only a few actually make a pragmatic approach sound inspiring and many designers inadvertently avoid working on the problem at hand while trying to be creative.

Gyo Obata, in discussing his proposal for the Air and Space Museum in Washington, D.C., identified the importance of knowing what kinds of problems to attack in large projects. This is especially important when economics are crucial and cost increases due to inflation alone can kill a project if it is not designed quickly enough. The major problem area that was identified in the Air and Space Museum was circulation and orientation for a very large number of visitors. The concept developed in response was a two-level street that connects a series of enclosed theme exhibit rooms. Three open multistory halls are located at intervals along the street, both to display the prime attractions and to entertain the viewer moving from one theme exhibit room to another. Visitors to the building have a choice of viewing order, because the collection is simply too large to be taken in at one time. The concept of a double-level, streetlike circulation pattern that would disperse people to all the various theme rooms was tested in the first few months of use. In fact, more than twice the projected number of visitors visited the museum in its first year. Without a clear concept of circulation as a prime issue, the whole building would have been less useful and would have created unnecessary frustrations to its millions of users.

Ideals

In contrast to the previous categories of concepts, which suggest that the architect look inside the problem or at a similar problem to discover appropriate concepts, ideal concepts are those that architects bring to the problem. If architects bring the right concept to the project, they are praised for their genius. If their choice is inappropriate, it becomes a preconception and their basic competence is questioned. Ideal concepts represent the highest aspirations and goals of the architect.

For example, an architect can bring to each project a series of ideal concepts about how to conserve energy in buildings. These concepts might include compartmentalizing, zoning according to need for heat, developing windowless backs of buildings that can be turned toward cold winds, angling surfaces for heat collectors, and designing for self-sufficiency of the whole system.

Another example of the potential for ideals to influence concepts is illustrated by the work of Mies van der Rohe. Mies developed the concept of an ideal building based upon large, open, unpartitioned spaces he called "universal space." Mies thought it was basically appropriate for each project he designed. Student unions, libraries, classroom buildings, and offices were expected to work best as versions of a universal space.

Ideals can have positive effects and if architects did not have them to refer to and use in conceptualizing and developing their designs, their task would be more difficult. Their previous experiences and insights would be useless, and each project would have to begin from scratch. This would aid neither the client nor the architect. Architects who are flexible and comfortable in emphasizing different ideals for different projects have an advantage in providing services to their clients

National Gallery, Berlin, by Mies van der Rohe. (Balthazar Korab).

SUMMARY

Notions, ideas, concepts, and scenarios form a continuum (of increasing complexity, appropriateness, and depth of thought) that can become an important basis for architectural design. Concepts integrate the various elements of a design into a coherent whole and allow the architect to direct his or her resources to the most important aspects of the design. Conceptual scenarios integrate a number of applicable concepts and are used for communicating ideas to one's self and to clients. Of course, the appropriateness of a concept or scenario is pivotal and it comes from a process of self-criticism.

There are five types of concepts: analogies or literal relationships, metaphors or abstract relationships, essences or intrinsic aspects, programmatic or pragmatic responses, and ideals or external values.

Most importantly, the search for appropriate concepts and their application in architectural design helps make good architecture.

NOTES

1. Charles Moore, "Self Portrait," *L'Architecture D'Aujourd'Hui,* no. 184, March/April 1976, p. XLV.
2. Louis I. Kahn, *Light Is the Theme* (Fort Worth: Kimbell Art Foundation, 1975), p. 15.
3. Edward Larrabee Barnes, in Paul Heyer, *Architects on Architecture* (New York: Walker and Co., 1966), p. 330.
4. Louis I. Kahn, *The Voice of America Forum Lectures: Architecture* (The U.S. Information Service, n.d) p. 39.
5. William J. J. Gordon, *Synectics* (New York: Harper and Row, 1961).
6. Eero Saarinen, *Eero Saarinen on His Work* (New Haven: Yale University Press 1962), p. 10.
7. Edward Larrabee Barnes in Paul Heyer, *Architects on Architecture* (New York: Walker and Co., 1966).
8. Eero Saarinen, *Eero Saarinen on His Work* p. 76.
9. Frank Lloyd Wright, *Frank Lloyd Wright: Writings and Buildings* (New York: Meridian Books, 1960), pp. 75–76.
10. Kevin Roche, in J. W. Cook and H. Klotz, *Conversation with Architects* (New York: Praeger Publishers, 1973). pp. 68–69.
11. Edward Larrabee Barnes, "Walker Art Center," *Design Quarterly,* 1971, No. 81, p. 10.
12. Louis I. Kahn in John Donat, ed., *World Architecture Today* (London: Studio Books, 1964), p. 35.
13. Charles Moore, "Self Portrait," *L'Architecture D'Aujourd'Hui,* No. 184, March/April 1976, p. XLV.
14. Gio Ponti, *In Praise of Architecture* (New York: F. W. Dodge Corp., 1960), p. 104.
15. Louis I. Kahn, in Stanford Anderson, "Louis I. Kahn in the 1960's," *Boston Society of Architects: Journal One,* 1967, p. 22.
16. Eero Saarinen, *Eero Saarinen on His Work,* p. 60.

FOR FURTHER READING

Bloomer, K. C., and Moore, C. W. *Body, Memory and Architecture.* New Haven: Yale University Press, 1977.

Cook, John W. and Klotz, Heinrich. *Conversations with Architects.* New York: Praeger Publishers, 1973.

Gilbert, Katharine. "Seven Senses of a Room," *Journal of Aesthetics and Art Criticism.* Vol. 8, No. 1, September 1949, pp. 1–21.

Giurgola, Romaldo, and Mehta, Jaimin. *Louis I. Kahn.* Boulder, Colo.: Westview Press, 1975.

Gordon, William J. J. *Synectics.* New York: Harper and Row, 1961.

Harris, Robert. "Bootstrap Essence-Seeking," *JAE Journal of Architectural Education,* Vol. XXIX, No. 2.

Heyer, Paul. *Architects on Architecture.* New York: Walker and Co., 1966.

INTRODUCTION TO ARCHITECTURE

Kahn, Louis I. *Kahn Talks with Students*. Houston: School of Architecture, Rice University n.d.

Kahn, Louis I. *Light is the Theme*. Fort Worth: Kimbell Art Foundation, 1975.

Le Corbusier. *Creation is a Patient Search*. New York: Praeger, 1960.

Leonard, Michael. "Humanizing Space," *Progressive Architecture.*, Vol. 50, April 1964, pp. 128–133.

Moore, Charles W., Allen, Gerald, and Donlyn, Lyndon. *The Place of Houses*. New York: Holt, Rinehart and Winston, 1974.

Moore, Charles, and Allen, Gerald. *Dimensions*. New York: Architectural Record Books, 1976.

Moore, Charles. "Architecture." John William Lawrence Memorial Lecture: New Orleans: School of Architecture, Tulane University, 1975.

Norberg-Schulz, C. *Existence, Space and Architecture*. New York: Praeger Publishers, 1971.

Ponti, Gio. *In Praise of Architecture*. New York: F. W. Dodge, 1960

Raskin, Eugene. *Architecturally Speaking*. New York: Delta Dell, 1966.

Rasmussen, Steen Eiler. *Experiencing Architecture*. Cambridge, Mass.: M.I.T Press, 1959.

Saarinen, Eero. *Eero Saarinen on His Work*. New Haven: Yale University Press, 1962.

Simonds, John O. *Landscape Architecture*. New York: McGraw-Hill, 1961.

Stern, Robert. *New Directions in American Architecture*. New York: George Braziller, 1969.

Stubbins, Hugh. *Architecture: The Design Experience*. New York.: John Wiley, 1976.

Thiel, Philip. "Processional Architecture," *AIA Journal,* February 1964, p. 23.

Venturi, Robert. *Complexity and Contradiction in Architecture*. New York: Museum of Modern Art, 1966.

White, E. T. *Concept Sourcebook*. Tucson, Arizona: Architectural Media, Ltd., 1975.

Zevi, Bruno. *Architecture as Space*. New York: Horizon Press, 1974.

CHAPTER 10

Perceptual Bases for Architectural Design

Frederick A. Jules

Buildings represent a form of communication, and, like language, they have vocabularies and syntax. Architects use these tools as they communicate the particular concerns or philosophy of society, a client, or the users of the building.

Architectural expression, like language, is continually evolving into new forms based on, or in contrast to, the past. Characteristics of past styles or building techniques that remain valid are carried into the present, while those that become antiquated are dropped from use.

This chapter explores the concept of buildings as communication, including the sources of architectural expression. The emphasis is on the appropriate visual image and the visual ordering techniques that can be used to create architectural statements.

ARCHITECTURAL STATEMENTS

Buildings that come to be recognized as good architecture are generally those that accommodate a number of communications into a totality and succinctly and elegantly express them. In essence, the quality of the communication becomes the basis for public criticism and the collective evaluation of a building. For example, the Acropolis is recognized as a powerful expression of its era. The Parthenon represents the development of the classic style to its epitome and symbolizes the mythology of the Greek people. In contrast to the Agora below, it differentiates between the commercial and religious aspects

The Parthenon, Athens.

of its society. A magnificent spiral approach up to the entrance of the Acropolis places it in correct juxtaposition to the rest of the society —the Acropolis is separate and closer to the heavens. This symbolism of pride and Athenian democacy is so strong that it has been carried through the ages to the present. Almost every town in the Unied States has its classic public building. Countless contemporary designs borrow the formality and power of the classic colonnade

A modern colonnade: Piedmont Junior High School, San Francisco Bay Area, by Marshall and Bowles, Chester Bowles (photo by Gerald Ratto).

while changing the column form to respond to the concerns of a different style.

Architects communicate concerns about buildings by emphasizing some forms while suppressing others, a technique that calls for subtle and often difficult decisions. The primary mode through which architects communicate is visual, partly because of the way the profession has evolved, and partly because vision is one of the clearest forms of perception. Thus, most of the symbols of society are received through sight. Form is revealed to the eye through light reflected from the form. Light directions, strengths, and colors can greatly affect the perception of form and therefore should be considered an intrinsic part of visual perception. Thus, lighting plays an important part in architecture and is part of the communication process for which the architect is responsible.

Other modes of perception that can be used by architects include the sensations of temperature and humidity, as well as touch and sound as they relate to texture and form in our environment. Comfortable ranges of temperature and humidity are well documented; the control of these has become the task of the mechanical engineer as well as of the architect. Electric lighting has also come into the domain of the engineer, but remains one of the architect's concerns because it affects the perception of form. Texture also conveys meaning; we expect certain reactions from various textures. For example, consider the sensations within a medieval castle. We expect a castle to be hard and cold as well as massive. These expectations are fulfilled by the characteristics of the building materials, which reinforce our visual and mental expectations. The stone of the building has a hard massive quality that makes sounds reverberate. It absorbs heat and condenses moisture, making surfaces cold and clammy to the touch. If these expectations were not fulfilled, we would conclude that the building was not a castle. If it were made of soft gray pillows, we might find it a delightful visual play or somehow feel cheated by its false imagery (as when smelling a plastic flower). Although our experience of an architectural place is a combination of all these sensations, our initial impression remains substantially visual.

One of the most important issues an architect faces is the image that the building will communicate. The choice of image will affect the attitude and behavior of the ultimate users of the building. In addition, each building may require a number of communicating elements to reinforce a total image or to separate and express different aspects of a single building. For example, a civic auditorium may express formality and acoustic clarity. An airport may facilitate easy access and circulation and express enjoyment and modernity.

Light and texture: Boston State Service Center, by Paul Rudolph (photo by Robert Perron).

After the architect selects an overall communication image, the relative importance of individual elements must be addressed. To do this, the architect may formulate a hierarchical list of the ideas or concepts that will form the building. A hierarchical list is simply an arrangement of concepts in order of importance. This design process ensures that a less important concept or element will not take precedence over a more important one.

Next, the architect should decide which of a number of design techniques to use on a particular project. This choice is based on the concepts and issues involved and may take divergent paths depending on the project. For example, a corporate office building may require formality, and thus structural expression and classical ordering techniques may be appropriate. In contrast, a community center may require participatory design techniques to involve the community in the process of identifying important concepts and suggesting the appropriate physical form. Architects must command a wide variety of design techniques and know when and where they are appropriate.

Although it is relatively easy to list concepts in hierarchical order and select design techniques, forming a total architectural composition can be extremely difficult. A building is a very complex object composed of a number of relatively small parts that have to be fitted together to produce a single architectural form. The parts may be potentially coordinated, but they have never before been assembled in the particular building configuration. The architect has to know a great deal about building components and how they go together, as well as how to visualize the final assemblage and its total expression. The communication content may be extremely subtle and require the careful balancing of form to create the right order. Although a successful composition of architectural form is seldom consciously appreciated by a user, this does not mean that it has not affected them in some way. Its orderliness may promote a sense of knowledge about and security in the environment. Some building parts, such as entries and paths to particular functions, can be visually defined in a way that provides participants with information, but at the same time they are not so aggressive that every user is distracted by them. The desire for information about the environment raises sensitivity to the nuances of form that will direct people to their desired goals. Since these nuances and hierarchies of order can be subtle (and they usually are if there is a wide range of information to transfer), there are many chances for error. However, the most common errors come from simple oversights. If the architectural form is not thought of as a total composition of components, strong contrasts can occur that will give totally misleading or irritating information.

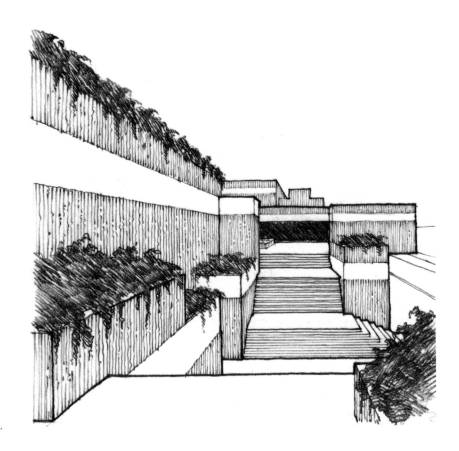

Strong entry: Police Memorial Building,
Jacksonville, Florida, by William Morgan.

As the building form develops in the design process, the architect must evaluate the appropriateness and success of the visual stimulus. Drawings and models of the building design facilitate critical evaluation. Although this process is difficult and time-consuming, visual information must be evaluated visually. There are no exact solutions—only alternatives that must be evaluated from many standpoints in a judgmental way.

THE SOURCE OF ARCHITECTURAL STATEMENTS

As discussed above, one of the first design issues involves selecting the substance of the architectural expression. Of course, many alternatives are available. The difficult task is choosing the one that will be most effective in giving the building the appropriate visual image. Three questions must be answered. The first involves the intended meanings of the building and the forms or images related to these meanings. The second involves the relative importance of the meanings to be expressed. Finally, there must be a logical order of building construction that will develop these images visually while providing good physical enclosure. Answers to these issues become the basis for the architectural design. These choices are critical in that they define a range of possible design solutions. An error at this stage of thinking will inevitably produce an error in the final solution, no matter how elegantly the concepts are expressed architecturally. An incorrect idea carried to its logical conclusion is still incorrect. The difficulty of the problem is compounded when one realizes that these decisions are open to a range of interpretation; much of the criticism of buildings is developed around the philosophies underlying these choices. For example, since the beginning of the modern movement in architecture, there has been debate over whether a clean, modern, efficient, and machined style is appropriate for residential design. Architects take both sides of this issue. Conventional wisdom holds that the average home buyer likes the traditional style over the modern, while the argument for the modern is based on the belief that there is a need to change peoples' value systems so that the culture can continue to develop.

This type of debate will be with us always, but there are many situations in which incorrect images have seriously affected the usability of the building. The Sydney Opera house is a prime example.

Sail imagery: The Sydney Opera House, by Jorn Utzon.

The applicable image was that of sailboats in the Sydney harbor. The opera house was designed as a shell structure that looks like a number of billowing sails. Is this an appropriate image for an opera house, and what, if anything, was sacrificed in achieving the image? The image question can be debated forever. The arguments for it say that it is a lyric expression responding to its siting; the argument against it is that the image should be developed from a base more closely related to opera—such as an appropriate acoustical envelope. However, the most serious criticism is based on the latter part of the question. What was sacrificed by choosing this image? There are many answers. The first sacrifice was that the sail image was not derived from a true shell structure, and therefore a number of structural problems within the design had to be solved by greatly overbuilding the structure. It *suggested* a shell structure, but it was not. This change in structure also made it visually heavier than the intended sail image and caused a significant budget overrun. There were difficulties in constructing these complex structural forms that added to the cost overruns and extended the construction time years beyond the expected completion date. As a result, Sydney has a controversial piece of modern architecture. It is a beautiful symbol for the city, but it poses questions about the appropriateness of modern architecture.

Thus, questions of image communication are important to architectural design. Approaches to solutions are found in essentially six places: the building program, the social imagery of the building type, the building site, the architect's individual style, environmental and behavioral research, and the character of building technologies. Depending on the particular nature of a design problem, any one of these may reveal the primary issue to be addressed by the building. However, they are all important generators of concepts, and, in most cases, each plays some role in clarifying the design problem. The designer is responsible for setting the relative importance of each of these areas. Criticism of the final solution arises as much from the importance the architect assigns to these issues as from how well the issues are addressed.

The Building Program

Programs for buildings are developed by professional programmers or architects. They include the proximity requirements of activity spaces, based on the use of the spaces or the fit with the site. An example of this is the logical flow of materials in a manufacturing process. The program would show room shapes and sizes, who uses the space and for how long, and any special equipment or environmental controls. It may implicitly or explicitly express the social order of the organization being housed as well as the flow of people and materials. These relationships are stated implicitly through the proximity requirements and must be explicitly verified with the client. They could become the basis for hierarchy to be expressed in the building. For example, the program has been the key generator of order in hospital and research facility design over the last twenty years. The reason for this is that these facilities require extreme flexibility and functionality to be as effective as they have to be; concepts that conflict with these programmatic issues must be given a second order of importance.

Building Type

Another answer to the basic questions may come from the symbolism of the building type within its context. Buildings can be grouped into categories, such as schools, houses, hospitals, banks, and churches. Each type is symbolic of its function in the society and has a traditional place in the context of that society. A symbol is an image that stands for a collective idea or set of ideas. Thus, a building type may have antecedents that are images symbolizing that building's function in society. It is important to note that the symbolism of a building is carried by images that have acquired meaning over time, and that these images are specific and refer to particular building form organizations. For instance, the location of a church in a New England town had considerable social meaning to the community. The church became the center of the town, usually faced the public common, and was the hub of social activity. Its form expressed this importance by its formality, elegance, and scale. The strength of the symbolism of particular building types within a community varies over time as the importance of the function to the community grows or diminishes. The architect assesses the symbolic importance of the building type being designed and decides whether or not the building should reaffirm, through symbolism, its position within the society. In many cases, the symbolism of a building type is apparent. However, some client groups may respond to symbols and symbolic places unfamiliar to the architect. In these instances, careful consultation with the client can elicit these images and locations, which in turn may become the basis for the design. The social imagery can be distinct from the functional utilization of the facility as stated in the building program, but good design integrates the concerns of both into a synthesized whole in which one part reinforces the meaning of all others.

Site

While the program and social symbolism of a building may suggest the appropriate site for a facility, the site itself can suggest particular form responses. A building site should be critically viewed for its potential to reinforce the activities within the building being designed. Site analysis is a standard activity of an architect. Much of this analysis involves gathering technical information concerning the site's potential for serving the proposed facility. Issues of soil-bearing capacity, surface water drainage, access to utilities, vehicular and pedestrian access, and other community requirements are all important. In addition, various state and local legal requirements (such as subdivision and zoning regulations) will affect the form of the building to be designed. However, beyond these technical constraints (which deal primarily with the protection of health and safety), the site may embody a certain imagery and meaning that can be used advantageously by the architect. For example, does a site have rolling landforms that suggest a bucolic situation, or is it a formal urban setting with existing buildings on every side? Do good views suggest a particular building orientation? Do the land forms and climate suggest a particular energy-saving building form?

Traditional building forms with strong images have evolved in response to particular site and situation constraints. For example, the colonial saltbox form evolved in response to New England's climate, tax laws, and available building materials. It has transcended that period, however, to become a strong image of home for much of the United States. Likewise, the adobe dwellings of the Southwest have become a strong residential image. Thus, the site itself can be a strong determiner of form and must be analyzed in terms of its potential for image generation.

The saltbox style.

The Architect's Style

The style of a design is most certainly an architectural statement. Style, in this context, means the distinctive qualities of form given a project that allow us to group projects as representatives of an individual's (or a group's) efforts. Thus, all buildings by Alvar Aalto can be recognized by his personal form-generating techniques, while buildings in the neoclassical style represent the form-generating techniques of a group of architects who relied on classical architecture for their inspiration. Style is a more general expression of concern than those generated from the program, and it usually creates the first impression of a building and its meaning. Styles are always in evolution; thus, stylistic choices embody an architect's philosophy about current and past design trends. They are comments on our society

Town Hall, Seinajoki, Finland, by Alvar Aalto.

and the art of architecture—a reaffirmation of some values and a criticism of others.

Le Corbusier, the father of the modern movement in architecture, was enchanted with the Parthenon. His architectural forms were reminiscent of the Acropolis while expressing the new technologies of building. At one and the same time, his buildings were criticisms of the current design styles and reaffirmations of the beauty of classic form. His attitudes toward technology, space, and social order mixed with his love of the classic form to produce a new form vocabulary that is now recognized as his style.

Le Corbusier's objective was not to develop a particular style but rather to express his concerns about architecture. In so doing, he developed a style. This is an important difference. Many designers adopt a popular current style for their buildings. They copy the apparent form without understanding the intentions behind the style. But it is the *intent* that forms the style and generates the correct application of that style in a particular setting. An individual evolves a style but does not adopt one; rather, style evolves from one's expressing new concepts of space, use, or building technology. A consistent philosophy about these elements will produce a style. If the style of a building is simply an application of form, it may not express the issues involved in the particular building or in the building process. These clashes between arbitrary and appropriate style produce little significant com-

Ronchamp Chapel, France, by Le Corbusier.

munication. Therefore, knowledge of the history of architecture and an understanding of the work of successful architects is an important part of architectural design. The rationales of particular architectural forms often remain as valid ways of thinking about architecture and therefore can be combined with other concerns to produce a building design.

Environmental and Behavioral Studies

A more recent area of professional and academic research has developed around studies of human behavior and the environment. Obviously, this research becomes an important source of architectural statements because it means that architects can predict behavior in a space as it is designed. For example, research has been done on the shape and size of conference tables relative to the level of participation by participants. This data can be used to form parts of a university conference center design, with reasonable confidence that it will work when constructed. Careful environment-behavior research has been conducted on many of the major building types such as schools, offices, and hospitals. In some cases, the resulting information is carefully integrated into a building program, but often it is not; it becomes the responsibility of the architect to find and use the appropriate research materials.

Building Technology

In recent years, major advances in building technology have had an important impact on architectural design. Technology has changed the basic form of office towers; great stadiums are moved to new configurations on cushions of air; and spaces are enclosed by air-supported fabric. The appropriate application of new technologies requires careful design consideration.

In the case of the floating stadium, there was a need to accommodate a wide range of sports and other activities and, thus, a wide range of seating alternatives—each with a particular form. Moving major sections of seating on cushions of air was a technological alternative to building a number of stadiums and was both programmatically effective and economically feasible. The need generated the application of technology. The recognition of need, an understanding of the range of technological alternatives, and the appropriate application of technology are clearly the responsibility of the architect. The importance of the visual expression of the selected technology must be considered, together with the elements of the building program and type, the site, and the architect's style. All these must fit into a hierarchy of importance. For example, in the stadium example, the architect might have chosen to express visually the technology that permitted changes in seating configuration. However, in terms of the communication to the user, the expression of pedestrian circulation was more important. The programmatic issue of easy access to seating was higher on the visual communication hierarchy. Thus, the circulation requirements elicited a strong formal order with a high degree of clarity, while the image of the extraordinary technology was suppressed.

Aloha Stadium, Hawaii, by Charles Luckman Associates.

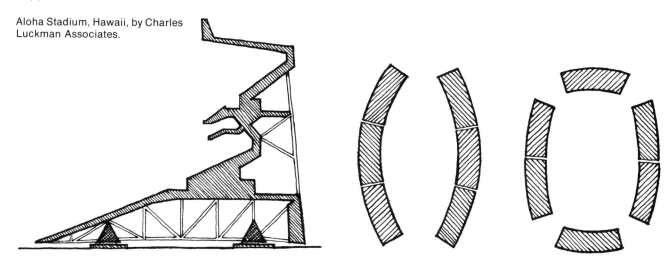

PERCEPTUAL BASES FOR ARCHITECTURAL DESIGN

VISUAL-ORDERING TECHNIQUES

After the architect decides on the substance of the expression or communication, the next step involves the selection and manipulation of building forms so that the correct message is conveyed. The building program lists all the spaces that are required in the building, their interrelationships, and in some cases, their form and significance. The designer can use this information and any of the following ordering techniques to express the intent of the building visually through its architectural composition. Essentially, these techniques are the methods architects use to mold the architectural composition so that it communicates the appropriate messages to the users of the building. They can be used to enhance the quality of the communication as well as to suppress undesirable visual communications.

Proximity Diagramming

Proximity diagramming is an analysis technique that is useful in generating a preliminary sense of the building's potential form. In this context, it is analogous to a sculptor's evaluation of a particular stone for its form potential. The proximity diagram usually will have a number of potential form combinations that will differ significantly in their visual expression. The architect develops the various alternative diagrams and selects the diagram that most closely matches the desired building expression.

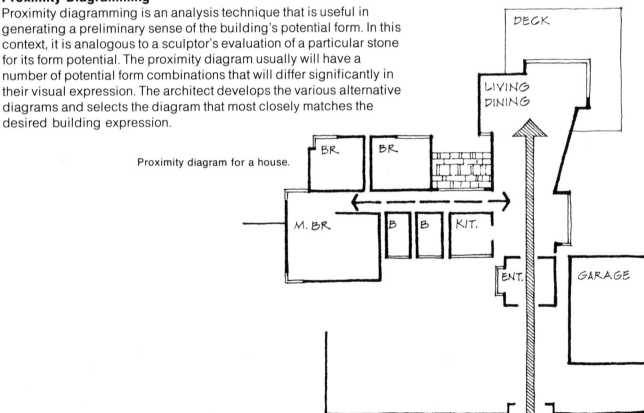

Proximity diagram for a house.

As stated earlier, requirements of adjacency are included in the building program. These can be augmented by requirements developing out of the site analysis and tentative construction type. A proximity diagram of these groupings can then be formed by manipulating the spaces and their location until most of the requirements have been fulfilled (that is, spaces that are supposed to be related, such as a kitchen and dining area, are next to each other, and rooms are facing the correct direction). Alternative diagrams can be drawn, because the requirements may be solved by different configurations, and architects usually generate a few alternatives so that the expressive potentials of each can be evaluated.

Depending on the building type and the severity of the requirements, either the site, the program, or the technological elements could be dominant. For example, technology is usually dominant in high-rise office structures, with site and program considerations taking a lower level of importance. The proximity diagrams represent the architect's best judgment as to the relative importance of the various design requirements.

Proximity diagrams usually have two hierarchies. The first is based on the scale of the different spaces of the diagram, with the larger elements having more importance. The second is the location of elements within a sequence of spaces. Beginning and end points in a progression are dominant over other spaces along the path. Path intersections produce a dominance wherever they occur, and compositions tend to have a center dominance. These, then, are the elements of a proximity diagram.

Consider two examples—first, a typical modern high school with a gymnasium. Although the internal orders in a high school can be very complex, this example will deal only with the external expression of the gym and the school. The proximity diagram for these two activities can treat the gym as a separate element or combine it with other parts of the school. In either case, the gym has dominance because it is large and has a strong physical form. However, the gym is not the most important reason for the school's existence. Thus, the architect might lessen the visual imagery of the gym and strengthen that of the total school. Locational techniques could lessen the visual importance of the gym. If something is hidden from the perception of the user, it has less meaning. The architect might simply control the users' approach to the complex so that the gym either is not seen or is seen only as a fragment with the school standing before it. Things in the foreground are dominant over things in the background, all other characteristics being equal. Higher locations are also sensed as being dominant over lower ones and have traditionally been used to express power. The gym could be buried or placed on a lower piece of land, thereby expressing its secondary nature. (See page 239.)

The second example is a traditional house in which the functional relationships suggest an order of entry, living, dining, and sleeping space. The end points of this proximity relationship are not equal. The entry is important but the sleeping area is not, so the progression from space to space must seem to be discontinuous at the living/dining space. This problem is usually solved by the fact that the living/dining space is the largest space in a home and therefore dominant. However, other techniques can be applied to strengthen this relationship. The simplest locational solution to this problem is to end the entry sequence in this space and to have a secondary pathway to the sleeping areas. Secondary activities or support functions can be given their relative importance by being appropriately located along these major or minor paths.

Proximity (and, therefore, location in a progression) is only a starting place for forming the ideas a building is to express. Other characteristics of form can now be applied to these beginnings to make the meaning of the building clear to its users.

Signs and Symbols

Signs and symbols are very direct methods of expression. They are used in architectural design to focus the attention of building users by conveying an understanding of the function of the building or spaces within the building. They range from simple exit signs to objects of representation for complex ideas and things. For example, the Parthenon has become a symbol for governmental functions; its style is classic. Likewise, the form of churches have been extremely symbolic and direct in their imagery. Other symbols can be more generally derived from the dominant characteristics of the activity being symbolized. For example, a number of airport designs symbolize flight and modernity, with upward curving and flowing forms and contemporary materials.

Symbolism has always been a major form-giving design technique and one that can be applied over functional and programmatic concerns with little conflict. It is widely used because it brings all the parts of a problem together to reinforce a meaning and give a wholeness to the total composition. Again, however, selecting the most appropriate symbol is the most difficult part of the problem. A mistake here can give us a sense that the building is out of place and in fact absurd. Returning to the high school example, a designer may think that the image of a book symbolizes the concepts of learning and, thus, try to incorporate its form into a roof structure. If this is done so that the roof truly looks like a book, most persons would agree that the

Sign and symbol: Broadview Cinema I, Savannah, Georgia, by Arkhora Associates.

symbol is too superficial and does not accurately reflect the learning function. A more successful attempt may symbolize the kind of setting in which learning has historically taken place. In this instance, the sense of seclusion might be symbolized by a naturalistic setting with paths and places to study. On the other hand, the philosophy of the school may be that learning is an active process much like being in a shopping center. In this case the imagery of stores may be appropriate.

There are numerous possible interpretations of what something should be and therefore what symbol might convey the correct image. It is important that image selection be based on the client, program, site, and construction issues previously presented. Schools are particularly difficult to symbolize because their functions are evolving at a rapid rate, and therefore no archetypical symbols have evolved. The house example, however, has a number of archetypical forms that do symbolize characteristics of home to reasonably large audiences. The words *saltbox, townhouse,* and *ranch* immediately bring images to mind. A client may very well want a particular image that, in some way, represents a particular way of life. The design problem then becomes fitting the program and site requirements into a shell with the correct imagery.

An architect's style is in itself archetypical in that it is symbolic of the attitudes the architect brings to any project. An astute client may select a particular architect because of the architect's style. A building produced by that architect will embody the concerns of his or her previous designs through the application of a consistent style.

Gestalts

While symbols speak of ideas, other specific form organizations express relationships between parts of a visual composition. A field of psychology has developed around the idea that the human mind is structured to perceive the environment in a way that organizes our visual field into distinct and related parts. This area of study is called "gestalt psychology"; the different pattern organizations we perceive are called "gestalts." The theories of gestalt psychology are of interest to architects because part of the design process is concerned with expressing the relationships between parts of the design. Each gestalt has a defined set of characteristics that can be manipulated by a designer to strengthen or weaken the visual relationship between parts of the composition. Understanding how particular configurations of form will be perceived allows the designer two opportunities. The first is in selecting parts of a composition that the designer wants to be perceived as related, and then in applying the characteristics of various gestalt patterns to the forms to ensure that they will be perceived as a group. The second opportunity is to use this understanding as an analytical technique. The designer may analyze a developing design to see what gestalt organizations are forming and whether they detract from or enhance the design concepts. If they detract, changes in their form can be made.

It is important to note that concepts of visual organization relate to what we can see at a particular moment. Therefore our relationship to the composition being designed must be carefully analyzed. Our relationship to buildings is continually changing as we use them. Gestalts can be used to organize perceptions and to guide us through a building, simplifying the process of recognizing our objectives in the building as well as enhancing our enjoyment of it. The following gestalts are those that have the widest range of application in the design fields.

Figure/Ground. We see figures on backgrounds. The figures are organizations in our visual field that look like things. For example, we recognize the boundaries of an object (such as a coffee cup) as that which gives it its thinglike quality. Ground, on the other hand, is unbounded and diffuse. It does not look like a thing. Figures are seen as being on (or in front of) grounds and are what we organize our view and understanding of the physical environment around. In architecture, figures can be simple recognizable things such as doors, or abstract compositions of window groupings on the elevation of a building. For example, if an entry needs visual expression (as it usually does), it can be formed as a figure against the background of a building. Our understanding of the building will organize around this figure and it will be immediately recognized for what it is. In contrast, there are numerous examples in architecture where there is no differentiation between the entry and the rest of the building, and therefore we are unable to differentiate the entry from other parts of the building. This can be extremely confusing and aggravating. The concepts of recognition embodied in the figure and ground relationship apply across the full spectrum of architectural design, from identifying a light switch to differentiating one building from another.

Center of Gravity. Individual forms and entire compositions seem to have centers that attract our attention. Our understanding of other parts of a form or composition develops from their relationship to the center. This concept can be used as a visual ordering technique in design by placing the more significant things in the center of the composition. One might want to make a reading room in a library embody the concept of "library" to someone within or without the structure. All other spaces might be considered as serving the reading function and therefore as being less important. In this instance, it would be logical to put the reading room in the center of the composition to give it visual importance. Within the building, the designer has to decide the importance of other major functions such as the information desk. It might be centered in one's field of vision to make it dominate the composition, or it could be put to one side to be available but unobtrusive.

Configuration. The concept of configuration holds that the mind will simplify the visual environment in order to understand it. Also, the

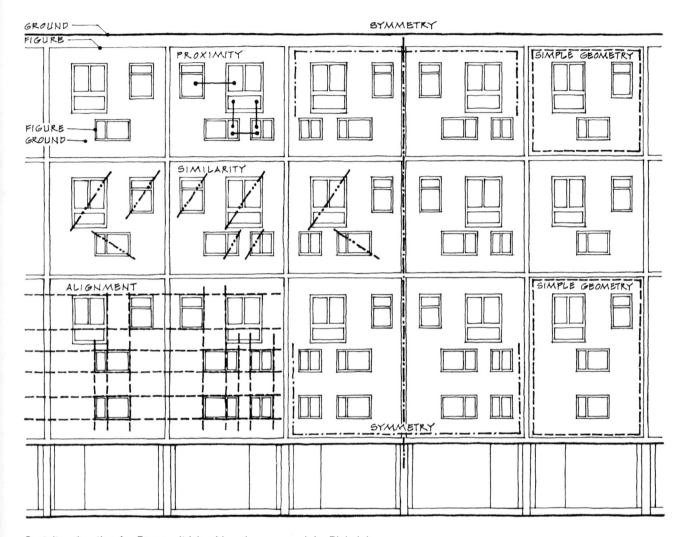

Gestalts: elevation for Roosevelt Island housing proposal, by Rick Jules.

most easily understood part of an environment is the most regular, the one that requires the least simplification. Simplification occurs everywhere. The edge of a brick wall is not really straight, but it is seen as straight. A rectilinear farmhouse is easily identified, while its rolling landscape is not as easily comprehended. An architect can make things clearer by using simple geometric forms, or disguise something by incorporating it into a larger form, or make it so visually fractured that its form is difficult to comprehend.

INTRODUCTION TO ARCHITECTURE

Similarity. Similar objects tend to group together. The characteristics of similarity can be the objects' form, color, texture, sense of mass, or cultural significance. For example, similarly shaped windows may be used to express similar activities occurring behind the windows, and contrasting shapes may be used to express a change of activity and separateness of function. Color may be used to relate two objects that have different forms (such as a table and chair set), or a color contrast can be used to bring out the importance of something in relation to something else.

An object's form, color, texture, sense of mass, and cultural significance are attributes that can be used to develop very subtle hierarchies in the relationships between it and other objects. Sequences of visual experience are developed by contrasts and

Center of gravity: a preliminary design for a shopping mall.

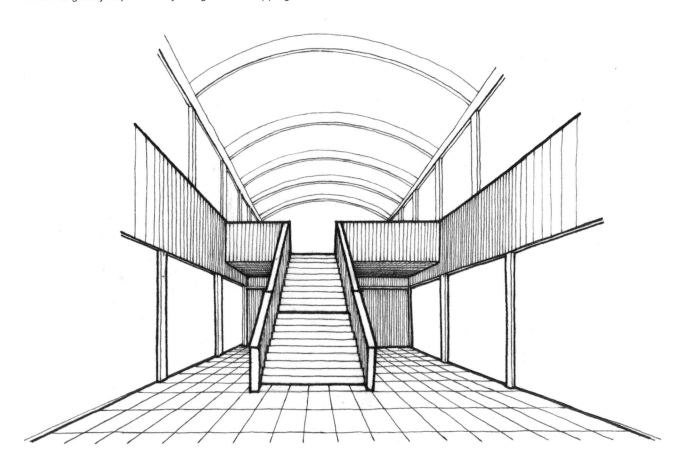

PERCEPTUAL BASES FOR ARCHITECTURAL DESIGN

similarities between these attributes of architectural spaces. The similarities make us see the relationship between the parts while the contrasts bring out the important differences. The sense of similarity between objects can be made stronger by making more of the objects' attributes the same. Objects can be separated from each other by making their attributes contrast. For example, a house may be developed as a sequential composition. The architect may decide that the major spaces should have the same proportion and be further related by identical connecting spaces. The contrasting characteristics in the composition might be the size of the rooms, the color, quality of light, and relation to exterior spaces. Cool colors may be used to make a relaxing bedroom while more active colors appear in the kitchen. This type of fine manipulation occurs continually in the design process until the building expresses the visual image desired by the architect.

Proximity. Objects in close proximity are seen as being related. This concept allows the designer to relate two dissimilar objects by placing them near each other. A school and a gym will always be related because they often appear beside one another. The architect may even want them to be indistinguishable and therefore will make more of their attributes similar. For example, both activities may be enclosed by the same wall with a standard texture applied to the entire surface. However, in some cases, spaces may need to be closely related on a functional basis, but not on a visual basis. This may be accomplished by controlling the user's views of the objects so that they are not seen together, but rather are seen one at a time. Or closer proximities can be developed between the two original spaces and other spaces to form separate visual groups that are stronger than the original proximity. For example, in multifamily housing, windows for each individual unit may be grouped in close proximity to separate them visually from other units. Thus, each living unit has a sense of identity within the larger building.

Symmetry. Symmetrically placed objects also seem to be related. Symmetry is a relationship to an axis. An object can be rotated around the axis, producing rotational symmetry, and it can be slid parallel to the axis to produce translational symmetry. Finally, it can be reflected about an axis to produce a mirror image of itself. These types of symmetry are used often to lend interest in a repetitive composition such as identical housing units or window locations on the elevation of a building. The symmetry produces visual groupings within other groupings to make the experience richer and therefore hold our attention and interest longer. Symmetry also lends importance to the axis that generates it because, as we saw earlier, centers of compositions attract attention.

Closure and Good Continuation. Some things are seen as objects with parts removed, while others look like complex shapes. The concept of closure involves the visual completion of incomplete objects. This visual completion tends to occur if an object is a simpler form when complete and if there is some kind of logical extension of the form that completes it. Rooms seem to enclose even though they have obvious openings. A high fence around a garden gives the sensation of volume even though there is no roof; the roof is implied because the top edges of the fence are in alignment. A stronger sense of closure could be accomplished in this instance by adding more substance to the "roof" with a trellis that aligns with the top of the fence but is freestanding in the space. This would make it simple to complete the rectangular space in one's mind, and therefore the sense of closure would be greater.

Good continuation is the concept of alignment. If things seem to be aligned, they are sensed as being related. Two horizontal windows that are in alignment will give a building a horizontal feeling; that is the effect of our sensing the continuation of one window to another. The more parts of a composition that are in alignment, the stronger the sense of relatedness we feel between those parts. Proximity plays a part in this, too, because the sense of alignment is stronger when two aligned objects are in closer proximity. In all cases, the simplest visual organization will be sensed.

Form Reproduction. The gestalt concept of form reproduction is less a design tool than a way of understanding how we remember spaces. The concept contends that if we have seen the complete form and then we only see part of it, we reproduce the rest of the image from memory. This means that a visual composition can be mentally retained and used for spatial orientation even if only part of the composition is visible. The strength of the image is based on the simplicity of the spatial form and the tight interrelationship of the composition, as well as on how well it contrasts with its context. The Guggenheim Museum, designed by Frank Lloyd Wright, is a good example whose forms are dramatic and thus contrast greatly with the rectangularity of the buildings around it. Essentially, it is a figure on the background of the cityscape. Seeing only a part of this building brings its entire configuration to mind. Because of this quality, it has become a landmark on Fifth Avenue.

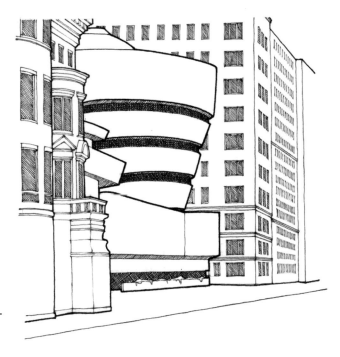

Contrasting image as memorable: Guggenheim Museum, by Frank Lloyd Wright.

Thus, gestalts represent design tools that allow the architect to group parts of a design so that they seem to be related and so that they convey a common message about their function. This direct link to our ability to perceive order makes gestalts extremely powerful design tools when manipulated by a skillful designer.

Vignettes

Vignettes are images of spaces that have emotional connotations. These images are usually powerful, but they are not exact in the way they are produced. They are what Charles Moore calls the order of dreams, for they have a dreamlike quality of being the perfect setting in which a particular activity should occur. The images are forms associated with past pleasurable experiences, and they are only generally remembered by their overall or dominant gestalts. The essence of the space has been preserved while the detail has vanished. Architects collect these images as they study buildings and places. In a lifetime of experiences many vignettes are recalled, and some can become the ideas around which spaces are formed. For example, many persons might remember the image of a good outdoor restaurant with a fine view, small round tables, bright canopies, fresh flowers, and soft-wood railings. These characteristics create the essence of the space; it does not matter much whether the canopies are yellow or orange as long as they are bright. This vignette can now be the genesis of a design for a similar setting. It can be successful only if the user of the space has the same emotional response to the vignette as the designer had. For this reason, such images must be carefully coordinated with the user before the final design is adopted.

Archetypes

Vignettes are images that suggest how a space could be formed, but many building types, such as churches and shopping centers, follow even more specific patterns based on careful research into the optimum form for their specific use. These patterns are called archetypes. Architects are continually looking for these optimum ordering

Vignette: a place to study. John S. Lehmann Building, St. Louis Botanical Garden, Missouri, by Hellmuth, Obata, and Kassabaum (photo by Barbara Martin).

Vignette: Greek Isle house.

patterns, both in the buildings they visit and in the preliminary
research they do for a particular project. For example, certain types of
shopping centers have a dominant pattern. They have two "magnet"
stores (large supermarkets or department stores that attract customers) at either end of a mall with smaller shops in between. The width of the
mall is well defined, depending on whether it is a one- or two-level
center. A great deal of study in merchandising has gone into identifying this pattern, and it is violated only after careful consideration.
Many other building types have more general patterns. High-density
housing, schools, hospitals, and, in fact, most building types have
somewhat typical patterns and forms. As previously mentioned, environment-behavior research produces archetypal patterns of behavior
in certain defined settings, and therefore can be useful in organizing
appropriate architectural forms. A starting place in many design efforts involves identifying the applicable archetypes for a particular situation.

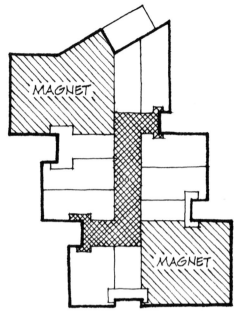

Archetype modified for visual interest: diagram for a shopping center.

Patterns

In building projects that are too new or complex to have archetypes,
carefully defined patterns of use can be abstracted from the building
programs to yield performance requirements that will define the building's enclosure, structure, and environmental control. Structural and
mechanical systems follow well-defined patterns, as does the process
of constructing a building. Each system has a pattern and range of
use that must be matched to the requirements of the function of the
building. An architect can choose to express any of these patterns as
they are applied to serve the needs of the building program, and in
fact these patterns may define very directly the form the building will
take. This choice, then, is a visual-ordering technique that lends emphasis to a particular aspect of the design for specific expressive purposes. In the 1960s the rationale of a usable bay size, structural pattern, and mechanical service formed the image of highrise office
buildings—usually with the structure expressed and the mechanical
distribution hidden. More recently, architects have been letting the
structure follow the building form, picking the appropriate structure
based on the requirements set by the form. In most cases the design is
a careful balancing of the requirements of many patterns, with the
architect deciding which patterns should be dominant. In our earlier
school example, the gym and school building may have very different
structural patterning because of the need for greater clear spans in

Expression of structural and mechanical patterns: Georges Pompidou National Center of Art and Culture, Paris, by Piano and Rogers (photo by Martin Charles).

the gym. However, the visual impression of continuity between the two elements may be maintained by not expressing the structure on the exterior and emphasizing instead a pattern of enclosure that is the same for both parts. An elegant building tends to integrate structure, mechanical, enclosure, and form issues so that they are sensed as a totality, always responding to the needs of the users of the building.

DESIGN OBJECTIVES

Good architects have high levels of skill in the application of the visual ordering techniques we have discussed. However, this alone is not enough to produce a good building. What is required is a well-structured criticism of the design as it develops, to ensure that the primary objectives are not being subordinated by unintentional over-emphasis of any particular part of the design. The following four primary objectives are the basis for such criticism.

The first objective involves maintaining the desired hierarchies between the parts of the building. The architect should be continually conscious of the design objectives and the way the form of space will convey these concerns to the user. Errors in expression at this point give users the wrong understanding of space use and importance. They are easily made, however, because the architect generally works on one part of the design at a time; if each part is not checked regularly against the rest of the design, the hierarchy may undergo an unwanted change. It is also important to note that there may be a number of areas in a design that are of equal importance, or of different importance to different users. This compounds the design problem and makes it doubly important that the desired hierarchies be kept in mind.

Exciting and enjoyable space: Peachtree Plaza, Atlanta, by John Portman (photo by Alexandre Georges).

The second general objective is to maintain clarity of expression in the design. Buildings must clearly state in visual terms the order of importance of the parts and direct people in their use of the building.

The third objective in designing is to develop interest and enjoyment in the design. People are not machines and do not have to be served in a purely functional manner. Buildings are a part of our lives, and they can and should enhance our enjoyment of life. The architect's task is not to totally control the behavior of individuals but rather to provide opportunities for people to experience a wide range of human feelings and, in general, to support the positive aspects of living and expand people's sense of options in the environment.

The final objective is to mesh the concerns of hierarchy, clarity, and interest with the requirements of physical enclosure. The architect should find and analyze alternative ways of expressing all the objectives and choose the best and simplest one. A good solution elegantly expresses the desired ideas in an appropriate manner, giving nothing more or less than what is required. The task is challenging, and meeting this challenge is the enjoyment derived from architecture.

FOR FURTHER READING

Attoe, Wayne. *Architecture and Critical Imagination*. Chichester, England: John Wiley & Sons, 1978.

Jencks, Charles. *The Language of Post-Modern Architecture*. New York: Rizzoli International Publications, 1977.

Moore, Charles; Allen, Gerald; and Lyndon, Donlyn. *The Place of Houses*. New York: Holt, Rinehart and Winston, 1974.

Prak, Niels. *The Visual Perception of the Built Environment*. Delft: Delft University Press, 1977.

Venturi, Robert. *Complexity and Contradiction in Architecture*. New York: Museum of Modern Art, distributed by Doubleday & Co., Garden City, N.Y., 1966.

EXAMPLES OF THE STYLES OF VARIOUS ARCHITECTS
Aalto, Alvar. *Alvar Aalto*. Zurich: Verlag fur Architektur, Artemis, 1963.

Bastlund, Knud. *Jose Luis Sert: Architecture, City Planning, Urban Design*. New York: Praeger, 1967.

Giurgola, Romaldo, and Mehta, Jaimini. *Louis I. Kahn*. Boulder, Colo.: Westview Press, 1975.

Roche, Kevin. *Kevin Roche, John Dinkeloo and Associates*. New York: Architectural Book Publishing Co., 1977.

Part Four
Building Science and Technology

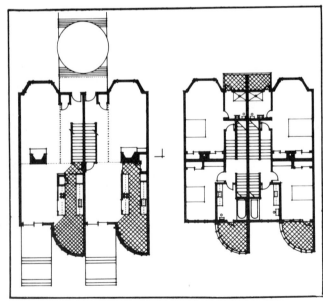

Clarissa Easton

Claudio Veliz

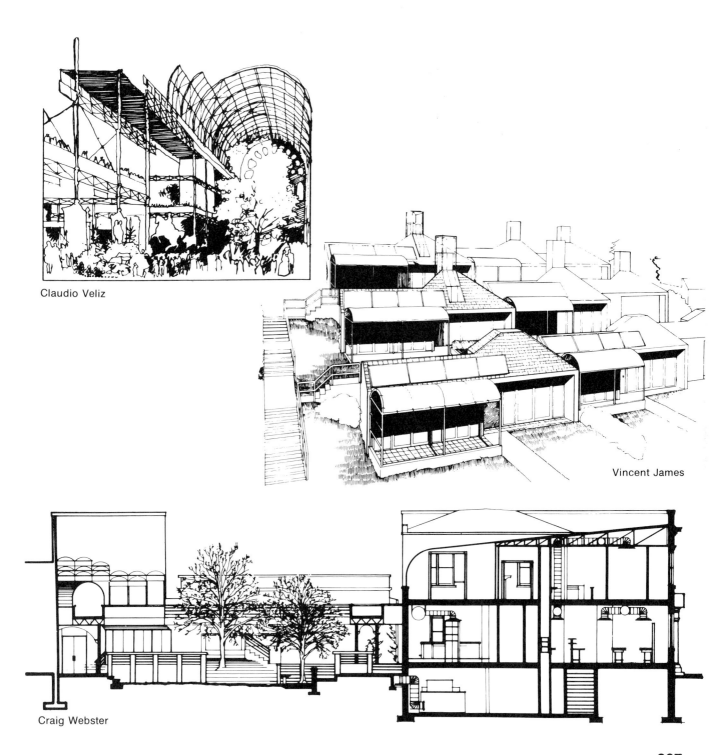

Claudio Veliz

Vincent James

Craig Webster

267

CHAPTER 11

Structural Considerations

David Evan Glasser

Structure in relation to architecture is one of the most compelling issues that architects have to resolve in building design. This relationship is complex and multifaceted. In strictly technological terms, structure may be considered as the means of translating external forces into internal load-carrying mechanisms in order to support and reinforce an architectural concept. Another, broader interpretation of structure might be one in which the means of support and methods of construction are seen as intrinsic factors and form determinants in the building design process. This chapter approaches structures from the broader perspective—as an integral part of architectural design.

Architects are faced, for the first time in history, with a bewildering array of structural and construction choices that are at once alluring and potentially misleading. Building design professionals of an earlier, simpler time had available only a limited choice of structural methods and materials that imposed spatial and visual constraints on the architecture of their society. Roman builders, for example, relied on compressive masonry arched structures, which imposed limits on single unsupported spans and determined much of the visual landscape we associate with ancient Rome today. In a similar way, the character of early American building was determined to a large extent by the limited availability of construction materials. The substantial supply of excellent timber at relatively low cost was a constituent factor in the development of indigenous American architectural prototypes such as barns, churches, town halls, houses, and similar buildings. In this regard it may be argued that the scale, character, and continuity of many early American communities, particularly in New England, owe their cohesive quality to structural considerations imposed by the limited building technology and narrow choices of construction materials.

The rigorous limits on building spans and architectural character imposed by these constraints no longer exist. Present theoretical potentialities of structural design are almost without limit. It is feasible to develop roof spans of 1,000 feet and construct a building a half-mile high. Recent international world expositions have demonstrated that it is possible to construct a building of virtually any shape. The issue, then, that every architect should consider is not merely how to incorporate structure into buildings, but also how to establish a basis for the selection of appropriate structural methods and materials in relation to building design. Since technological means are at hand to make every structural solution possible, an increasing burden of responsibility has been placed upon architects to make rational choices with respect to structure in buildings.

RELATIONSHIP OF STRUCTURE TO ARCHITECTURE

Structure as Form Determinant

In all buildings it is necessary to carry external loads and forces from roofs, floors, and walls through an internal load-carrying mechanism to the ground. The design and development of the structural system in relation to a building concept constitutes one of the major formal decisions made by the architect. The importance of structure as a form determinant may be seen in the central business district of almost any large city in the world. The shape and scale of most major office buildings has been decided almost exclusively by considerations of column spacing, efficiency of spanning members, and wind loading.

It is important to make the observation that, as buildings increase in size, the issue of structure as a principal form determinant becomes increasingly persuasive. It will be recognized that at the scale of individual residences it is possible, and in many cases desirable, to subordinate structural issues. On the other end of the scale—as in the case of arenas, auditoriums, and stadiums—it is equally clear that a conceptual design without a rigorous and well-integrated structural framework would be specious.

Some architects and engineers insist that to be considered an excellent work of good architecture, a building must provide an in-

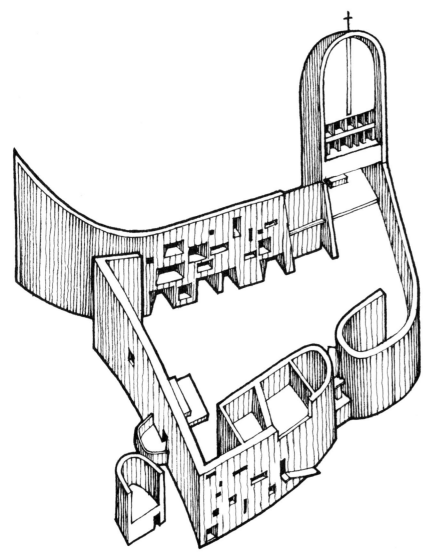

Ronchamp Chapel, France, by Le Corbusier.

terlocking fit between spatial, conceptual, and structural design concerns. This point of view suggests that the structural system provides an encompassing framework for the successful incorporation of all the other elements that together form the basis for architecture. In this regard, structure is viewed as a dominant factor in the design process and, as such, provides the basic aesthetic character of buildings.

There are, at the same time, buildings whose primary form determinants may be metaphorical, sculptural, spiritual, or symbolic, where structure plays a subordinate role in the design. A building such as

INTRODUCTION TO ARCHITECTURE

the Ronchamp Chapel by Le Corbusier derives its character from its treatment of space and light rather than through articulation of structure.

Irrespective of these divergent points of view, there can be no dispute as to the importance of structure in architecture and the need for the architect to understand fundamental structural design principles and their application. Substantial differences may arise with respect to the nature and extent of structural expression on any architectural project, but most architects will agree that structure constitutes one of the organizational aspects of building design.

Structure as Organizing Principle

Structure may be thought of as an organizing design principle as well as a load-carrying mechanism. In this regard structuring implies the act of establishing hierarchy and order simultaneously in terms of architectural space and physical force translation.

One of the earliest decisions made during the building design process is the establishment of the structural bay size. Usually this determination is made in relation to projected space utilization patterns and incorporates flexibility, where practicable, in anticipation of future changes. Structural bay sizes in commercial office buildings provide an excellent illustrative example.

The bay size, which determines column location, generates the appropriate sizes not only of all structural members, but of all components and subsystems as well. For example, a building consisting of *x* number of bays in width and *y* number in length might consist of

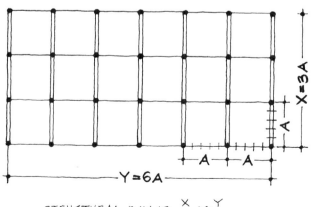

Structural bay sizes.

a number of components, each in a specific ratio to the dimensions of the basic bay. The relationship of each part to the entire structure provides a satisfying and unifying architectural character as well as a mechanism for the logical distribution of forces.

A great many issues have to be considered in the design of a building. Urban design, environmental behavior, and other concerns have been added to the traditional requirements for "firmness, commodity, and delight." In this regard, architectural design may be seen to depend on an increasing number of variables. To give equal attention to each of these building design concerns is inappropriate and, in fact, impossible. Design priorities are established by the architect in relation to specific program requirements for each project. It is safe to say that in the majority of buildings, selection of structural systems is usually one of the highest priorities in the design process. Thus, the early determination of a rational and logical structural system can provide the basis for more effectively dealing with the full range of design priorities.

Natural and Built Forms

Natural forms of plants and animals provide the designer with valuable insights into structure and design. All forms in nature may be viewed as load-carrying mechanisms, with their characteristics being the results of internal structural responses to external load conditions. In fact, when one examines the evolutionary history of plants and animals, it becomes clear that those without suitable structural responses to external stimuli were unable to survive. The development of appropriate and successful structural systems in natural forms now around us accounts for their continued presence.

A tree is a convenient example to analyze from a structural standpoint. Upon examination we can see that the trunk is both thick and strong enough to carry vertical loads from the branches to the ground. It is at the same time flexible enough to withstand fairly high lateral wind loads. The branches are stiff enough to extend laterally and support the leaf system, yet not so heavy as to sag unduly under snow and ice. The root structure spreads radially below the ground to distribute the total weight of the tree simultaneously to a wide area of earth and to create a substantial anchor against overturning due to wind. Thus the tree offers an insight into the architectural design task of designing a force-responsive system in which every component serves its appropriate local structural function and all together form a comprehensible and serviceable entity.

The relationship of natural forms to those selected by builders

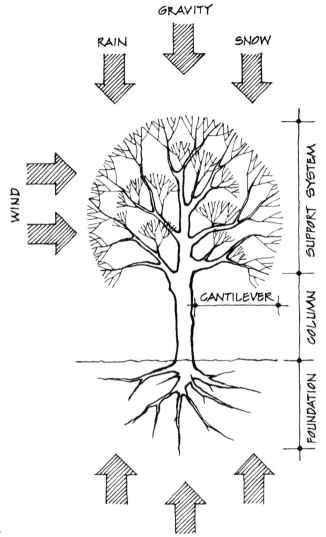

Structural analogy.

and designers over the centuries is more than coincidental. Just as natural stone caves led, in all likelihood, to the idea of the arch as a construction method, so also did elements in nature lend their conceptual identities to current structural ideas. Thin-shell concrete construction and egg shells are perceptual homonyms, as are spiders' webs and cable net structures, blow fish and air-supported structures, and leaf cell structure and isostatic ribbed slab systems. Wherever we look it is possible to make inferential connections between natural forms and built structures.

STRUCTURAL CONSIDERATIONS

In examining these analogous structural ideas, we might notice that a straight line does not appear anywhere in nature. Architecture, on the other hand, employs linear and planar elements to a great extent. On the surface this appears to be a major inconsistency. In one respect, nature offers a wide range of structural insights and forms for designers to use. However, architects often employ systems and forms that are noncongruent with those perceived in nature.

The dichotomy between made and natural forms with respect to structure and design may be accepted somewhat more easily if the designer is willing to recognize the implicit and fundamental distinctions between them. The propensity of nature would appear to be the successive generation, suppression, and regeneration of forms. In this rigorous process, the hardiest specimens survive; the weakest perish. The architect's intentions are more deterministic. Buildings represent an effort to withstand natural forces rather than to accommodate them. Structural forms are designed to provide climate-controlled, weather- and wind-resistant environments that deliberately exclude natural tendencies for cyclical deterioration. Architecture requires structural permanence in the context of uncontrollable natural forces.

LOADS ON STRUCTURES

Why Structures Exist
Buildings are made to create controlled internal environments capable of withstanding external forces. They are designed to accommodate a specific number of functions and house human activity. Some buildings, such as barns and sheds, only serve to provide shelter. Others are quite specific and complex, as, for example, sports stadiums. Well-designed buildings facilitate and amplify their intended functions. There is a wide variation in primary school building design, for instance; to a large extent the quality and character of teaching is determined by the environment created in each school. In this last regard, we recognize that buildings perform a larger service than mere shelter. Ideally, they serve to enrich our spirit and ennoble our activities.

Structure as Response to External Forces
The structural system exists as a response to certain unavoidable external forces. Principal among these is gravity. The weight of a structure and its occupants tends to pull it towards earth, and the function

of every component in a building is to resist this tendency. In addition to known loads from building materials and the users, there are loads due to natural forces that can only be statistically predicted but that have to be accommodated nevertheless. Snow is a gravity load that varies with geographical location. Wind and earthquakes affect buildings differently from gravity loads. Wind has the potential of inducing horizontal loads, which tend to displace a building laterally. Seismic or earthquake loads have somewhat the same lateral load characteristics as wind, but theirs are of much shorter duration and much greater magnitude.

A building must develop a structural mechanism responsive to all forces upon it. In this respect all structural systems may be viewed as three-dimensional force response systems that are adjusted to accommodate external loads from any direction.

Construction history abounds with case studies of structures that failed because of inaccurate prediction of projected loading conditions. One of the most spectacular of these failures was the Tacoma Narrows Bridge, built in 1940 and known to engineers and failure aficionados as "Galloping Gertie." At the time of its erection, Tacoma Narrows was the third longest suspension bridge in the world—2,800 feet between supports. Wind tunnel tests made prior to construction failed to reveal the fact that a sustained wind load of moderate velocity against stiffening trusses along the roadway would develop increasing oscillations in the bridge, leading to collapse of the main span. While architects cannot be expected to determine exact magnitudes and duration of all loading conditions, a basic conceptual and practical understanding of loads and their impact is fundamental in order to develop an appropriate structural design concept.

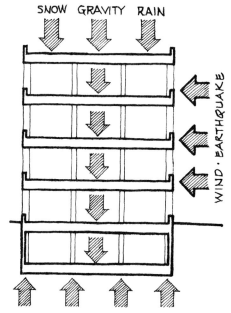

Force-resisting system.

Kinds of Loads

Static Loads. In general there are two types of loading conditions that concern building designers—*static* and *dynamic*. Static or stationary loads constitute the preponderant conditions in most buildings. Typical static (nonmoving) building loads include fixed machinery weights, anticipated occupant load, and building materials. This means that the architect can anticipate loads of predictable magnitude and duration and design a system that readily responds to these known conditions. Dynamic or moving loads, as in the case of wind or a locomotive crossing a bridge, present more difficult structural design tasks in that both magnitude and duration of loading are predictable only within limits.

Live Loads. Live loads are design loads that represent empirical statistical assumptions regarding anticipated future use of a planned space.

Live loads include all loads other than the weight of the building structure—occupants, furniture, equipment, and machinery. Snow, rain, wind, earthquake, and water pressure are live loads that vary in magnitude and duration. In order to simplify structural analysis, a statistical average live load is assigned to represent the *static equivalent* of these dynamic loads.

Since it is virtually impossible to predict accurately the exact use pattern of a building (for example, the number of occupants and amount of furniture), it becomes necessary to make reasonable assumptions regarding the *worst* possible future condition that might arise. Architects are not generally called upon to make these assumptions. Building codes and many nationally recognized structural manuals incorporate recommended minimum, uniform-distributed live loads for each type of proposed occupancy. For example, commercial offices require a live load of 50 pounds per square foot (50 psf), but a corridor in the same building would require a live load of 100 psf. The logic behind this is clear. An office can only hold a certain number of people and amount of furniture and still function. A corridor, on the other hand, might be completely filled in the event of an emergency. The live load figures reflect this variable potential.

Dead Loads. The weights of structural materials and components that make up the force-response system are dead loads. Architects can select from a wide range of construction material alternatives, each of which has varying configurations, density, and weight characteristics. One of the principal concerns of architects and engineers is the dead load–live load ratio in structure systems. Structural efficiency would seem to demand a low percentage of dead weight to imposed live loads. On the other hand, concern for fire safety and construction system constraints often dictate dead loads that considerably exceed design loads. For example, a 6-inch-thick concrete slab, which is a common floor element in many multifamily residences, weighs 75 psf and may carry only a 40 psf static equivalent live load. An accurate determination of building dead loads thus constitutes one of the principal factors in structural analysis.

Wind Loads. Wind loads are actually dynamic loads but are treated in analysis as *equivalent static loads,* that is, as statistical average assumptions. Wind loads are more complicated to assess than floor loads because of several factors. For example, negative or suction pressures on the leeward sides of structures tend to increase the effect of direct wind loading, and the duration of load application has a profound effect on the structural design of a building. For instance, a short hard gust of wind will have twice the impact of an equivalent force wind applied over a sustained period. The siting of buildings also has an effect on wind pressure. For instance, a 100-foot-high building on a downtown urban site would be subject to a live load of 18 psf as a result of a 100 mph wind speed. This same building, if located in an open, coastal region, would sustain a live load of 44 psf in relation to the same wind speed. This suggests that collective siting of major buildings seems to have compelling structural as well as urban design justification.

The accurate and safe determination of wind loads is a matter of judgment and experience. Architects and students are advised to use equivalent static loads for wind conditions with some degree of caution.

Seismic Loads. The National Council of Architectural Registration Boards (NCARB) now requires all architects to be aware of and conversant with provisions for making buildings safe against seismic (earthquake) loads. A seismic load is usually of high intensity and short duration. Thus it tends to have a much greater impact on a structure than would the same load applied over a longer period. This phenomenon occurs because of a property manifested by all structures—the *fundamental period*. This period of time, which might vary from one-tenth second to ten seconds, is the duration in which the structure will oscillate completely from side to side and return to its original position. All structures, even tall office towers, are flexible to some extent and undergo vibrations of certain duration depending on structural rigidity and other factors. If a sharp, short shock, such as a seismic load, is applied to a building so as to be the same as or shorter than the fundamental period, the building will be subject to dynamic rather than static loads.

Dynamic loads on buildings require provision for increased stiffness of individual members and for the structural system to transfer loads readily throughout the structure. By having a structure with continuous (rigidly connected) joints, a building becomes better able to resist the effect of seismic loading. Poured concrete buildings, which are monolithic and therefore intrinsically continuous, are excellent in this regard. (An atomic blast approximates earthquake shock in larger magnitude. Films taken of the aftermath of Hiroshima and Nagasaki show that the only buildings to survive the regrettable holocaust were of poured concrete.) Provision for these major short-lived lateral loads must be made in certain designated areas of the globe where past experience and geological structure suggest the probability of earthquake.

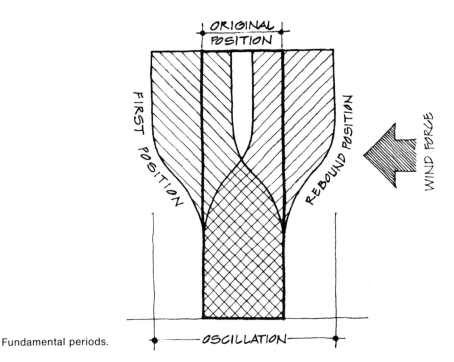

ORIGINAL POSITION

FIRST POSITION

REBOUND POSITION

WIND FORCE

OSCILLATION

Fundamental periods.

Thermal Loads. Thermal loads are induced by temperature changes, which tend to modify the shape and dimensions of structural elements in accordance with time and season. Each material has a particular *coefficient of expansion* (unit of dimensional change for each degree change of temperature) related to its unique molecular properties. For example, structural steel has a coefficient of linear expansion of 0.0000067/inch°F, which is to say that for a 100°F change a 1-inch-long steel bar would elongate (or shorten) 0.00067 inch. This may not appear to be significant, except when we consider that many buildings are situated in climates with annual extremes in excess of 100°F, and that the size of many buildings is such that these dimensional changes become significant. For instance, a 200-foot-long building would experience a dimensional change of more than $1\frac{1}{2}$ inches in a 100°F variation.

Since every material expands and contracts, architects are faced with the choice of providing details that permit free movement of building components or providing for rigid constraints that would

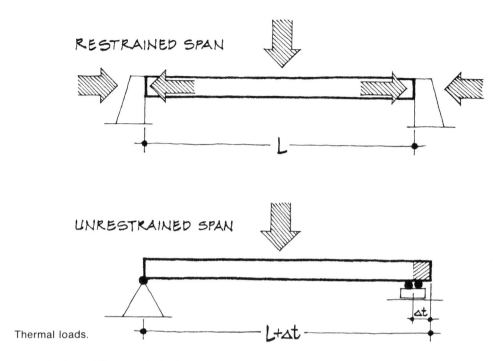

RESTRAINED SPAN

UNRESTRAINED SPAN

Thermal loads.

require treating thermal changes as induced live loads in the structure. The second approach often proves to be counterproductive in that one-half of the load-carrying capacity of structural members is sometimes utilized to withstand thermal loads, instead of having full capacity available to sustain normal live and dead loads. For this reason, prudent designers make provisions for expansion joints in structures in order to accommodate accumulated dimensional changes at designated parts of the structure without unnecessarily stressing principal load-carrying members.

LOAD-CARRYING STRATEGIES

Structural Options Available to the Architect
After the magnitude and direction of all loads that will affect the building have been identified, the architect, usually with the collaboration of a structural engineer, will determine a suitable structural system to resist these forces. A structural system implies an organization of spanning (horizontal) and support (vertical) members to provide a spatial framework for transferring all loads to the ground.

In the most general terms, there are relatively few fundamental structural approaches the architect can manipulate in relation to building design. In fact, there are only two principal strategies architects use to solve most building design problems. These are based upon linear or point-supported systems. The basic distinction is made between available systems in relation to the manner in which vertical loads are transferred to the earth.

A linear support system is a load-bearing assembly in which the majority of the exterior walls serve to both enclose and continuously support floors and roof. Until the twentieth century, the overwhelming number of significant buildings were of this type. It is true also that many buildings, particularly those of modest size and scale, are still built using this time-tested approach. Continuous support or wall-bearing systems have two basic characteristics: openings in the support walls require structural attention and architectural expression; and foundations must be linear in nature to provide continuous load distribution to earth.

A noncontinuous support system is a load-bearing assembly in which horizontal spanning loads are transferred first to point supports (columns or posts) and then vertically to earth. The resulting framework or skeleton makes possible the clear distinction between load-bearing and non-loading-bearing elements. A noncontinuous or point support system has two salient characteristics: the exterior enclosing walls may be treated as non-load-bearing, weather-resisting components that are different in character from supporting elements; and point-supported foundations may also be noncontinuous, that is, directly related to column locations and loads. The ability to employ point-supported modes is often of advantage, particularly on difficult building sites, where irregular terrain or unusual subsurface conditions make it necessary to develop specialized foundation conditions.

Although choices are limited with respect to alternative support systems, a broad range of spanning alternatives is available to the architect. These vary with respect to load-carrying capability, dimension, material, weight, scale, and character to such a substantial degree that the architect must develop a clear set of design criteria to serve as the basis for the selection of appropriate spanning systems and structural elements.

Structural System Criteria

The list that follows is neither all-inclusive nor arranged in order of importance. However, few buildings are designed without serious regard for the following criteria:

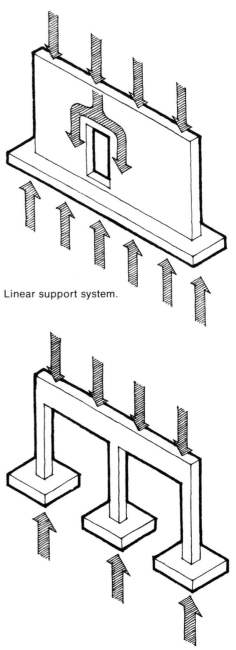

Linear support system.

Point support system.

1 *Structural safety.* Are the total system and the individual members properly sized to carry the design loads?

2 *Fire safety.* To what extent is the system resistant to fire?

3 *Ease of construction.* Are the methods of construction simple and straightforward? If the construction techniques are elaborate, are difficulties outweighed by the inherent benefits of the proposed system?

4 *Durability.* Will the system and components withstand the ravages of time and weather? Will the material continue to be attractive in the future?

5 *Availability.* Are the necessary materials and structural elements readily available in the vicinity of the building site?

6 *Scale.* Are the system and its components appropriate in size and character to the building design? Do the building elements relate to the human occupants?

7 *Integration.* Every structural system exists in relationship to parallel and interlocking building systems that must be accommodated. How well does the system interact with electromechanical distribution networks, circulation patterns, and building enclosure systems?

8 *Rigidity.* Is the total structure sufficiently stiff to withstand wind and/or seismic loads? (Sometimes this characteristic is called *racking strength*.) Are the individual members rigid enough to keep deflections (vertical deformation) within acceptable limits?

9 *Economy.* Is the relative cost of the system in balance with the total building cost? More to the point, is the cost of the structure appropriate to the benefits to be obtained?

10 *Visual.* Do the completed structure and its components together serve to enhance and extend the architectural building concept?

To illustrate how these criteria might affect the choice of structure for a building consider two examples, a 10-story multiple dwelling and a 70-story commercial office structure. The choice of structure for the first might reasonably be poured concrete, with uniform thickness of slabs used throughout. In accord with the above criteria, the reasons for the selection might be as follows:

MULTIPLE DWELLING / PROPOSED STRUCTURAL SYSTEM

1 Spans are relatively small (20 feet maximum), and flexible column spacing is both desirable and possible with this system. Uniform flat slab construction is appropriate and easy to construct.

2 The building uses available materials. Concrete and steel reinforcing are universally obtainable.

3 The integration of mechanical systems is possible. Flat slab is not particularly accommodating in this respect, but the scale of heating and electrical elements is fairly small, and they will have relatively minor impact on the structure system.

4 The system is rigid as a result of being a continuous concrete framework and will be wind resistant.

OFFICE BUILDING / PROPOSED STRUCTURAL SYSTEM

The larger-scale office building, with its greater occupancies and need for flexibility in planning tenant subdivisions, requires a very different structure. An appropriate system might consist of a concrete-protected rolled steel skeleton framework, with columns on a 30 × 30-foot grid. The reasons for selecting this system are as follows.

1 The rapid speed of erection of steel would lead to real economies, since other building trades can proceed within accelerated time schedules.

2 Fireproofing of steel can be accomplished by spray application; it is therefore less time-consuming and cheaper than forming each member in concrete.

3 Large bays will result in relatively deep floor-framing members. The size of members is in relation to large occupancy spaces.

4 Deep members in steel may be designed with internal openings located so as to maintain structural safety and accommodate electromechanical systems.

5 Steel frames may be made rigid to resist wind loads, either by welding (producing continuity) or by installing wind-bracing elements. These are diagonal elements which tie spanning and support members together.

Building Materials

The primary structural materials used in construction are steel, aluminum, wood, concrete, and masonry. While plastics, fabrics, and other specialized materials are being increasingly employed in construction, the materials listed above represent basic materials in current use.

These materials vary considerably with respect to their structural properties and strength and incorporate a number of specific characteristics that have to be identified in order to form a basis for comparison. Every material has a specific density (*molecular weight*) and individual molecular construction that determines its unique structural characteristics. The importance of material characteristics in relation to structural design is evident. An imposed design load must be equalized or, more properly, equilibrated by the action of the load-carrying mechanism of the structural system. The external load requires an internal force response of equal magnitude within the structural member. In order to do this, structural members are stressed (that is, they generate unit strength characteristics) within predetermined limits of safety.

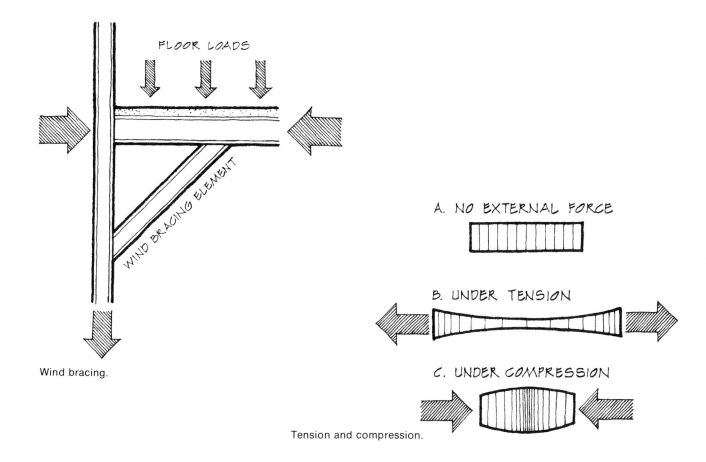

FLOOR LOADS

WIND BRACING ELEMENT

Wind bracing.

A. NO EXTERNAL FORCE

B. UNDER TENSION

C. UNDER COMPRESSION

Tension and compression.

Materials may be subject to a wide range of stresses, several of which are universally considered as principal factors in the selection of appropriate construction materials. The following list describes such stress characteristics.

1 *Tension or tensile stresses.* Tensile stresses tend to lengthen or elongate members. Cables in a suspension bridge are examples of materials in tension.

2 *Compression or compressive stresses.* Compressive stresses tend to shorten or flatten members. A load-bearing column in a building is an example.

3 *Bending.* Horizontal load-carrying members or beams tend to bend away from the loaded edge of the beam. In this event the upper edge of the beam tends to shorten (compress) and the lower edge to elongate (tense). This combination of opposing stresses is common to all beams.

STRUCTURAL CONSIDERATIONS

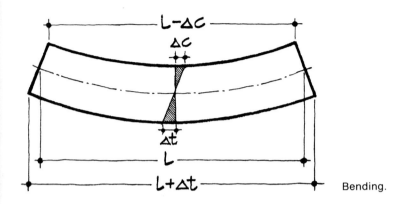

Bending.

4 *Shear.* Structural spanning members have the universal propensity to move downward under force of gravity in direct proportion to the magnitude of load carried. This movement is resisted at the support conditions of all spans. The system of counteracting forces tends to produce tearing or shear stress in members. Shear is a phenomenon that can be viewed in two distinct ways. At the gross behavior level, loads tend to shear the beam downward at the supports. Looking more closely, we can see that the gravity loads tend to distort the beam in such a way as to induce both tension and compression stresses at right angles to each other. Shear stress occurs at an angle of approximately 45° to the direction of both span and support. Sometimes shear is referred to as diagonal tension, since the governing factor for most materials will be limited by tension rather than by compression. This factor becomes significant particularly in relation to wood, which has very low shear strength relative to bending.

5 *Deformation.* Another basic material characteristic that architects and designers are concerned with is the amount of change or deformation a material will sustain in relation to applied loads. Every material will deform (elongate or shorten) in direct proportion to the amount of stress induced, within certain limits. This means that doubling induced stress on a member will produce twice the deformation or strain. Conversely, halving the stress in a member will produce one-half the strain. In this respect we can state that stress and strain are directly proportional.

This is another way of saying that within proportional limits members will return to their original state after loads have been removed. If materials did not have this elastic property, successive periods of loading would induce additive deformations that over the course of time would inevitably result in structural failure.

This characteristic elastic quality of each material is designated as the *modulus of elasticity*, a term derived from a ratio of unit stress to unit strain. The modulus of elasticity (E) is generally taken as $E = 30 \times 10^6$ psi for structural steel, for example. This figure, obtained through careful and frequent

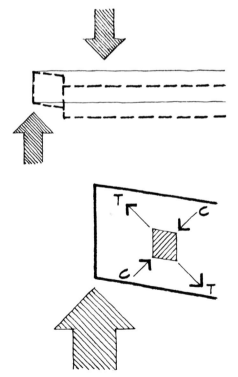

Shear: gross and micro behavior.

laboratory testing, shows that a stress of 30,000,000 psi would theoretically produce a deformation of one inch in a section of material 1 inch square and 1 inch long. By contrast, timber with an average $E = 1.5 \times 10^6$ psi would take only 1,500,000 psi to produce the identical deformation. From this observation it will be apparent that the elastic property of materials simultaneously describes both stress and deformation characteristics.

A list of principal construction materials with allowable unit stresses is provided in Table 11-1. A comparison of the stress values listed there reveals several remarkable material characteristics.

1 *Steel.* Steel is extremely strong in all categories. Deformation is one-third that of aluminum and approximately one-tenth that of concrete under equal loading conditions. Also noteworthy is the relatively high value of steel in shear: 60 percent of allowable bending stresses. The significance of this is apparent in a comparison with wood, whose shear strength is about 5 percent of its value in bending.

2 *Aluminum.* Strength characteristics of aluminum are very close to those of steel, particularly with respect to bending strength and shear. Moreover,

Elasticity.

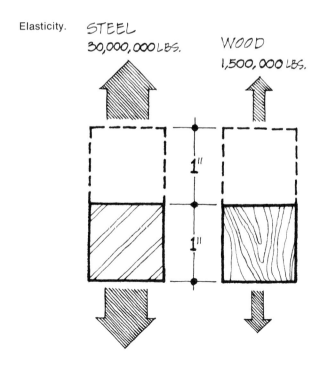

Table 11-1

Allowable Unit Stress for Materials,* Pounds per Square Inch (psi)

Material	Bending f_b	Tension f_t	Compression f_c	Shear f_v	Modulus of elasticity E
Steel, mild	24,000	22,000	22,000	14,500	30×10^6
Steel, high strength	33,000	30,000	30,000	20,000	30×10^6
Aluminum, typical alloy	21,000	19,000	20,000	14,000	10×10^6
Wood (average strength)	1,500	1,050	1,200(a)	85	1.3×10^6
Concrete	1,125–2,250(b)	80–113	1,125–2,250	55–78	$3–5 \times 10^6$
Masonry/brick (average strength)	48–72(c)	22–32	320–480	34–68	$2–3 \times 10^6$
Concrete block (average strength)	32–78(c)	16–39	1,500	23–24	$2–3 \times 10^6$

(a) Note that compression values listed for wood are in conditions where loads are parallel to the direction of the grain. Values for compression applied perpendicular to the grain are about one-fourth of these.

(b) These values for bending in concrete assume that tensile forces in bending members are carried by reinforcing steel, since concrete sustains negligible tension stresses.

(c) These extraordinarily low values are for tensile stresses in bending. They assume unreinforced walls and are therefore the limiting factor in the design of masonry structures where bending is a factor.

* The term *allowable* describes a unit stress that is taken at a certain percentage below the ultimate or failure stress of the material. This provides for a safety factor that varies with each type of material.

this high strength is achieved with material weights one-third those of steel. Considering the weight/span ratio, aluminum is an almost ideal material. On the other hand, aluminum deflections (which are three times those of steel) impose certain constraints on its use. Both steel and aluminum require covering with fireproofing materials in order to obtain conditions of fire safety.

3 *Wood.* Wood generally has uniform bending, tension, and compressive stress characteristics within a specific species and grade. Note that wood carries extremely low values in shear. Unlike the other materials reviewed, wood is nonisotropic, which is to say that its strength is not equal in all directions (as is true for steel, for example). The determining factor is the shear strength parallel to the wood grain. Shear stress across the grain is approximately four times greater.

4 *Concrete.* It is immediately apparent that concrete without added reinforcement has negligible tensile and shear stress capability. The development of reinforced concrete structures and components flows naturally from this physical property. The excellent tensile strength of steel can be combined with the compressive qualities of concrete to make a composite member in which each material is used to its best advantage. Its high fire-resistance rating and plasticity make concrete a highly attractive structural medium.

Steel, aluminum, wood, and masonry are all manufactured products with stock profiles, cross-sectional areas, and dimensions. With respect to these, the architect is basically involved with selecting a prefabricated component in response to a designated set of design conditions. In the case of concrete, individual members as well as the entire structure may be shaped to respond to design loads in highly specific configurations. Further, by modifying concrete strength and adjusting sizes and position of internal steel reinforcing, infinite variations are possible.

With increasingly sophisticated technology, concrete application has expanded considerably beyond its initial use in structural frames. Entire buildings with exposed concrete surfaces are becoming less exotic and more acceptable to the public.

5 *Masonry*. Brick, concrete, clay, and other masonry construction systems rely for their strength on the bonding together of many units and the positioning of each element in the wall to develop a structural entity. Mortar in masonry work is intended to provide a plastic embedment for irregular elements and should not be considered as a "glue" between units. Building components assembled from masonry units have, to a large degree, the same virtues and faults as concrete. They are weak in tension and shear. To the extent that masonry is employed in direct-load bearing compression, it is both desirable and efficient. Because of its poor qualities in other respects, it requires the addition of steel reinforcing in order to extend its capabilities. Reliance on unit masonry construction for the principal vertical support system in major buildings has been supplanted to a substantial degree by steel- and/or concrete-framed structures.

SYSTEMS CHOICES

Having established a range of structural design criteria and a number of basic structural materials, we can move on to examine a range of systems that might be employed in various types of buildings. First, however, we will examine the concept of a system in relation to structural elements.

Structural Systems

A system is an organization of elements that work together for a common purpose. A road system, for example, is thought of as an interconnecting network of circulation routes, each scaled for the anticipated traffic, and with each component designed to facilitate movement between all designated points within the system. The size and character of the road construction is as much part of the system as the overall pattern. In this regard the road system may be seen as an assembly of elements (the roads) and their organizational arrangement in space which forms the network. Viewed in this way, within any system, separate notions of product (structural elements) and process (arrangement in space) become mutually interdependent.

In relation to a building, a structural system incorporates the same notions. In specific terms, a building structure should be able to:

1 Provide conditions of safety and support.
2 Accommodate the means of enclosure (weather protection).
3 Accommodate environmental control systems.
3 Utilize appropriate methods and materials of constructions consistent
4 with the architect's design intentions.
5 Establish a coherent visual framework.

Implicit in any system are built-in constraints and limitations that the designer should recognize and appreciate. No single system can accommodate every factor with equal success. The ability to evalu-

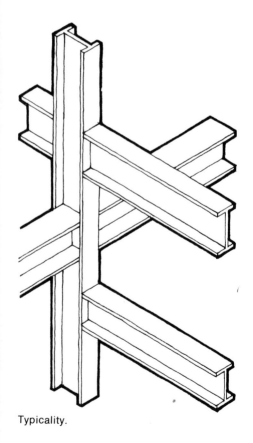

Typicality.

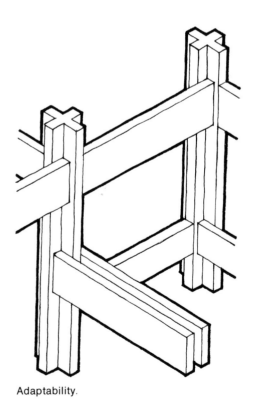

Adaptability.

INTRODUCTION TO ARCHITECTURE

ate and select different structural systems for individual design situations is one of the most important skills of the architect.

When a building structure is conceived as an entity, rather than as a series of isolated events, several major design advantages are derived.

1 *Repetition.* Dependence on industrial technology and economy of manufacture make the use of modular, repetitive units possible. The production of large quantities of elements allows builders to obtain high-quality building components at reasonable cost within acceptable time limits.

2 *Typicality.* The recurrence of similar conditions in a structural system generates details and connections that tend to be uniform throughout the building. Typical details are economical and desirable from an architectural standpoint. They provide one of the important elements of building design vocabulary and establish visual continuity and consistency in an architectural project.

3 *Adaptability.* Within the characteristics and constraints of any system, certain options and possibilities exist that may be used to accommodate specific architectural tasks. Turning a corner of a building or incorporating a stairway are universal design issues. Reliance upon a structural system often dictates, and thus simplifies, the manner in which these conditions are resolved.

Alternative Spanning Systems.

Structural design choices are related to two fundamental issues: span and support. Available choices for spanning systems are much greater than those for support.

While particular structural spanning solutions may vary as to materials, connections, and configuration, spans are accomplished in two basic ways: as one-way or as multidirectional spans. Unidirectional or one-way structural elements, such as wood beams, have inherent strength in the linear direction of the span. Multidirectional spanning elements, such as concrete flat slabs or masonry domes, may be thought of as spanning in a concentric rather than in a linear pattern.

In any spanning system, the basic task of structure is to carry vertical (gravity) loads by means of horizontal members that in turn transfer their loads to the support system of columns or bearing walls. The initial translation of vertical forces to horizontal members is done through bending. The load on the member simultaneously stresses the upper beam edges in compression and the lower ones in tension; these combined stresses are described as bending stresses. The stress characteristics of spanning materials determine the upper limits of bending stretch for any member. This explains why a concrete beam requires steel reinforcing. Concrete, which is poor in tension but good in compression, cannot function in bending without the addition of steel reinforcing bars to repair this deficiency.

Unidirectional Spanning Systems

All single-directional spanning systems are hierarchical in nature. As the span of each component increases, its cross-sectional area and depth must increase correspondingly. For example, the depth of floor or roof decking is generally shallow, varying anywhere from 3/4 inch, in the case of plywood, to 2 or 4 inches for concrete decking. For reasons of economy and ease of handling, decking elements generally will be lighter and thinner than required elsewhere in the assembly. These shallow deck elements naturally will have limited spanning capability and require structural supports (beams) spaced at regular intervals in order to carry the loads from the decking. The spacing of beams in any one-way spanning system is entirely dependent upon the decking structural characteristics. Shown in Table 11-2 is a range of deck types and resulting beam spacing, assuming typical loading conditions.

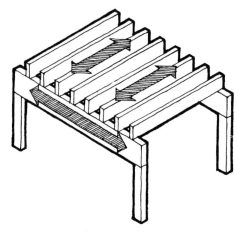
One-way spanning system.

TABLE 11-2
Deck Type and Beam Spacing

Deck type, in inches	Beam spacing, inches
$\frac{1}{2}$ plywood	12–16 on center
$\frac{3}{4}$ plywood	20–24 on center
$2\frac{1}{2}$ concrete plank	48–72 on center
2 wood decking	60–72 on center
$1\frac{1}{2}$ steel decking	84–96 on center

Multidirectional spanning system.

Supporting beams spanning at right angles to the deck span must be supported in turn by other load-carrying members, that is, by girders that provide the final transfer of all collected loads onto column supports. Since there are fewer girders at larger space intervals, it follows that these members will be the most substantial elements in the system. As in the case of deck and beam load transfer, the beam-to-girder relationship is one in which the beams are perpendicular, or normal, to the direction of the supporting girders.

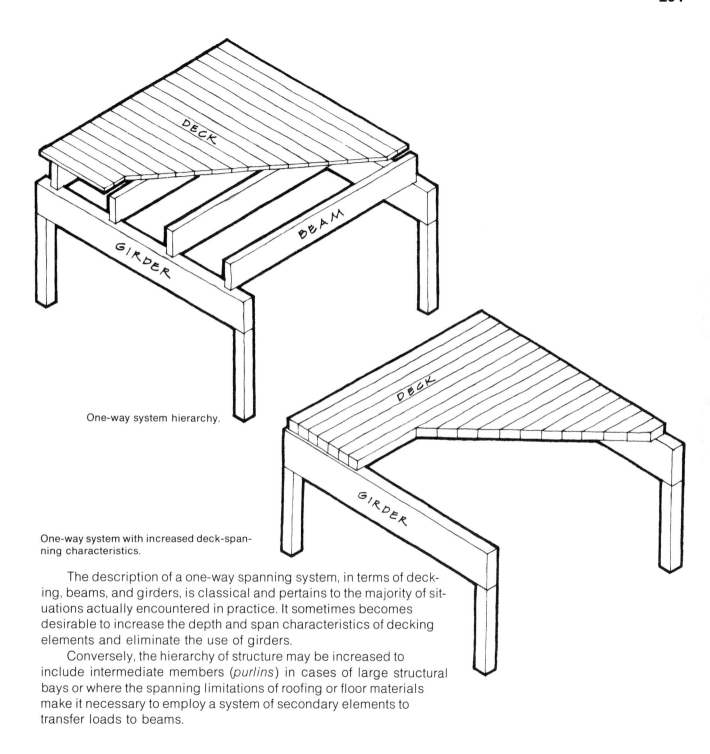

One-way system hierarchy.

One-way system with increased deck-spanning characteristics.

The description of a one-way spanning system, in terms of decking, beams, and girders, is classical and pertains to the majority of situations actually encountered in practice. It sometimes becomes desirable to increase the depth and span characteristics of decking elements and eliminate the use of girders.

Conversely, the hierarchy of structure may be increased to include intermediate members (*purlins*) in cases of large structural bays or where the spanning limitations of roofing or floor materials make it necessary to employ a system of secondary elements to transfer loads to beams.

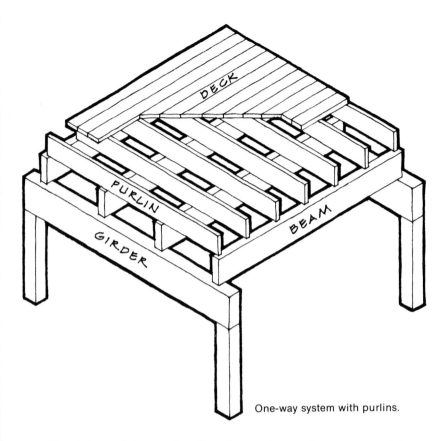

One-way system with purlins.

The virtues of single-directional spanning systems are considerable. Most available structural materials are linear and prismatic in nature (that is, of constant cross-section). Wood, steel, and aluminum shapes are easily obtained and of predictably high quality. Erection techniques and connections are standardized. The building industry produces an enormous variety of stock components. It thus becomes attractive, with respect to speed of erection and economy, for designers to use single-span systems. Single-span beam and girder elements naturally have limits beyond which they cease to be efficient or even feasible. In general, as the span increases, the weight and cost of the member will increase in geometric rather than arithmetic progression. The efficiency of any structural system can be measured to a large extent by the weight-to-span ratio, as discussed earlier. In sizing spanning elements, if other conditions remain constant, a doubling of span will produce a fourfold increase in structure weight. As spans increase, a point of diminishing returns develops, at which members of substantial weight and cross-section will be required to carry relatively light loads. In response to this condition, a special class of beams has been developed that demonstrates excellent weight-to-span ratios and has additional benefits as well. These special elements are defined as *trusses,* which are, in effect, custom-fabricated beams made up of an assembly of individual components proportioned to respond to applied loads. This is accomplished by removing material that is not stressed to its maximum carrying capacity.

In the previous discussion of beam action we saw that bending stresses induced under loading conditions produce high compression stress in the extreme top fibers and high tension stress in the extreme lower fibers of spanning members. Trusses incorporate maximum material at the top and bottom in order to accommodate this stress distribution pattern. The diagonals, which are intrinsic to every truss, serve to provide rigidity (triangles cannot deform as parallelograms can) and to carry shear stresses. By varying the height, angle, and spacing of the internal components of the truss, it is possible to develop a specialized element that can provide an infinite number of patterns in response to different loading patterns.

Trusses have the additional advantage of being able to accommodate environmental control systems in buildings. The use of the typical beam and girder bay system requires the allocation of space below framing levels for the passage of ducts and piping. The use of trusses permits the incorporation of these elements within the structure depth. With proper planning this can result in reduced overall building height and volume.

Truss concept.

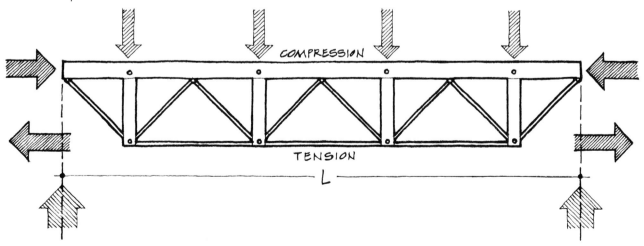

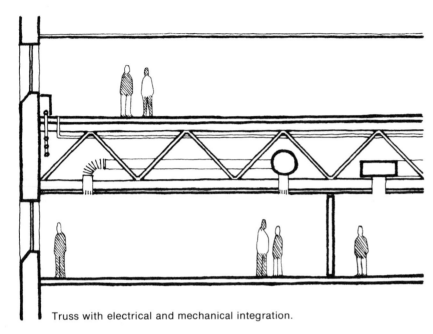

Truss with electrical and mechanical integration.

Trusses can be custom-made to a wide variety of configurations. They are also available in stock sizes and shapes for spans up to 100 feet for typical loading conditions. These are designated as *open web joists* or *steel joists.*

Multidirectional Spanning Systems

The distinction between single and multidirectional spanning systems is made evident in the difference between an arch and a dome. The arch, a load-carrying member, can carry only directly applied loads and can transfer loads in a linear manner to its supports. The dome, on the other hand, which may be viewed as a rotated arch, can transfer loads in a radiating or omnidirectional pattern. The three-dimensional character of the structural form produces a nonlinear load-distribution pattern.

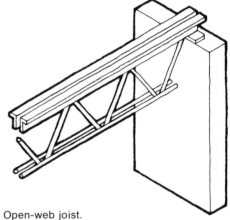

Open-web joist.

Domes, of course, have a somewhat limited application. They are not feasible for use in floor systems, for example. However, the implied nonlinear stress distribution characteristic is instructional. Structural systems that have the potential of continuity, such as those in poured concrete and welded steel, can develop multidirectional load-carrying capacity. In such systems, a load applied at any point may be visualized as being distributed concentrically from the point

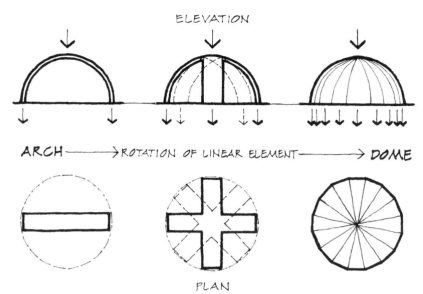

ELEVATION

ARCH ────→ROTATION OF LINEAR ELEMENT────→ DOME

PLAN

Multidirectional spans: the arch and the
dome.

of application to all perimeter support members. Unlike the case of
single-directed linear systems, loads may be shared and stresses
generated in a network or grid pattern within the bay.

That multidirectional systems must be inherently efficient is evident. In a two-way system, every load is supported by a minimum of
four points rather than two. As a result, the size of each member may
be accordingly reduced. Two-way and multidirectional spanning systems have architectural implications that differ substantially from
those of single-span systems. Single-span systems are hierarchical
and linear in nature. These characteristics invariably produce buildings and spaces with a polar or directed character. In general, single-
span structures have major and minor axes that serve to differentiate
building components in relation to orientation.

Multidirectional systems operate as network grids. The relationship of components is therefore nonhierarchical and, subsequently,
nonpolar. The structural system can thus offer greater flexibility with
respect to internal spatial subdivisions, integration of mechanical
systems, and accommodations of exterior enclosure elements.

In linear systems the available structural choices consist of decking, slabs, beams, girders, and/or truss elements. Equivalent choices
are available in nonlinear systems as well. Plates or two-way slabs,
beam grids or ribbed plates, and space frames comprise the basic
structural vocabulary in multidirectional span systems.

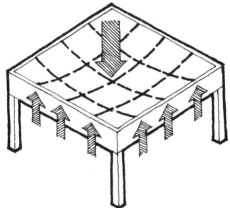

Network distribution in grids.

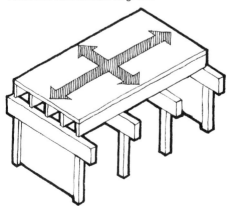

Polarity in single-directed structure.

STRUCTURAL CONSIDERATIONS

The characteristics and implications of each element can be described as follows. Plates or flat slabs, made of reinforced concrete, incorporate within a uniform depth a pattern of steel that serves to distribute applied loads in two directions, generally at right angles. Plates do not require continuous or evenly spaced perimeter support conditions, but they do require special attention to shear at all edges.

Beam grids, ribbed plates, or waffle slabs all have the same characteristics as plates but also incorporate an expressed network of beams that provides increased spanning and strength characteristics. The coffered pattern inherent in these systems offers potentiality for the incorporation of lighting and acoustic baffles.

Finally, there are the two-way equivalents of the truss—the space frame and three-dimensional truss. These have the virtues of linear trusses with regard to electromechanical system integration, together with the efficiency of plates. Once regarded as a structural novelty brought out for display at international World's Fairs, space frames are now commonly being selected by architects for both floor and roof systems. Moreover, support points for space grids may be randomly located, permitting extraordinary freedom in building planning.

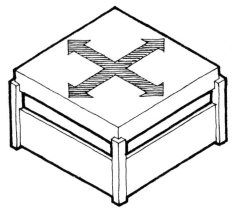
Nonpolarity in multidirectional structure.

Framing Systems

Up to this point, conditions of span and support have been treated separately. In practical structural applications, this distinction is not made. In a building, vertical and horizontal members are assembled in such a way as to provide mutually supporting characteristics.

When a spanning member or beam is carried by supports or columns, the nature of the connection has a substantial impact upon the nature of the total assembly. If the connections are designed to permit movement (rotation), they are designated as hinged joints and are incapable of transmitting stresses from beam to support. A typical nailed or bolted joint in timber would be considered as hinged, for example.

This basic configuration of three members, with joints free to rotate, is referred to as a post and lintel system. The term "lintel," in this case, is synonymous with "beam." In practical architectural terminology, lintel is usually reserved for the special class of beams that span windows and door openings. When the lintel is subjected to bending, the posts remain in their vertical position and are incapable of carrying anything but direct gravity loads. Lateral loads, such as wind or seismic, cannot be accommodated by this arrangement. If, however, the joints among the three members are made rigid, the post and lintel assembly behaves monolithically and can accommodate both gravity

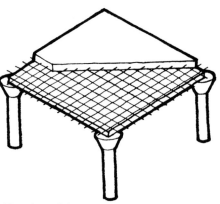
Flat plate slab.

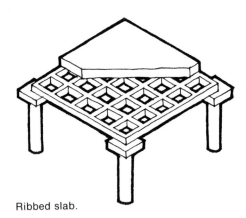
Ribbed slab.

and lateral loading. The development of fixity at the joints transforms the arrangement of spanning and support elements into a *rigid frame* or *portal*. The application of vertical loads onto a rigid frame induces bending into the posts as well as the beam. With all members working together to resist the external loads, individual components can obviously be made smaller than would be required to sustain the loads independently.

The greatest advantage of rigid frame action is its resistance to lateral forces. In a simple post and lintel assembly the wind loads must be taken entirely by the posts, since bending loads cannot be transferred through hinged joints to other members. In a rigid frame, wind load is partially absorbed by the beam as well as by the interior column, which shares the load with the exterior column.

No building consists of single rigid frames. Three-dimensional multiple frames are employed, adding the benefits of continuity to those of rigidity. Continuity makes possible the distribution of stresses to adjoining bays and members. Continuous behavior can exist without fixed joints. For example, a wood beam continuous across three spans will require a smaller section than would single beams for each separate span. If, at the same time, rigidity is present with continuity, even greater structural efficiency is obtained, since loads from any direction will be transferred into all members in the system.

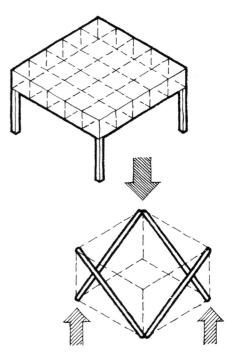

Diagram of space frame with detail of one bay.

Post and lintel.

Frame with fixed joints.

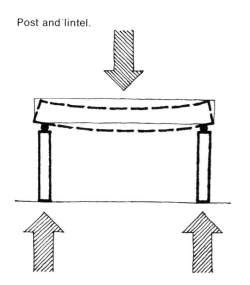

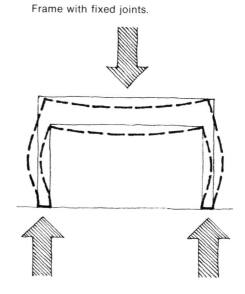

STRUCTURAL CONSIDERATIONS

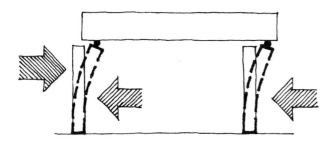

Post and lintel: wind loaded.

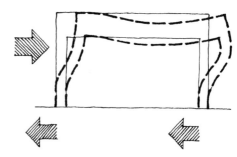

Fixed joint frame: wind loaded.

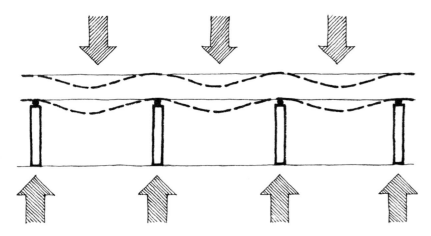

Continuity of span.

The methods and materials of construction selected will determine the feasibility of obtaining three-dimensional frame action for any building. It is almost impossible, for example, to obtain completely rigid joints in wood construction. It is more feasible in steel, but it requires the use of elaborate field welding to obtain fixed-end conditions. Welding, if properly done, provides joints whose strength exceeds that of the steel. However, to ensure a high standard of welding quality, most building codes require that all field joints be x-rayed and that licensed welders be recertified every six months.

The most feasible and widely used means of obtaining frame action in buildings is poured and reinforced concrete. No building can be poured in a single day. In order to provide bonding between each successive day's work, steel rod projections are placed, to which subsequent reinforcing is tied. This method of construction produces the conditions of continuity and rigidity automatically as the system becomes complete.

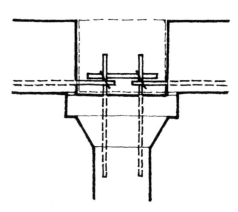

Continuity and fixity in concrete.

PREFABRICATION

Building construction invariably consists of a combination of factory-produced and field-installed elements. In that sense, all buildings are, to some extent, prefabricated. Lumber is sawed and dressed (preprocessed) at the mill. Steel beams are rolled, punched, cut, welded, and presized at the shop. Even brick can be said to be prefabricated. What is generally meant or implied by this term is the use of industrial methods to produce larger building components that include enclosure and structural elements and are assembled from different parts.

Recognizing the need to achieve time, cost, and quality control, the building industry continually develops construction systems and components that can be produced and erected quickly. Where industry has been most successful is in the area of simple factory buildings, which can be seen in many industrial areas. Many firms produce and market high-quality, relatively inexpensive systems that include spanning and support members and all enclosure elements. Usually a variety of building configurations is available, formed from a set of basic elements that are designed to be interchangeable and adaptable, limited as to types in order to minimize connection variations, and sized to carry stresses of transportation and erection as well as ultimate design loads.

Occasionally serious efforts have been mounted to carry the benefits and potentialities of prefabrication to other sectors of the building industry. Many experiments have been tied in with small homes. The federal government's program to stimulate production of high-quality, low-cost multiple dwelling units, known as Operation Breakthrough, is the best example. The fact that few units were found to be feasible was due to a number of complicated factors, including union labor practices, transportation difficulties, scale of operation, and initial start-up costs versus production quantities, as well as other problems.

The virtues of prefabricated construction are not universally appreciated. Many see the process as leading to the eventual dehumanization of building by reducing all choices to a minimum of standard components of limited size and character. The notion of mass-production raises issues of quality as well. Ford Motor Company or General Motors has to recall millions of cars if a brake is found faulty. Similar problems in industrialized building components are awesome to contemplate. For example, a concrete additive used in modular schools in the United Kingdom was found to cause deterioration of the structure, so that several buildings actually collapsed. Investigation is now underway to determine how many schools were affected.

The concept of prefabrication is perhaps one that should be philosophically accepted by building design professionals. We may be soon reaching the point at which a hand-crafted building will be beyond the reach of most clients. For the most part, building design professionals have taken a passive role in the control and utilization of prefabrication. This aspect of architecture may provide expanded design capabilities and credibility to students who see themselves in a nontraditional role in the profession.

METHODS IN STRUCTURAL DESIGN

It is useful to consider that in any structural design, the architectural design intentions are the first issues to be accommodated. The size of bays, floor-to-floor heights, and lengths of span are all decisions made by the architect in response to program requirements. The structural engineer does not establish the overall size relationships. Analysis and design of individual members is done only after basic planning decisions have been made.

Once major spatial determinations have been made, the methods of analysis are quite straightforward. Each member is isolated and examined, in relation both to the loads that will be applied to it and to the internal resisting forces that will have to be induced in order to keep the member in equilibrium. This method of analysis, sometimes called *free body analysis,* is possible because

Free body analysis.

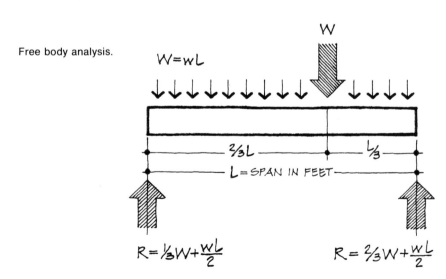

not only must the entire structure be in equilibrium, but so must each and every part. Once all the known forces have been reconciled with the internal resisting forces, it is possible for the designer to size and select individual members with properties that will satisfy the stress requirements indicated by the free body analysis.

As a practical matter, buildings are structurally designed in the exact reverse order in which they are built. The roof system is designed, then the floors, then the column or support system, and finally the foundations that transfer the entire building load onto the soil. The design process is an accumulative one, in which each transfer of load is added to successive members as they approach their ultimate or maximum conditions of support.

As a practical matter, few architects undertake the detailed structural analysis of buildings. Most prefer to develop a working relationship with a structural engineer early in the design process. The structural engineer, like any specialist, has specific concerns and training. Thus, he or she is better able to perform efficient structural calculations than the majority of architects. On the other hand, the intensive technical training of most engineers does not often provide them with a generalized and comprehensive overview of the architectural design process.

The Case for the Study of Structures

Since structural systems comprise a substantial portion of most building projects, and since their selection and design are of high priority in the building process, it will be readily apparent that architects require considerable knowledge of the subject. In this regard, an understanding of basic physics, with particular regard to kinematics and statics, is essential. Courses in the strength and characteristics of materials are also highly desirable.

There was a time when it was possible for an architect to acquire all the skills and perceptions needed to single-handedly carry out a major project from concept through implementation. The larger scale and time constraints of most current architectural projects make necessary collaboration with various building design professionals, including civil, structural, mechanical, and electrical engineers; lighting and acoustic consultants; interior designers; and other specialists. This formidable array of talent requires direction and leadership, which the architect traditionally provides. By training, the architect is a humanist and a generalist. All factors that affect the built environment are included in most professional programs: law, programming, human behavior, sociology, planning, environmental control issues, anthropomorphics, history, construction, and structural design, as well as basic building design. Given this broad range of concerns, the architect has evolved as a manager or team leader in the building process. From this standpoint it is highly desirable that the architect be conversant with all available major choices and form determinants within each specialist's province.

The wide use of structural engineering consultants by architects should not suggest an abdication of responsibility in this area, but rather the contrary. The greater the expertise of the engineer, the more judgment required on the part of the architect to make intelligent choices from available alternatives. It can be effectively argued that there is no practical need for architects to have technical skills paralleling those of their engineering collaborators. At the same time, there is a clear need for every architect to be aware of and familiar with the implications of structural systems. In practical terms, architects should be cognizant of a wide range of structural issues.

FOR FURTHER READING

Callender, John Hancock, ed. *Time-Saver Standards for Architectural Design Data*. 5th ed. New York: McGraw-Hill Book Co., 1974.

Cowan, Henry J. *Architectural Structures: An Introduction to Structural Mechanics*. New York: American Elsevier Publishing Co., 1971.

Parker, Harry. *Simplified Design of Reinforced Concrete*. New York: John Wiley & Sons.

————. *Simplified Design of Roof Trusses for Architects and Builders*. New York: John Wiley & Sons.

————. *Simplified Design of Structural Steel*. New York: John Wiley & Sons.

————. *Simplified Design of Structural Timber*. New York: John Wiley & Sons.

————. *Simplified Engineering for Architects and Builders*. New York: John Wiley & Sons.

————. *Simplified Mechanics and Strength of Materials*. New York: John Wiley & Sons.

Parker, Harry, and MacGuire, John W. *Simplified Site Engineering for Architects and Builders*. New York: John Wiley & Sons.

Salvadori, Mario. *Structure in Architecture*. 2d ed. Englewood Cliffs, N.J.: Prentice-Hall, 1975.

Salvadori, Mario, and Levy, Matthys. *Structural Design in Architecture*. Englewood Cliffs, N.J.: Prentice-Hall, 1967.

CHAPTER 12

Environmental Control Systems

Jeffrey E. Ollswang

Environmental control systems (ECS), as their name implies, have one fundamental objective—to maintain those environmental conditions in which the human occupants of buildings are most comfortable. In that statement rests the sole justification for the application of environmental control technologies in architecture, that is, human occupancy and comfort. As long as there is human occupancy, the various environmental control systems must provide the thermal, visual, auditory, and sanitary conditions necessary for the comfort and efficient performance of the occupants.

This chapter introduces the fundamental concepts common to all environmental control systems, including the four primary subsystems: fluid distribution, heating–ventilating–air-conditioning (HVAC), lighting, and acoustics. A major concern is, of course, integrating these systems with architectural design.

Architectural technologies in general have had direct, and often radical, impacts on architectural design. Too often architects and designers take them for granted, and no where is this more true than with regard to environmental control systems. Most architects and designers accept the role that the Otis elevator (and the emergency safety break) played in the development of the modern high-rise building. Consider, though, the work of Willis Carrier, involving the development of the scientific principles of air-conditioning. Would the common glass-curtain wall building be feasible without the aid of modern air-conditioning systems? How many architects recognize and appreciate the names of Wallace Sabin (acoustics), H.R. Blackwell (lighting), or Thomas Crapper (sanitation)? It could be justifiably argued that these scientists and inventors had as much influence on modern architecture as did the more familiar names of Wright, Gropius, and Le Corbusier.

Architects should spend considerable effort on the design and selection of appropriate ECS to provide the physical comfort of the building's occupants, especially since these components represent as much as one-third of the total cost of a modern building. Traditionally, architects have not taken an active role in environmental control systems, because the increasing scientific and technological base of ECS has removed them somewhat from systems design and application. There is some justification for this absence, since architects often lack the rigorous scientific and engineering skills required for the design of ECS. Having said that, however, we should recognize that a fundamental misconception is posed here regarding the architect's role and responsibilities. There is a considerable difference, for example, between architectural lighting design and the engineering design of a lighting fixture. The architect's principal functions are the stating of human comfort goals and objectives to be met by the various ECS and the evaluation of architectural implications of the individual systems, *not* the engineering design of any given component of the system itself.

WATER SYSTEMS

The single objective of any water distribution system is to provide a prompt and generous supply of water for the building's occupants. This is accomplished by ensuring sufficient water pressure throughout the system to operate the various plumbing fixtures. Assuming the quantity and quality of the water supply (and source) is sufficient, the first issue to be addressed is, how does the water get from the source to the occupant? Then, once the water has been used, how is the resulting waste product (sewage) collected and removed from the building? Both the supply and disposal are accomplished by a building's water distribution system. This system can be imagined initially as a network of pipes and equipment that has two distinct sides separated by a use function. The supply and distribution side of the network is a mirror image of the collection and disposal side. The use function refers to the various points (plumbing fixtures) at which the

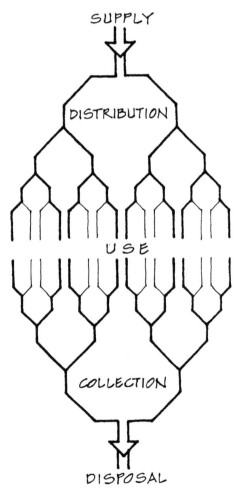

Fluid distribution network.

water is drawn off for consumption. The supply and distribution system is itself comprised of several subsystems, for example, hot and cold water supply, hot water/steam heating, and fire protection systems. Other water supply subsystems may be included in a building, depending upon specific acitvities or environmental conditions. For example, in places where there is a limited amount of potable water, there may be two cold water supply systems providing potable and nonpotable water.

In any discussion of water distribution systems, two critical factors must be understood and appreciated: water always travels in one direction through the system, and the two sides of the network must at all times be carefully separated. Both factors reflect concern for the health and safety of the occupants. Any cross-connections or backflow may introduce noxious gases or toxic waste water back into the supply side of the network.

A great amount of energy and time has been spent in developing the means by which *separation* may be achieved. As a case in point, consider the recognition and accolades awarded to Thomas Crapper (allowing him to display the Royal Crest of King Edward VII of England) for his perfection and marketing of the sanitary toilet. The water seal or trap incorporated by Crapper into his toilet bowl design ensured sanitary separation by preventing the backflow of noxious gases from the waste pipes into the bathroom.

Water Supply

In the water supply/distribution side of the network, there exists a series of sequential stages through which water must pass before it reaches the occupant at any given plumbing fixture. These stages are reflected in the variety of pipes, valves, and equipment that together constitute the physical network.

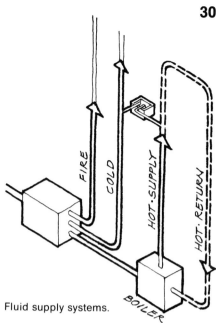

Fluid supply systems.

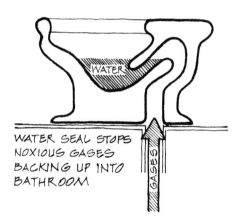

WATER SEAL STOPS NOXIOUS GASES BACKING UP INTO BATHROOM

Components and flow in water systems.

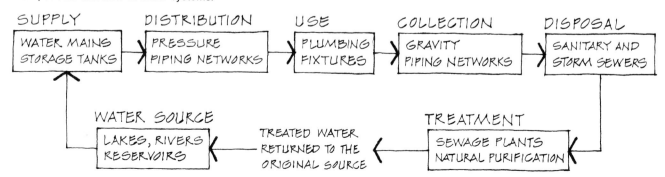

Specific building networks may vary somewhat depending upon the building form and size, occupancy, and activities to be performed. The fundamental components of water supply/distribution are common to all buildings, however. The order in which they are presented suggests a possible sequence of stages through which the water passes on its way to the occupant: treatment, pumps, storage, pipes and fittings, valves, and fixtures. These stages and their related components represent a complete water supply network. Several deserve greater attention, especially those that are most commonly misunderstood, and those that have the most direct architectural implications.

Pressure. Just as the human body requires a normal blood pressure to operate efficiently, so does a building's water supply/distribution system require pressure. If the building's pressure is too low, the various plumbing fixtures will not function efficiently. In the simplest terms, pressure is required to raise and force water through the system, from the supply to the fixtures. The pressure may come from the city water main, or it may be developed by pumping water within the building.

Components of water pressure.

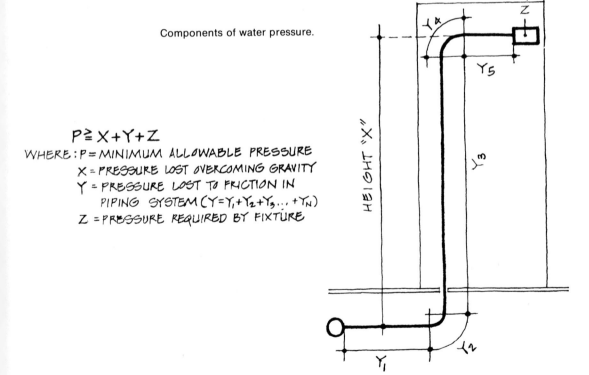

$$P \geqq X + Y + Z$$
WHERE: P = MINIMUM ALLOWABLE PRESSURE
X = PRESSURE LOST OVERCOMING GRAVITY
Y = PRESSURE LOST TO FRICTION IN PIPING SYSTEM $(Y = Y_1 + Y_2 + Y_3 \ldots + Y_N)$
Z = PRESSURE REQUIRED BY FIXTURE

The amount of pressure required in any water system is governed by the amount of pressure lost in overcoming two forces—gravity and friction. That is, how high must the water be lifted, and how much friction is developed between the pipes and fittings and the water? Remember that each time the water is forced around or through a fitting, additional friction is generated, resulting in pressure loss. After the forces of gravity and friction are overcome, there must be enough pressure remaining to operate the given plumbing fixture.

Storage. Storage is important since it serves as the basis upon which the various water supply systems are classified. There are only two generic categories into which water supply systems fall—*upfeed* and *downfeed*. As these names imply, the classification is based upon the location of the major storage and pressure components in relation to the fixtures.

The architectural implications of the issues of pressure and storage are direct and immediately apparent. Water is very heavy (1 cubic foot = 62.4 pounds), and people and their activities require a great deal of water. Consequently, the location of water storage becomes important, specifically in terms of size, space, and the associated structure required to support the enormous weight accumulated in water storage tanks.

Treatment. A variety of water conditions may require treatment before the water can be introduced into a building's supply and distribution system. These are generally the result of impurities common to most of our water resources. Treatment for the purposes of health and safety generally occurs before the water enters a city's water supply system. Some limited treatment (for hardness, odors, turbidity, and so on) may occur within the building. When this is the case, additional equipment (such as water softeners and filters) is introduced into the building's water supply system.

In any case, there is at least one treatment procedure that is included in all building water supply systems—heating. Since hot water is essential for any building encompassing human acitvities, hot water generation, storage, and distribution are required components of a supply system. The implications are simple: every building will have at least two separate and distinct water supply subsystems, each including all the required treatment, storage, piping and fitting, and valving components of a comprehensive supply/distribution network. One important difference should be noted. Unlike the cold water supply system, the hot water supply can be a closed and constantly circulating system. The purpose of a return piping system is

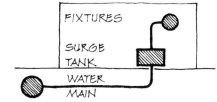

UPFEED: MAIN PRESSURE

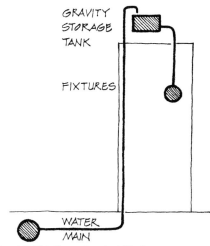

DOWNFEED: GRAVITY

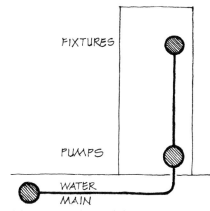

UPFEED: CONSTANT PRESSURE

Water supply systems classification.

to conserve energy. Returning hot water requires only a boost to raise its temperature before it reenters the hot water supply system.

Control. The next issue to be addressed is the control of the flow of water. That is, what components or devices are employed to control the direction, speed, and amount of water flowing through the system? Where are the control components placed within the supply system? The control function is simply accomplished by the introduction of a series of valves, each one with its own particular control function.

One very important factor governing the placement or location of valves within a water supply system is the ability to isolate the fixture (or fixtures) from the rest of the supply network. This includes the ability to isolate the entire building from the water supply system if necessary. Such a capability facilitates the repair and/or replacement of any fixture (or fixture group) without the need to shut off the water supply to the entire building.

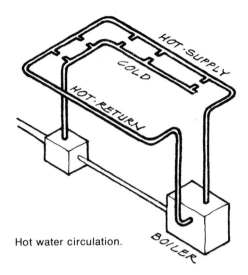

Hot water circulation.

The architectural implication of this aspect is one of access. Wherever valves exist in a water supply system, a means of physical access from the building to the valve and piping network must be considered by the architect.

Sizing. While not often considered within the realm of architectural design, the sizing of a water supply system and its associated components has important architectural implications, especially since it concerns the size, location, and spatial requirements of the various treatment, pressure, and storage components of a supply network. The procedures involved in determining the sizes and capacities of the components are simple and are based upon the concept of *probable maximum demand,* which simply states that the greater the number of fixtures in any building, the less likely is their *simultaneous* use. It is important, then, to understand that systems are sized upon the probable amount of water that may be required by the occupants of a building and not the possible maximum amount of water demanded.

Sanitary Systems

The supply/distribution system terminates after the water has been drawn off for consumption at any given plumbing fixture. At this point, the water (now carrying off the wastes produced by the occupants and their activities) enters the other side of the network—the collection and disposal system.

The use of water in a closed system of pipes to carry off human wastes was perhaps first implemented by the Minoan king Minos at

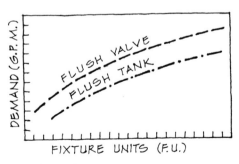

Flow demand curves.

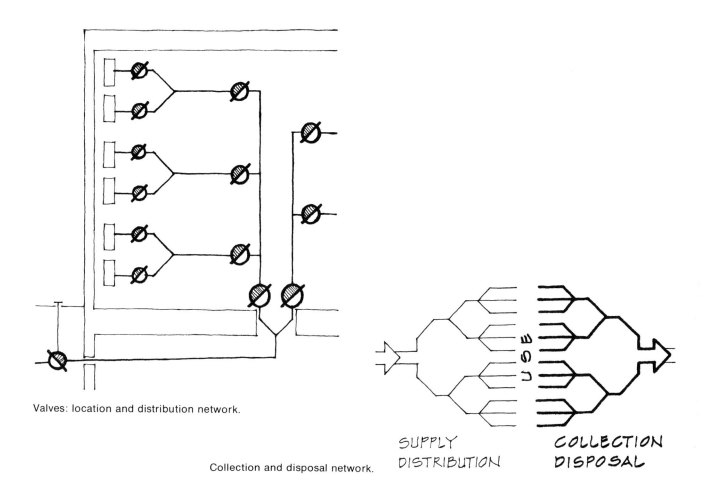

Valves: location and distribution network.

Collection and disposal network.

SUPPLY
DISTRIBUTION

COLLECTION
DISPOSAL

his palace at Knossos on the island of Crete. This major step toward sanitation was implemented in the queen's chambers. In her suite, the queen had a bath and a toilet (with a flushing mechanism) that were connected to a drainage system by a series of earthenware pipes. This closed collection and disposal system for carrying of waterborne wastes was built over 3,500 years ago.

By providing a closed network in which waterborne wastes—the effluent—are collected and carried out of the building, sanitary systems fulfill their sole objective—to provide the occupants with a safe and healthy environment. The essential word *closed* must be emphasized. It simply refers to the fact that at no point are the occupants exposed to the potentially noxious and toxic waterborne wastes.

Piping Network. Piping networks through which the effluent must fall are significantly different from water supply/distribution piping networks. This difference manifests itself in three basic ways. The pipes are generally much larger than supply/distribution pipes, have minimum allowable horizontal runs, and have minimum allowable types and amounts of turns. All of these differences reflect the principal need for easy, unobstructed passage of the effluent. Simply, it must have the ability to drop freely out of the building. The architectural implication of *stacking* fixtures is apparent. This planning guideline facilitates an easy, unrestricted flow of the effluent.

There are no valves to control the direction of flow. Instead, traps or water seals are employed. The inclusion of traps is essential to ensure that there is no backflow of gases and germ-laden air. Each time the fixture is used, the water in the trap is carried off with the effluent and replaced by fresh water. The entire collection/disposal system must be vented to the air. The purpose of venting is to guard against siphoning, that is, to prevent the water seal (produced in the trap) from being drawn off. Vents are also restricted in the number of turns, bends, and horizontal runs that are acceptable.

In point of fact, then, the collection/disposal system is comprised of two distinct piping networks, both of which have imposed restrictions that suggest long, uninterrupted, straight, vertical pipes. One carries the effluent down and out of the building, and the other travels upward through the building and must penetrate the roof to get to the open air. The architectural implications of the latter are direct and often frustrating to the architect. It means that the pristine, elegant roof of the building must be penetrated (often more than once) by vent

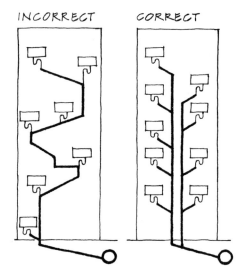

Sanitary network layout.

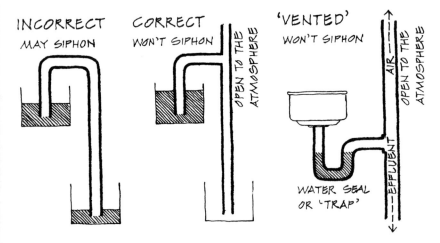

Venting and siphoning.

pipes. The actual sizing of the collection/disposal systems is normally governed by local plumbing and health codes, and it is based upon experience and safe practice.

HVAC SYSTEMS

The second major distribution network to be addressed is the air sup-ply system—that is, the heating, ventilating, and air-conditioning (HVAC) system. The goal for this particular environmental control sys-tem is to provide the occupants with healthy and comfortable thermal and atmospheric conditions, achieved by treating and distributing conditioned air throughout the building. Normally, conditioned air is thought of solely in terms of its temperature. In fact, temperature repre-sents only one of five treatments that thoroughly conditioned air should undergo before delivery to the occupants. These five separate treatments reflect the thermal and atmospheric conditions that most directly affect human comfort. Thermal conditioning regulates temper-ature, moisture, and air distribution. Atmospheric conditioning regu-lates purity and controls odors.

Unlike the other distribution networks that travel throughout a building, the HVAC system and its component parts require a signifi-cant amount of space. If for only this reason, understanding and ap-preciating the implications of the HVAC system is important for archi-tects. In addition, this system has recently received a great deal of at-tention due to its implications regarding energy use and conservation.

Thermal Comfort
Consider the human body as an inefficient heat machine, one that is continually generating too much heat. Thermal comfort is directly related to the ease with which the human body can dispose of this excess heat. In normal conditions, this transfer of heat occurs between the body and the ambient air. Fortunately, the human body has natural defense mechanisms that are constantly working to main-tain the necessary balance between heat generation and waste heat disposal. These mechanisms (sweating and shivering) function to maintain a normal body temperature of 98.6°F, by controlling the rate at which the waste heat is disposed. For example, if the rate of heat

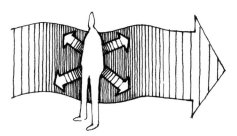

Waste heat dissipation.

loss is too slow, we perspire. This increases the rate of heat loss due to evaporation. Conversely, if the rate of heat loss is too fast, we begin to shiver. This mechanism attempts to increase the rate of heat generation to balance against heat loss.

It is apparent, then, that the less stress placed upon these mechanisms, the greater the level of comfort attainable. The architect should understand and appreciate the ways in which the human body transfers heat to the ambient air and the atmospheric and thermal conditions that facilitate (but not accelerate) the rate at which the waste heat is transferred.

Heat Transfer. There are four methods of heat transfer employed by the human body: *conduction, convection, evaporation,* and *radiation.*

1 Conduction. Conduction is heat transfer resulting from direct contact between surfaces. The body may either gain heat from the environment or lose heat to it based on conduction. This occurs simply by touching or contacting warm or cool surfaces.

2 Convection. Heat transfer based upon fluid motion is called convection. In this case the fluid is air; heat may be either gained or lost depending upon the temperature of the air passing over the body.

3 Evaporation. In heat transfer based on evaporation, the body can only lose heat. This occurs because the moisture on the surface of the skin evaporates as air passes over the body.

4 Radiation. Radiation is heat transfer based upon electomagnetic waves. The body will gain radiant heat from any surface of higher temperature, and it will lose or radiate heat to any object or surface that is cooler than itself. Radiant heat gain or loss is not affected by air motion, nor by the air temperature between radiating surfaces or objects.

The amount of total heat transfer produced by each of the methods is almost entirely governed by the existing environmental conditions. For example, saturated air cannot accept moisture from the body; thus heat transfer cannot occur through evaporation. The HVAC system must therefore facilitate and ensure reasonable *rates* of heat transfer between the occupant and the ambient air. The conditions should increase the rate of heat loss when the occupants are too warm and decrease the rate of heat loss when they are too cold. This objective is achieved by treating and delivering air that is comfortable in terms of temperature, moisture content (humidity), and velocity (air motion and distribution patterns). Air purity and odor removal (through ventilation) are additional comfort conditions that must be controlled by the HVAC system.

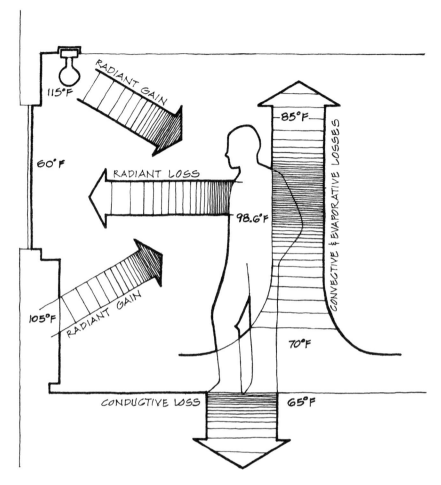

Heat transfer.

In order to provide constant comfort conditions inside a building, the HVAC systems must maintain a balance between the internal thermal and atmospheric conditions and the continually changing climatic conditions outdoors. In the summer, the system must provide enough cool air to overcome the heat gained from the outside; in the winter, it must provide enough warm air to replace the heat lost to the outside.

Heat Flow Calculations. It is necessary at this point to introduce the fundamentals of heat as an energy form and explain the

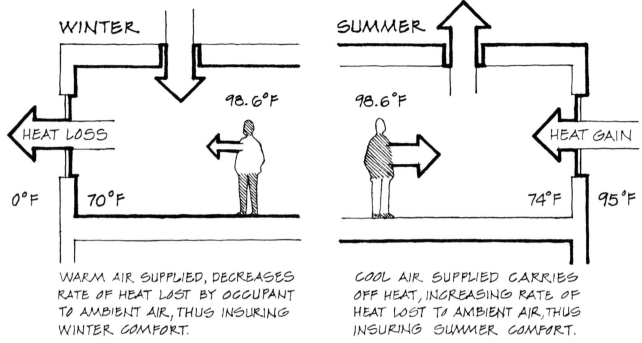

WINTER

SUMMER

98.6°F

98.6°F

HEAT LOSS

HEAT GAIN

0°F | 70°F

74°F | 95°F

WARM AIR SUPPLIED, DECREASES
RATE OF HEAT LOST BY OCCUPANT
TO AMBIENT AIR, THUS INSURING
WINTER COMFORT.

COOL AIR SUPPLIED CARRIES
OFF HEAT, INCREASING RATE OF
HEAT LOST TO AMBIENT AIR, THUS
INSURING SUMMER COMFORT.

Heat flow and comfort, winter and summer.

vocabulary used to define and describe heat flow and its control.
First, it should be understood that heat always flows in one direction—away from its source. That means that heat always flows from a
point of higher temperature toward a point of lower temperature.
Amounts of heat are measured in British Thermal Units (Btu). A Btu is
defined as the amount of heat required to raise the temperature of
one pound of water from 60°F to 61°F. Translating this measurements
to the metric scale, the amount of heat required to raise the temperature of one gram of water one degree Celsius (from 15°C to 16°C) is
one *calorie,* so 1 Btu = 252 calories.

The total heat content of the air is comprised of two components—*sensible heat* and *latent heat.* Sensible heat refers to the heat
content of dry air and is measured in temperature, dry bulb (T_{db}), by
an ordinary thermometer. Latent heat deals with the heat content of the
moisture present in the air. The combination of the air's sensible and
latent heat—or the total heat content—is called the *enthalpy.* This is
an important concept because it directly affects human comfort. For
example, raising the relative humidity from 20 percent to 50 percent in
a room at 70°F adds 5 Btu's per pound of air. Thus, winter comfort con-

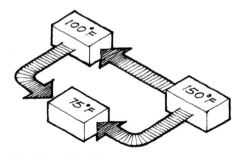

Direction of heat flow.

ditions may be partially achieved by lowering or maintaining the ambient air temperature while raising the humidity. The converse holds true for summer comfort, because lowering relative humidity increases the rate of evaporation and its cooling effect on the body. The energy implications are clear.

Thermal conductivity, K, refers to the rate of heat flow through any given homogeneous material. It is measured in Btu/hour/square foot/°F/inch thickness. For example, brick has a K value of 5.0 per inch thickness; therefore 6 inches has a total K of 30.0. This means that for every degree Fahrenheit, 30 Btu will pass through 1 square foot of brick every hour. Resistance, R, is the property of any material to retard or reduce the rate of heat flow and is therefore expressed as the reciprocal of K:

$$R = \frac{1}{K}$$

The rate of heat flow through construction (a combination of materials) is expressed as the U factor. This U factor is the reciprocal of the combined total resistances of the individual materials.

$$U = \frac{1}{\Sigma R_T}$$

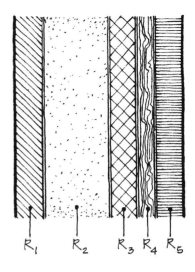

$$U = \frac{1}{R_1} + \frac{1}{R_2} + \frac{1}{R_3} + \frac{1}{R_4} + \frac{1}{R_5}$$

Resistance (R) and the U factor.

One of the objectives of any architectural enclosure is to control the rate of heat gain or heat loss. This is becoming more and more important to architects, for the rate of heat flow has a direct relationship to the rate at which energy is consumed.

Mathematical formulas and computations are used to predict the rate of heat gain or heat loss of any proposed building. These computations are of great value to the architect. Heat gain/loss calculations not only establish the gross heat flow (in Btu's per hour), but they are also able to define and locate any major leaks in the building envelope. As one might expect, these leaks—or rapid heat flow—generally occur at the windows of the building. Moreover, heat gain/loss computations assist the architect in the selection of building materials, especially the choice of insulation, which can significantly reduce the rate of heat flow. Consequently, these computations, and the associated issue of insulation, deserve special attention. Consider the comparison of the U factors of two similar wall sections, one with and one without insulation. The results are immediately apparent; the wall with 2 inches of insulation added has more than three times the resistance to heat flow as the uninsulated wall.

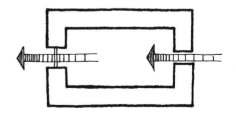

Enclosure and heat flow.

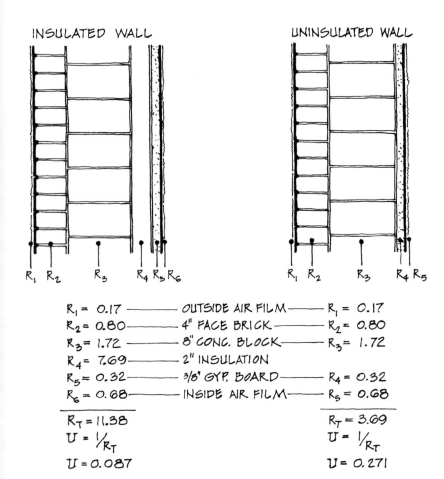

INSULATED WALL

UNINSULATED WALL

R_1 R_2 R_3 R_4 $R_5 R_6$ R_1 R_2 R_3 R_4 R_5

$R_1 = 0.17$ ———— OUTSIDE AIR FILM ————	$R_1 = 0.17$
$R_2 = 0.80$ ———— 4" FACE BRICK ————	$R_2 = 0.80$
$R_3 = 1.72$ ———— 8" CONC. BLOCK ————	$R_3 = 1.72$
$R_4 = 7.69$ ———— 2" INSULATION	
$R_5 = 0.32$ ———— 3/8" GYP. BOARD ————	$R_4 = 0.32$
$R_6 = 0.68$ ———— INSIDE AIR FILM ————	$R_5 = 0.68$

$R_T = 11.38$ $R_T = 3.69$

$U = 1/R_T$ $U = 1/R_T$

$U = 0.087$ $U = 0.271$

Insulation, resistance, and U factors

A number of calculations are used to establish the total heat flow through an existing or proposed building envelope to evaluate its thermal characteristics (heat gain and loss). Once established, this heat flow assists the architect in determining the required capacity of the HVAC system and its component parts.

Air-Conditioning Systems

HVAC systems are classified into four generic types: all-air, air-water, all-water, and direct refrigerant. The designation is based upon the fluid (air, water, or refrigerant) that is delivered to each space for the purposes of air-conditioning. It is essential that architects develop an understanding and appreciation of each of these systems for two reasons. First, their characteristics will govern their applicability and appropriateness for any given building; second, each system carries its own set of architectural implications.

All-Air. All-air systems are those in which totally treated air is delivered to the space to be conditioned. The required treatment of the supply air occurs at a location separate from the conditioned space, generally in a centrally located mechanical room. The treated air is delivered from the mechanical room to the individual spaces through a network of air ducts. The supply air is introduced through registers or diffusers that control the air distribution within the conditioned space.

One energy conservation feature of all-air systems deserves special attention. It is possible to recycle a percentage of the return air into the system. This reduces the amount of energy required by the system to elevate the incoming air to the required conditions. In addition, one of the principal advantages of the all-air system is the high degree of possible treatment of the supply air.

Of all the HVAC systems, all-air systems generate the greatest spatial demands upon the building. Not only are mechanical rooms

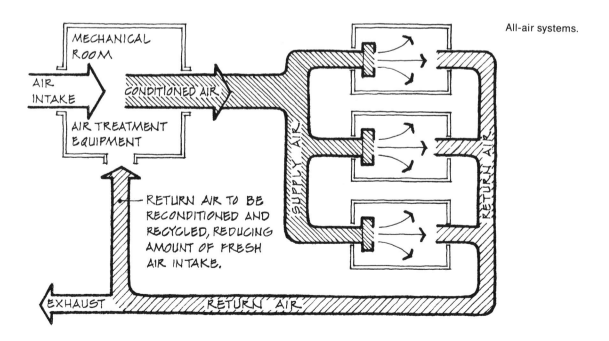

All-air systems.

required, but the air distribution networks (ducts) also must penetrate the building both horizontally and vertically. These ducts are often large enough to cause architectural problems.

Air-Water. In some ways the air-water system is similar to the all-air system, in that it requires a mechanical room that is separated from the conditioned space. The principal difference, however, relates to the fact that in the air-water system the major percentage of the *thermal* conditioning of the air occurs *within* the conditioned space.

In this system, the mechanical room delivers hot and/or cold water to the space through a network of pipes. It also supplies, through ducts, suppiementary air that is partially treated for purity, humidity, and so on. (These ducts are generally significantly smaller than those used in all-air systems.) The introduction of supplementary air serves two purposes: it provides necessary ventilation, and it induces a mixture of the room air and supplementary air to circulate over either the hot or cold water pipes. At this point the major percentage of the required thermal conditioning occurs. The architectural advantage of this system, as compared to the all-air system, is that considerably less space is required. For example, there are fewer air ducts, they are normally smaller, and the amount of air-handling equipment in the mechanical room is reduced.

However, some degree of control over the quality of treatment, especially in terms of thermal conditioning, has been lost. In addition, this system relies on induced air circulation and thus has limits regarding the even distribution of air throughout the room. Therefore, its application in terms of the size and volume of the conditioned room is limited.

All-Water. The all-water system treats the air entirely within the space to be conditioned. The only element delivered to the space is hot and/or chilled water. Generally, ventilation is achieved by introducing outside air at each conditioned space. Through the use of fans and natural convection currents, a mixture of outside and inside air is passed over the hot or cold pipes, thus achieving thermal conditioning.

All-water systems have almost no spatial requirements. They require no mechanical equipment for air handling or treatment, and there are no air ducts. As might be anticipated, though, their application is limited to rooms that have exterior walls through which outside air may be introduced. The ability to achieve uniform air distribution patterns is even more limited than in air-water systems, which employ supplementary air. In addition, the degree of comprehensive air treat-

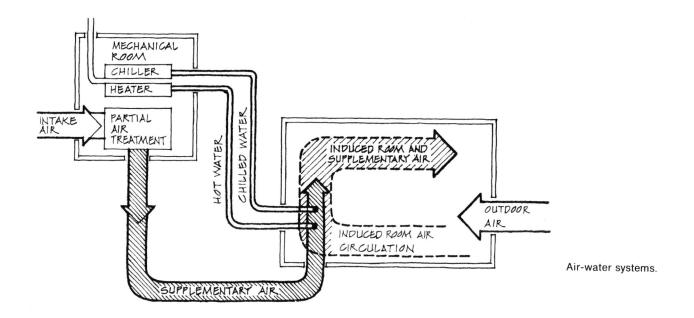

Air-water systems.

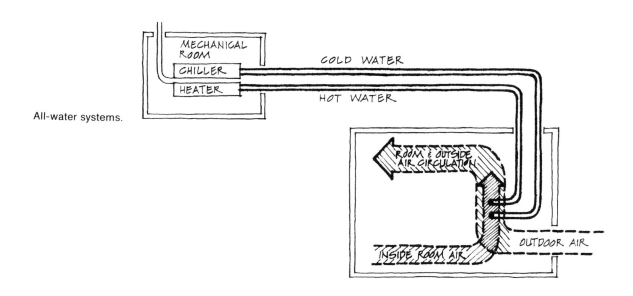

All-water systems.

ENVIRONMENTAL CONTROL SYSTEMS

ment is at a significantly lower level than in the all-air or air-water systems. For example, it is difficult to control humidity levels in all-water systems.

Direct Refrigerant. The last of the four categories is the direct refrigerant system. This system requires only gas or electricity to function, and the air-conditioning is accomplished by a self-contained package that contains all the packages, or units, required to produce the conditioned air. These components are generally immediately adjacent to the space to be conditioned or within it. They require minimal ducting, if any. Outside air is drawn through the unit, where it is conditioned and then delivered immediately to the space. This system may be imagined as being comprised of small, individual, mechanical rooms at each space to be conditioned. The application of direct refrigerant systems has limitations, again in terms of its ability to achieve uniform air distribution throughout the conditioned room.

Duct Sizing
Since air ducts are often large and cumbersome and must pass vertically and horizontally through a building, the space they require is of immediate importance to architects. The size of ducts is governed by two factors—the amount of air (in cubic feet per minute, cfm) required to balance the heat gain or loss of any space, and the velocity at which the air travels through the ducts (in feet per minute, fpm). The theoretical size of any duct may be established by dividing the amount of air by its velocity:

$$\frac{cfm}{fpm} = \text{Theoretical cross-section area of duct}$$

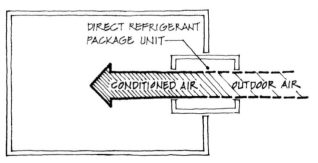

Direct refrigerant.

The actual size of ducts is always larger, due to pressure drops resulting from friction.

The spatial implications are evident: the higher the velocities, the smaller the duct. The apparent architectural solution would be always to select high velocities for the delivery air, since the duct sizes would thus be correspondingly smaller. Unfortunately, the answer is not that simple. Air velocities have direct effects on human comfort. The consequences of high air velocities include noise and the possibility of uncomfortable drafts. In most circumstances, then, the selection of air velocities is based upon a compromise between human comfort criteria and architectural spatial requirements.

Zoning

One of the characteristics of an HVAC system that influences its applicability is its ability to serve different *zones* within any one building. Zoning refers to separating a building into areas that exhibit similar air-conditioning requirements. Often within a building there may be several zones that require different air treatments, especially in terms of thermal conditioning. Consider, for example, a building that has large amounts of glazing. While the east, north, and west façades lose heat at a rapid rate in the winter, the south façade, in direct sunlight, may actually gain heat due to the penetration of large amounts of sunlight. In this case, one zone may require heating while another, simultaneously, requires cooling.

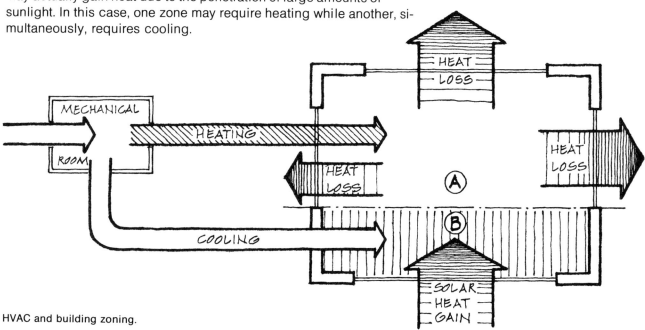

HVAC and building zoning.

System Selection

Let us review the two factors that most directly affect the selection of any particular HVAC system. Interestingly, both factors address the issue of the architect's, responsibilities.

The first factor deals with the architect's ability to appreciate and clearly define the human thermal and atmospheric comfort requirements to be met by any given system. It is important to note that these requirements are constant regardless of the architectural context. They include both thermal conditions (temperature, moisture, and air motion) and atmospheric conditions (purity and control of odors). Comfortable environments can only be achieved by the uniform distribution of these controlled conditions throughout the space.

The second issue involves priorities. Since some of the basic parameters may be in conflict with one another (such as the desired degree of air conditioning versus the associated costs), the architect must be able to establish priorities as well as to state specific comfort criteria. For most situations, the basic evaluative parameters may be described as follows.

1 The HVAC system's ability to successfully respond to stated comfort criteria.

2 The architectural implications of each system, that is, its ability to be integrated successfully into the architectural design.

3 The direct and indirect costs of the system (such as its initial and long-term operational costs and its rate of energy consumption).

In the final analysis, for any given architectural situation, the appropriate selection of the HVAC system should be predicated upon the various criteria and requirements of the occupants, the client, and the architectural design.

LIGHTING

The architect's primary responsibility in lighting involves the establishment of comprehensive lighting design criteria and the selection of lighting systems that will satisfy the stated criteria. This activity should be based upon an architect's ability to define and appreciate the visual tasks and activities to be performed by the occupants of any given space—as well as the relationships that exist between light, a lighting design, and the spatial enclosure.

This requires the architect to have a working knowledge of the

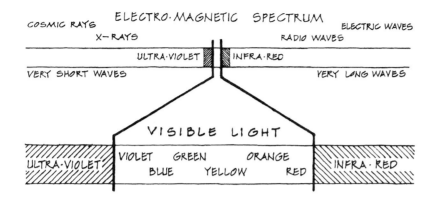

Electromagnetic and visible spectrums.

behavior of light and the mechanisms of vision as well as of the current technologies and equipment available for architectural lighting design.

Light and Vision

The human eye is a sensitive (though tolerant) sensing device. It is able to discern light only in a very narrow portion of the entire electromagnetic spectrum, referred to as the *visible spectrum.* Within this narrow band, however, the human eye can perceive minor variations in both color and relative intensities of light.

The human eye is composed of many parts, each with its own specific task concerned with the reception and perception of light. It is important to understand that each eye functions separately but that both function simultaneously. This is of special interest to architects, for it relates to how much we see at any one time. The term used to describe how much we see is *visual field.* Consider also that visual *acuity* (fine-detail discrimination) drops off rapidly from the very

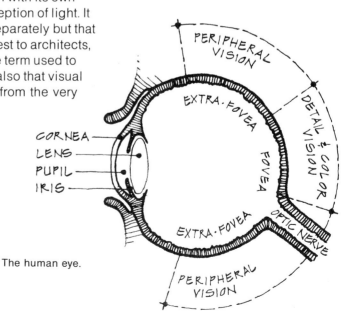

The human eye.

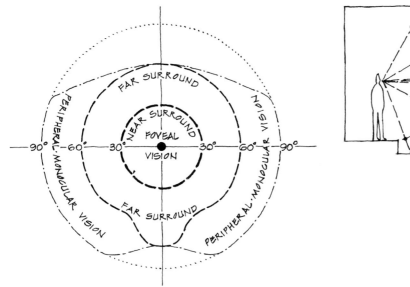

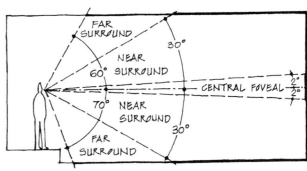

Visual field.

center of the field. Finally, the extreme or peripheral vision perceived by one eye has, at best, a marginal ability to perceive any detail at all. The translation of this visual field to an architectural context has important implications. It illustrates exactly how much of any one space we actually see at one time and the manner in which we see it.

Another aspect of light and lighting design deals with perception, that is, how we register and associate that which we see. To facilitate this set of tasks, the intensity of light alone is not sufficient. The eye must be able to perceive and discriminate between form, outline, texture, and color, for example. The more our understanding and appreciation of light and vision grow, the more evident it becomes that, in terms of vision, brighter light is not enough. Higher levels of illumination are no insurance against poor lighting conditions. Too much light may aggravate the conditions produced by a poor lighting design.

Visual Comfort. There are fundamental questions the architect should address with regard to the *quality* and *quantity* of light produced by a lighting design. The questions are as follows.

1 What are the visual tasks to be performed in a given space?

2 What are the visual and spatial characteristics of the space in which these tasks are to be performed?

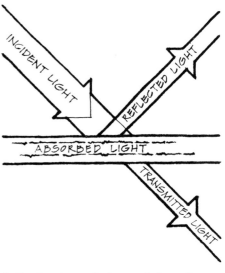

Reflection, transmission, and absorption.

INTRODUCTION TO ARCHITECTURE

3 What are the lighting performance criteria necessary to ensure comfortable and efficient performance of the tasks?

4 What is the visual atmosphere created by the combined effects of lighting on the space?

The answers to these questions will suggest the most appropriate method of illumination for any given space.

Visual Tasks. Comfort is governed by our ability to perform visual tasks. Architecturally, all visual tasks may be classified into two broad categories: those requiring spatial perception and those requiring detail discrimination. Spatial perception deals with our ability to see and appreciate surfaces, spaces, shapes, enclosures, and activities. Detail discrimination refers to the ability to perceive and appreciate fine detail, such as is encompassed in the tasks of reading, drafting, or writing. A careful analysis of visual tasks should preceed and serve as the basis for the establishment of visual comfort criteria, especially since each type of visual task requires its own specific lighting conditions. For example, as one might expect, the comfortable performance of fine detail discrimination is largely dependent upon high levels of illumination and the absence of visual distractions in the 30° cone of vision.

Regardless of the task to be performed, however, the one way to ensure some degree of comfort is to avoid repeating the familiar faults experienced in many lighting designs. We can list most of these based upon our own set of visual experiences. Among the most common are shadows that *obscure,* reflections that *conceal,* high brightnesses from the source in the field of vision that *distracts,* and excessive contrast between the task and its immediate surroundings.

Behavior of Light. The behavioral characteristics of light in space, after it has been generated by the source and before it has been perceived by the eye, are of particular interest to anyone responsible for lighting design. The transmission path and behavior of light are determined by the properties of the surfaces the light encounters. The incident light is either reflected, absorbed, or transmitted. In an architectural context, light is normally partially reflected, partially absorbed, and partially transmitted, depending upon the characteristics of the surface. It is essential to note at this point that our perception of color is governed by *selective* reflection, absorption, or transmission of the incident light. Light may, in addition, be focused, bent, or spread out, again depending upon the surface characteristics. The ar-

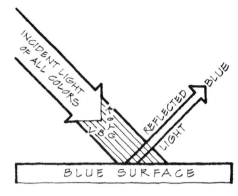

BLUE SURFACE ABSORBS LIGHT OF RED, ORANGE, YELLOW, GREEN AND VIOLET WAVELENGTHS - REFLECTING ONLY BLUE LIGHT.

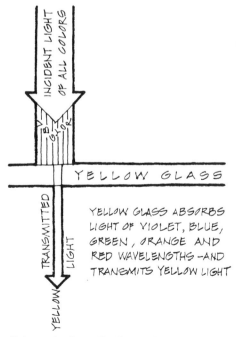

YELLOW GLASS ABSORBS LIGHT OF VIOLET, BLUE, GREEN, ORANGE AND RED WAVELENGTHS —AND TRANSMITS YELLOW LIGHT

Color: selective reflection and transmission.

ENVIRONMENTAL CONTROL SYSTEMS

REFLECTION

SPECULAR
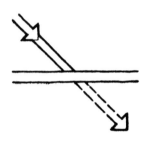
POLISHED SURFACE

DIFFUSE

ROUGH SURFACE

COMBINED
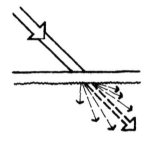
MATTE SURFACE

TRANSMISSION

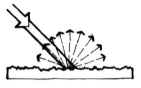

CLEAR, TRANSPARENT   ROUGH, TRANSLUCENT   SMOOTH, TRANSLUCENT

Types of reflection and transmission.

chitectural implications are evident. The surfaces and materials chosen by architects to create the enclosure of any space govern to a large degree the behavior of light in the space.

Light Sources
Understanding and appreciation of the sources of light are needed to facilitate the architects' ability to manipulate, select, and appropriately employ the wide variety of lighting tools at their disposal. First, let us introduce four definitions.

1 Lamp—the initial source of light.
2 Bulb—the glass envelope.
3 Luminaire—the complete lighting fixture.
4 Lumen—a measurement of the quantity of light.

INTRODUCTION TO ARCHITECTURE

FLUORESCENT LUMINAIRE

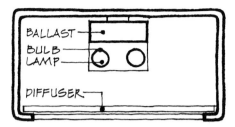

INCANDESCENT LUMINAIRE

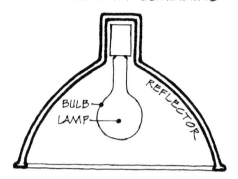

Fluorescent and incandescent luminaires.

Lamps. All lamps used in architectural lighting may be classified into two basic categories—incandescent and gaseous discharge. Regardless of the wide variety of incandescent lamps, all basic lamps consist of a bulb, filament, and base. The filament glows as current is passed through it and emits at least some light in all the wavelengths in the visible spectrum. Consequently, incandescent lamps produce a continuous or homogeneous spectral emission, and what is generally accepted as "warm" light.

As the lamp is used, the filament gradually evaporates. Thus, as the lamp grows older, there is less and less filament, and in turn, less and less light. The diameter of the filament is directly related to the rating (watts) of the lamp. The thicker the filament, the higher the possible operating temperatures, and the higher the efficiency of the lamp. This has important implications for energy conservation. For example, the efficiency of a standard 1,000-watt incandescent lamp is more than twice that of a standard 50-watt incandescent lamp. Efficiency has another implication—heat. The operation of electric lights generates heat at the rate of 3.14 Btu's per hour per watt.

One might ask why, if the efficiency of standard incandescent lamps is so low, are they so commonly employed? The answer is simple—incandescent lamps have certain properties that are very desirable. Among the advantages of incandescent lamps are the following.

ENVIRONMENTAL CONTROL SYSTEMS

1 The wide variety of filaments and bulbs available, each with its own light generation and distribution characteristics.

2 The interchangeability of lamps.

3 The ability to operate the lamps directly from standard circuits.

4 The ease with which the lamps may be dimmed.

5 The continuous spectral emission produced by incandescence.

The nature of incandescent lamps should suggest to the architect both their possible applications and their limitations. Incandescence is desirable where varying levels of illumination are required from point sources. Simply, incandescent lamps are appropriate for specific effects rather than for general area illumination.

Gaseous Discharge Lamps. A second category of light sources is the gaseous discharge lamp. This category includes neon, fluorescent, sodium, and mercury vapor lamps—although only the most commonly used fluorescent type is discussed here.

In the 40 years that fluorescent lamps have been available for architectural lighting, they have almost entirely supplanted the incandescent lamp as the principal lighting source. This is due to a combination of three factors: the desire for higher general levels of illumination; the fact that, by their very nature, fluorescent lamps are an area rather than a point source; and the significantly higher efficacy of fluorescent lamps.

The energy efficiency of fluorescent lamps is obvious. In addition, the heat generated by various lighting systems must also be considered. That is, heat generated by lighting sources may have to be re-

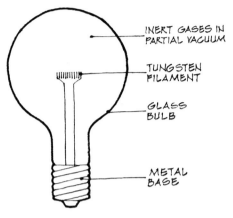

INERT GASES IN PARTIAL VACUUM

TUNGSTEN FILAMENT

GLASS BULB

METAL BASE

Incandescent lamp.

Light sources: approximate efficiencies.

EFFICACY — LUMENS PER WATT

	0	10	20	30	40	50	60	70	80	90	100	110	120
1910 EDISON LAMP													
STANDARD INCANDESCENT													
TUNGSTEN–HALOGEN				INCANDESCENT									
MERCURY VAPOR							GASEOUS DISCHARGE						
STANDARD FLUORESCENT													
HIGH PRESSURE SODIUM VAPOR													

A. ONE 40 W. FLUORESCENT

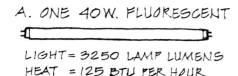

LIGHT = 3250 LAMP LUMENS
HEAT = 125 BTU PER HOUR

B. SEVEN 50W. INCANDESCENT

LIGHT = 3360 LAMP LUMENS
HEAT = 1100 BTU PER HOUR

C. TWO 100 W. INCANDESCENT

LIGHT = 3500 LAMP LUMENS
HEAT = 630 BTU PER HOUR

Comparison of **lamps**: light and heat generation.

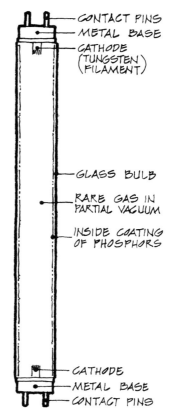

Standard fluorescent lamp.

moved by the building's HVAC system. For example, if 3,250 lumens are required, one could select one 40-watt standard fluorescent lamp generating 125 Btu's per hour, or two 100-watt standard incandescent lamps generating approximately 630 Btu's per hour.

The light source of gaseous-discharge lamps is developed by a glowing gas-electron arc. A property of any glowing gas is that it produces a discontinuous spectral emission; that is, the light generated does not include all the colors within the visible spectrum. For example, the characteristic color of neon gas is pink, and sodium vapor is yellow. Much of this problem of color rendition has been at least partially solved by fluorescent lamps, which generate a more complete spectral emission than other gaseous discharge lamps.

Another characteristic that has been known to cause problems is the stroboscopic flicker effect inherent in all gaseous discharge lamps. This is caused by the change in direction of the electron flow resulting from the use of alternating current. The gas-electron flow changes direction 60 times each second. Initially this is no problem, but as the lamp and ballast age, the flickering becomes more and more noticeable. Needless to say this is an extremely unpleasant lighting condition.

The selection of the light source is governed by the variety of properties exhibited by individual types of lamps, with both quality and quantity dimensions.

Lighting Criteria

The goal of a lighting design is to provide a pleasing and comfortable visual environment that facilitates the efficient performance of visual tasks without stress or strain. Part of this comfortable environment includes the occupant's ability to perceive and appreciate the architectural enclosure. The criteria by which a lighting system may be chosen include intensity and quality.

Intensity. Intensity refers to the *quantity* of light, defined as the amount of incident light coming from or falling on any given object. Technically, intensity is expressed as density of luminous flux and is measured as footcandles (fc). The intensity of light is an essential ingredient in any lighting design. As we have said, however, it alone cannot ensure comfortable lighting conditions. Historically, the approach to lighting design has been to provide ever increasing levels of illumination. In some cases, the result has been the provision of sufficient light to read architectural drawings in the bathroom or perform surgery in a supermarket.

It is generally agreed that previously accepted intensity levels were often too high and that, rather than alleviating visual strain, excessively high levels of illumination can aggravate it. Consequently, recent trends have been away from high general levels of illumination, and more and more attention is being paid to the quality of light.

Quality. In terms of architectural lighting, *quality* refers to all those factors other than the intensity of light. These factors are often more important than quantity. The term *brightness* refers to the subjective response to the light produced on or from a surface and is measured in footlamberts (fl). This is important in terms of architectural design because occupants define and interpret their spatial enclosure through brightness relationships, for example, the ratio of brightness between floors and walls or between walls and ceilings. In addition, the human eye is involuntarily drawn first to the object or sur-

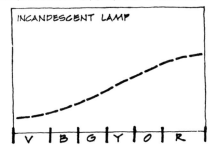

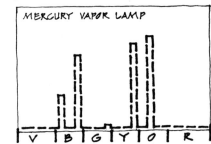

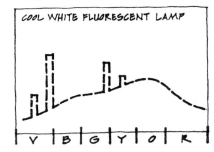

Spectral emission of typical lamps.

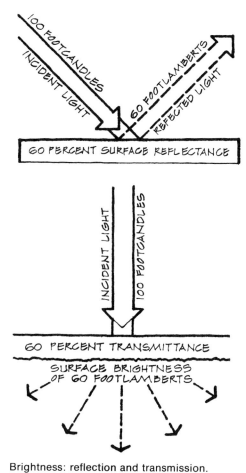

Brightness: reflection and transmission.

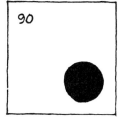

BRIGHTNESS RATIO = 5:1

BRIGHTNESS RATIO = 90:1

BRIGHTNESS RATIO = 1:5
ALL FIGURES ON DIAGRAMS
REPRESENT REFLECTANCES

Brightness ratios.

face of the highest brightness. The architectural implication is that the lighting design has the inherent ability to draw and direct the eye to any predetermined object or surface.

One of the most important aspects of brightness relationships is that they produce contrast. Contrast is defined in terms of brightness ratios; the higher the ratio, the greater the level of contrast. This is a critical factor in visual performance, for it directly affects our ability to discriminate and delineate outline, size, details, and so on.

Comfort limits are partially established by the level of contrast and by where in the field of vision the highest contrast exists. Generally speaking, high contrast is desirable within the area in which a task

ENVIRONMENTAL CONTROL SYSTEMS

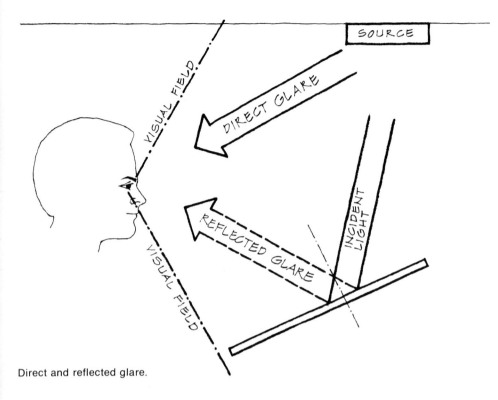

Direct and reflected glare.

is done and undesirable between the task and its immediate surroundings. If the surroundings are too bright, the eye may be drawn away from its appointed visual task. There exists in many architectural environments just such unfortunate visual conditions. This is one of the most common of the faults that produce visual stress and strain.

The issue of brightness and its developed contrast raises another common lighting problem—glare. Technically, glare is produced when background brightnesses exceed the brightness of the task. By this definition alone, glare is a condition to be avoided. One way of approaching the solution to the problem of glare conceptually is to increase the task brightnesses and simultaneously decrease the brightness of the immediate surrounding surfaces.

Lighting Design

The next issue facing the architect or designer involves the selection of an appropriate method of illumination. The selection should be based not only upon comfort criteria, task analysis, and lamp or luminaire characteristics, but also upon the desired aesthetic effects produced in the space.

There are two generic methods of illumination available for the designer—general and local. These may be employed singly or in combination and can be defined as follows.

1 *General* implies a system for even, uniform distribution of light throughout the space. General illumination further suggests the use of area sources (such as fluorescent lamps).

2 *Local* implies a system for varying the intensities of light throughout the space. Local illumination suggests the use of point sources (such as incandescent lamps).

One aspect of illumination that deserves special attention is the amount of light produced by the source that actually reaches the task surface. This has become a critical issue, for it directly relates to lighting efficiency and energy consumption. To facilitate this discussion, it may help to image a space as being analogous to a luminaire. Consider the surfaces of the space as the light-controlling devices that govern the amount of light reflected or absorbed. If the surfaces are predominantly dark and absorptive, most of the light produced by the source will be lost before it reaches the task. In some ways that would be similar to painting the reflector in a luminaire a dark color and using a dark smoked glass for the diffuser.

Methodology. Many variations exist in the methodologies employed in architectural lighting design. Perhaps the best would be one that existed somewhere between inspirational and computer-

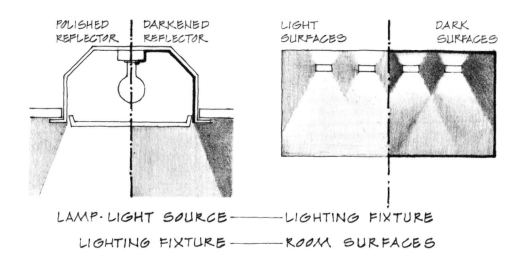

POLISHED REFLECTOR | DARKENED REFLECTOR

LIGHT SURFACES | DARK SURFACES

LAMP · LIGHT SOURCE ————— LIGHTING FIXTURE

LIGHTING FIXTURE ————— ROOM SURFACES

Analogy: luminaire and room surfaces.

ENVIRONMENTAL CONTROL SYSTEMS

aided design. In any case, there are procedures and sequences common to most comprehensive approaches to architectural lighting. The methodology should be comprised of three basic sequential procedures: analysis, selection, and calculations. It is important to mention that the architect's responsibilities normally apply to the first two procedures, whereas the last task falls to the lighting specialist.

The first step is to analyze the visual tasks and the architectural environment in which they are to be performed. This involves, at the very least, the analysis of the following.

1 *Occupancy:* the users of the space and their activities.

2 *Visual tasks:* the spatial and detail tasks to be performed by the occupants.

3 *Quantity of light:* the intensity of light required to perform the tasks efficiently. This is of particular importance when the task requires a high degree of visual acuity.

4 *Quality of light:* the issues of comfort and visual atmosphere desired by the occupants and by the designer.

5 *Physical characteristics of the space:* the surfaces and materials, specifically as they affect the reflection, absorption, and/or diffusion of the light.

This is perhaps the most important aspect of the lighting design process for the architect. It serves as the basis for lighting design and performance criteria as well as establishing the relationships between lighting and architectural design.

The second step is to select for consideration alternative methods of illumination and the associated lighting equipment. This procedure involves both the selection and evaluation of:

1 Methods of illumination.

2 Lamps.

3 Luminaires.

4 Location and placement of luminaires.

The ultimate selection of any combination of the above should be based on their ability to fulfill the comfort requirements established by the first procedure. Further, consideration of the architectural implications, energy requirements, and costs should serve as additional guidelines for the selection.

The final step involves discrete calculations and is normally the responsibility of the architect's consultants. The calculations include, among others, the computations required to establish the following.

DIRECT

SEMI·DIRECT

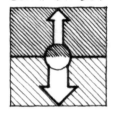
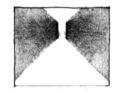

GENERAL DIFFUSE

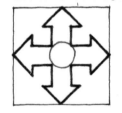
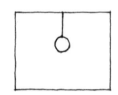

SEMI·INDIRECT

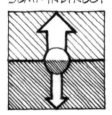

WHERE REFLECTING SURFACE SERVES AS LIGHT SOURCE

INDIRECT

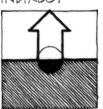

WHERE REFLECTING SURFACE SERVES AS LIGHT SOURCE

Methods of illumination: light distribution.

| | DISTANCE FROM SOURCE | INTENSITY AT SOURCE | INTENSITY AT DISTANCE 'D' |

A. POINT SOURCE

$$I_2 = I_1/D^2$$

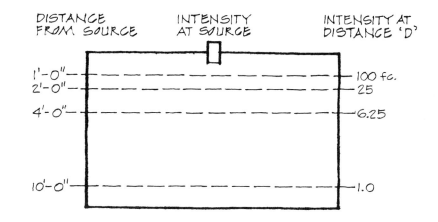

1'-0"	100 fc.
2'-0"	25
4'-0"	6.25
10'-0"	1.0

B. LINEAR SOURCE

$$I_2 = I_1/D$$

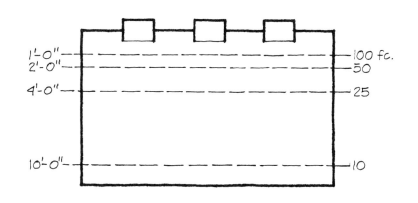

1'-0"	100 fc.
2'-0"	50
4'-0"	25
10'-0"	10

C. LUMINOUS CEILING

$$I_2 = I_1$$

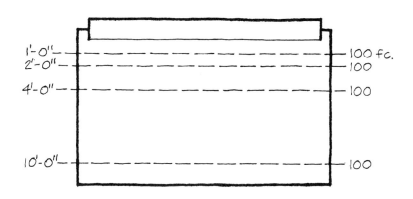

1'-0"	100 fc.
2'-0"	100
4'-0"	100
10'-0"	100

Distance and intensity.

ENVIRONMENTAL CONTROL SYSTEMS

1 Number of specified lamps.

2 Number of specified luminaires.

3 Placement of luminaires.

4 Heat generated by the lamps/luminaires.

5 Electrical energy required to operate the lamps/ luminaires.

These calculations are of great value to the architect or lighting designer. The results are one way of measuring the success of the proposed lighting design in meeting the objectives and criteria produced by the first two procedures.

In the final analysis, good lighting is as much the result of the absence of faults (which produce visual stress and strain) as the presence or application of any specific lighting technology.

ACOUSTICS

The design of the luminous (visual) and auditory (hearing) environments have many similarities. This is due to the fact that, in an architectural context, the behavior of light and the behavior of sound are analogous. It is safe to assume that good acoustical conditions result as much from a lack of defects as from the presence of any specific device or technology. Further, the most common acoustical defects are the result of unwanted, uncontrolled sounds, those that interfere with or detract from the desired listening task.

It must be emphasized that once a major acoustical problem has been recognized, its successful repair and correction is too often only partially attainable. Perfect results can sometimes be obtained only through a major redesign effort, with its associated costs. (Such costs, it might be added, are substantial.)

A recent and highly publicized example of this problem was the renovation of Avery Fisher Hall (then Philharmonic Hall) at Lincoln Center in New York City. Upon its completion in the early 1960s, the hall was found to be acoustically unsatisfactory. After several analyses and attempted solutions, it was finally agreed that the only satisfactory remedy was a comprehensive acoustical redesign and corresponding architectural renovation. The hall was literally gutted and rebuilt! The redesign and renovation costs were literally in the millions of dollars. The hall was only 14 years old when it was reopened. While this may be an extreme and disturbing example, it effectively stresses the necessity of avoiding acoustical mistakes

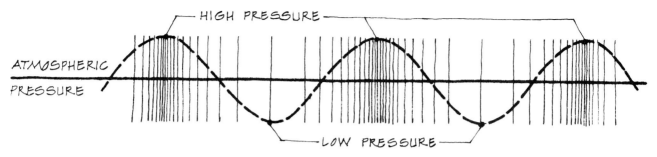

Sound waves and pressure.

before they can result in unsatisfactory and unacceptable auditory and acoustical environments.

Sound and Hearing

The first task at hand is to define sound, then to introduce the basic terminology or vocabulary used to describe sound and its behavior in architectural spaces.

Sound is a kinetic form of energy generated by vibration. These vibrations, in turn, produce alternating high and low air pressure waves. The difference in pressure between the air waves is miniscule—less than 1/1,000,000 of a variation from normal atmospheric air pressure. These air pressure waves move outward spherically from their source until they encounter some obstacle or surface in their path. When the waves reach the human ear, they cause the eardrum (a highly sensitive membrane) to be alternately pushed and pulled. This vibration of the eardrum produces the sensation of hearing.

One of the most frustrating problems facing architects in dealing with acoustics is the vocabulary employed in the discipline.

Intensity. The intensity of sound is governed by the rate at which energy is being generated. The subjective response to intensity is the relative loudness of sound. Intensity is measured in watts divided by square centimeters and is analogous to intensity level, measured in decibels (db). For example, consider the figures in the adjacent table.

Frequency. Frequency is defined as the number of sound pressure waves generated per second. It is described simply as waves per second (wps) or cycles per second (cps) and is measured in hertz (Hz). The subjective response to frequency is pitch. The greater

Intensity level (decibels, db)	Perceived loudness
140 db	Deafening, physical pain
130 db	Threshold of pain
110 db	Subway noise
100 db	Industrial plant noise
80 db	Noisy office
70 db	Average street noise
60 db	Average office
40 db	Private office or classroom
30 db	Bedroom
10 db	Sound of normal breathing
0 db	Threshold of hearing

ENVIRONMENTAL CONTROL SYSTEMS

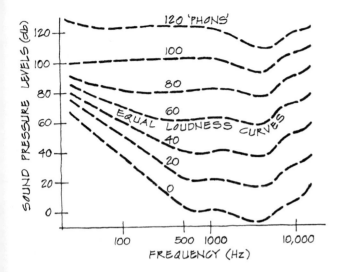

Equal loudness curves.

the number of waves per second, the higher the perceived pitch. The human ear is sensitive to sounds that have frequencies between approximately 20 Hz and 20,000 Hz.

An important relationship exists among frequency, intensity, and loudness. The human ear is more sensitive to certain frequencies. Therefore they require less intensity to be heard, while other frequencies that are not readily perceptible require high intensities. This relationship can be illustrated in a graph of equal loudness curves, called "phons." This relationship is describing the *audible spectrum*. The audible spectrum is to the ear what the visible spectrum is to the eye—the limits of perception. It lies between the loudest and softest and the highest and lowest sounds that can be heard. These limits are described in terms of thresholds—the threshold of hearing at the low end, and the threshold of auditory pain at the high end.

Wavelength. The physical wavelength of a sound is governed by three factors:

1 The distance traveled by sound in one second.

2 The frequency of the sound.

3 The velocity of sound in air (and for the purposes of architectural accoustics, the velocity of sound in air may be assumed as 1100 feet per second).

INTRODUCTION TO ARCHITECTURE

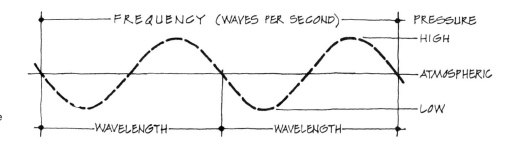

Frequency, pressure, and wave lengths.

The wavelength of any sound (λ) is the velocity divided by its frequency. The wavelength of sound has important architectural implications that deal with the ability to control the reflection of sounds that have a wavelength of five feet or less. Sounds with stacle equal to or larger than the wavelength of the sound. For example, a surface with a maximum dimension of five feet will reflect sounds that have a wavelength of five feet or less. Sounds with wavelengths larger than five feet will ignore the wall and pass by virtually undisturbed.

Noise. One of the most difficult terms to define is noise. When should a sound be considered a noise? It could be argued that the easiest way to classify noise and all sounds would be in terms of their structure and order. The factors influencing this classification would primarily be intensity, frequency, and generation (continuous versus random) patterns. In this case the most structured sounds would be music, and the least structured sounds would be noise. Speech patterns would rest somewhere between the two extremes.

Perhaps the simplest way to define noise is as any intrusive sound that interferes with or detracts from the desired auditory task. This definition, which is appropriate for the purposes of architectural acoustics, will be the one we use in this section when discussing noise control.

Behavior of Sound

One of the major problems facing architects in the field of acoustics is the difficulty of understanding the behavior of sound in space. Architects must understand the behavior of sound if they are to successfully control and manipulate it. This is a primary concern, for the great majority of acoustical problems are the result of unwanted, uncontrolled sound. In addition, the behavior of sound is directly

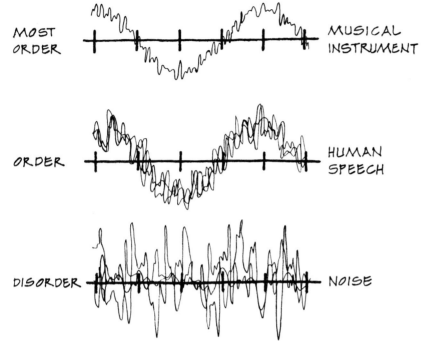

MOST ORDER — MUSICAL INSTRUMENT

ORDER — HUMAN SPEECH

DISORDER — NOISE

Music, speech, and noise.

related to a space's surfaces, which are the product of architectural design. At this point, the similarities between the behavior of light and that of sound become interesting. The area of architectural acoustics that employs the light-sound analogies is referred to as *geometric acoustics*. The field of geometric acoustics is based upon three fundamental assumptions:

1 The angle of incidence equals the angle of reflection.

2 Sound waves may be assumed to travel in straight lines as they move outwards spherically from their source.

3 Sound waves will be reflected, focused, spread, absorbed, and transmitted in much the same manner as light waves.

While these analogies are valid for the most part, they have their limitations. The limitations refer specifically to sounds that have frequencies below 250 Hz and corresponding wavelengths larger than 4 feet. The behavior of these low-frequency sounds cannot be accurately predicted by a geometric acoustical analysis.

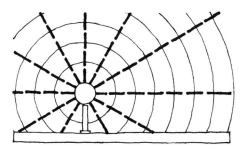

Radial path.

Angle of incidence.

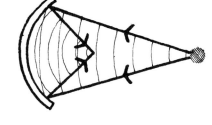

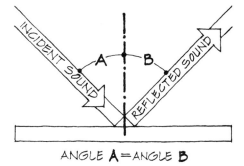

ANGLE **A**=ANGLE **B**

Geometric acoustics.

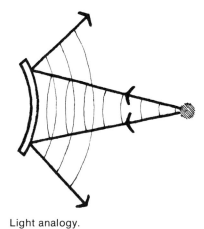

Light analogy.

Intensity and Distance. As sound spreads outwards from its source, its intensity level decreases markedly. One of the important behavioral properties of sound is the rapidity at which its intensity levels decrease as the distance between the source and listener increases. This is governed by two factors that operate simultaneously. First, the rate at which intensity levels decrease is governed by the *inverse square law*. In other words, the intensity of a sound in a free field (that is, in the absence of any reflection or absorption) decreases with the square of the distance away from the source. Secondly, while this is occuring, the area over which the sound must spread is increasing.

The architectural implications of these phenomena are extremely important. Much of the sound heard by listeners in any space is the result of sound reflections that reinforce the direct sounds that are heard, especially as the listener moves farther and farther from the originating source.

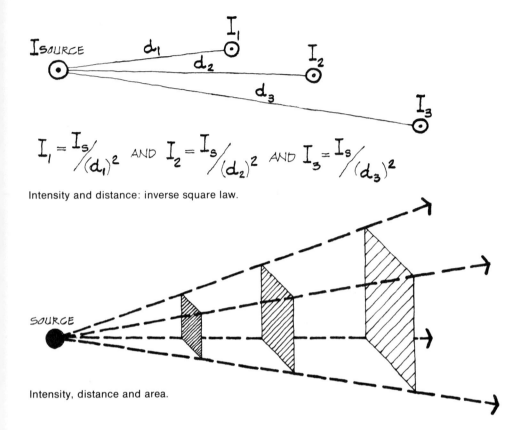

$$I_1 = \frac{I_s}{(d_1)^2} \quad \text{AND} \quad I_2 = \frac{I_s}{(d_2)^2} \quad \text{AND} \quad I_3 = \frac{I_s}{(d_3)^2}$$

Intensity and distance: inverse square law.

Intensity, distance and area.

Reflection, Transmission, and Absorption. Sound radiates outward from its source until it encounters an obstacle or surface in its path. Upon striking the obstacle or suface, sound behaves much as light does. The incident energy is partially reflected, transmitted, and/or absorbed. A significant part of architectural acoustics is involved with the question of how much of the incident sound is reflected, transmitted, and absorbed by the obstacle or surface. The answer determines in what manner the sound will arrive as well as how much of the incident sound will be heard by the listener.

The amount of sound reflected, transmitted, or absorbed is governed by two factors—the nature and properties of the surface the sound encounters, and the angle of incidence. The properties that influence the behavior of the incident sound are the surface's density, mass, and composition. As one might expect, hard, dense, or rigid materials reflect most of the incident sounds, while soft, porous, and resilient materials absorb and transmit most of the incident sound.

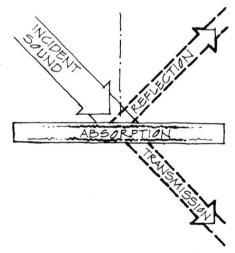

Reflection, absorption, and transmission.

INTRODUCTION TO ARCHITECTURE

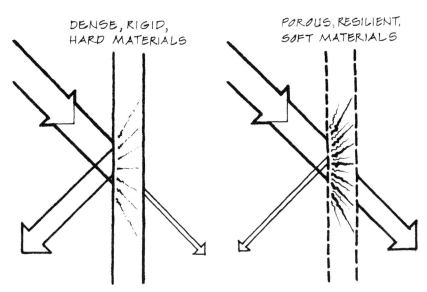

Reflection, absorption, transmission, and materials.

The degree of the angle of incidence also influences the amount of sound energy reflected. The greater the angle of incidence, the greater the corresponding amount of possible reflection. The smaller the angle, the greater is the possibility of transmission and/or absorption. This phenomena may be likened to skimming a rock on the surface of a body of water. If the angle is shallow enough, the heavy rock will skip or bounce across the surface before it eventually sinks.

Shapes and Surfaces This phenomenon leads to another issue—that of shapes and surface configuration. As stated previously, sound and light react to surface shapes in a similar manner. In addition, sound waves are easily diffracted or bent. When sound waves encounter the corner of an obstacle, they are easily bent around it. It is difficult to create acoustical shadows, especially with low-frequency sounds. In addition, sound that passes through small openings in a wall (such as electrical outlets or cracks under doors) tends to spread out uniformly on the other side.

Architectural Acoustics

There are two fundamental goals for architectural acoustics—to enhance and reinforce desired sounds, and to reduce or eliminate in-

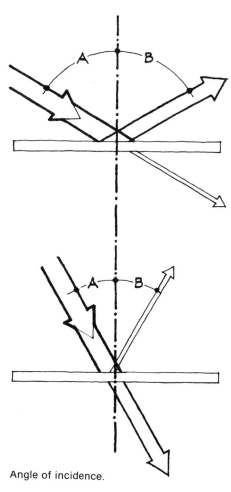

Angle of incidence.

trusive and undersirable noises. The first may be referred to as *room acoustics;* the second as *noise control.*

Room Acoustics. Room acoustics deals primarily with the control and manipulation of sounds that are generated within a space. To establish good room acoustics, one should reduce undesirable background noises while preserving and reinforcing desired sounds. This can be achieved effectively by the control of useful sound reflections. In any space, the listener will first hear direct sound, and then a series of reflections of that sound. In fact, most of the sounds heard in a space are the result of sound reflections rather than of direct sound. Therefore, a principle function of the enclosing surfaces of any space is to control sound reflections. First, reflective surfaces should be chosen and placed for the purpose of directing and distributing sound throughout the room. Secondly, absorptive surfaces should be designated and placed to prevent the continued presence of reflected sounds that are no longer useful for reinforcement.

The continued presence of sound in a room after the source has ceased generating it is *reverberation.* Reverberation (R_t) is defined as the time it takes for a given sound to diminish to a level at which it is no longer perceptible in the space. There is an important relationship, therefore, between reverberation and background noise levels. This raises two questions: when does a desirable sound reflection become an undesirable noise, and where and when should sound reflections be absorbed and terminated? The answers to both questions are simple. After the listener has heard the direct and reflected sounds, it is no longer helpful or advisable to have them persist in the room. At that point, sound reflections should be absorbed. Otherwise their continued presence may interfere with the perception of the next desired sound.

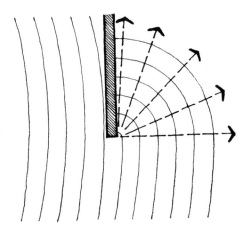

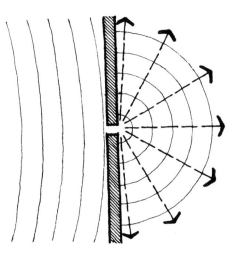

Diffraction and secondary waves.

Direct and reflected sounds.

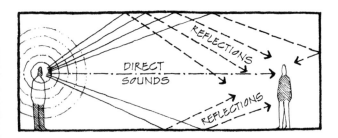

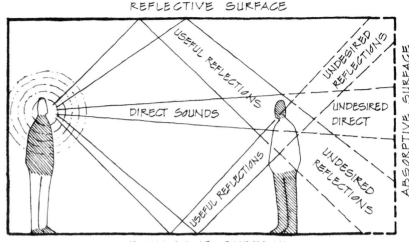

REFLECTIVE SURFACE

REFLECTIVE SURFACE

ABSORPTIVE SURFACE

Reflective and absorptive surfaces, and background noise levels.

If sounds are immediately absorbed after they have been heard, the corresponding background noise levels (and R_t) may be significantly reduced. There is, however, the serious question of how much noise should be removed by absorption; that is, how quiet does one wish the room to be, or how much acoustical isolation is desireable? One might argue that it would be highly objectionable to reduce the background noise level to a point at which the loudest noise in a room is the scratching of a pencil on a piece of paper. The reason for mentioning this point is to raise the issue of *acceptable* background noise, that is, just enough *white noise* in a space to mask or cover other less desirable noises. For instance, the pleasant noise of soft music might be desirable in an office if it were loud enough to mask someone else's conversation but not loud enough to distract or interfere with one's own concentration at a given task.

This aspect of room acoustics has been developed empirically over an extended period of time. The relationship between auditory comfort and acceptable background noise levels may be found in recommended *preferred noise criteria* (PNC) tables. PNC relates to what might be anticipated for given situations as acceptable, even desirable, background noise levels.

Noise Control. Assuming the successful control of sounds within a room, the next issue to be addressed is noise control. This involves keeping out unwanted sounds that might interfere with the auditory tasks to be performed. The principal objective of noise control is to shield the occupants of a room from noises generated outside the space. The task of architecturally achieving acoustical privacy is becoming more and more difficult. This is due primarily to architectural trends toward lighter and lighter construction.

The best (and often the only) place to effectively control noise is at its source. This is perhaps the single most important rule to learn regarding noise control. Once noise has radiated throughout a building, its control requires large amounts of design ingenuity, technology, and money. Even then, the solution may be only partially successful. Whenever and wherever possible, one should isolate and control the noise at the point of origin.

To achieve the goal of effective noise control, architects must recognize and define potential sources of noise and understand and appreciate the paths that noise may take through a building. There are basically two paths that noise (and sound in general) may take. The first is through the air, and the second is through the structure of a building.

In terms of airborne noise control, the physical behavior of sound must be reemphasized. Airborne noise will enter a space through any opening it is afforded, regardless of the size, shape, or location of the opening. Among the more common openings are HVAC ducts; cracks around doors, windows, or partitions; and electrical outlets. Consequently, the attainment of any degree of airborne noise control must begin with the effective blocking of these openings.

Structure-borne noise is by far the most difficult to control. This is due in part to the speed with which sound travels through solids. The velocity of sound in air is approximately 1,130 feet per sound, while its velocity through stone, for instance, is about 12,000 feet per second. In addition, once sound has entered a structure, the only way to block its path is literally to break the structure. Therefore, the only ef-

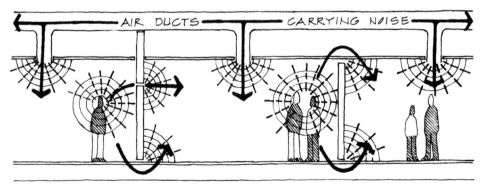

Airborne noise paths.

fective way of controlling structure-borne noise is to isolate the source and prevent its initial entry into the structure. This isolation includes not only structural separation but also remote location. Where possible, discontinuous structural systems, which do not transfer sound vibrations from one member to the next, are of great value. Every separation has the potential to impede the path of structure-borne sound.

Assuming that all direct sound paths (airborne and structure-borne) have been blocked, the next area to be addressed is of special interest to the architect—the role the enclosure system plays in preventing the intrusion of noise into the room. This factor deals with how much reduction in the transmission of noise may be expected of the walls, floor, and ceiling of any room. The tendency of the enclosure system to reduce sound is referred to as the *sound attenuation* properties of construction. The question facing architects is twofold—first, how much sound attenuation is feasible, and second how much is desirable? The answers to these questions are predicated upon human comfort criteria for acoustical privacy, available construction technologies, and associated costs. Decisions are made by evaluating potential sources of noise and their associated intensities, and by establishing the desired or acceptable sound levels for the given space and its activities. The difference in sound levels between the two will govern the *sound transmission class* (STC) required for the given enclosure. The STC rating of any construction simply describes the theoretical amount of insulation that may be expected. Due to the variability of construction practices, it is advisable to specify an STC rating higher than that actually required.

The factors that govern the STC rating of any construction component are material weight, mass, and rigidity. The greater the weight,

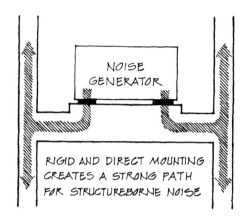

UNACCEPTABLE

RIGID AND DIRECT MOUNTING CREATES A STRONG PATH FOR STRUCTUREBORNE NOISE

ACCEPTABLE

ISOLATORS AND RESILIENT PAD DAMPENS AND REDUCES NOISE ENTERING STRUCTURE

Structure-borne noise.

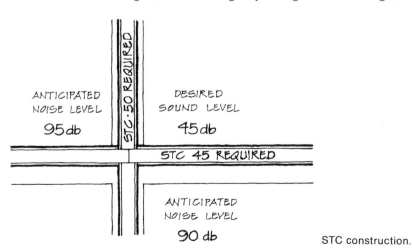

ANTICIPATED NOISE LEVEL
95 db

STC 50 REQUIRED

DESIRED SOUND LEVEL
45 db

STC 45 REQUIRED

ANTICIPATED NOISE LEVEL
90 db

STC construction.

mass, and rigidity, the greater the corresponding attenuation produced. For example, the attenuation value increases by almost 5 db for every doubling of the weight (per square foot) of the construction. This illustrates the difficulties in achieving acoustical privacy in buildings that employ lightweight construction.

To ensure effective noise control, architects should consider the issue of noise during the initial design phase. A useful noise control methodology for architects may be said to consist of four sequential procedures:

1 Locate and define potential noise sources, specifically in terms of their anticipated intensities.

2 Evaluate possible direct transmission paths for structure-borne as well as airborne noise.

3 Employ construction detailing and available technologies and plan to isolate and impede these various noise paths.

4 Select appropriate STC-rated construction, based upon the desired degree of attentuation between spaces.

By using this simple methodology and expanding it to include such factors as human comfort criteria, architects could produce auditory conditions in spaces that would be significantly better than most we commonly experience. The ability to evaluate and address potential auditory and acoustical problems before they occur is invaluable.

FOR FURTHER READING

Banham, R. *The Architecture of the Well-Tempered Environment*. London: Architectural Press, 1969.

Carrier Air Conditioning Company. *The ABCs of Air Conditioning*. 1st rev. ed. Syracuse, N.Y.: Carrier Air Conditioning Co., 1972.

Doelle, L. *Environmental Acoustics*. New York: McGraw-Hill Book Co., 1972.

Flynn, J., and Segil, A. *Architectural Interior Systems: Lighting, Air Conditioning, Acoustics*. New York: Van Nostrand Reinhold Co., 1970.

Lam, W.M.C. *Perception and Lighting as Formgivers for Architecture*. New York: McGraw-Hill Book Co., 1977.

Kaufman, J. E., ed. *IES Lighting Handbook: The Standard Lighting Guide*. 4th ed. New York: Illuminating Engineering Society, 1966.

Fitch, J.M. *American Building: The Environmental Forces That Shape It*. New York: Schocken Books, n.d.

McGinness, W., and Stein, B. *Mechanical and Electrical Equipment for Buildings*. 5th ed. New York: John Wiley & Sons, 1971.

United States Gypsum. *Sound Control Construction*. 2d ed. Chicago: United States Gypsum, 1972.

CHAPTER 13

Energy, Architecture, and Buildings

Stephen D. Dent and John Schade

Energy has become a critical factor in national and global economic development. Whether or not there is a true energy crisis at this time may be debated, but it is certain that the era of plentiful and cheap fossil fuels is ending. Also ending with it will be the extravagant use of energy to create interior comfort conditions and lighting within buildings that largely ignore the natural environment. We are now beginning to develop an architecture that is more responsive to environmental factors and is much less dependent on the ever more valuable fossil fuels. Some call this *energy-conserving* design, but a better term may be *energy-conscious* design, since we will still be constructing energy-consuming buildings—only at a much lower level of consumption per unit area. This trend is not only related to the market pressures of rapidly increasing operating costs, but it is also being actively encouraged and enforced by newly developed codes, regulations, and guidelines that are being adopted in increasing numbers at all levels of government.

Building energy consumption amounts to about one-third of the current annual fossil fuel consumption in the United States. Since it is often quite feasible to reduce consumption by 50 percent or more with recent practices of design and construction, it is easy to understand the pressure for improved building energy performance. The necessity for reduced energy consumption is, of course, not limited to new construction. Of at least equal importance is the existing stock of buildings, many of which are true energy gluttons. Thus, the design profession has the twofold task of applying principles of energy-conscious design to new construction and of rehabilitating existing structures.

There is no single approach to energy-conscious design, just as there is no single approach to the formal or functional aspects of building design. The design process that leads to good, working, energy-conscious buildings is inherently a more quantitative design process than the architectural practitioner is accustomed to. In that sense, it is a challenge to the architectural profession. Yet at the same time, the chance to develop new, energy-related design vocabularies is a significant opportunity for the profession.

If the ultimate judge of an energy-conscious design is the amount of energy consumed per square foot per year, then the challenge is to create architecture that still meets the classical dictum of "firmness, commodity, and delight" within this new framework. Greater technical proficiency in the areas of site climate, thermal comfort, heat gain and loss, innovative and alternative energy systems, and building economics is now being demanded. The architect who has mastered these topics will see them not as limits, but as the basis for developing a new aesthetic for energy-conscious building design.

RESOURCES AND VALUES

In the United States, as in most developed countries where high levels of energy consumption in buildings are problematical, we have very few reminders of our dependence on the earth as a provider of life-sustaining and life-enhancing resources. Our primary connection to thermal comfort is the thermostat and the monthly utility bill. The processes that lead to our comfort are overwhelmed by the energy-intensive economic and industrial system that supports and extends it. We are detached.

Before convenient and cheap sources of energy or the technology to use it were available, design guidelines were clear. Adaption to extreme climate conditions was necessary or one would have to confront the full force of the elements. Throughout the world there are examples of vernacular architecture that responds to external climatic conditions with the materials at hand. Native American shelter serves as an example of the highest order. It displays not only a sense of technical aesthetic regarding energy resources, but also, along with cultural and economic customs, a spiritual aesthetic. The earth and its gifts were sacred.

For the pre-nineteenth-century Sioux Indian, winter comfort was a result of the teepee, conceived as an insulator. Protection was provided by buffalo skins for the outer membrane, brush to insulate the air space between the inner and exterior skins, and wood for fuel. Summer comfort on hot, open plains was provided by the teepee as an air conditioner. There was no brush between the layers, the outer base

Acoma Pueblo, New Mexico.

flaps were rolled up, and a multidirectional top vent assisted the natural chimney cooling effect of the conical shelter. Not only did the basic materials for shelter and comfort come directly from the earth, but the shelter was designed to respond to the natural energy processes occurring around it. It behaved much like the animals and plants of the plains.

Ralph Knowles has investigated the solar design apparent in many pueblos in the Southwest.[1] Building form and construction were designed to receive and use a maximum of sun energy during the winter. Knowles shows that at Acoma Pueblo in New Mexico, the energy-receiving south walls are virtually shadow-free during the winter months, allowing the mass of the walls to store and transmit heat energy to the interior. A "solar ethic" is apparent in the placement of buildings within the village. Spacing between the buildings increases as buildings become taller, so that shading of a neighbor's source of heating is minimized or avoided. The high summer sun strikes the roofs, which are insulated with layers of twigs and branches, and the end walls, which have been minimized by building "row houses" on an east-west axis.

Examples of cultures whose architecture reflects dependence on and a corresponding use of natural energy flows extend well beyond the Western United States. By reviewing so-called primitive forms of shelter, we can begin to understand the kind of design ethic that exists when our link with the earth is apparent. That link is the value base of energy-responsive design.

Contrast the primitive shelter with the modern skyscraper. Rather than responding to natural climatic factors, the skyscraper turns the same facade to widely different conditions of solar heat gain and is totally sealed against any possible helpful breezes. It is probably overlighted, to levels of illumination that create internal heat gain problems. The skyscraper provides very high levels of thermal comfort control at all times, but at a constantly increasing cost. One would think that these great glass towers would have immense heating problems in winter, but internal lighting and human occupancy in the core of the building actually require cooling while the perimeter is being heated. In summer, the entire building is being cooled with expensive electricity, even when beneficial breezes could be used. There is no link between natural energy flows and the building's occupants. Comfort is produced by the central HVAC system, the building operation engineer, and fossil fuels.

There is usually a direct correlation between independence from fossil fuel use and greater personal involvement in creating comfort conditions. Since we have become so dependent on our mechanical servants for creating thermal comfort, it may be difficult for us to move to lower consumption and higher involvement. But, as we will see, both high- and low-technology solutions are being developed. The choice by the user will be between greater involvement and lower cost, or greater convenience and higher cost.

World Trade Center, New York.

Energy and the Biosphere

How, then, as architects, do we find a way of recognizing the natural energy and resource flows that support our lives? An appropriate starting point would be to study the basic life cycles and energy flows that maintain the spaceship Earth. We cannot begin to cover this immense topic here, except to outline the relationship between the energy cycle and shelter design.

The sun is the driving force behind all climatic and life forces on earth. The macrolevel transfer of energy begins when incoming solar energy strikes the outer level atmosphere. About 30 percent of this energy is reflected back into space by the atmosphere and clouds. About 20 percent is absorbed by water vapor, dust, and water droplets in the lower troposphere. The remaining 50 percent is absorbed by the earth's liquid and solid surfaces. It is the outward movement of this energy from the earth's surface by long-wave radiation, conduction, and lateral energy flow in the form of water vapor that begins the dynamic climatic process of the atmosphere.

The reduction of incoming solar radiation toward the winter pole means there is an excess in radiation heating in the summer hemisphere and a corresponding deficit at the winter pole. This heat gradient is the major force driving large-scale atmospheric and oceanic currents to move heat energy toward the winter pole. The north-south gradient will cause heated air to move toward relatively lower-pressure areas heated by sinking masses of radiantly cooled and contracted air. The warmer air mass will then sink gradually and complete the loop cycle, returning toward the thermal equator. Precipitation often occurs during the downward movement of air, when the air mass gives up latent heat stored in water vapor. Summer heat storage in the oceans and the earth's crust and its release during the winter helps to moderate large climatic zones.

Although this description is simplified, it serves to illustrate the complex interaction of various forces that make major climatic patterns. Two points are important to the architectural designer. The first is that the power source for those patterns is incoming solar energy. The second is that the architect is dealing with a set of variable factors (temperature, solar radiation, air movement, humidity, and precipitation) that demand flexible design responses for optimum performance. The important generalization to be made regarding the architect's overall role is that the buildings we design become parts of biospheric cycles. Depending on their design with respect to energy and resources, they may either coexist and conform to those cycles or ignore and fight them.

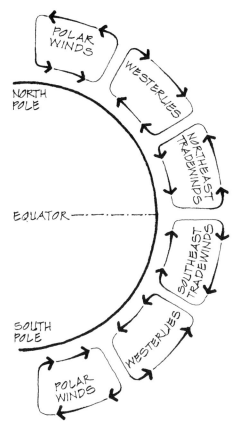

Global wind patterns.

THERMAL COMFORT

Buildings serve as the barrier between major climatic cycles and the activities of people. To do this, they must be designed to respond to both external environmental conditions and the comfort requirements of the user. Those comfort requirements are usually defined in terms of thermal characteristics—air temperature, relative humidity, air motion, and radiation. Humans, like other organisms living in the biosphere, use the short-term solar energy fixed by photosynthesis to do work, build body tissue, and maintain a constant temperature of 98.6°F. Because the body uses only about 20 percent of its generated heat internally, the remaining 80 percent must be released to the surroundings. At the same time, there is a thermal exchange taking place with those surroundings. This demands that the thermal gains equal the losses in order to maintain a stable body temperature.

TABLE 13-1

Human Heat		Percent loss at typical
Gains	Losses	room temp. (68°)
Metabolism	Convection	30
Shivering	Radiation	45
Radiation	Evaporation	25
Convection	Conduction	Negligible
Conduction		
Activity		

Skin surface temperature is about 92°F. Therefore, temperature colder than that will cause the body to use energy in order to maintain its heat, while with a temperature warmer than 92°F, the body will be asorbing heat. The importance of the different methods of heat gain or heat loss vary. As illustrated, evaporation through sweating becomes the only technique for losing bodily heat at high temperatures. Conversely, heat loss at lower temperatures can be slowed by higher surface temperatures or increased humidity. Air conditioning, of course, will solve either problem, but with the necessity of mechanical energy input.

It is especially important to note that there is no single set of conditions that constitutes comfort, but rather a range of conditions. Com-

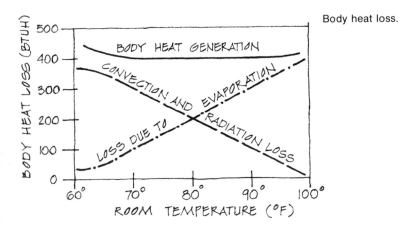

Body heat loss.

fort, for any one individual or group of individuals, may vary considerably according to the culture, age, clothing, sex, and health of those involved. The energy-conscious designer must then respond to the needs of the specific client at the specific location.

There are four primary responses the designer may use as a means of coordinating building thermal environments (and the resultant energy use) with the comfort needs of the user. These are the manipulation of site climate, building membrane, building use, and mechanical and natural thermal modification.

SITE CLIMATE

An architect is concerned with the climate on the particular building site; thus site climate is even more specific than a local microclimate. By relating site climate conditions over the entire year to human comfort, one can determine appropriate responses in type and time for site planning, landscaping, and architectural form and construction.

The essential climate data for the closest city or airport can be obtained and will be generally applicable to the specific site. An inspection and analysis of the site should reveal conditions that might cause local deviation. An excellent indicator of the particular site climate variations is the existing type and condition of vegetation.

Climatic data that should be collected and plotted would include:

1 Temperature—normal, maximum, minimum, average, and extreme temperatures by month to determine heating and cooling requirements.

2 Solar radiation—hours of sunshine, clear and cloudy days, insolation data (if available), and a slope and orientation analysis to determine the amount of solar gain, the site exposure, and the need for shading.

3 Wind—direction and velocity by monthly averages at three-hour intervals and site features that would modify airflow patterns in order to define ventilation possibilities and protection requirements.

4 Humidity—monthly morning and afternoon averages and site features, particularly water bodies, swamps, or vegetation that would modify it, to determine the need for humidification or dehumidification.

5 Precipitation—rain or snowfall by monthly average and extremes to determine need for special design responses.

Modification of the site climate to the greatest extent possible is the first response required if comfort conditions are to be achieved within the limits of minimum energy consumption. Of course, individual sites will have various possibilities for modification. A crowded urban parcel may have none, while a rural one may have many, the most important of which may be the selection of the exact location for the structure. The location should be chosen to meet the maximum number of design and planning requirements while minimizing negative site climate effects.

There are many techniques for controlling or modifying climatic factors. Vegetation can be used to intercept solar radiation, either direct or reflected, before it strikes building surfaces. Deciduous trees are excellent shading devices, because they respond to the local climate: they lose their leaves when sun is wanted and provide shade when it is not. Plants diffuse and reflect radiation due to their multifaceted and generally rough, dark surfaces. Placement of low shrubs or lawns can be critical in controlling reflection from water or paving surfaces.

Anyone who has walked from a parking lot into a forest on a hot summer day can attest to the cooling effect of vegetation. This is accomplished by the canopy shading of trees and the continual process of transpiration. In colder weather, the forest will be warmer than open land, because of the reduced wind velocities and the trapping of warm air by the overhead vegetation. Insulating dead-air spaces can be created next to buildings to utilize such effects and reduce building heat loss. Vegetation can be used to reduce temperature buildup in paved areas, particularly where it will radiate its heat to adjacent buildings.

Humidity on a site can be increased, but it is very difficult to decrease it due to the overall importance of the encompassing

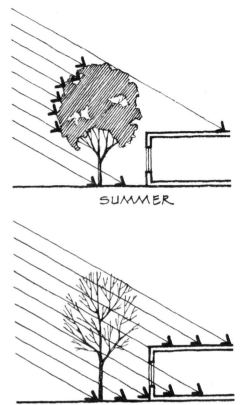

SUMMER

WINTER

Incident solar radiation and vegetation.

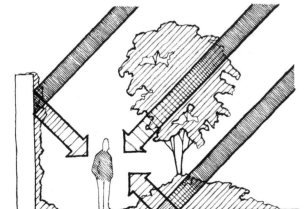

Incident solar radiation and vegetation.

INTRODUCTION TO ARCHITECTURE

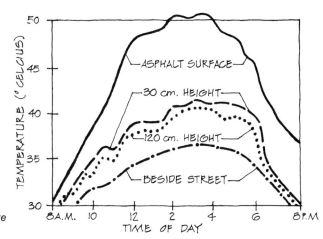

Climate near ground (after Rudolph Geiger, *The Climate Near the Ground,* 1950).

macroclimate. Eliminating vegetation to decrease humidity would also eliminate beneficial shading, wind protection, and air purification functions. Humidity in arid regions may be increased with the addition of water ponds or water-intensive planting. Best use is made of these techniques in contained areas such as courtyards or atriums, where natural ventilation will assist in cooling and exposure to drying winds and sun is reduced.

Masjid-e Shah, Isfahan, Iran.

ENERGY, ARCHITECTURE, AND BUILDINGS

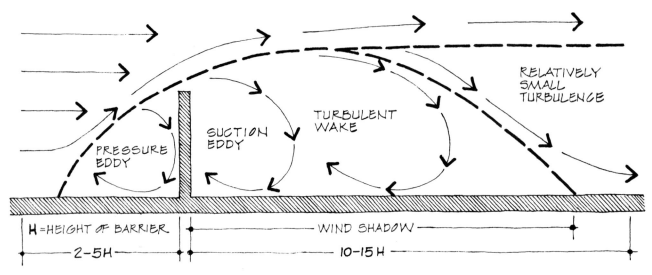

Windbreak effects.

Airflow on a building site may be controlled by obstructions, deflectors, or filters made by trees, hedges, berms, and other buildings or structures. Unwanted winter winds can be slowed or deflected and cooling summer winds can be guided into a structure. A windbreak will reduce downwind air speed up to 75 percent for a distance of ten to fifteen times its own height. Vegetation and walls outside a building can be used to assist in natural ventilation or to mitigate the full effect of strong winds. Extensive research has been done on this aspect of airflow control. Much less work has been done on the effect of groups of buildings on airflow.[1a] This is undoubtedly because of the immense number of variables in climate, topography, building size, and spacing. A good rule to follow is to have wind tunnel testing done on any large project to determine airflow patterns, not only for ventilation but also for structural wind loading and pedestrian comfort.

The site planner may use knowledge about the local climate and possibilities for its on-site modification in the selection of a site for a particular use. When site selection is part of the design process, it is necessary first to state clearly the design goals for the project and then to thoroughly investigate the off-site factors, legal and fiscal restraints, and surface and subsurface conditions. In this procedure, the important steps for energy-conscious design are making a clear statement of energy-related design goals and a thorough evaluation of the site for factors that would affect a building's energy performance. Conditions such as exposure to north winds, cold-air dams, north-facing slopes, or shading of welcome winter sun would increase winter energy consumption. Unshaded west slopes, exposed sites, vegetation blocking summer breezes, or sites with reflected radiation from large paved areas or adjacent buildings are some conditions that will increase summer heat gain and energy consumption.

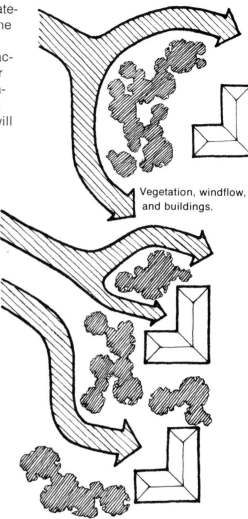

Vegetation, windflow, and buildings.

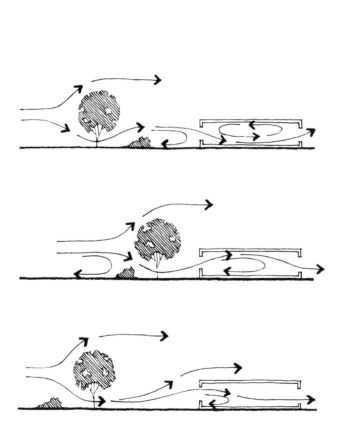

Vegetation, windflow, and buildings (after R.F. White).

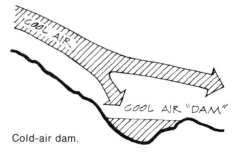

Cold-air dam.

BUILDING MEMBRANE

A building's outer surface, which separates user activities from biospheric conditions like rain, snow, heat, cold, and wind, is often called the "envelope." A more dynamic concept in tune with the organic nature of energy is "membrane." This biological analogy is conceptual as well as practical, and dynamic instead of static. One approach is to regard the building as an organism designed to survive in the specific site climate. An instructive design exercise is to investigate the physical characteristics of plants and animals that thrive on that site or a similar one and, where possible, to integrate these characteristics into the building design. It is a helpful way to generate new design concepts based upon natural energy patterns.

In the analysis of typical buildings, the architect or engineer tests the performance of the membrane by analyzing its heat gain or loss. Using John Yellott's acronym,[2] we can show total gain or loss by:

$$Q_{SCEMP} + Q_{VENT} = \text{Heating or Cooling Load}$$

where:

Symbol	Definition	Heat flow
Q_S	Solar heat gain	Heat flow is inward; may reduce heating load in winter but adds to summer cooling load
Q_C	Conduction heat flow opaque areas	Flow is from warmer to cooler spaces; generally outward in winter and inward in summer
Q_E	Electric heat from lights & equipment	Internal gain; may reduce winter heating load but will increase summer cooling load
Q_M	Miscellaneous heat gains from gas stoves, etc.	Same as Q_E
Q_P	People's heat generation	Same as Q_E
Q_{VENT}	Ventilation or infiltration airflow	Bringing outside air into building for health and odor control adds to heating load in winter and cooling load in summer

Since mechanical systems for heating or cooling are sized for close to the worst possible conditions, Q_{SEMP} is often not considered to contribute to interior heating because its factors may be unreliable. Exceptions are made where fixed conditions such as high artificial lighting levels or high occupancy loads (both of which are present in office buildings) can be relied on. As we shall see later, buildings designed as solar collectors themselves may use Q_s for all or part of their heating.

INTRODUCTION TO ARCHITECTURE

The basic formula used to determine conduction heat gain or loss (Q_c) through the membrane is:

$$Q_C = UA(t_i - t_o)$$

where: U = overall coefficient of heat transfer through the membrane
A = area of membrane
t_i = interior surface temperature
t_o = outside surface temperature

(Note: Resistance to heat flow is the R value. The inverse of the sum of the individual R values of each element of construction is the U value; $U = 1z...\Sigma R$)

A review of this formula will reveal that the architect has control of two of the variables—the surface area and the U value. One concerns the overall form of the building and the other is determined by the details of its construction. These, of course, are significantly different approaches to reducing energy consumption for thermal comfort requirements.

Form responses to natural environmental forces is perhaps a more interesting subject for the designer in the search for improved membrane performance. The most basic concept here is that of surface to volume ratios. It is easy to understand that for two equal volumes, the one with the least exposed surface area will gain or lose the least amount of heat to its surroundings. Geometrically, a sphere has the least surface area per unit of volume of any form. But since a circular or curved geometry is not always appropriate in terms of construction, space use, or accoustics, its qualities may be approximated with straight line geometries. Note that a curved surface dilutes the solar radiation falling on it by spreading it out over more surface area. Thus, a curved geometry would be a help in a hot, arid region.

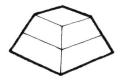

House forms based on climate conditions: thermal retention (after Donald Watson, *Designing and Building a Solar Home*, 1977).

Afghan home.

Conceptually, in temperate climates of the northern hemisphere, a good rule to follow is to make the building small to the high summer sun and large to the low winter sun. The relative emphasis on summer cooling or winter heating needs will modify this dictum according to the local climate.

The orientation of the building should vary with its local climatic factors in order to gain maximum benefit from natural heating and cooling techniques. An excellent source is the work of Victor Olgyay in his classic text, *Design With Climate*.[3] Illustrated are his recommendations for building orientation in four climatic zones. Where solar gain is extreme, the opportunity—indeed the necessity—for shading of glazed areas can lead to a richly varied architecture, as shown by Le Corbusier at the Secretariat at Chandigarh, India.

Secretariat at Chandigarh, India, by Le Corbusier.

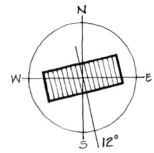

COOL · MINNEAPOLIS

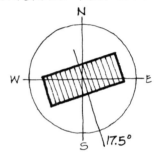

TEMPERATE · NEW YORK

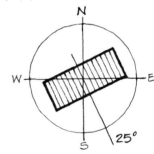

HOT–ARID · PHOENIX

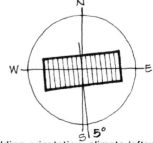

HOT–HUMID · MIAMI

Building orientation: climate (after Victor Olgyay, *Design with Climate*, 1963).

In a study of house forms, Donald Watson has generated responses to the parameters of maximum thermal retention, maximum solar heat gain, minimum wind resistence, and maximum internal airflow.[4] The results have been interpreted in terms of conventional forms for construction and begin to show some of the many possibilities, especially when the various forms are combined for various climates.

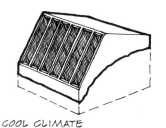

COOL CLIMATE

MAXIMUM THERMAL RETENTION
MAXIMUM SOLAR HEAT GAIN
MINIMUM WIND RESISTANCE

TEMPERATE CLIMATE

MODERATE THERMAL RETENTION
MODERATE SOLAR HEAT GAIN
SLIGHT WIND EXPOSURE
MODERATE INTERNAL AIR FLOW

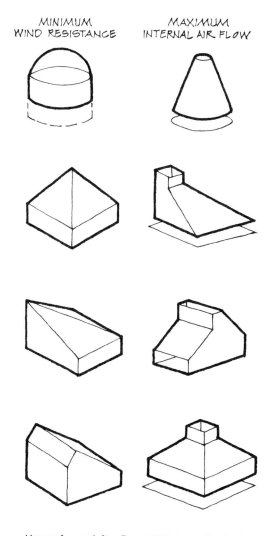

MINIMUM WIND RESISTANCE   MAXIMUM INTERNAL AIR FLOW

House forms (after Donald Watson, *Designing and Building a Solar House*, 1977).

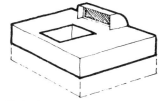

HOT-DRY CLIMATE

MINIMUM SOLAR HEAT GAIN
MODERATE WIND RESISTANCE
MODERATE INTERNAL AIR FLOW

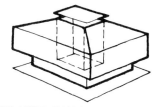

HOT-WET CLIMATE

MAXIMUM WIND EXPOSURE
MAXIMUM INTERNAL AIR FLOW

House forms (after Donald Watson, *Designing and Building a Solar House*, 1977).

ENERGY, ARCHITECTURE, AND BUILDINGS

Construction techniques and materials may not be as exciting for the designer as form response, but they are at least as important. Critical factors to be concerned with are the insulative qualities of all construction sections, benefit for heating or lighting by windows, time lag, and thermal storage requirements of the building mass.

Typical membrane heat loss and total energy budget descriptions for typical residential and office buildings are shown below. Table 13-2 shows where energy is used and that heating needs in both cases are more than 50 percent of the total energy budget.

The table also shows that there is considerable potential for considering the membrane a dynamic surface rather than a static one. The residential case can be used as a fairly clear example. Windows typically account for over 40 percent of the building's total heat loss. In cold climatic regions of the United States, it is reasonable to assume that during the eight-month heating season, windows are used for their primary functions of light and visual enjoyment for less than half of the twenty-four-hour heating day. If, instead of being fixed and static, they were designed to change their nature from a light (and possibly heat) source during the day to an insulator at night (and during periods when the home is unoccupied), major reductions in heat loss by both conduction and infiltration could be achieved. A good insulating shutter, for example. could reduce window heat loss by 50 percent or more.

Membrane responses can also be sensitive to daily and seasonal movement of the sun around the building. Changes in membrane characteristics can occur on either the exterior or interior of the building—shades, awnings, shutters, movable or fixed exterior fins and overhangs on the outside; curtains, blinds, shutters, and vents on the inside. The result would be building façades that vary not only with their orientation, but also with local climate factors, creating a regional architecture that functions in harmony with the biosphere.

The massiveness of the construction becomes a factor wherever climatic conditions involving substantial diurnal temperature fluctuations are present. The most obvious example, mentioned earlier, is the Pueblo architecture of the Southwest United States. Diurnal temperature differences range from 30°F to 40°F during a large portion of the year, and mass can be used to temper the seasonal heating and cooling loads. During the winter day, a high-mass membrane of thick adobe acts to absorb and store solar energy. This heat migrates slowly through the thick walls to provide heat during the cold nights. In summer, this time lag effect acts to even out the high temperatures. Even in conventional construction, massive buildings

TABLE 13-2

Lifespan Energy Budgets
(Recent Conventional Construction)

Residential	Percent of budget
Space heating	55.0
Water heating	14.6
Refrigeration	5.8
Cooking	5.0
Air conditioning	4.0
Clothes drying	2.0
Other	10.6
Construction	3.0

Office buildings	Percent of budget
Heating	52.0
Lighting	23.0
Equipment	13.0
Cooling	6.0
Hot water	3.0
Construction	3.0

Source: American Institute of Architects, *Energy and The Built Environment*, 1974, AIA, Washington, D.C.

are more stable in thermal terms. As shown, the interior temperature in a massive house will fluctuate much less than that in a light frame house. As might be guessed, in warm humid climates, high mass would be detrimental, for it would stabilize temperatures at a level above the comfort zone, prevent the passage of cooling breezes, and absorb moisture and thus maintain humidity.

Design for natural ventilation has largely been ignored since the mid-1950s, when air conditioning became affordable in all types of construction. The winter task is relatively simple: to minimize wind and infiltration. Tight construction, including weatherstripping and caulking, exterior shelterbelts, and protected and/or vestibule entrances will accomplish the task. But much more thought and effort must go into the design if it is to take advantage of breezes for ventilation and cooling in warm periods.

The membrane of the building should act to control and direct airflow within the building, and its form should assist in generating supplemental air motion during periods of calm. From the detailed site climate analysis, the architect can determine times when wind will be helpful and what its direction and velocity will be. In many parts of the country, this will reveal that mechanical refrigeration is often overused or not required. Before attempting to cool by natural means alone, architects should take two steps to reduce heat gain—insulate the building well and shade it.

Natural cooling will not be very effective at low humidities and high temperatures since one would already be getting the maximum benefit of evaporation with just slight air motion. Nor will it be helpful at high relative humidities (above 85 percent), where unpleasant indoor air speeds would be required to create an effective evaporation rate. Air speeds of greater than three miles per hour are generally unacceptable indoors, thus further limiting the range of natural cooling possibilities.

One basic rule in natural ventilation is that without an outlet, there is no airflow. Effective cross-ventilation requires a free flow of air through the building, minimal interior obstructions, and openings on opposite sides of the building. Air speed is increased when the inlet is smaller than the outlet, and the inlet itself should face the wind and direct the airflow toward the occupants. Olgyay has determined that the height of the outlet opening has little do do with the airflow within buildings. This is true except when the "stack effect" is utilized to create air motion during calm periods. This effect depends on the height and temperature difference between inlet and outlet, with greater height increasing the airflow.[3]

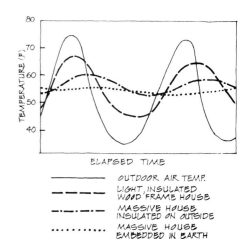

Building mass and temperature fluctuations (after Bruce Anderson, *The Solar Home Book* 1976).

ENERGY, ARCHITECTURE, AND BUIL

BUILDING USE

A key problem in energy-conscious design is to develop an integration of building form, mechanical system, and membrane that will use energy only under the conditions and to the extent that people using the building need it. Every building has a pattern of use that varies over the day, the week, and possibly the season. A building that is responsive to natural climatic factors will be used most intensively at a particular time when the orientation or exposure is best for that use. To do this, the architect may first describe the use pattern of each defined space, then correlate it with the expected variation in indoor and outdoor climate. Particularly important is sun exposure for both light and heat.

    Little-used rooms or those with low thermal requirements can be used to buffer other spaces from cold or hot exposures. A further refinement of this concept is internal zoning. By putting together in one area all the spaces with similar thermal requirements, we can heat or cool them to different degrees of specificity. A limited example of this

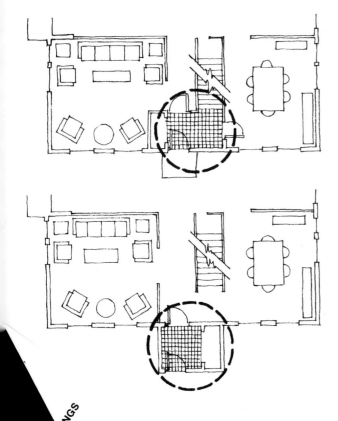

Enclosed entries: the vestibule.

would be the placement of all the bedrooms in a house on the second floor, allowing them to be only partially heated to comfort conditions when not in use. This requires the ability to control the mechanical system for each individual zone and the need for thermal barriers, such as doors or partitions between zones.

Individual rooms may themselves function as separate zones. The old-fashioned vestibule entry with two doors is an excellent thermal buffer zone from interior to exterior. An attached solarium or greenhouse may be allowed to go unheated, only being used when comfort conditions permit. If properly coupled to the main structure and insulated at night, it may also act as a solar heat collector and storage space.

More intensive use of buildings is another way of reducing overall energy consumption. Multifunctional buildings reduce the cost (in both dollars and energy) of constructing and operating separate facilities. To carry over the daytime heating of a school building for evening community use is more efficient than heating two individual buildings. Another approach is to limit hours to those of intensive use, permitting an energy cutback over a longer period of nonuse. In either instance, the key is to get maximum use, then lower the thermostat when the building is not in use, rather than operating it for the benefit of only a few users.

Building reuse, renovation, or rehabilitation is usually a net energy saver over new construction. The work and energy expended in demolition, hauling, manufacture of new products, and new construction are convincing arguments for revitalizing older buildings, not to mention the need for preserving architectural character. Partly because of rising energy costs, the economic arguments are now often in favor of reuse.

MODIFICATION FOR COMFORT

Mechanical

Mechanical and electrical systems supply the differences between conditions within the building membrane and conditions required for user comfort and activities. They are powered either by fossil fuel energy or renewable energy sources. Energy is used for temperature and humidity control, ventilation, power requirements needed for specific work processes, and lighting. Design development of the mechanical system for space conditioning is inseparable from the aspects of climate, use, and membrane. Since it is only mechanical and electrical systems activities that require external sources of energy, many individuals consider this area of energy-efficient design to be the most important. Hence, considerable emphasis should be placed on a comprehensive approach that integrates building design and mechanical system design.

Heating is the primary consumer of residential energy, while in most commercial and institutional building uses, cooling, lighting, and ventilation are the primary energy loads. Commonly, energy for these needs is supplied either directly or indirectly by the fossil fuel sources of natural gas, fuel oil, and coal. Much less commonly, energy comes from a renewable energy source through solar, wind, or geothermal devices. The delivery of conditioned air, with the one exception of direct solar gain, requires a delivery medium— either air, water, or refrigerant. In the case of gas, oil, or electrical heating systems, air or water is heated at a central furnace or boiler. The heated air or liquid is then transported to spaces in buildings as needed. In an all-air system, heat energy is moved by electrically driven fans and distributed directly to the spaces from supply ducts. In an all-water or hydronic system, the heated liquid or steam is moved to the space by electrically powered pumps. In an air-water system, the water is piped to the space, and air passing over a heat exchanger distributes the heat to the space. Direct-resistance heating is another option. Though this method converts electricity to heat in the space at 100 percent efficiency, the overall efficiency from power plant to user is closer to 35 percent. Fuel oil and natural gas heating systems operate at overall efficiencies of 60 to 75 percent.

Cooling, ventilation, and air purification are usually powered by electricity. Since so many other functions require electricity year-round the addition of summer cooling loads for buildings creates the peak demand for electrical generating plants; hence the importance of reducing these cooling loads. The distribution system is the same as for heating, with the exception of the direct refrigerant system. In these, each space may have a separate refrigeration unit, eliminating the distribution system. When not in use, the space may not be cooled, but if they are used constantly, many small refrigeration units will be much less efficient than a large central chiller. Major reductions in cooling requirements can be made through the membrane design responses previously suggested—shading, insulation, mass, and natural ventilation.

Many buildings now have HVAC systems that heat or cool incoming air whether or not the buildings are occupied. Another common waste has been the use of refrigeration equipment to cool air for the interior zones of large buildings even in the middle of winter. But new equipment and controls are becoming much more sophisticated and energy conscious in their response to variable interior and exterior thermal conditions. Unoccupied buildings may now be simply shutting off their heating and cooling equipment and providing only the minimum necessary ventilation air, while outside cold air is used for cooling interior zones directly when possible. Variable air volume systems respond to highly sensitive room thermostats to provide only the minimum required amount of heating or cooling airflow. Exhaust heat generated by large HVAC equipment is now often used to preheat incoming air.

Lighting/Electrical System Impact. Electrical energy for lighting may be a double energy load, initially in the lighting and then in the cooling load to compensate for waste heat given off by lighting fixtures. Lighting energy can account for a significant portion of the energy budget for commercial and light industrial building types. The potential for conservation in this area is high.

An energy-efficient lighting system should have three objectives. The first is to reexamine suggested standard lighting requirements. Many of these standards were developed in the days of cheap energy and can be reduced without significant task interference. Lower overall lighting levels with local task lighting can replace the commonly used general illumination techniques without any loss in performance for the user. The second objective is to accomplish as much of the indirect lighting load with natural lighting as possible, while minimizing heat loss through glass areas. The third is to utilize waste heat given off by necessary fixtures, either directly or by recovery for storage or other uses. Electrical energy that powers building and office equipment can be reduced by using demand limiting and electrical load-controlling devices.

Control Systems. Continuous fine tuning of large HVAC and lighting systems for energy conservation is possible with automated controls. Such controls can constantly monitor conditions and adjust operating efficiencies and sequences, shed unnecessary loads at critical peak loading periods, optimize fan and pump outputs, adjust to various zone loads, and provide constant monitoring of performance. These computer-aided or computer-operated systems can be used to maintain a dynamic correlation between building use, membrane, and climate. The successful building is exciting to both architect and engineer, for its dynamic response over time is like an organism's seeking to minimize the use of resources in its environment.

Natural

Alternative Energy Systems. The classification of energy systems that are powered by renewable resources as "alternative systems" is undoubtedly a temporary terminology. By about 2025, the United States may have exhausted its reserves of oil and natural gas that can be recovered cost-effectively. Before that time we will probably see these fuels being reserved more and more for uses that require their highly concentrated energy potential or their unique properties in producing lubricants, medicines, plastics, or fertilizers. Use of the low-intensity energy in the renewable sources of sunlight and wind is highly appropriate to the relatively undemanding process of heating and cooling buildings. Other possibilities include water power and biofuels, both of which have limits of location and/or technology that lessen their potential for widespread use in building construction.

Our ability to link technological evolution to natural energy patterns of the biosphere is limited by legal, economic, and financial constraints that were developed in the oil-based growth of the past century. Our national and global economies are now oil-based, and their resulting structure protects and subsidizes fossil fuel interests. Thus solar and wind energy now appear less economically competitive. But that picture is changing and its potential impact on architecture is great.

Passive Solar. The technological and economic constraints on using solar energy for space heating and hot water production are fast disappearing, as the result of the recent wave of federal and privately funded projects will attest. Current terminology differentiates between "active" and "passive" solar systems. The energy flow of an active system is forced by pumps, fans, or motors requiring an outside energy source, however small. The thermal energy flow in a totally passive system is by natural means. Adding a fan or mechanical controls to a passive system to increase its efficiency or ease of operation creates a "hybrid" system. The definition of the system is, of course, less important than its operation, economics, or architectural implication.

No matter which system is used, thermal energy must flow from collection to storage to the conditioned space. Collection is limited by the low-intensity nature of the solar energy striking the earth. Solar energy seldom exceeds 300 Btus per hour per square foot or 3,000 Btus per day per square foot, compared with about 140,000 Btus per gallon of #2 fuel oil. The solar energy itself is free, but its collection is not since large areas of collector surface are required. The most basic concept in passive solar systems is that the design of the building should itself facilitate the collection and storage of solar energy and at little extra construction cost.

The simplest of passive systems is *direct gain*. In it the sunlight passes to the occupied space to heat the space directly and to be absorbed in the mass of the structure for continued warmth. It requires a large glazed area that faces the low winter sun path and a large thermal mass in floors, walls, or ceiling to store heat. Its greatest problems are lack of control and overheating. And the effectiveness of the mass storage is greatly reduced when covered with carpets or furniture. Some degree of control is obtained by shading to prevent overheating in summer, by ventilation, and by night window insulation to prevent massive loss of heat in cold weather.

In order to obtain a higher degree of control, *indirect* passive systems intercept the solar energy in a collector-storage mass placed between the sun and the space. Three basic types, though there are many variations in detail, are the mass or Trombe wall, the water wall, and the roof pond. The Trombe wall is a south-facing, dark-colored masonry or concrete mass with a covering of glass to minimize outgoing long-wave solar radiation emitted by the heated mass. Slotted openings in the top and bottom of the wall allow for a natural thermosiphoning process to transfer heat to the adjacent space. Cool air enters the bottom, rises when it is heated by the sun and by contact with the wall, and exits at the top. The wall itself absorbs a great deal, of heat, which migrates slowly to the inside surface where it provides time-delayed radiant heating.

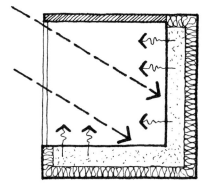

Direct solar gain.

The Trombe wall.

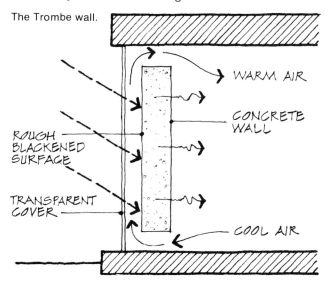

WARM AIR

CONCRETE WALL

ROUGH BLACKENED SURFACE

TRANSPARENT COVER

COOL AIR

The water wall operates in a similar fashion but has a much higher heat capacity per cubic foot and has little time lag. Additional heat may be added to both walls by adjustable reflectors that increase the collector area. In many cases these reflectors also act as operable night insulation to keep the heat in the structure at night or cloudy periods. In Trombe wall or water wall systems, views may be obstructed or eliminated, and the orientation of the wall is critical.

Roof ponds have long been used to protect buildings from summertime overheating, but their greatest potential may be in heating. Harold Hay's Skytherm system uses water contained in plastic bags on top of a steel roof deck to collect solar heat on sunny winter days.[4] Operable insulation panels cover the water at night and the collected heat is radiated to the interior. In summer the insulated panels are closed in the day and open at night. Cooling is produced by radiation of heat to the night sky and is increased by evaporation of water sprays or flooding. Thus, the system offers year-round air conditioning. In colder climates, where snow is a problem, the water bags are placed in an attic with a south-facing glass or plastic roof opening. The effectiveness of this method for summer cooling in colder climates is severely limited, but the cooling load in this case would be much less. Architecturally, the large area and weight of the water must be dealt with, as well as the problem of waterproofing. The horizontal orientation of the water is not an efficient winter collector and thus requires larger areas than if it were vertical or tilted. Roofs need not be completely flat but can be stepped, though doubling the height of the room would decrease the radiation heat transfer by a factor of four, that is, the square of the distance.

A third passive system is the *isolated gain* type, which separates the collector and storage from the space and permits much greater control. The two most common isolated gain systems are solar spaces and thermosiphoning collectors. A solar greenhouse, atrium, or sun-porch must be sun-facing with a large glazed area and thermal mass provided by masonry, earth, or water. The temperature is usually allowed to fluctuate much more than if the space were used full-time. When there is a surplus of heat, it may be circulated to the rest of the building by simply opening doors or windows. Occupancy of the space will vary with the thermal conditions. There are many ways in which the space will fit into the building and as many possibilities for the thermal connection. Thermal transfer may be by convection, conduction, or radiation. Shading from summer sun and ventilation to prevent overheating, and night insulation to prevent conduction losses in winter, are required for optimum performance.

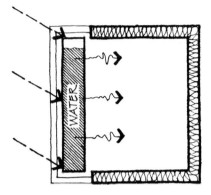

The water wall.

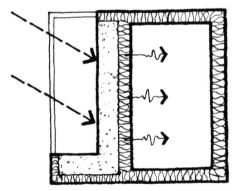

Isolated gain.

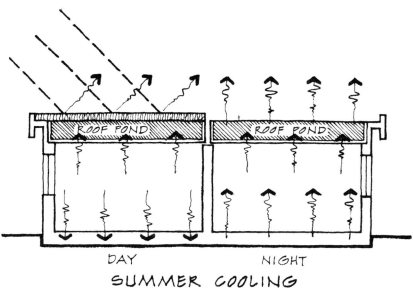

DAY   NIGHT

SUMMER COOLING

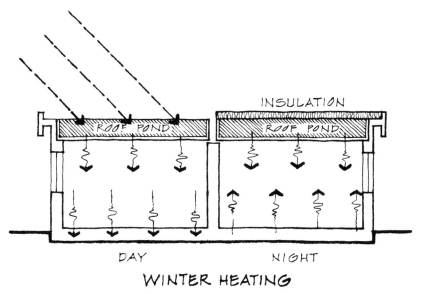

DAY   NIGHT

WINTER HEATING

Roof pond collector, summer and winter (the Skytherm System).

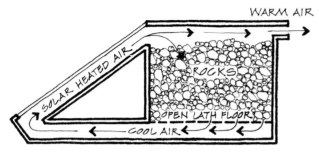

Air loop rock storage system.

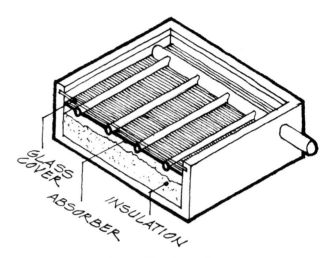

Liquid-type flat plate collector.

A thermosiphon operates by the natural convection currents created by rising hot air and falling cool air. This phenomena can be utilized to generate heat from a flat plate collector without the use of fans or pumps. Though less predictable than an active system, a thermosiphon has the greatest amount of control for a passive system when coupled with a storage mass. The heated air rises from the collector to the storage area, where it may be circulated through the rock bed, giving off its heat and then repeating the cycle. Or it may be passed on to the interior space, where natural convection currents must be allowed to circulate freely through the entire space.

Beyond these basic types of systems are unlimited options and combinations, many not yet designed. Possibilities for hybrid systems, in which mechanical aids are used to control or distribute thermal flows within any passive system, are numerous and are only limited by the designer's inventiveness.

Active Solar. The most widely used and accepted solar technology today is the flat-plate solar collector. The common flat-plate collector consists of five components, whether it is circulating air or liquid:

1 Glazing—glass or plastic.

2 Fins or tubes to conduct heat from inlet to outlet.

3 Absorber plate that conducts heat to fins or tubes and thence to heat transfer fluid.

4 Insulation, to minimize heat loss from the back of the collector.

5 Collector frame.

Solar radiation passes through the glazing and heats the plate, which is painted or coated to absorb as much heat energy as possible. Heat is conducted to tubes that carry liquid or to fins that increase the surface area for heat transfer to air. Fans or pumps then move the working fluid either to storage or to the heated space. (In a thermosiphon collector, natural thermal forces move the heat.)

The collector is tilted at an angle to optimize collection for the appropriate use. For heating, use the angle of the local latitude plus 10 to 20°; for domestic hot water use the local latitude angle; for powering of cooling equipment use the angle of the local latitude minus 10 to 20°. The heat collected must be enough to carry over at least until the next day or possibly for several cloudy days. Consequently, heat storage is of great importance. The most commonly used storage materials are water and rock beds. The pressure for thermal storage advances is not for small buildings, but for large systems that require very large storage volumes. Thus much research is being done on phase change and other innovative techniques that store large amounts of heat in small volumes.

The choice of system type (air or water) depends on the size of the building, the distribution system, and the climate. For large buildings, the quantities of heat needed would require large ducts or high velocities. Collection efficiency falls off at higher temperatures, indicating the economy of collecting more heat at lower temperatures but increasing air duct size over that of conventional systems. The same holds true for a liquid system, but a 50 percent increase in pipe size has much less impact on space planning than a corresponding change in a duct. Consequently, most large buildings use a liquid system.

These lower operating temperatures of a solar system, typically 110°F to 160°F, limit some of the choices for the distribution system in the conditioned space. Small baseboard convectors that use water at

Schematic diagram of an indirect solar system.

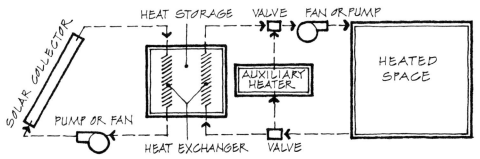

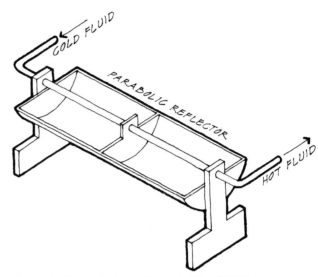

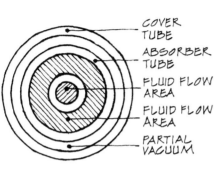

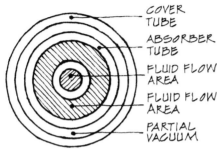

Cross-section of tubular collector.

Concentrating collector with parabolic reflector.

180°F are inappropriate, and larger radiators are required. Fan coil units may be used but will require extra heat transfer area. Air systems, though, can directly heat the conditioned space.

There are very few locations in the United States that are not subject to occasional freezing and thus to the accompanying problems of using water as a heat transfer fluid. To solve these problems, ethylene glycol (antifreeze) is added. Its high cost limits it to the collector-storage loop, thus requiring a heat exchanger to transfer collected heat to storage. In locations with few freezing days per year, a system that drains down when not in use can be used. Air systems do not require these precautions.

There are numerous variations in plumbing, ducting, control, collection, and distribution beyond these basic systems. Some of the more important possibilities include concentrating and evacuated tube collectors that permit much higher operating temperatures and thus the potential for also powering refrigeration equipment. Trickle-type water collectors, popularized by Harry Thomason's Solaris system, can be good performers even when fabricated on site by nonprofessionals.[5] Solar cells that directly convert solar radiation to electricity are the subject of much current speculation regarding their potential for becoming an economically feasible energy source. Dr. Karl W. Böer of the University of Delaware, a leader in direct energy conversion research, predicts that by the early 1980s we will see solar cells at $2 per watt and at $1 per watt a few years thereafter, the threshold of widespread use.[6]

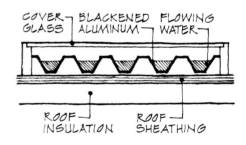

Section of solar water heating.

This discussion has so far ignored the issue of auxiliary heating. It is usually not economical to provide 100 percent solar heating, and the remaining variable percentage must be made up by other sources. Auxiliary heating is often designed to heat the entire building in case of an extended period of cold, cloudy weather. Indeed, lending institutions may require it. An appropriate marriage of technology is the use of a heat pump with the solar system to provide the backup heat. The heat pump can extend the usefulness of the collected solar heat by withdrawing heat energy from storage at temperatures much below those that could be used for direct heating.

Wind, an indirect form of solar energy, has great potential for providing direct electrical or heat energy conversion for primary or backup systems. Wind-powered electrical generators work best when the wind is in the range of 12 to 25 miles per hour, consequently limiting the number of usable sites. Luckily, there is often a strong correlation between high wind speed and heating needs. Sites for towers should be clear of all obstructions for about 300 feet and the plant should be at least 30 feet above ground to eliminate local turbulence. Generated power may either go into a storage battery system or be fed into the local electrical power grid. The future will see significant technological changes and greater availability of economical package systems. But wind power will tend to be rural and will always be limited by the capricious character and low-energy density of moving currents of air.

SYNTHESIS

Governmental agencies in increasing numbers are passing guidelines and regulations that mandate energy budgets or standards. A national program to establish energy performance standards for buildings is being developed for the Department of Housing and Urban Development. The result will be a matrix relating a range of designed energy consumption levels to major building types in particular climates. This range will then be used as a standard by design teams working on particular building projects. In addition, energy use standards are being adopted in many states and local jurisdictions. The implication of these trends is simply greater responsibility and accountability for the design team in developing energy-efficient buildings that can be operated by the owner to perform according to stated design objectives. This is a reasonable goal as energy and its management take on higher economic value, since a greater investment in the form of physical plant capital and design time is justified.

In response to the complexities of long-term financial decisions, life-cycle costing techniques have been developed. These are particularly useful in demonstrating the advantages of capital investment in energy conservation over the life of the building. They represent significant departure from the usual approach to building economics, particularly in speculative construction that minimizes first cost, down payments, and monthly financing costs while ignoring operating costs. As utility costs rise, they become a larger, more significant portion of owning and operating costs.

In this developing era of greater accountability for both energy and economic performance of buildings, the architect is in a pivotal position. Leadership from the architectural profession can bring about a creative working partnership among engineers, clients, builders, lenders, and architects that will lead to solutions of beauty and economy. The conventions of the architectural design process often result in completion of schematic design documents before any contact with specialized consultants has been made. An earlier communication among the involved professionals, particularly the architect and the engineer, is one way of improving energy-conscious design. The higher challenge, though, goes beyond communication to an understanding of the new environment that we are facing.

We are in an era when the limits of the earth to sustain growth as we know it are being made known. The impact of the knowledge that fossil fuel resources are finite is beginning to be felt globally. The inability of the earth's balanced ecosystem to continue to support biospheric life under the pressures of oil-fueled industrialization is also becoming apparent. It is inevitable that these trends will have a direct impact on the buildings that shelter life activities—and on the activities themselves.

Although the process of global change is long-term and diffuse, it will affect populations in direct relation to their level of reliance on the energy resources that they use for maintaining basic cultural lifestyles and standards of living. The United States is prototypical for the Western world, consuming one-third more energy per capita than its nearest competitor. Having grown in a century of cheap energy and resources, the United States will feel any change more quickly and more sharply than its neighbors. The architecture profession will be involved in developing new environments and in adapting old ones to new lifestyles. The challenge is great, but so are the possibilities, and therein lies the excitement of the future.

NOTES

1. Ralph Knowles, *Energy and Form: An Ecological Approach to Urban Growth* (Cambridge, Mass.: M.I.T. Press, 1974).

1a. Robert F. White, "Effects of Landscape Development on the Natural Ventilation of Buildings and Their Adjacent Areas," *Texas Engineering Experiment Station Research Report* 45 (College Station, Texas: Texas Engineering Experiment Station, 1945).

2. John Yellott, "Solar Heating and Cooling Systems," (Memorandum to Arizona Chapter, American Institute of Architects, 1976).

3. Victor Olgyay, *Design with Climate* (Princeton: Princeton University Press, 1963).

4. Harold Hay and John Yellott, "International Aspects of Air Conditioning with Movable Insulation," Solar Energy, vol. 12, 1969, pp. 427–438.

5. Solaris system details and license are available from Edmund Scientific Company, Barrington, New Jersey.

6. "An Interview with Karl Böer," in *Solar Age,* vol. 3, no. 2 (February 1978), pp. 32–35.

FOR FURTHER READING

Anderson, Bruce, and Michael Riordan. *The Solar Home Book.* Harrisville, N.H.: Cheshire Books, 1976.

Egan, M. David. *Concepts in Thermal Comfort.* Englewood Cliffs, N.J.: Prentice-Hall, Inc., 1975.

Fitch, J. M. *American Building: The Environmental Forces That Shape It.* New York: Schocken Books, 1975.

Geiger, Rudolph. *The Climate Near the Ground.* Cambridge, Mass.: Harvard University Press, 1950.

Givoni, B. *Man, Climate, and Architecture.* London: Applied Science Publishers Ltd., 1976.

Knowles, Ralph L. *Energy and Form, An Ecological Approach to Urban Growth.* Cambridge, Mass.: M.I.T. Press, 1974.

Koeningsberger, O. H. and others. *Manual of Tropical Housing and Building, Part I Climatic Design.* London: Longman Group Ltd., 1973.

McGuiness, William J., and Benjamin Stern. *Mechanical and Electrical Equipment for Buildings.* New York: John Wiley & Sons, Inc., 1971.

Olgyay, Victor. *Design with Climate.* Princeton: Princeton University Press, 1963.

Robinette, Gary O. *Plants/People/and Environmental Quality.* U.S. Department of Interior, National Park Service. Washington, D.C.: Government Printing Office, 1972.

Ruegg, Rosalie T. *Solar Heating and Cooling in Buildings: Methods of Economic Evaluation.* U.S. Department of Commerce, National Bureau of Standards. Washington, D.C.: Government Printing Office, 1975.

Scientific American. *The Biosphere.* San Francisco: W.H. Freeman and Company, 1970.

Watson, Donald. *Designing and Building a Solar House.* Charlotte, Vt.: Garden Way Publishing, 1977.

Wright, David. *Natural Solar Architecture.* New York: Van Nostrand Reinhold Co., 1978.

CHAPTER 14

Computers in Architecture

Anthony J. Schnarsky

The important impact of computers on modern society is well known. While many argue, and will continue to argue, about the long-run merits and problems associated with a computer-oriented society, the fact remains that the computer has vastly increased our ability to store and process information. Numerous mundane, manual tasks have been automated, and complex computations and analyses have become simple and routine. As initially heavy research and development costs are recovered, the cost of hardware decreases—and computing capability extends to more and more applications.

Architects as a group are generally attuned to trends; they are quick to try a new material or process and struggle with its expression. So it was with computers. In the mid-1960s, computers offered great potential to architects. However, promise often exceeded performance; numerous firms tried, evaluated, and rejected computer applications. Nevertheless, more recent applications and products suggest a reemergence of computing in architecture—with remarkable results and significant potential. This chapter describes the basic elements of computing systems and presents numerous applications for architecture.

THE INTRODUCTION OF COMPUTERS TO ARCHITECTURE

In the early introduction of computers to architects, two conferences were important: the Boston Computer Conference (1964) and the Yale Conference on Computer Graphics in Architecture (1968). The participants were practicing architects, educators, students, researchers, and computer specialists. Two groups were formed, not the expected ones of practicing architects versus educators or computing specialists versus others, but believers versus non-believers. There were two conference agendas—the conversion of nonbelievers, and the carefully guarded exposure of new applications. The proceedings were stimulating and provocative; the demonstrations were seductive. There was much prophesying and much selling.

Murray Milne said about the papers of the 1968 conference:

> The work . . . is just the beginning. In fact, if development continues at the present rate, most of these papers will be classified as history in four or five years.[1]

By 1970 Nicholas Negroponte devised an artificially intelligent design partner, played with it, cast it in a movie called *Urban Aid,* then laid it to rest as a good start from which much was learned. His book *The Architectural Machine* explores, provokes, prophesies, criticizes, and gropes for fundamental relationships between humanity and a designing machine in architecture.[2]

By 1975 Kaiman Lee, in his book, *The State of the Art of Computer-Aided Environmental Design,* enumerated 334 distinct programs or packages in 13 areas of application. One hundred forty-two of these were developed before 1973.[3] The period of the mid-1960s to the mid-1970s saw a sudden and enthusiastic expression of computer usage.

What were all of these computing programs like? Negroponte described three characteristic levels of programs as they relate to human capability.

> *Level I*   Programs that mimic human ability to solve a problem or to act.
> *Level II*   Programs that use generic algorithms that few humans would attempt by hand.
> *Level III*   Programs that act upon problems in a completely autonomous fashion. They have independent sources of perception, built-in values, and decision capabilities.[4]

Most early programs belonged in Level I. Intrigued by the computing machines, programmers devised explorations involving processes that were very familiar to users. (These programs were analogous to the early uses of iron. In the 1850s there were no precedents for iron, so architectural forms made of the new material often adopted traditional wood and stone motifs.) Soon, however, many Level II programs evolved, especially when problems could be modeled and simulated using numerical analysis techniques. Computer graphics is an example of Level II applications, where a designed form can be viewed from a multitude of vantage points that few would attempt to construct by hand. Finally, a few researchers attempted Level III and met with little success. Perhaps they tried this advanced level without realizing the magnitude of the effort. Despite this high level of developmental activity, integration into the architectural profession was relatively slow.

The other historical insight that should be considered is the nature of the sales pitch. Why were the believers so intense and persuasive, and yet the evidence of acceptance by the practitioners so slight? The proponents for computers claimed that computers would do all of the following.

1 Save the architect and designer important time.

2 Free humans from mundane tasks and allow them to concentrate on the more humanistic aspects of architectural practice.

3 Allow exploration of a higher number of design alternatives.

4 Be user-oriented, interactive, generic, flexible, versatile, convenient, efficient, responsive, open-ended, economical, common data-based, user-controlled, graphical, and realistic.[5]

5 Reduce office errors and omissions.

6 Extend the offering of services, including the leasing of excess computer time to others.

7 Encourage more orderly approaches to data acquisition and methods of design.[6]

Almost from the beginning there were such claims. Although some of these were valid, something was missing. The demonstrations became more seductive and the sales pitch increased, but still the conversion of nonbelievers was slow and tentative. Why?

It is clear that, at least in the early days of development, architects were being asked to commit considerable resources to a tool that offered considerable potential—as opposed to proven ability. In a sense, they were being asked to underwrite the development of computer applications implicitly. Computers required new and different skills (and staff) and signaled changes in traditional work processes. Such developmental work is common in many industries. However, most architectural firms are small in size; new equipment and staff represent a major financial commitment. Thus, many computer applications were developed by academics and experts outside architectural firms and subsequently sold to the architect as a service or product. This apparently generated the extensive claims that were seldom matched by performance. In addition, the economic slump of the early 1970s caused contraction of architectural services; services based on expansion were postponed. However, the more recent improvement in the economy and the subsequent expansion of architectural work have opened the door for computing applications. Even though architects have not fully explored the value of computers, it is clear that we are facing a geometric growth in architectural applications, coupled with a more realistic appreciation of the nature and potential of the tool.[7]

ATTRIBUTES OF COMPUTERS

For the architect and student seeking to understand the essential nature of a computer, there are some fundamental concepts, devices, and characteristics worth discussing.

Characteristics

Computers are binary and finite. Their fundamental capability depends upon the ability to sense *on/off, $\emptyset/1$, or $+/-$*. Complexity and significance of larger numbers or symbols builds on sequences or patterns of on/off sensors. Compare this to the way one human brain cell may work. We can close our eyes and remember a scene from the past, its color, smell, moisture, and temperature. Our brain senses along a continuum of possible values. A computer requires thousands of on/off switches to store one instant. In order to recognize or infer a new instant or a new context, as our brains can in a fraction of a second, a computer would require capacity still not evolved.

Computers depend upon encodement to recognize meaning. Numbers, symbols, and alphabetic letters are encoded using international conventions. For example, the letter *b* equals a 12/2 punch on a computer card that, in turn, is stored as a series of bits in an organization called a word. Words can be of varying types and significance. A machine's capacity is often rated by its word capacity—which could mean how many numbers it can store, or how many letters of text it can handle in its high access memory.

Computers are programmable. The evolution in computer science is that the languages that allow the user to build an algorithm are growing easier, more powerful, and more subtle. It is becoming less difficult to use a computer in a problem-solving process. Users can design their own problem-orientated language and instruct computers regarding the syntax and vocabulary.

Once entered, data can be stored, copied, moved, transformed, retrieved, sorted, merged, deleted, analyzed, and edited. When converted to an electronic data-processing form, information of the numeric, symbolic, or alphabetic type can be manipulated in hundreds of controlled transformations. Multibased data structure represents a most challenging problem in the use of computers in architecture. It allows data to be related in a way such that the descriptive data for one program becomes useful for another. For example, as a building design evolves, the user can describe and model each new decision and then continue to interact with more and more definitive computer programs. In more sophisticated data structures, the results of one processor are automatically added to the project's file. Thus, the process is one of buildup and accumulation of descriptive information about the project. Ultimately, computing devices may draw and print instructions on how to build the project directly from such a file.

Graphics

Besides the standard encodement of numbers, symbols, and letters, other relationships can be built into a computer. An example is the instructions required to make a vector or line on a *plotter* (an automated drawing device) or *cathode ray tube* (CRT). The start and end locations of a line are ordered pairs that are the physical coordinates of the line in space. These coordinates can be computed and stored in machine representation. The graphical inference causes a graphic device to move its marking head to the start of the line and then mark to the end of the line. This gives visible differentiation of all the points contained in the line, with only two sets of numbers stored in memory. Thus, the drawing of a wall, floor plan, or other physical object can be accomplished by identifying a series of points in space.

Another example of graphic inference is a color technique that allows the user to mix the hue and brightness of each facet in the representation of an object. With each new view from a particular vantage point, each facet is projected relative to the view. The associated color is automatically recalled and regenerated on the screen of a color CRT.

A final example of inference is the input of graphic information using a digitizer. Suppose the problem is to describe polygonal planes that are the enclosure parts of a building. A device called a digitizer and a small microprocessor can be used for the task. The digitizer senses the location of a pointer moved by the user and converts this into an X-Y coordinate in space. To start, the user will tag the plane, name it, give it some global origin, and decide what principal plane it belongs to. The user then signals that the first digitized point is to be strobed. The user would continue from point to point until the first point is strobed again. Upon sensing this the processor would complete the description and file the plane in storage. From this action the following could be computed: perimeter, area, compactness, convexity, and graphic projection from any view. These examples demonstrate the basic potential of designed computer inferences as they relate to the description of physical form and internal machine representation.

APPLICATIONS

The following examples represent the current range of applications of computers in architecture. Of course, the most sophisticated uses are found in large and innovative architectural firms, universities, and specialized consulting firms, for many smaller firms may have little or no computer capability. However, a growing number of firms of all sizes are finding significant uses for computers, from management and accounting systems to structural analysis to computer graphics. Often this occurs with the help of specialized consulting firms; more and more it involves the in-house expertise of architectural school graduates with training in computers or other computer specialists.

Site Analysis. Plan, section, and aerial perspective drawings for building sites or larger areas can be produced on a line plotter. These allow for the analysis and presentation of both natural features (topography, vegetation) and made features (structures), including the analysis of sun angles.

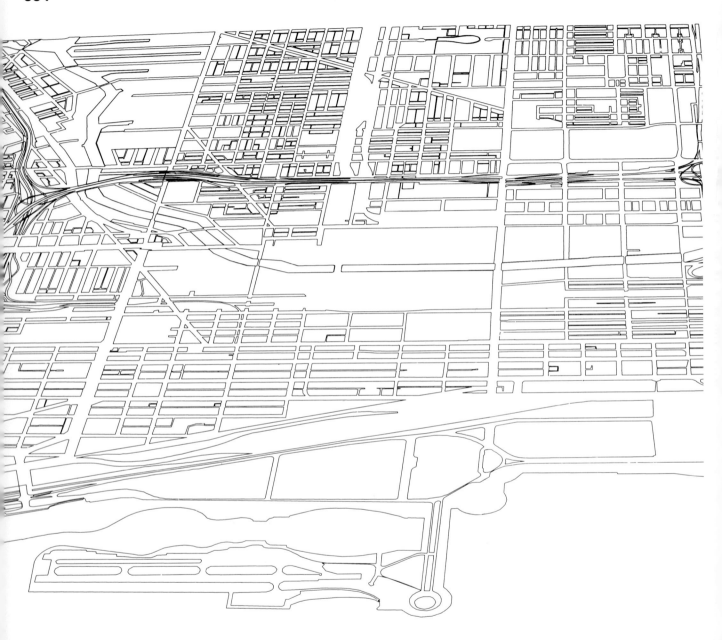

Computer Drawing: Chicago, by Skidmore, Owings, & Merrill.

COMPUTERS IN ARCHITECTURE

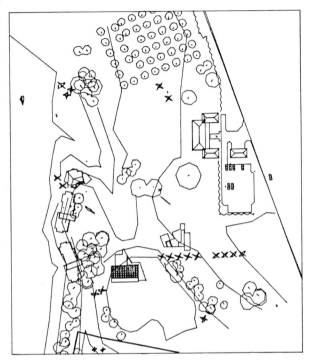

A simple site plan, by Architectural Design Graphics.

Site topography, by Architectural Design Graphics.

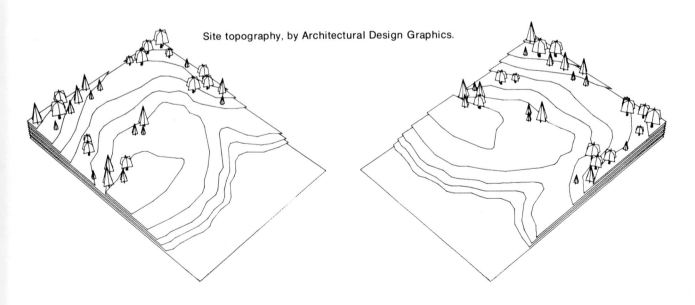

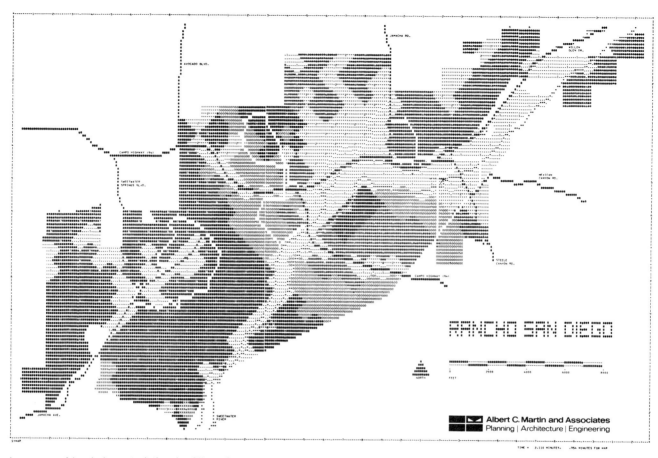

Area map of land characteristics, by Albert C. Martin and Associates.

Areal Mapping. Map drawings can be generated on printers, plotters, or CRTs. These are usually visual representations of values for a number of variables, such as environmental data (slope, vegetation, soils) or demographic data (population density, income, land cost). In addition, variables can be combined into complex factors to represent such things as ecologically critical areas, potential for development, and so on.

Sun Angles. The orientation of buildings on a site is an important aspect of site and building design, particularly with respect to energy conservation. Various graphic programs facilitate the generation of sun angle drawings, whereby one views the site and building from the angle of the sun at various times of day and year. This provides the designer with the kind of information required to select an appropriate orientation.

COMPUTERS IN ARCHITECTURE

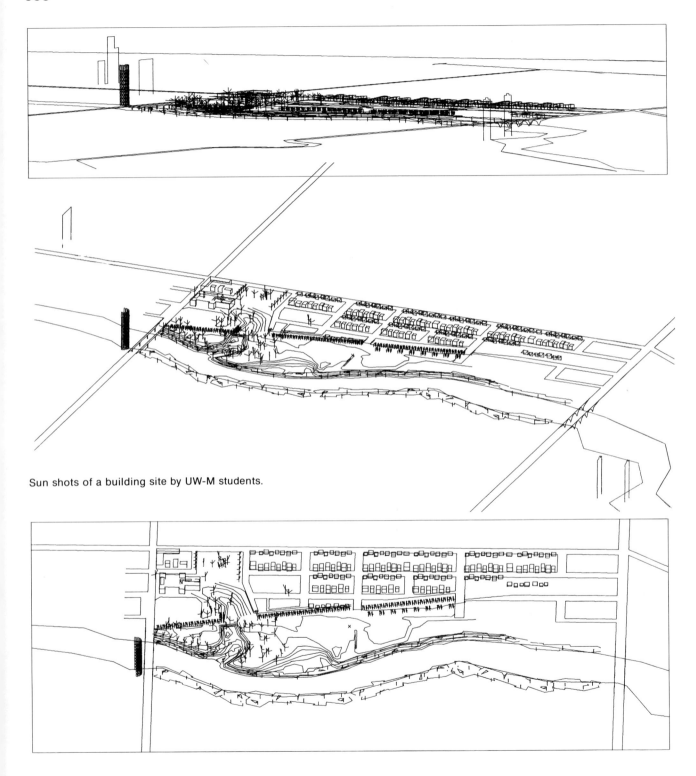

Sun shots of a building site by UW-M students.

Visualization. Predigitized library elements and digitizers facilitate the construction of visual models of buildings—which can be viewed from any position—in perspective, plan, and elevation. This type of visualization allows the designer to study

Office building perspective, by Skidmore, Owings, & Merrill.

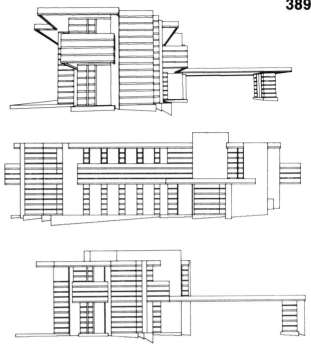

Perspective and elevations, by Architectural Design Graphics.

Interior perspective, by Ron Foran and Architectural Design Graphics.

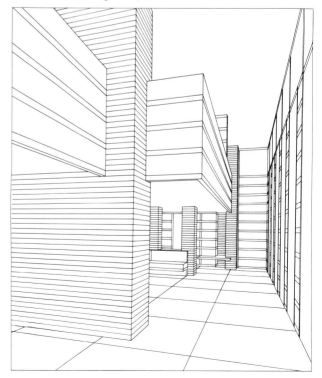

and evaluate a design from more views than are otherwise possible, with the capability to alter the design as it is viewed. In addition, these visualizations can be copied and used in client presentations.

Building Form Composition. As an extension of graphic visualization techniques, building form composition involves the generation of physical form models directly on a CRT. That is, a floor plan,

building mass, or even furniture can be designed, modified, and viewed in a number of ways. The images may be plotted at appropriate intervals. Components can be designed individually and added to a composition, or drawn from predesigned library elements.

Automated Drafting. Automated drafting involves a particular type of computer graphic whereby working and/or presentation drawings are

Floor plans, by Architectural Design Graphics.

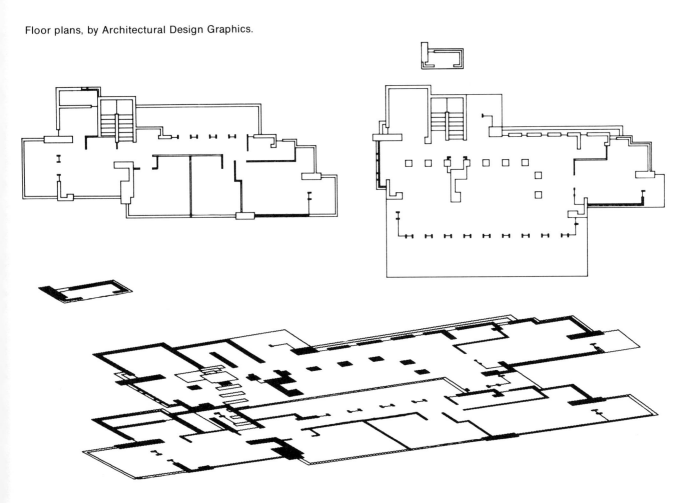

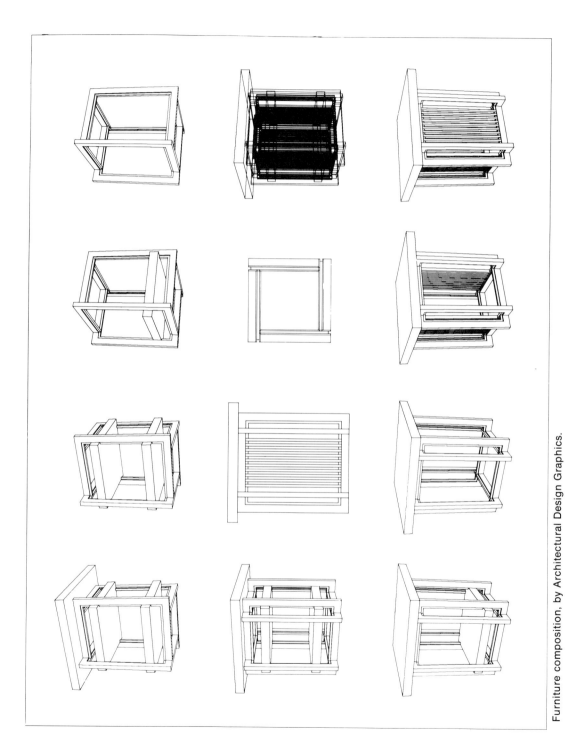

Furniture composition, by Architectural Design Graphics.

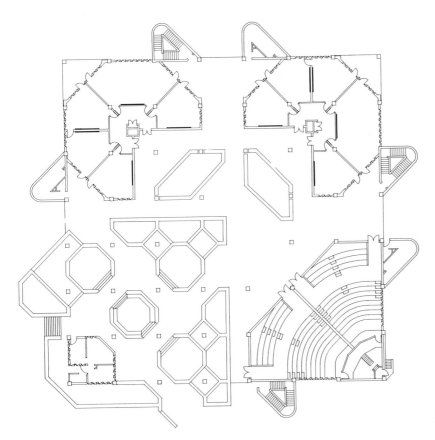

Computer plotted floor plan: Blida University, by Skidmore, Owings, & Merrill.

constructed by a plotter. These may include extensive drawings that might otherwise require an inordinate amount of drafting time, or base working drawings with appropriate annotations and titles. These drawings exhibit a high degree of accuracy and can replicate almost anything that can be done by hand, often in a shorter time.

Technological Packages. A wide range of structural, mechanical system, lighting, and acoustic analysis packages exist that allow the architect to explore the implications of numerous building alternatives as well as to design and size particular components. Computer languages for these packages

are user-oriented; analyses can often be performed on desk tops or mini-computers. This capability is well developed in the profession, with trends toward multiple analyses with a single, integrated data base (such as engineering or costs).

Building Economic Analysis and Cost Estimating. For early stages of building proposals, there exists programs for the analysis of financial consequences of alternative sites and buildings, including site development, construction, operating costs, tax implications and so forth. In the design phase, other programs are used to generate detailed

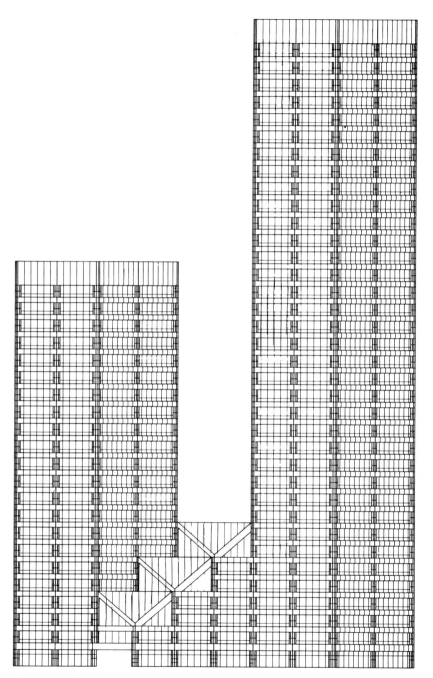

Computer plotted elevation, by Skidmore, Owings, & Merrill.

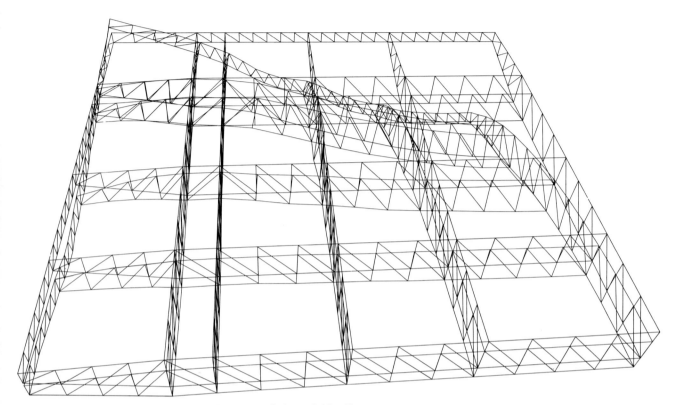

Deflected structural system analysis, by Skidmore, Owings, & Merrill.

Sample cost estimates, by Cost System Engineers, Inc.

```
                TYPE PROJECT: 82 SHOP, AUTOMOTIVE        FRAME:COMMERCIAL   MAS LO
                LAST HISTORICAL DATE:-10/76  AVE ESCL/YR     %    REPORT DATE:- 8/ 1/77

                ESCALATION (L-  0.00%),(M-  0.00%) TO  9/1977

                FLOOR AREA :        2000 SF      NO.FUNCTIONAL UNITS:     1 SHOPS
                MILWAUKEE,WIS 7/77       COST/SF:-   63.94, BASE COST/SF:-   54.59
```

SYSTEM	SYS MEAS	SYS UNIT	FLSF/ SYS U	DIR COST/ SYS U	% LAB COST	% MAT COST	% TOT COST	DIR COST/ BLDSF	TOTAL COST/ BLDSF	LABOR COST	MATERIAL COST	TOTAL COST	M/HRS
02 FOUNDTN													
B- SITEWORK		1.00		0.35	76.76	23.24	0.73	0.35	0.47	542	164	707	58
C- CONCRETE		1.00		1.19	32.54	67.46	2.48	1.19	1.58	775	1608	2384	74
D- MASONRY		1.00		0.49	44.61	55.39	1.01	0.49	0.65	433	537	971	40
G- MOISTR PROTECTION		1.00		0.05	68.02	31.98	0.10	0.05	0.06	65	30	95	6
SUB-TOTAL	2000BLDSF	1.00		2.08	43.70	56.30	4.32	2.08	2.76	1817	2341	4158	178
03 FLOOR													
C- CONCRETE		1.00		1.74	37.51	62.49	3.61	1.74	2.31	1302	2169	3472	126
E- METALS		1.00		0.19	44.70	55.30	0.39	0.19	0.25	166	205	372	14
F- CARPENTRY		1.00		0.01	68.49	31.51	0.03	0.01	0.02	19	8	28	2
G- MOISTR PROTECTION		1.00		0.00	49.81	50.19	0.00	0.00	0.00	1	1	2	0
I- FINISHES		1.00		0.23	64.95	35.05	0.47	0.23	0.30	296	159	455	26
L- FURNISHINGS		1.00		0.47	33.29	66.71	0.97	0.47	0.62	311	624	936	28
SUB-TOTAL	2000BLDSF	1.00		2.63	39.81	60.19	5.47	2.63	3.50	2097	3170	5268	196
17 EL W/AC													
P- ELECTRICAL		1.00		2.75	37.12	62.88	5.72	2.75	3.66	2045	3464	5509	149
SUB-TOTAL	2000BLDSF	1.00		2.75	37.12	62.88	5.72	2.75	3.66	2045	3464	5509	149
TOT DIR COST	$96239.				100.00	48.12				40341	55897	96239	3361
MARK-UP	$31634.				32.87	15.82				13260	18373	31633	
TOTAL COST	$127873.				132.87		63.94			53601	74271	127873	

```
                TOTAL DURATION(CREW WORK DAYS), ALL TRADES =    65 CREW/DAYS
```

cost estimates of particular design alternatives (for example, concrete or steel construction). Finally, computer programs are used to estimate final costs for purposes of bidding.

Management. There exists a large variety of computer programs related to the management functions of architectural firms. Many of these deal with the internal functions of personnel assignment, budgeting, accounting, and payroll, while others cover the scheduling of construction projects (Pro-

gram Evaluation and Review Techniques and Critical Path Methods). While the large architectural firms generally have this capability in house, many firms subcontract with consultants for these services.

Other Applications. There are a number of important additional applications of the computer in architecture. For example, there are a large number of "package," easy-to-use, statistical analysis programs that facilitate the processing of large bodies

Architectural manpower analysis, by Skidmore, Owings, & Merrill.

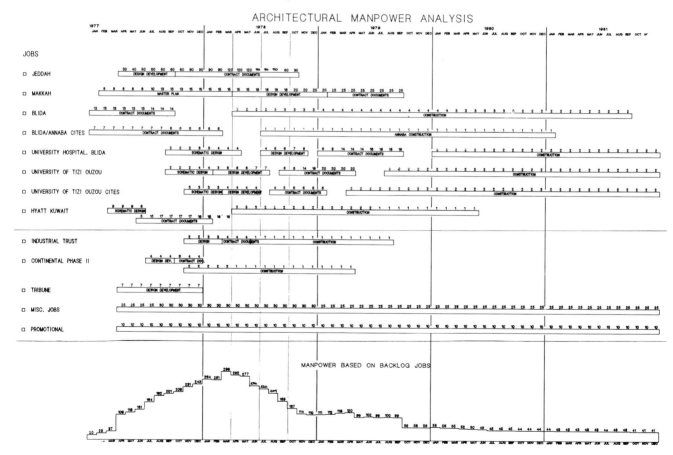

of data. The social, economic, and physical attributes of a neighborhood can be described, analyzed, and presented in a statistical format. The computer also finds application in the analysis of existing or proposed building uses in terms the interactions of users and spaces. This type of information is important to the general task of programming existing and proposed buildings. Lastly, many architectural offices have an automated specification system. That is, designers use key words to specify particular processes or materials from a library of standard specifications. The computer converts the key instructions to full specifications for contract purposes.

Building use analysis, by Albert C. Martin and Associates.

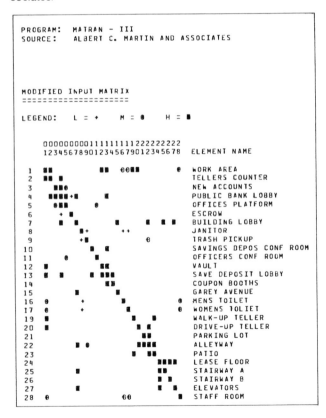

FUTURE USE

These examples demonstrate the growing use of computers in architectural practice. The early era of believers and nonbelievers is over. The pragmatic issues of the cost of hardware, language limitations, limited capability, and program instability no longer represent significant problems, even to small architectural firms. The miniaturization of electronic circuitry and diminishing development costs have led to the minicomputer. A machine that once required a room now sits on a desk top. Sophisticated machines are within the range of many architectural offices. Likewise, numerous standard software programs and easy-to-use languages can now be generated. Also, there are large numbers of persons with expertise in both architecture and the use of computers; nearly every school of architecture has some sort of computer lab and various related courses.

By now, many architectural tasks have been programmed. Some of these have been developed, used, and dropped, either because the ratio of benefits to costs was too low, because too few insights were realized, or because the tool did not fit the task. However, numerous applications have become relatively standard. Patterns of innovative, efficient, and successful use are beginning to emerge. Research and development continue. There is still a great deal of prophesying, but there is now a high correlation between what the believers are offering and what is being accomplished.

Several role models exist and will continue to exist in architectural practice. First, there is the computer specialist, who has some familiarity with architecture but whose primary training is in computer science or systems analysis. This person may work in an architectural firm, as a consultant, or in a software development firm. His or her job is to select and develop the appropriate hardware-software capability for the firm, and to develop applications for particular architectural tasks. For example, such a specialist might develop and install a structural analysis or computer graphics capability. A second role model is the architect-computer specialist. This person most likely is an architect or engineer with substantial experience in computers. He or she uses the computer for various architectural tasks, depends on the computer specialist for new developments, and transfers knowledge to interested but less-skilled colleagues. This person is an architectural specialist in applications.

Of course, the ultimate user is the practitioner. Without knowing the details of the hardware or programs, he or she will determine the applicability of the computer for various uses and, depending on the immediate situation, use the computer as an aid to the practice of architecture. This in turn requires an overview of computer capabilities and enough experience to become an efficient user or manager of computer systems.

NOTES

1. Murray Milne, ed., *Computer Graphics in Architecture and Design* (New Haven: Yale School of Art and Architecture, 1968).
2. Nicholas Negroponte, *The Architecture Machine* (Cambridge, Mass.: M.I.T. Press, 1970).
3. Kaiman Lee, *State of the Art of Computer-Aided Environmental Design* (Boston: Environmental Design and Research Center, 1970).

4. Negroponte, *The Architecture Machine.*
5. Lee, *State of the Art.*
6. Robert Mattox, "Computing," in *Current Techniques in Architectural Practice,* ed. Robert Allen Class and Robert E. Koehler (Washington, D.C.: American Institute of Architects, 1975).
7. William Mitchell, *Computer-Aided Architectural Design* (New York: Petrocelli-Charter, 1977).

FOR FURTHER READING

Eastman, C. M. *Spatial Synthesis in Computer-Aided Building Design.* New York: John Wiley & Sons, 1976.

Class, Robert Allan, and Koehler, Robert E., eds. *Current Techniques in Architectural Practice.* Washington, D.C.: American Institute of Architects, 1975.

Lee, Kaiman. *State of the Art of Computer-Aided Environmental Design.* Boston: Environmental Design and Research Center, 1970.

March, L., and Steadman, P. *The Geometry of Environment.* Cambridge, Mass.: M.I.T. Press, 1974.

Milne, Murray, ed. *Computer Graphics in Architecture and Design.* New Haven: Yale School of Art and Architecture, 1968.

Mitchell, William. *Computer-Aided Architectural Design.* New York: Petrocelli-Charter, 1977.

Negroponte, Nicholas. *The Architecture Machine.* Cambridge, Mass.: M.I.T. Press, 1970.

Part Five
Research and Evaluation

THEORY AND RESEARCH IN THE SOCIAL AND BEHAVIORAL SCIENCES	THEORY AND RESEARCH IN ENVIRONMENT-BEHAVIOR STUDIES	APPLIED ENVIRONMENT-BEHAVIOR RESEARCH	COMPILATION, TRANSLATION, & DISSEMINATION
Anthropology Geography Psychology Sociology	Man-Environment Studies Environmental Psychology Environmental Sociology Resource Management Social Ecology Social Geography Urban Anthropology Urban Sociology Human Factors	Building-Type Research, User Studies	A GAP? Extension Worker
Basic theory and research from extant disciplines	Derivation of principles, concepts, and hypotheses	Often by research-oriented planners or architects	

Research, design, and evaluation for people in environments, by Gary Moore.

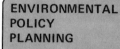

ENVIRONMENTAL POLICY PLANNING	ARCHITECTURAL PROGRAMMING	DESIGN DEVELOPMENT	POST-OCCUPANCY EVALUATION
Long-Range Planning Feasibility Studies Social Impact Assessments	Space Programming Behavioral Programming	Architecture Urban Design Schematic Design through Construction	Technical Functional Behavioral Social
	A GAP?		A GAP?
			University researchers plus consulting firms
	Architects in their offices plus consulting firms		In relation to behavioral program and other user behaviors and desires

CHAPTER 15

Research in Architecture

Uriel Cohen and Lani van Ryzin

Research is the systematic investigation of a subject in order to ascertain facts that add to the body of knowledge about that subject. While investigation is a natural human activity, research is more rigorously prescribed in terms of methods and products.

Research has always been a part of the building industry, but it has not been a large part of typical architectural practices. That is, research has been done *for* architects (by universities, research institutes, and product manufacturers) rather than *by* them. Recent years have brought significant changes:

> Research used to be considered an activity for Ph.D's in white coats, but that's changing. Many architects are getting involved in research and development these days, and. . .there is room for more.[1]

Clearly, many architects are becoming involved in conducting research for both traditional and nontraditional clients in areas such as solar applications, residents' satisfaction with housing, vandalism, environmental management, structural systems, the needs of children and elderly, and so on. In addition, a growing number of professional organizations and journals are focusing on research in environmental design and architecture, and an increasing number of government-funded projects are requiring research as a basis for design decision. Lastly, many schools of architecture offer courses in research methods; several offer doctoral degrees with a research emphasis.

RESEARCH

Inquiry is a natural human activity. People wonder about the world around them. They discover patterns or regularities as they observe the environment, and they collect ideas about how things work and are ordered. Ideas are cumulative; the body of knowledge grows.

There are several classic ways of describing the acquisition of knowledge. For example, things can be said to be known intuitively. That is, they are internalized, derived in the context of immediate experience, and described as inspirational, imaginative, and creative. Such was Plato's comprehension of the ideal. Another way of acquiring knowledge rests on authority. That is, if an expert says it is so, then it must be so. Although this may appear to be superficial, a great deal of our knowledge is handed down from generation to generation by word of mouth and recorded documents. Another form might be described as the artistic approach, whereby an artist attempts to organize complex information into a new structure, presenting in a symphony or sculpture a subjective expression of a view of the world. Lastly, there is acquisition of knowledge from reason and laws, based on an appeal to objective evidence and on logical deduction and inference, as Aristotle taught. This is termed the scientific approach.

Goals of Science

Scientific research represents a special form of inquiry, with a rigorously prescribed method. The goals of scientific research are the construction of a theory or a systematic explanation of how certain phenomena relate to each other, and the prediction of future relationships. In other words, the goal is to increase the understanding, and thus the predictability, of how things or people perform and behave. The establishment of fact in science is based on the simple question, "Do you see what I see?" That is, research findings must be universal; identical inqui-

ries under identical conditions must yield the same results. This universality of findings or replication requires a rigorous methodology; an accepted set of rules governs the process of gathering, analyzing, and presenting findings. Scientific research methodology attempts to increase the validity (does the research actually measure what was intended?) and reliability (universality) of this form of knowledge acquisition.

Theory Building From Research

In the strict classical sense, scientific research method is derived from a coupling of deductive and inductive reasoning. Deductive reasoning derives a belief about a singular situation from the general situation. That is, something existing in general must also exist for a particular case (for example, structures fail when loaded in a certain way to a certain level, and so this structure will fail if so loaded). Inductive reasoning derives general beliefs from a number of singular cases (this structure failed when loaded in a certain way, therefore any and all identical structures so loaded will fail). These ways of reasoning are coupled in a four-step process: generate hypotheses, deduce consequences, test by experiment, and confirm or fail to confirm.

Hypotheses are simply proposed theories about what is, based on initial observations, intuitions

The process of scientific research.

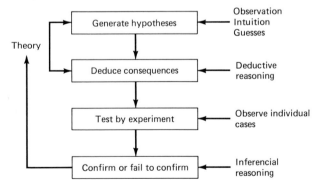

(which are part of the scientific method of research), or guesses. For example, we might hypothesize that overcrowding in public housing is associated with a high vandalism rate. If we believe this to be true in general, then it must be true in singular situations (deduction). Therefore, given the general theory that overcrowding is associated with vandalism, we might expect a particular overcrowded housing project to exhibit a high level of vandalism. In the next step, this theory is tested by an experiment (empiricism)—let us say, by measuring the rates of overcrowding and vandalism at a sample of housing sites. If the correlation of the two variables, measured statistically, is high in these individual cases (that is, if the theory holds true in the individual cases), then we might infer by inductive reasoning that the theory holds true in the general sense. The theory originally hypothesized has been substantiated. If the general theory does not hold in the experiment, then the theory has not been substantiated. This does not mean that the theory is false —only that it has not been proved.

In this way theories are developed, confirmed, and expanded; accepted theories form a base of scientific knowledge. The process is self-correcting and cumulative. The rigor of the four-step process above is not always appropriate. Yet, the orderliness and consistency of the classic concept is generally accepted as good research method. The word *research* implies a systematic method with some base in scientific inquiry.

THE FORM AND SEQUENCE OF RESEARCH ACTIVITY

Although research projects vary in a number of ways, they often follow the same form and process. The following framework illustrates a proposed plan of research or a research report organization.

1 *Context*
  Definition of the problem
  Statement of research objectives, hypotheses.
  What is already known—a literature search.
2 *Procedure*
  Research design—the strategy
  Procedures, methods, instruments.
  Data analysis—quantitative and qualitative techniques.
3 *Findings*
  Results of the investigation
4 *Conclusions*
  Hypotheses tested, confirmed
  Validity and reliability.
  Interpretations.
  Implications.
  Fit with existing knowledge.
  Support or development of theory.

The following list presents the typical process of research in terms of three stages: planning, conducting, and reporting.

1 *Planning*
  A Definition of the problem
    1 Describe the broad issue of concern.
    2 Establish the significance of the problem.
    3 State the research problem.
  B Establish the framework
    1 Review the related literature.
    2 Describe current research in terms of related work.
    3 State research questions and hypotheses.
    4 Define terms.
  C Design the study
    1 Describe the procedure to be used.
      a Selecting subjects and settings.
      b Data collection procedures.
      c Data analysis procedures.
      d Testing of instruments.
    2 Assign resources.
    3 Schedule.

2 *Conducting the Study*
  A Preparation for the study
    1 Obtain permissions, make arrangements.
    2 Organize participants, instruments.
  B Data Collection
    1 Administer instruments, make observations.
    2 Record data.
  C Data Analysis
    1 Organize and prepare data for analysis.
    2 Conduct analyses.
    3 Derive conclusions.
3 *Reporting*
  A Discussion of results
    1 Summarize results.
    2 Discuss limitations, validity, reliability.
  B Interpretations and implications
    1 Relate the findings to the research questions.
    2 Interpret findings in larger context of reviewed literature.
    3 State conclusions.
    4 Suggest applications.
    5 State implications for future study.
  C Communication of results
    1 Select format and style of presentation.
    2 Draft, edit, criticize, and revise.
    3 Disseminate.

Purposes of Research

The reasons for conducting research are probably as numerous as the projects being conducted. Each project is motivated by one or more of the following general goals: exploration, description, and explanation.

Exploration. Exploratory research is conducted in order to familiarize the researcher, and subsequently the audience, with a new topic or situation. Satisfying curiosity, testing the feasibility of undertaking a more detailed study, and developing methods for a more elaborate study are some of the reasons for exploratory research.

For example, the tenants of a large housing project may be complaining persistently about a variety of poor conditions. The researcher might wish to learn more about the situation. How widespread is the complaining? What are the main targets of the complaints? An exploratory study might be undertaken to get approximate, but seldom definitive, answers to these questions. In addition to collecting information regarding the complaints (checking the site, interviewing tenants), the researcher might explore other housing case studies, relevant literature, and other information sources. In summary, exploratory research is the attempt to develop an initial general understanding of some phenomenon.

Description. Descriptive research is the careful and rigorous observation and reporting of what exists—situations or events. For example, in the case of the housing project, a descriptive research study might attempt to report accurately the precise number of tenant complaints, classify the types of complaints and characteristics of the tenants and complainers, and report on the physical conditions of the setting.

Explanation. Explanatory research deals with the discovery of relationships among the various aspects under study. Essentially, this is the search for the "how." In our housing example, identifying and measuring the relationship between certain physical features and tenant satisfaction would constitute an explanatory study.

The relationships between factors or variables in a study can take several forms, usually expressed as mathematical functions. The weakest form of relationship is correlation, whereby two factors occur together (crowding and crime are correlated if crime is higher where crowding is higher). Correlation is not in itself explanatory; the fact that two factors behave similarly does not imply any causal relationship between them. A somewhat stronger relationship is implied with a probabilistic function in which one factor affects another with some frequency or likelihood. For example, a probability function might describe the relationship between crowding and tenant dissatisfaction. Lastly, the strongest type of relationship is called deterministic. A deterministic function holds that one factor causes another in a direct relationship. Actually, most relationships in the real world, and certainly in the social sciences, are described with correlation and probability functions. Deterministic relationships imply a certainty about the state of the world that simply does not exist in our range of knowledge. However, all three types of relationships allow for prediction, which is essential to scientific research method. Probability and deterministic functions both are explanatory and allow for tentative assumptions of causality. For example, if a study showed that long dark corridors in public buildings tended to yield high levels of vandalism, a designer might use that knowledge to design corridors in such a way as to avoid that problem.

Research Designs

A research design is a specific plan for answering research questions. The design will vary depending on the nature of the questions asked. There are three basic types of research design: controlled experiments, field experiments, and field studies.

Controlled Experiments. Testing relationships between different components of a situation often requires the maintenance of a relatively pure environment, isolated from outside interferences. This requires a strict control over the research setting, usually in a laboratorylike situation. This type of research design implies that many variables are under the control of the researcher, as with highly technical research topics. For example, the testing of the strength of structural members or the heat retention value of building materials would require a highly controlled research environment.

Field Experiments. Sometimes it is preferable to conduct research experiments in a more realistic setting, with a number of variables. In this case the researcher controls fewer of the components of the situation. This type of research design implies a less

technical situation and less accuracy of measurement. For example, a field experiment might involve identifying and measuring the relationship between lighting levels and job performance in a hospital or factory, or the effect of various patterns of public spaces on residents' social behavior in a home for the elderly. Each situation might require a number of observations to be made at various times of the day or days of the week to average out the effects of uncontrolled variables.

Field Studies. Field studies most often deal with observing and recording the perceptions, attitudes, or behavior of individuals or groups in real life situations with little or no control by the researcher. Control is not exercised either because it is not required (a windshield survey of building condition), because it is not possible (observing behavior of pedestrians leaving a stadium), or because it would result in some undesirable interference (observation of spontaneous children's games).

Emphases of Research

Research projects can be classified in terms of their research emphasis or conceptual approach. Some of the better-known distinctions relevant to architectural research are *basic* versus *applied* research, and *technical* versus *behaviorally based* research.

Basic and Applied Research. Basic research is usually aimed at the generation of new knowledge and theory building, whereas applied research seeks an answer to a practical, immediate problem. Testing a particular theory of the way children develop cognitive maps of their environment would be classified as basic research. The results would have general application. In contrast, a field experiment testing the direction-finding behavior in alternative settings of a complex hospital would have direct application to the design of circulation, signing, and other features within that specific facility. This would be classified as applied research.

Technical and Behaviorally Based Research. Some research, although ultimately contributing to human service, is related more to the characteristics of objects than to human interactions. Technical research in architecture examines topics such as the thermal conductivity of various glass types, structural strength of various bricks, or the performance of various outdoor lighting systems. This type of research is often called engineering research. Behaviorally based research, on the other hand, involves the interaction of people with components of the environment. An example of this type of research is the investigation of the developmental needs of exceptional children and the relation of these needs to the school setting.

In summary, the distinctions among the purposes, designs, and emphases of research form a convenient classification system. Actual research projects often fall between and borrow from all of the classifications. The attention of the architect is often focused on the exploratory, descriptive, and applied types of research, due to the nature of information needs in programming and design tasks. Nevertheless, it is important to remember that basic research is essential for the advance of knowledge and that it thus provides the base for applied research.

Methods of Collecting Data

Most research involves the analysis of some type of data. The collection of data is often the most time-consuming and costly part of research. The collecting of data for architectural research calls upon methods and techniques shared by many disciplines. For example, many techniques for collecting data in real-life situations are based on ecological and anthropological approaches, including making field observations, looking for physical traces of past behavior or present attitudes, and observing natural individual or group behavior. Techniques developed in the life and physical sciences are oriented to controlled experiments in the laboratory, although field applications are also common.

Techniques for data collection in the social and behavioral sciences rely heavily on individual and group responses. These include interviews, questionnaires, and tests that attempt to measure opinions, attitudes, and perceptions.

In the continuing search for new ways to answer research questions, various innovative techniques have evolved. Unobtrusive methods, such as observing physical traces in an activity space or measuring the wear on floor tiles as evidence of traffic patterns, are now in common use.[2] The most basic, popular, and cost-effective techniques in architectural research are observing and questioning. These two techniques can be used in a wide range of studies from rigorous, large-scale experiments to brief exploratory research.

Research Instruments and Analysis

The researcher is always faced with the problem of selecting the appropriate instrument for a specific study. Each instrument implies the collection of data in a particular form and consequently a specific method of analysis. Because data collection and analysis often are time-consuming and expensive, it is important that efficient combinations of instrument and method be selected.

Research instruments are too numerous to review here, but they can include questionnaires, observation checklists, behavioral maps, drawings, activity logs, recording machines, cameras, environmental measuring devices (to measure sound, light, temperature, humidity, and so on), scale models of buildings, and others. Methods of analysis are used to convert data to information. In the case of numeric data, statistical analysis is used to describe the data, test hypotheses, and draw inferences. In fact, a vast majority of research analysis depends on mathematical and/or statistical manipulation. However, graphic and literary analysis techniques are found as well in architectural research.

The adjacent figure represents various research techniques in terms of the extent of structuring and intervention needed by the researcher.

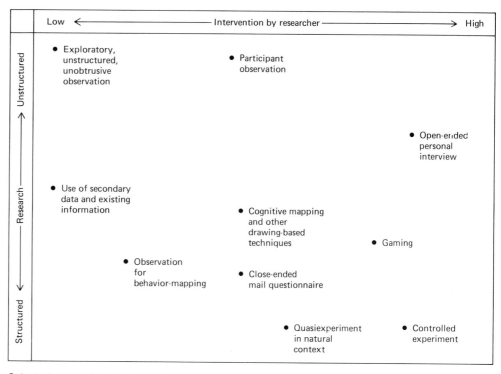

Selected research techniques by level of intervention and structuring.

RESEARCH IN ARCHITECTURAL PRACTICE

Human Needs

Although significant amounts of time and attention in architecture are devoted to purely technical and mechanical aspects in the design process, it is important to recognize that the ultimate goal of planning and design is the accommodation of human needs. As described by Robert Bechtel, "There is no such thing as the design of space or spaces: behavior, not space, is enclosed by architecture."[3] It is appropriate, then, to view all architectural research questions and objectives in a person-environment relations perspective.

Primary Domains in Architectural Research

Within the broad area of person-environment rela-

tions, there are a number of primary areas where research is needed to improve architectural design. For example, housing projects for ethnic and income mixes, barrier-free buildings, and energy conservation are just a few areas where more information is needed. All involve the interrelated components of the person-environment system.

Table 15-1 and the figure on page 408 show the main factors that influence human behavior, perception, and experience. External forces include factors in the physical environment, such as heat and humidity, and social and cultural factors, such as norms for privacy. Internal factors include physiological conditions, such as health, and the person's psychological state, which determines how all of these factors are being perceived. The relationships among these factors form the domains of architectural research.

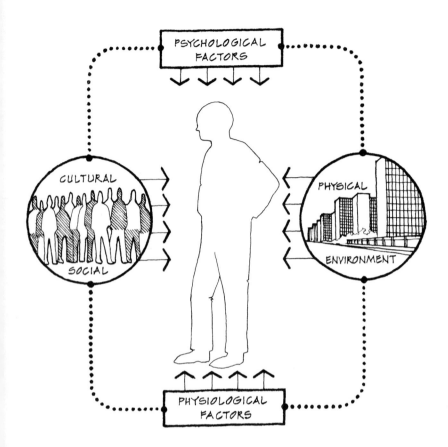

Simplified model of person-environment relationships: domains of potential research.

Research For Programming

The programming process often necessitates acquiring new information about the project users, their characteristics, their activity patterns, their preferences, and the functions for which the space is being designed. Programming researchers typically ask, "Who is doing what, with whom, where, when, and how?" The need for new information depends on various factors: the complexity of the design context, its uniqueness, the quality of available informa-tion relevant to the design in this context, and the special needs of the client. These needs will dictate the type of research required—exploratory, descrip-tive, or explanatory—as well as the scope of the research. For example, in programming a new hos-pital, the information requirements are quite com-plex. The programmer has to deal with many users—patients, nurses, doctors, aides, administra-tors, and visitors—whose needs are often conflict-ing. Rapidly changing medical technology and

TABLE 15-1

Domains of Architectural Research and Examples

Primary relationship	Example of Needed Research	Example of design application
Physiological-Physical Environment	Wheelchair users' capabilities and limitations in negotiating ramps and other circulation paths.	Design of paths, corridors, and building entrances and exits.
Social/Cultural Factors-Psychological Factors	Internal differences in norms and comfort standards for temperature; crosscultural differences in perception of crowding and density.	Design of air-handling systems and temperature levels for various tasks and contexts; space allocation and floor plan design of housing for migrant workers.
Social/Cultural Factors-Physiological Factors	Crosscultural differences in anthrophometrics.	Design of microspaces and furniture.
Psychological Factors-Physical Environment	The way spatial-perception and cognitive maps of the environment are developed.	Design of coherent circulation paths in complex facilities such as hospitals.
Social/Cultural-Physical Environment	Crosscultural differences in homemaker roles.	The design of kitchens and dining areas in ethnically dominated, working-class housing projects.
Physical Environment	Heat gain and heat loss of various glass-types.	Window design for energy conservation.

procedures require constant study and updating of information. In this case, programming cannot rely totally on past experience or existing knowledge but requires research that is uniquely applicable to the specific situation. Answering who, what, where, when, and how can provide a valuable bank of information concerning the users; their activities, needs, and preferences; and the processes and procedures that must take place in the new facility.

Research for Design

Research in the design phase involves the search for design concepts, principles, and ideas. It is concerned with the implications of the information gathered in the programming phase and with the discovery of principles for incorporating this information into the design solutions.

A design principle is a research-based guideline. It is a statement of characteristics that the built environment should have in order to respond to design problems. It serves as the link between information gathered and the design solution and presents the research data in a more general and applicable form. For example, understanding that exceptional children need spaces that will accommodate varying sizes of social groups may be helpful information for the generation of design solutions. Consider the following principle:

> *A Range of Social Scale*
> **Exceptional children have a great diversity of needs. A range of spaces in terms of size, type, and enclosure, but most especially in terms of the social scale or size of group they will contain, would provide greater opportunity for different individual and interpersonal experience and for different kinds of activities. Possibilities include open playing fields, hedges, enclosed small sand areas, a very private tree house.**

Research in design may also take the form of building typology studies. These involve the systematic collection and generation of prototypical floor plans, basic spatial configurations, or images of the building type in question. From such studies it is possible to survey the hypothesized design options available. The pattern work of Christopher Alexander and his associates captures not only the behavioral regularities in the interaction between people and their environments but also provides image-evoking illustrations.[4] Both graphic and verbal, these images can stimulate the designer's creativity and further design exploration.

Research for design should not be confused with the typical idea or solution search undertaken by the architect, which lack the rigor of research. These searches parallel the scientist's initial literature search in many ways, serving as a review of projects similar to the one being contemplated. As such, they can incorporate site visits, review of basic reference source books, and a scan of architectural magazines for examples of similar building types. However, if information gathering is limited to such searches, there is always the risk of adapting solutions that are not necessarily successful or that overlook the unique needs of the user group involved. Since the circumstances in each project are somewhat different, adapting solutions without a real understanding of their rationale creates the potential for serious misfits.

Research in Postoccupancy Evaluation

Building evaluation, postoccupancy evaluation, and *buildings-in-use* are terms describing research that focuses on completed building projects. The objectives of this type of study are to discover how the completed and occupied structure performs; to determine possible misfits, mistakes, or omissions; and to accumulate information for future programming and design efforts. Traditionally, architects receive little feedback about buildings, except from the satisfied or dissatisfied client. Because actual users often differ from clients, evaluation by the users is important for better design.

NOTES

1. John P. Eberhard, "Editorial," *Research and Design* 1 (January 1978).
2. E. J. Webb, D. T. Campbell, R. D. Schwartz, and L. Sechrest, *Unobtrusive Measures: Nonreactive Research in the Social Sciences* (Chicago: Rand McNally, 1966).
3. R. B. Bechtel, *Enclosing Behavior* (Stroudsburg, Pa.: Dowden, Hutchinson & Ross, 1977), p. vii.
4. C. Alexander, S. Ishikawa, and M. Silverstein, *A Pattern Language* (New York: Oxford University Press, 1977).

FOR FURTHER READING

Scientific Method and Research

Conant, J.B. *On Understanding Science: An Historical Approach.* New Haven: Yale University Press, 1947.

Kuhn, T.S. *The Structure of Scientific Revolutions.* Chicago: University of Chicago Press, 1970.

Research Methods and Their Application

Bechtel, Robert. *Enclosing Behavior.* Stroudsburg, Pa.: Dowden, Hutchinson and Ross, 1977.

Michalson, William. *Behavioral Research Methods in Environmental Design.* Stroudsburg, Pa.: Dowden, Hutchinson & Ross, 1975.

Webb, E.J.; Campbell, D.T.; Schwarts, R.D.; and Sechrest, L. *Unobtrusive Measures; Non-Reactive Research in the Social Sciences.* Chicago: Rand McNally, 1966.

Reporting about Environmental-Design Research Case Studies

Lang, J.; Burnette, C.; Moleski, W.; and Vachon, D. *Designing for Human Behavior.* Stroudsburg, Pa.: Dowden, Hutchinson & Ross, 1974.

Environmental Design Research Association. Annual Conference Proceedings, under different titles, annually since 1969.

Journals: *Man-Environment Systems*
            Journal of Architectural Research
            Environment and Behavior
            Research and Design

CHAPTER 16

Postoccupancy Evaluation

Harvey Z. Rabinowitz

Although postoccupancy evaluation is a relatively new term in architecture, the concept has already had a significant impact. Modern buildings are structurally sound, free of fire hazards, and sanitary. These attributes were much less common before the advent of building codes, which are based on evaluations. These codes and subsequent building evaluations have great influence on building design. For example, the use of asbestos for fireproofing, design for energy conservation, sprinklers for fire protection, access for the handicapped, and lower quantities of artificial lighting are some of the features now being evaluated in terms of building code modifications, which in turn will affect building design.

Although building codes are an obvious example of the influence of evaluation on architecture, other types of evaluations are common. Building owners often conduct such studies, as do architectural critics. The users of a building certainly evaluate their environment. However, the subject of this chapter is the type of evaluation that produces codes —that is applied, rigorous, disseminated, and above all, useful in the design process in terms of technical and functional decisions and the way the building can affect user behavior.

Buildings are evaluated for the same important reasons that products are—to prevent failure (which in buildings can result in accidents, disfunction, or misfit), to provide good value for the building users and accountability for those responsible for its implementation, and to provide real increments of progress in terms of advancing the field or product.

Buildings provide a safe, protected, and sanitary environment with enough area for anticipated activities. They also create a setting in which privacy and social interaction are accommodated. They provide space for the implements that we need to carry on our activities, and an image that is appropriate and appealing for the uses to which they are put. They can contain an emotional context of awe, delight, trust, solidity, comfort, or richness. Buildings are also part of a continuing aesthetic legacy. Finally, they are extremely expensive, and mistakes stay with us for a long time.

Given that the built environment is always with us, and that architects are responsible and accountable for a large part of this environment, the importance of building evaluation in architecture cannot be overstressed. However, architects and others responsible for building design rarely examine, in a formal and comprehensive manner, the environment they have helped create, even though such examination is one of the primary methods through which better buildings can be created.

THE DEVELOPMENT OF POSTOCCUPANCY EVALUATION

As part of the architectural design and building process, programming plays a key role in suggesting and defining many basic design parameters. Programming is the perscriptive tool used by designers in developing solutions. One step is missing, however, in the existing view of the process—an evaluation or diagnostic step to monitor the quality of the building. We need a diagnosis before we can prescribe. Postoccupancy building evaluation is the new diagnostic step in the process. Its goal is analagous to that of the use of precedents in law or the case study method in business; that is, to make better decisions with a knowledge of the consequences of decisions made in the past. We want to learn from past experience. As Oscar Wilde put it, "Experience is a word we use to describe our mistakes."

Architectural programming techniques, first developed in the late 1950s and early 1960s, had evolved considerably by 1970. It is said that quantitative changes eventually lead to qualitative changes. So it was with many programming tech-

niques; they outgrew their efficiency and usefulness when they became overly systematic and rigorous. They evolved into postoccupancy evaluation, more formal research based on an analytical field of inquiry. The first formal and comprehensive postoccupancy evaluations took place in Great Britain. The Pilkington Research Unit at Liverpool University and the Building Performance Research Unit at the University of Strathclyde in Glasgow studied office buildings and high schools.[1] These studies included technical, functional, and behavioral eval-

The building process.

The building process with evaluation.

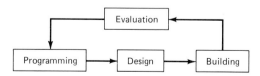

uations. In the United States, at the Buildings in Use Study at the University of Wisconsin-Milwaukee, Department of Architecture evaluated four elementary schools.[2] The common denominator of these studies was a rigorous approach to diagnosis and a comprehensiveness in examining numerous factors—technical, constructional, material, functional, and behavioral. These comprehensive studies are the exception. More numerous are studies concentrating on a few aspects of the entire spectrum of variables. Clare Cooper's *Easter Hill Village* and Oscar Newman's *Defensible Space* are among the most extensive of these studies.[3] They both concentrate on the relationships between physical design and behavior.

Postoccupancy building evaluations are now slowly becoming institutionalized and acknowledged. The *Architects' Journal,* a British weekly architectural magazine, has carried and even sponsored such building appraisals since the late 1960s.[4] The *American Institute of Architects Journal* began a series of evaluations in 1976.[5] This may signal the beginning of a cycle that, like programming before it, may take a decade or more to become a standard part of architectural practice.

Types of Evaluation

Postoccupancy evaluation focuses primarily on three factors—technical evaluation, functional evaluation, and behavioral evaluation. These relate to the architect's concerns in building design and to the classification of architectural literature, as well as to the perception of the building by both client and inhabitants.

Technical factors are the buildings' background environment; the often unnoticed backdrop to our actions and behavior. How often are fire exits, lighting fixtures, or air conditioning diffusers consciously noticed? Although we expect a high level of performance from this background environment, the object of our attention is more often the functional aspect of the environment. *Functional factors* support the activities within the building. For

example, book storage is a key item in a library; shopper circulation is a prime functional consideration in a store. *Behavioral factors* can have a great effect on the users of the building. The quality of behavioral factors such as morale, security, and communication can be affected by building design.

TECHNICAL EVALUATION

Buildings must provide basic shelter and a sustaining environment. Early shelters created an "inside" to keep the outside (elements and animals) "outside." This remains the highest of building priority—to exclude heat, cold, rain, snow, animals, and vermin. We also expect our buildings to be sanitary, safe from collapse, and safe from fires. We expect them to provide satisfactory illumination, control of sound, and thermal comfort. Finally, we expect these attributes to last for the lifetime of the building.

Building Codes

The attributes we expect from the built environment are taken for granted; they represent a minimum level of expectation. That virtually all of the environment meets these standards is the result of an excellent evaluation and feedback process, reflected in building codes that regulate structure, sanitation, ventilation, health, and fire safety in buildings. In addition, we have a society that can afford to build to meet these code requirements. Though they are sometimes perceived as being engraved in stone, building codes are always changing to reflect technological advances, research findings, and societal needs. Behind these legal strictures is an apparatus of many organizations, including the National Bureau of Standards (a government agency doing basic research on building materials and systems); the American Society for Testing and Materials (devising tests and standards for building products); regional code groups such as the Southern Building Code Group (which develops and pro-

			Scale of Physical Environment		
			Equipment	Rooms and Spaces	Entire Building
Categories of Research	Technical	Exterior wall Roof Energy Fire safety Structure Interior finishes Illumination Acoustics HVAC		▒▒▒	▒▒▒
	Functional	Workflow Human factors Storage Flexibility and change Circulation	▒▒▒	▒▒▒	▒▒▒
	Behavioral	Use Proximity Territory Privacy Interaction Image		▒▒▒	▒▒▒

Matrix: types of evaluation.

mulgates building standards especially responsive to regional characteristics); the National Fire Protection Association (an organization sponsored by insurance companies that develops standards concerning fire aspects of building codes); and other organizations including manufacturers, industry associations, unions, building owners, architects, and contractors. Sometimes even building users, such as the handicapped, can exert influence to change codes. Change in building codes sometimes comes slowly because health, safety, and welfare are often taken for granted. However, failure in this area can be catastrophic. For example, particles of asbestos used for fireproofing and acoustical purposes have been found in the air of some buildings; asbestos is now believed to be a carcinogen and may be harmful to the occupants of these structures.

Noncode Regulation

Some technical factors are either not regulated or only minimally regulated. Problems or failures with exterior walls, roofs, interior finishes, lighting, and acoustics may make a building undesirable, expensive to operate, and to some degree unusable, but they are not in the code purview of protecting individuals and society from harm. Though more flexibility exists in these areas, there are also many organizations promulgating standards, devising tests, and conducting research and evaluation. For instance, the U.S. Department of Housing and Urban Development (HUD) has Minimum Property Standards that must be met in government subsidized or guaranteed housing, and financial institutions giving mortgage loans often have standards in these areas. Organizations such as the Illuminating Engineering Society (IES) have lighting standards that are commonly used. Many of these noncode technical factors, though not legally binding, are monitored through a number of mechanisms that almost have the force of a building code.

Evaluation of Technical Factors

Most evaluation of building performance now occurs in the technical area. Technical factors are the easiest to evaluate with instruments and thus the results are most objective; this area is most important to evaluate because of the potential for less than useful or even dangerous buildings if problems or failures occur. In addition technical solutions are the least amenable to adaptation or modification in the physical sense; they must be done right the first time. One of the architect's prime concerns is to ensure adequate performance of the components of the building in this most basic area of responsibility. That many common problems continue to occur is due to the almost complete lack of formal, or even informal, evaluation and feedback in the design process.

Technical factors in buildings lend themselves easily to evaluation by instruments and rigorous examination, since they are directly concerned with the materials and construction methods of the background environment for which there are precedents in measurement, analysis, and performance. An example is the way acoustics are evaluated. Acoustics are measured primarily within rooms, and, for sound transmission, between rooms. Four acoustical tests are usually administered—for ambient or background noise, for reverberation, for sound transmission, and for equipment noises. Since most existing tests are laboratory based, field test versions are developed (although in acoustics there are some standard field tests). A sound level meter and octave band analyzer are used to gather data. Finally, the results are compared to standard criteria, and an evaluation is made.

The technical factors most commonly evaluated are exterior walls, roofs, fire safety, structure, interior finishes, illumination, acoustics, and HVAC (heating, ventilating, and air conditioning) systems.

Exterior Walls. Exterior walls, along with roofs, constitute the enclosure part of the building. Not only must walls prevent weather from affect-

PHYSICAL ENVIRONMENT
ROOMS, SPACES: eg CLASSROOMS

RESEARCH CATEGORIES
TECHNICAL: eg. ACOUSTICS

1. AMBIENT NOISE — dbA/NC
2. ATTENUATION — db.
3. REVERBERATION — R_T
4. SPECIAL: eg. BALLAST, MECH.

Matrix Intercept.

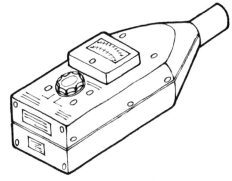

Test Instrument: sound level meter.

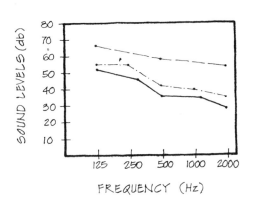

ROOM 'A' — — — —
ROOM 'B' — · — · —
RECOMMENDED ———

Results and criteria.
Acoustical tests.

ing the interior, but they must also resist deterioration due to temperature, moisture, wind, and vandalism. Typically, the critical points in this evaluation are joints, such as at material changes, doors and windows, and expansion joints. Some tests in this area include weathering, moisture penetration, wind infiltration, and heat loss. Wind infiltration and temperature transmission, traditionally unregulated, are now found in most codes due to the efforts of public and private agencies, manufacturers, and individuals in supporting and developing standards to respond to the energy crisis.

Current energy research and standards promulgation is probably the most explicit example of the use of technical postoccupancy evaluation. Evaluations of the use of energy are now being performed—formally and informally—by a large number of building owners. The building is usually measured as a whole, with the gauge being the fuel bill; the result is almost always poor performance. The amount of energy expended can be determined individually for loss through walls and roof, heating during nonuse hours, outside air usage, energy storage effects, lighting, water heating, and so on.

The architect's role in energy conservation is especially germane. The form of the building; its orientation, materials, and surfaces; the design of its lighting, heating, air conditioning, and ventilation, are all affected if energy is to be conserved. This area is especially amenable to predictions of energy use before construction, made by comparing the design alternatives to projected energy budgets.

Durability, another measure of performance, is important in evaluating exterior walls. Although walls are designed to last forty years or more, the immediate and cumulative effects of expansion, contraction, moisture, and frost can cause a range of unwanted results. Cracks, spalling, buckling, straining, and leaks are typical problem conditions. Aesthetics must also be considered, because the exterior wall provides the principal image of the building.

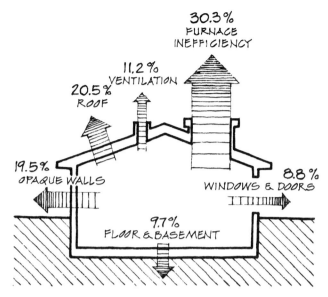

Energy loss.

For instance, dirt flowing off exterior window sills during rains can produce the undesirable effect of "whiskers" at window locations.

Roofs. Though quite similar to exterior walls in function, roofs have some particular requirements. Roofs provide an impervious, jointless, and monolithic surface, much like a tent, to keep water out of the building. They are the most exposed of all building components because of their horizontal, or near horizontal, character and the relatively "soft" nature of their materials. Roofs have the most frequent problems and failures of any building element because of their vulnerability; thus, they require extreme care in design and construction. Though problems can occur almost anywhere on exposed surface areas, roof penetrations (vents, exhausts, and skylights) and joints with exterior walls are especially susceptible. Human activities on roofs, however infrequent, can also damage fragile surfaces.

Roof failures become self-evident as water leaks inside a building; usually they can be traced to the offending area. Deterioration of roofing materials, such as cracking, blistering, peeling, and the like, is easily visible upon visual examination. Ponding (when considerable water remains on the roof surface) is also clearly evident. All these conditions undoubtedly shorten the life of a roof.

The high frequency of roofing problems, which are often frustrating and costly to repair, is one of the key technical areas for architects, clients, and evaluators to consider in terms of providing increased performance capabilities. Often, this factor is not given sufficient attention. Because failures can occur (due to construction defects and stresses during the life of the building) designing for durability in excess of typical standards should be considered for roofs.

Fire Safety. Fire safety in buildings is evaluated by careful examination of the architect's design (drawings) to determine whether the building meets the criteria set forth in the building code. The circulation, construction type, and materials must

Roof ponding.

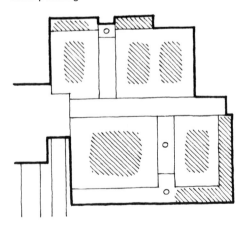

 AREAS OF PONDING

meet standards for fire exits, fire resistivity, flame spread, and amount of smoke produced. Failure to comply in this area is rare because of strict enforcement. However well buildings are evaluated before and during construction, the use of some buildings may, in fact, change over their useful lives. Fire exits and corridors may sometimes be used for storage or activities instead, and wall coverings with a high flame spread can cover original and safer surfaces. Fire doors are sometimes closed and locked for security reasons, creating a most dangerous condition. Also, overoccupancy can become a problem. Even the paper in an office, exposed and present in large quantities, can be a serious hazard. Postoccupancy evaluation in these areas is fairly straightforward and involves inspections by fire marshalls—but it does not always occur. Fire research and building failures in this area are now having an effect on building codes. Codes once regulating fire spread alone now recognize that injuries and death caused by smoke, superheated gas, and toxic products are more frequent occurrences. Also recently recognized are fire safety problems brought about by the unregulated use of interior furnishings. Nonregulated items may produce high amounts of toxic gas and smoke and increase flame spread. Furniture specifications are beginning to include fire-related criteria, especially important in hospitals and other institutions.

Structure. Like fire safety, structural concerns are most rigorously regulated by building codes. While on occasion failure may occur during construction, failure during occupancy is very rare under normal conditions. However, inadequate structural design may occur, and this is compensated for by the use of safety factors in building codes (in a sense, mandatory overdesign.). Even so, failures still occur. For some years in Britain, a high alumina content was used in reinforced concrete; it eventually deteriorated the steel reinforcement, causing structural failure. This concrete can be found in thousands of buildings in Britain, and though a number have collapsed, it is not really known if all are in danger.[6]

Interior Finishes. Interior finishes include the finishes of the floors, ceilings, and interior walls. The evaluation of these finishes is important more because of contact between the users and these surfaces than because of code considerations. The floor must have strong resistance to indentation, scratch, and wear, as well as providing resiliency for user comfort. Other attributes neccessary for the floor, and to a lesser extent for the walls and ceilings, include cleanability, stain resistance, slip resistance, cigarette burn resistance, abrasion, adhesion, color fastness, lack of static discharge, delamination, water absorption, scratch resistance, brittleness, resiliency, and impact resistance.

Sometimes, unanticipated conditions are found during evaluation. A study that included the evaluation of the wall of an elementary school found a line of dirt some 2 feet above the floor on the otherwise white walls. In another wing of the same school, the same phenomonen occurred, but some inches higher. Pupils of different ages occupied these respective wings and ran their hands on the walls as they walked. Brightly painted stripes at the appropriate heights were recommended to alleviate the condition.[7]

Most testing in this area is done by minute observation of existing conditions. If possible, samples of unused original materials are compared with those in place. The concept behind this and some other areas of technical factors is that the building environment has already been thoroughly tested. For instance, flooring surfaces have been tested by the building occupants for years by being stained, scratched, abraded, and otherwise used; we only have to examine the results of this testing. This method is more accurate than laboratory simulation tests, though it takes a longer time.

Illumination. The evaluation of illumination in buildings should go far beyond measuring quantity and must include measures of direct and reflected glare. Today only minimal and quantitative lighting standards are required by building codes. Quantitative lighting standards have been increasing for years; offices with over 100 footcandles of general illumination are not uncommon. Recently, however, because of concern over energy, these high levels have been seriously questioned. They are costly in terms of energy and may be only marginally productive in terms of additional visual acquity. Qualitative factors have proven as important as the quantity of lighting in providing visual comfort, and a shift to specific task lighting, minimizing general illumination, is taking place.

The quality and the quantity of existing lighting can be accurately evaluated with instruments. Although criteria are available, they too are undergoing further study in view of the energy crisis and new research in the field. Many new buildings do not do much more than meet the recommended quantita-

Isolumens and light distribution.

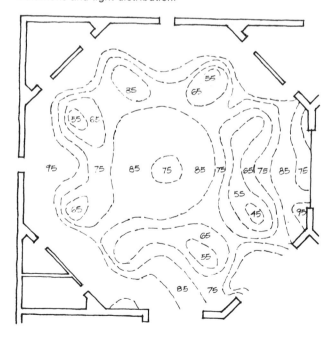

420

tive criteria. Quantitative measurements (in footcandles) are still made, but these are only one aspect of an evaluation that now includes sources of direct glare (including windows), reflected glare, and contrast ratios.

Acoustics. Generally, the subject of acoustics is not even represented in building codes, even though it is an important part of building design. Sound control includes regulating the background or ambient sound levels, the transmission and absorption of sound between areas (to ensure privacy) and any reverberation of sound or "echo" that affects clarity and loudness. Sound transmission from building machinery such as motors, fans, pumps, and lighting must also be considered. Acoustical problems are common, and no one type seems to predominate. A long-term trend to lighter construction methods and the increasing use of large open spaces in offices and schools may exacerbate some acoustical problems. Test methods and solutions are well known and can be applied to traditional rooms. For large and unusual spaces, there are few precedents and recognized standards. Field evaluation of background noise, equipment noise, and sound transmission and attenuation can be made with a sound level meter and existing field test procedures. More complex conditions, such as reverberation, structure-borne vibration, open plans, and auditorium acoustics, require professional consultation. Clients must be made aware of the necessity for proper acoustical design, in view of the frequency and persistance of shortcomings in this area.

Heating, Ventilating, and Air Conditioning. While a large number of heating and cooling sources, media for delivery, and terminal devices exist, their common goal is to deliver thermal comfort. This requires having proper temperature and humidity, air movement, and radiative effects. Typical standards in this area are quite high, so lower

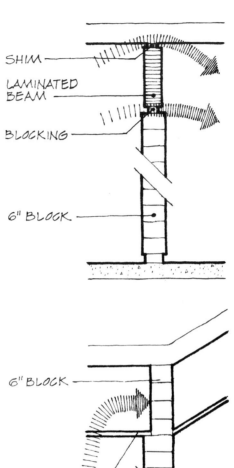
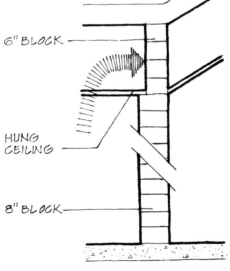

Airborne noise.

standards brought about by concern for energy use are still within the range of acceptability. In fact, rates of ventilation even lower than code standards have not been perceived by building users, indicating the existence of general overdesign in this area. Evaluation is based on results obtained from instruments; good criteria do exist, though, and as mentioned earlier, existing practice goes beyond these standards in many situations.

FUNCTIONAL EVALUATION

Functional factors are those aspects of a building that directly support user activities and organizational performance. For example, floors, ceilings, and acoustics do not directly support user activity; they constitute the background environment. But storage and the placement of adjacent areas to enhance work flow directly support user activity and organizational performance. Functional considerations are integral to the overall success of the building. Unsatisfactory design decisions can inhibit functions and result in monetary loss or serious inefficiencies. Failure here, unlike the failure of technical factors, can be subtle or produce ungainly adaptations.

The architect, dealing with function, is concerned with the connection between areas and activities inside the building; access for users and materials; the provision of services, such as utilities; storage; and the correct dimensional fit of the environment for specific user groups. In addition, specific building types require an emphasis on special needs such as security, supervision, flexibility, materials movement, and queuing. Many building types have guidelines for design that emphasize functional factors. However, few are based on adequate research and evaluation; many are too general to be of sufficient use in architectural design. Some exceptions exist. For example, many supermarket corporations have impressive design rulebooks based on extensive evaluations of their facilities, as do some fast-food chains.

Precedents, official tests, measures, and criteria are not as prevalent in the functional realm. Certain measures, such as dimensional fit, are quite direct and have adequate criteria; others, such as flexibility, have not had the benefit of sufficient research.

The range of measurement techniques varies widely. Here, we begin to employ direct observation of user activities. In measuring workflow and occupant movement, we observe the building users over some time, record their activities, and analyze the data to see if inefficiencies exist. Also used are unobtrusive measures, or indirect clues to user activities. For instance, the informal network of paths worn on the grass lawns of college campuses can be an unobtrusive indicator of an unfilled need for circulation routes. Recorded data is also used to measure functional factors. For example, hospital renovation records may help to determine the need for flexibility in future hospital designs.

Locational Grouping. Workflow is a most critical issue in the functioning of any facility. This is the concept of grouping or separating areas in the building in order to influence communication and the movement of people and work. The architect's design decisions in this area can seriously affect the delivery of services or goods by an organization. For example, classes adjacent to the library in many elementary schools tend to use that facility more often than other classes. Likewise, open office plans use proximity as a technique for arranging desks in an open office, based on work flow and the need for communication. An extensive study of these patterns is required before such a plan can be developed.

Circulation. Like functional grouping, circulation is an important factor in building design; it is a key factor in building function. The design of circulation can influence the utilization of various parts of a

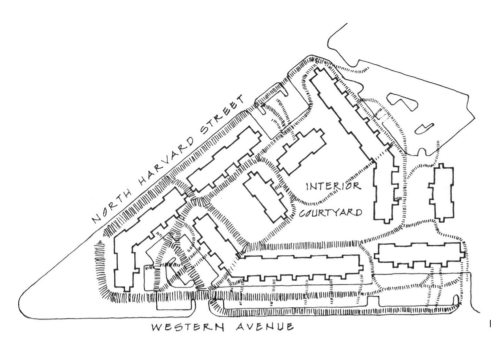

NORTH HARVARD STREET

INTERIOR COURTYARD

WESTERN AVENUE

Pedestrian circulation in housing.

building, as well as crowding, security, orientation, and operating costs. For example, inefficient circulation of personnel in hospitals produces very high costs, which can be reduced through design. A rigorous study of hospital circulation that built three floor plan configurations as an experiment found that a radial plan yielded the least amount of unnecessary circulation and better patient care.[8] In supermarkets, maximizing circulation, or workflow, is extremely important in generating additional sales. Inevitably, the staples such as dairy products, eggs, and bread are placed in the most remote part of the store, thus increasing the amount of circulation necessary and exposing the shopper to the largest possible number of goods. Efficient circulation is also critical to building owners in making the most of usable area. Industry standards calling for 85 percent leasable office building space or 90 percent efficient apartment building space are widely used.

These types of evaluations, both formal and intuitive, have produced excellent information for architects, but they are limited examples in highly structured building contexts. More evaluation is needed in less structured situations with more decision choices. For example, many major buildings have both front and back entrances, with the back entrances having little visual significance and fewer doors. Yet in many cases, the back door is used almost as much as or more than the front entrance. *Charlesview Housing,* a study by Zeisel and Griffin, documents the fact that circulation paths in many cases may not be congruent with the architect's design intentions for paths and spaces.[9]

Human Factors. The study of human factors is a discipline concerned with developing standards and designs that match the dimensions, configurations, and materials of the environment to its users. The bulk of human-factors evaluation takes place in the area of equipment design, but some important work is being developed in architecture. Kiras' rigorous work on bathrooms is a classic example.[10] Traditional bathroom equipment is shown to be poorly designed from a number of viewpoints; new designs, quite free of existing precedents, are presented.

Although most building users can adapt to dimensions and configurations that may not conform to correct human-factors criteria, there are uses and users for whom such close tolerances are critical. An evaluative study of cardiac care facilities made many recommendations for improving efficiency and performance during emergency procedures, when time and accuracy are critical.[11] Likewise, evaluations of buildings for use by handicapped persons have revealed many needless deficiencies; based on these evaluations, most building codes now require that architectural design accommodate handicapped users.

Improvised storage.

Storage. Storage is important in almost all activities within a building, yet it has not had much evaluation. Studies that have included this factor have usually found provisions for storage to be deficient; usually insufficient capacity is the problem, but other variables include location, allocation, and configuration. Storage can usually be evaluated by unobtrusive measures, because there are adequate signs of performance in this area. One study of schools found that some teachers actually brought their own storage cupboards to school or improvised storage space from existing materials.[12] Sometimes storage overflowed into hallways; coat storage cupboards were appropriated for teaching materials; and almost every horizontal surface was laden with assorted items. In one school with quite large amounts of classroom storage, there was adequate capacity for that use. However, additional storage for teachers' materials was necessary. We can also categorize storage by the size of the objects sorted and the frequency of their use. Both the study of schools and the St. Francis Square Housing Study found specific needs in these categories unsatisfied.[13]

Flexibility and Change. Flexibility is an increasingly important consideration in architectural design. Potential and anticipated changes in function, philosophy, size, or area must all be accommodated. The past two decades have seen significant changes in organizational structure and processes and in attitudes towards the use and reuse of older buildings. For example, open school and office plans, a departure from tradition, have become common; older, more compartmentalized buildings cannot accommodate the required large spaces. More recently, there has been a tendency to subdivide the open schools. Obviously, educational philosophy changes faster than buildings—which often last forty to eighty years or more. Hospital and laboratory design has also responded to flexibility. One evaluative study of hospitals found that interstitial servicing floors between normal activity floors are less expensive for specialized departments, such as radiology, because of the high potential need for changes in servicing infrastructure.[14] Studies such as these also point out, however, that there are many functions that should *not* have a high degree of built-in flexibility.

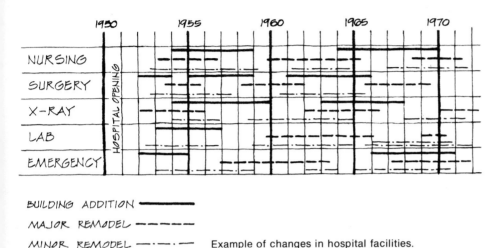

BUILDING ADDITION ●——————

MAJOR REMODEL ——————

MINOR REMODEL ——·——·—   Example of changes in hospital facilities.

Information about functional factors is primitive compared to what is known of technical factors. Only certain proprietary uses, such as supermarkets and hotels, have had rigorous and continuous study. Other building types, such as housing for the elderly and for families, facilities for the handicapped and the retarded, preschools, elementary schools, and playgrounds are now being formally and comprehensively evaluated. While functional factors are more directly related to organizational goals, the evaluation of behavioral factors has a conceptual framework focused more on users' responses.

BEHAVIORAL EVALUATION

Behavioral factors emphasize the relationship between behavior and the physical environment. Some of the issues explored in this area are: Is the building being used as intended in the original design? How does the size of the facility affect its users? What does the building's image imply to the users and the community? How does the proximity of areas in the building affect the frequency of their use? Does the configuration of rooms and materials affect user behavior? How do other factors combine with the physical environment to affect users?

Research and evaluations indicate that the physical environment can profoundly affect behavior. Such research efforts are growing rapidly in universities and in government, but applications are rare in architectural practice. Though decisions made by architects strongly affect the users of buildings and the economic success or failure of the building, the architect's use of behavioral design input is infrequent. What are the reasons for this lapse?

We are really talking about a problem of the architectural profession as a whole and not of the individual practitioner, who, notwithstanding his or her intentions and ideals, does have limited resources. The profession does not now have a research bias, appropriate resources, or a sufficient cadre of persons involved in such work. Only recently have some changes begun that may correct this state of affairs, but even with such changes, sufficient penetration of these ideas in the profession will take some time. One problem has been the small amount of information in this area applicable to design. The classic 1948 study by Festinger and others that linked physical design and social relationships in housing stood as a singular example in the field until the late 1960s.[15] This important work was not enough of a critical mass to move the architectural profession off base. So there have been dual problems—the lack of evaluative research understandable to architects and applicable to their design projects, and an attitude in the profession that is not conducive to research.

The first trend towards inclusion of behavior information in design might be traced back to Alexander and Chermayeff's *Community and Privacy* and much of the subsequent work of Alexander. *Community and Privacy* included extensive lists of user needs, requirements, and patterns that helped prepare the framework for later architects' evaluative studies. By the 1970s such user needs studies were common programming devices in architectural practice.

"Evaluative" studies of behavioral factors began emerging in the late 1960s; *Dorms at Berkeley* by Sim Van Der Ryn and Murray Silverstein, *Personal Space* by Robert Sommer, and *Big School, Small School* by Roger Barker and Paul Gump were influential.[16] In England, the Pilkington Research Unit at the University of Liverpool and the Building Performance Unit at the University of Strathclyde, Scotland, conducted comprehensive building evaluations that were later published. John Zeisel at Columbia University and Clare Cooper at the University of California, Berkeley were also involved in essential work.[17] Government agencies such as the National Bureau of Standards under John Eberhard, the National Institute of Mental Health, and in England the Ministry of Housing and Local Government were also funding significant research and publications. Finally, the Environmental Design Research Association (EDRA) was formed in 1969, giving more formal recognition to the field and a "home" to many architectural researchers, and providing a necessary forum for communication.

Form Follows Fiasco (1970) and *The Master Builders* (1962), both by Peter Blake (a noted architect and writer), together represent a barometer of how far architectural attitudes have changed.[18] Constance Perin's *With Man in Mind*, Brent Brolin's *Failure of Modern Architecture,* and the Royal Institute of British Architects' *Crisis in Architecture*, written by Malcolm McEwan, all further reinforce the need for reviewing priorities in the profession, and especially the need for building evaluation and the use of behavioral input in building design.[19] Another strong institutional indicator of a change in attitude towards building evaluation is a series of such case studies begun in 1977 in the *American Institute of Architects Journal.*[20] This is the first extension of the AIA into this area. As the number of such studies increases and the evidence of tangible benefits grows, greater architectural application may make evaluation a common aspect of professional services as programming is today.

The Context of Behavioral Factors

While technical and functional factors produce results that are often direct cause-and-effect relationships, are uninvolved with values and philosophies, and relate to well-known goals and requirements, behavioral evaluations are more tenuous and elusive in all of these areas. Establishing and measuring the relationships between physical environment and resulting user behavior in that environment is difficult. In many situations, other nonphysical environment variables may be more important to behavior. Hertzberg's theories on motivators in the work environment place the physical environment low on the list as a "neutral" motivator.[21] In any environment, the organizational rules, leadership, compensation, tasks, climate, and other factors may all effect behavior more than the physical environment does.

Relationships between environment and behavior are also difficult to establish because they can be voluntary. Environments in which behavior is largely procedural and sequential, such as airport departure gates, yield responses that are largely automatic, although there are a few voluntary components. Voluntary behaviors predominate, however, if free choice exists. Behavior will not be automatic or even consistent; in fact, some environments may produce infrequent but important responses, making relationships even more difficult to ferret out.

A final complication is the diminished effect of environmental stimuli on behavior through habituation. An amusement park may be absolutely thrilling on the first or even the second visit, but constant contact will have a satiating effect. Our typical environment is often less stimulating than an amusement park, and a satiating effect can come much more quickly. The physical environment, the most obdurate of all influences in terms of change, must then have an effect in more basic and lasting attributes.

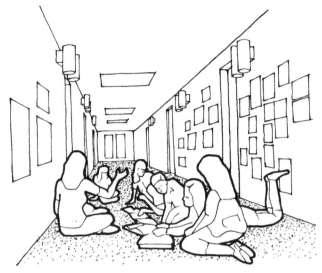

Use: corridor as classroom.

Objects of Evaluation

The evaluation of relationships between the physical environment and behavior requires the collection and analysis of information about what activities occur in the environment, who participates in them, the areas in which they occur, circulation, and equipment used in the environment. Methods employed in measuring behavioral factors usually consist of direct observation of behavior, interviews, and questionnaires. Unobtrusive measures are also used here, especially in examining the adaptations that users make in the environment.

Building Use. The evaluation of building use employs a method similar to that developed by Barker and Gump as behavior settings.[22] By very carefully collecting and analyzing data on activities, Barker and Gump were able to show the significant influence of the size of an organization on behavior. For example, students in small and large high schools were found to exist in almost different cultures. A more architecturally oriented study using this methodology was the Buildings in Use study that examined four elementary schools.[23] Results in-

dicated that various areas of these schools enjoyed different amounts of use, whether they were designed for such use or not. For example, corridors contained a large amount of classroom-type activity. Many other studies have shown the same syndrome. Spaces intended for activity are not being utilized, while other spaces relegated to service—such as corridors—have a surprising amount of use, especially considering the lack of amenities or equipment. Zeisel and Griffin in *Charlesview Housing* found centrally located courtyards unused, as were the student lounges in dorms at Berkeley.[24] On the other hand, the *St. Francis Square Study*, by Cooper, found the courtyards quite well used in this housing project.[25] The buildings in use project mentioned above also studied an unassigned indoor area at one school—the forum—that had quite a bit of use. Finally, Willems, in a rehabilitation hospital study, reported that some of the most meaningful behavior of patients (independent behavior, considered most significant in allowing patients to be productive in the outside world) took place in the corridors and not in the therapy rooms.[26] As these studies indicate, there is much work to be done in examining even this most basic of behavioral phenomena.

Proximity and Territory. Two factors crucial in determining the utilization of areas within the building are the attributes of proximity and territoriality—combined here because proximity so often implies a territorial influence. The strong inherent effect of proximity and territory is well known to parents. If you live in a good neighborhood your children will meet other good children and befriend them. Join the correct club and you will be among the correct people. Festinger's classic study pointed out the power of proximity in forming friendship patterns.[27] A study by Lee, also at the urban scale, demonstrated that people living closest to community facilities tended to use them the most.[28]

Decisions concerning proximity and territoriality are an ever-present architectural and behavioral concern. In schools, this concern may involve the necessary relationship between a teaching area and an instructional resource center; in hospitals, it may involve the nurses' station and the patients; in shopping environments, it dictates the maximum exposure of goods. The importance of these factors is presented by Oscar Newman in *Defensible Space*.[29] Newman found that low-rise housing developments in which the inhabitants could survey public outdoor areas and in which the housing form defined these areas had lower crime rates. In fact, the tenants of this kind of housing felt that such an area was part of the building's territory and not an entirely public space. One would guess that potential perpetrators must have thought likewise.

Privacy and Interaction. Privacy and interaction among users can be key concepts for enhancing productivity and morale in office situations, for satisfaction in many housing situations, and for success for open-plan schools. Until recently, stan-

Proximity and defensible space.

dards for prison design allowed multiple-user cells, resulting in serious physical privacy problems. Dormitory standards often include shared rooms, and students must go to great lengths to protect their privacy in these situations. Likewise, open schools do not always have areas with few aural and visual distractions for concentrated study or special activities. Often, the lack of privacy in open-office environments is cited as the largest single cause of dissatisfaction.

Interaction among users is also strongly influenced by proximity in house unit groupings, and in office environments. Interaction can also be generated in special high-use spaces. Grouped bathrooms in dormitories are strong sociopetal areas; they bring people together, notwithstanding their location. Other examples include laundry rooms, coffee rooms, and even dormitory lounges if correctly designed.

Image. Lynch's *Image of the City* provided the basic impetus towards the development of this area of behavioral evaluation.[30] People's perceptions of the physical environment were found to be key determinants in their use of and satisfaction with it. This has been especially well documented in housing—the building type most closely related to a person's life. A poignant example is the study by Boudon of Le Corbusier's housing at Pessac, France built in 1926 in the International Style and extensively modified by its owners to conform to typical housing.[31] More than half the strip windows have been changed to typical window proportions, and extensive modifications have been made to the open plan of the interiors. Much decoration has been added to the exterior of the houses. Cooper and Becker, in two separate studies of multifamily housing projects, found similar ideas expressed by residents in terms of image.[32] Upkeep, landscaping, and building scale (high-rise or low-rise) were the strongest influences on the residents' images of housing. Variations in the heights and colors of the buildings were also strong determinants. Especially interesting was the fact that certain attributes valued by architects—such as differences in stair railings and roof color, and even the staggering of facades—were seldom noticed.

Studies of image such as these are relatively few, but they are gaining increased attention because of the powerful cues they present to the public and building users. Architects, for whom the only input to the design of a building's exterior consists of formal and stylistic variables, should find image

studies a significant tool in creating buildings based on a more humanistic and rational basis.

Architects can influence a certain amount of behavior through physical design; that such influence can be significant is obvious from the results of recent studies and from personal observation. Much of the success or failure of many buildings depends on the use of areas within the building, accommodations for privacy and social interaction, and the provision of a design image that fits the user.

Future Directions

Formal and comprehensive building evaluation should be a routine part of the architectural profession because of its potential to yield a better environment. Like other innovations, however, it must be made marketable before it can be accepted. This bodes well for evaluation over the next decade, because professional circumstances will mandate this type of direction. Architectural programming, once done as an exotic activity by research organizations and a very few architects, is now a traditional service in many firms. Building evaluation and research is still in an early stage. Clients and users, having to live with too many building problems, are realizing that the evaluation of existing

House by Le Corbusier, France, as built.

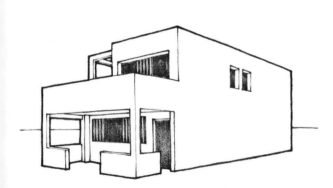

The same house after remodeling.

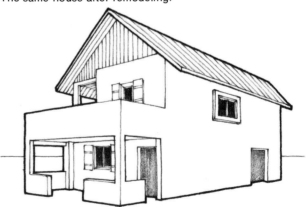

buildings has real advantages, for both renovation and new construction. Evaluation, often conducted at a relatively low cost, can produce significant saving for clients and users. The payoff from evaluation is not limited to the technical area, such as savings in repair and replacement costs, but also includes the functional area, where inefficiencies in planning, communication, and production can cost time, money, and additional effort. Even in the behavioral area, research results have demonstrated

the basic relationships of physical design to security, privacy, sociability, and space utilization.

Building evaluation, like programming, will become a solid part of architectural practice. The inclusion of evaluation in architecture curriculums, the expansion of programming activities in architectural offices, the new awareness of building owners and users, and the critical requirement for more energy-efficient buildings will all help bring about the change.

NOTES

1. Peter Manning, ed., *Office Design: A Study of Environment* (Liverpool: Department of Building Science, Liverpool University, 1965); T. Markus, P. Whyman, et al., *Building Performance* (New York: Halstead Press, 1972).

2. Harvey Rabinowitz, *Buildings in Use Study, Vol. 1 Field Test Manual; Buildings in Use Study, Vol. 2 Technical Factors; Buildings in Use Study, Vol. 3 Functional Factors* (Milwaukee: Department of Architecture, University of Wisconsin, Milwaukee, 1976).

3. Clare Cooper, *Easter Hill Village: Some Social Implications of Design* (New York: The Free Press, 1975); Oscar Newman, *Defensible Space* (New York: Collier Books, 1973).

4. Conrad Jameson, "Social Research for Architecture," *Architect's Journal* (Oct. 27, 1971). Also see replies in issues of Nov. 17, 1971, Dec. 8, 1971, and Feb. 2, 1972.

5. *American Institute of Architects Journal* (Washington, D.C.: American Institute of Architects).

6. Scott Geoffrey, *Building Disasters and Failures* (Hornby, England: Construction Press, Ltd., 1976).

7. Rabinowitz, *Buildings in Use, vol. 2 Technical Factors.*

8. David Trites, Franklin Galbraith, Jr., et al., "Influence of Nursing-Unit Design on the Activities and Subjective Feelings of Nursing Personnel," *Environment and Behavior,* 2:3 (December 1970).

9. John Zeisel and Mary Griffin, *Charlesview Housing, a Diagnostic Evaluation* (Cambridge, Mass.: Architecture Research Office, Graduate School of Design, Harvard University, 1975).

10. Alexander Kira, *The Bathroom* (New York: Viking Press, 1976).

11. Colin Clipson and J. Wehrer, *Planning for Cardiac Care* (Ann Arbor, Mich.: The Health Administrator Press, School of Public Health, University of Michigan, 1973).

12. Rabinowitz, *Buildings in Use, vol 3 Functional Factors.*

13. Clare Cooper, *Resident Attitudes Towards the Environment at St. Francis Square, San Francisco: A Summary of Initial Findings* (Berkeley, Calif.: Center of Planning and Development Research, University of California, Berkeley, 1970).

14. Herbert McLaughlin, John Kibre, and Raphael Mort, "Patterns of Physical Change in Six Existing Hospitals," *in Environmental Design: Research and Practice,* W. Mitchell, ed. (Los Angeles: EDRA Conference, 1972).

15. L. Festinger et al., *Social Pressures in Informal Groups* (New York: Harper & Row, 1950).

16. Sim Van Der Ryn and Murray Silverstein, *Dorms at Berkeley* (Berkeley, Calif.: Center for Planning and Development Research, University of California, 1967); Robert Sommer, *Personal Space* (Englewood Cliffs, N.J.: Prentice-Hall, 1969); Roger Barker and Paul Gump, *Big School, Small School* (Stanford, Calif.: Stanford University Press, 1974).

17. Brent Brolin and John Zeisel, "Social Research and Design: Applications to Mass Housing," in *Emerging Methods in Environmental Design and Planning,* Gary Moore, ed. (Cambridge, Mass.: M.I.T. Press, 1970); Cooper, *Resident Attitudes.*

18. Peter Blake, *Form Follows Fiasco: Why Modern Architecture Hasn't Worked* (Boston: Little, Brown, 1977).

19. Constance Perin, *With Man in Mind* (Cambridge, Mass.: M.I.T. Press, 1970); Brent C. Brolin, *The Failure of Modern Architecture* (New York: Van Nostrand Reinhold, 1976); Malcolm Macewen, *Crisis in Architecture* (London: RIBA Publications, 1974).

20. *American Institute of Architects Journal* (An evaluation article now appears each month.)

21. Frederick Herzberg, *Work and the Nature of Man* (Cleveland: World Publishing Co., 1966).

22. Barker and Gump, *Big School, Small School.*

23. Rabinowitz, *Buildings in Use, vol. 3 Functional Factors.*

24. Zeisel and Griffin, *Charlesview Housing;* Van Der Ryn and Silverstein, *Dorms at Berkeley.*

25. Cooper, *Resident Attitudes.*

26. Edwin P. Williams, "Place and Motivation: Independence and Complexity in Patient Behavior," in *Environmental Design, Research and Practice*, W. Mitchell, ed. (Los Angeles, University of California, Los Angeles, Proceedings of 3d EDRA Conference, 1972).

27. Festinger et al., *Social Pressures*.

28. Terence Lee, "Urban Neighborhood as a Socio-Spatial Schema," in *Enviromental Psychology*, H. Proshansky, W. Ittleson, and L. Rivlin, eds. (New York: Holt, Rinehart and Winston, 1970).

29. Newman, *Defensible Space*.

30. Kevin Lynch, *The Image of the City*. (Cambridge, Mass.: M.I.T Press, 1960).

31. Philippe Boudon, *Lived-in Architecture*. (Cambridge, Mass.: M.I.T Press, 1972).

32. Cooper, *Residential Attitudes;* Franklin C. Becker, *Design for Living* (Ithaca, N.Y.: Center for Urban Development Research, Cornell University, 1974).

FOR FURTHER READING

Alexander, C., and Chermayeff, S. *Community and Privacy*. New York: Doubleday, 1963.

Barker, R., and Gump, P. *Big School, Small School*. Stan-Mass.: M.I.T. Press, 1972

Boudon, Phillippe. *Lived-in Architecture*. Cambridge, Mass.: M.I.T. Press, 1972.

Brolin, Brent. *The Failure of Modern Architecture*. New York: Van Nostrand Reinhold, 1976.

Clipson, C., and Wehrer, J. *Planning for Cardiac Care*. Ann Arbor, Mich.: The Health Administration Press, School of Public Health, University of Michigan, 1973.

Cooper, Clare. *Easter Hill Village: Some Social Aspects of Design*. New York: The Free Press, 1975.

Markus, T.; Whyman, P.; et al. *Building Performance*. New York: Halstead Press, 1972.

Newman, Oscar. *Defensible Space*. New York: Collier Books, 1973.

Perin, Constance. *With Man in Mind*. Cambridge, Mass.: M.I.T. Press, 1970

Scott, Geoffrey. *Building Disasters and Failures*. Hornby, England: Construction Press, Ltd., 1976.

Epilogue

This book has provided the beginning architecture student with a wide variety of topics for initial study. It can also provide a survey for students and professionals in related fields such as urban planning, landscape architecture, environmental design, engineering, and the fine arts. The topics were selected through an analysis of what is being taught in architectural schools and represent the state of the art. The book does not pretend to be a complete introduction, since each subject requires more intensive and thorough examination, even at the introductory level. It does not begin to incorporate the total educational needs of architects—the social sciences, the arts, the humanities, and the physical sciences. However, we view this book, along with its companion volume (*Introduction to Urban Planning*), as the first comprehensive treatment of the subject—a basis for further study and direction for the serious student.

Current signs and trends indicate significant changes over the next decade. To list but a few examples:

1 While the federal government and other sources predict a good job market for architects through the 1980s, there are more students entering the field than ever.

2. Related fields, such as landscape architecture, engineering, the social sciences, and management, are expanding to include important areas formerly within the exclusive province of architecture, while the education and practice of architecture is expanding to include many aspects of those fields.

3. A widening of interests and curricula is taking place in architecture schools.

4 The search to better define and describe architectural education continues. Complete agreement in this area appears unlikely.

These trends are further complicated by recent events that have led to a reaffirmation by architecture schools of traditions, values, and skills that were decried as socially irrelevant during the 1960s. Current students of architecture are demanding "marketable skills." Employers and clients are asking for graduates who can start work on technical matters without the need for extensive on-the-job training. Yet, many architectural faculties maintain that such technical skills quickly become obsolete, and that it is more important to educate for future jobs than for first jobs. Somehow, these seemingly paradoxical demands will have to be reconciled in the years ahead. Architecture schools will be called upon to produce graduates with adequate skills to be employable and useful, yet with sufficient flexibility and adaptability to meet future needs and changing markets and conditions.

These issues form a set of fluid characteristics of architectural education. A sifting and winnowing process is taking place that seeks both truth and understanding. It is probably best to consider architectural education as *inclusive,* rather than exclusive, of a variety of concerns. If errors are to occur, it may be better to err on the side of attempting to do too much. Architecture is already a broadly defined profession and area of interest, and it is changing rapidly. New architectural services pertaining to such areas as urban revitalization, energy conservation, environmental protection, technological change, and regional development are certain to be in demand. Expanded services in architectural design, programming, and technology, as well as in building construction, environment-behavior studies, and evaluation are inevitable. For these reasons alone, an architectural education oriented to the future is prerequisite.

Thus we conclude with a sense of change and expectancy. Yet we would be remiss if we did not restate our fundamental optimism in architecture. This optimism was best expressed by one of the greatest American architects of this century, more than seventy years ago:

> To stultify or corrupt our architectural possibilities is to corrupt our aesthetic life at the fountainhead. Her architecture is the most precious of the susceptibilities of a young, constructive country in this constructive stage of development; and maintaining its integrity in this respect, therefore, distinctly a cause. (Frank Lloyd Wright, *In the Cause of Architecture,* 1908)

Index

Index